BIG BOOK of CROCHET

Featuring the Best of Crochet With Heart Magazine

Wonderful designs … great variety … clear instructions … beautiful afghans … adorable layettes for baby … fashions for the family … gifts to please everyone … and home accessories to hand down for generations …

These are just a few of the reasons so many people loved **Crochet With Heart** magazine from Leisure Arts.

Now here in one big book are all our favorites from these categories: afghans, baby, fashion, gifts, and home. These 124 designs are the best of the best, carefully selected by our editors for their beauty, practicality, and timeliness.

We start with afghans, those warm and cozy wraps that make us feel at home. There are choices for all skill levels, as well as elegant ones, casual ones, and super-fast ones made with a Q hook.

Baby is covered from birth to toddler stage, with cloud-soft blankets and outfits, as well as sweet shower gifts. The fashion scene features sassy selections for teens, chic apparel for ladies, colorful sets for kids, and even a jacket for the family dog.

Gifts range from bedside guardian angels to bags, bookmarks, and baby toys. And to enhance your home, there are charming doilies and table toppers, handy kitchen helpers, and plush pillows and rugs.

Take a few minutes now to browse and mark the designs that touch your heart the most. Then gather up some gorgeous yarn and get started. Enjoy!

LEISURE ARTS, INC.
Little Rock, Arkansas

EDITORIAL STAFF

Vice President and Editor-in-Chief:
Sandra Graham Case
Executive Director of Publications:
Cheryl Nodine Gunnells
Senior Publications Director:
Susan White Sullivan
Special Projects Director:
Susan Frantz Wiles
Director of Retail Marketing:
Stephen Wilson
Director of Designer Relations:
Debra Nettles
Crochet Technical Editor:
Linda Luder
Senior Art Operations Director:
Jeff Curtis
Art Publications Director:
Rhonda Shelby
Senior Production Artist:
Rebecca J. Hester
Art Imaging Director:
Mark Hawkins
Imaging Technicians:
Stephanie Johnson and Mark Potter
Publishing Systems Administrator:
Becky Riddle
Publishing Systems Assistants:
Clint Hanson, Josh Hyatt, and John Rose

BUSINESS STAFF

Chief Operating Officer:
Tom Siebenmorgen
Director of Corporate Planning and Development:
Laticia Mull Dittrich
Vice President, Sales and Marketing:
Pam Stebbins
Director of Sales and Services:
Margaret Reinold
Vice President, Operations:
Jim Dittrich
Comptroller, Operations:
Rob Thieme
Retail Customer Service Manager:
Stan Raynor
Print Production Manager:
Fred F. Pruss

AFGHANS

TABLE *of* CONTENTS

BABY

FASHION

GIFTS

HOME

HEARTS APLENTY AFGHAN

*Airy rows of filet hearts make this afghan perfect
for Valentine's Day — or any day. Crocheted with cotton yarn,
it's sure to warm your heart and the rest of you, too!*

◼◼◻◻ **EASY**

Finished Size:
46" x 61" (117 cm x 155 cm)

MATERIALS
100% Cotton Medium/Worsted Weight
 Yarn [2¹/₂ ounces, 127 yards
 (70 grams, 116 meters)
 per skein]: 16 skeins
Crochet hook, size F (3.75 mm) **or** size
 needed for gauge

GAUGE:
16 dc and 8 rows = 4" (10 cm)

Note: Each row is worked across length
of Afghan.

AFGHAN
Ch 213.

Row 1 (Right side)**:** Dc in back ridge
(Fig. 1, page 205) of fourth ch from
hook **(3 skipped chs count as first
dc, now and throughout)** and each
ch across: 211 dc.

Row 2: Ch 5, turn; dc in fourth ch from
hook and in next ch, dc in next dc,
★ ch 2, skip next 2 dc, dc in next dc;
repeat from ★ across, add on 3 dc *(Fig.
6, page 205)*: 217 sts.

Row 3: Ch 5, turn; dc in fourth ch from
hook and in next ch, dc in next dc, ch 2,
skip next 2 dc, dc in next dc, ch 2, dc in
next dc, 2 dc in next ch-2 sp, ★ dc in
next dc, (ch 2, dc in next dc) 5 times, 2
dc in next ch-2 sp; repeat from ★ 10
times **more**, (dc in next dc, ch 2) 3
times, skip next 2 dc, dc in last dc, add
on 3 dc: 223 sts.

Row 4: Ch 5, turn; dc in fourth ch from
hook and in next ch, dc in next dc, ch 2,
skip next 2 dc, dc in next dc, (ch 2, dc in
next dc) twice, 2 dc in next ch-2 sp, dc
in next 4 dc, 2 dc in next ch-2 sp, ★ dc
in next dc, (ch 2, dc in next dc) 3 times,
2 dc in next ch-2 sp, dc in next 4 dc, 2
dc in next ch-2 sp; repeat from ★ 10
times **more**, (dc in next dc, ch 2) twice,
skip next 2 dc, dc in last dc, add on 3 dc:
229 sts.

Row 5: Ch 5, turn; dc in fourth ch from
hook and in next ch, dc in next dc, ch 2,
skip next 2 dc, ★ (dc in next dc, ch 2)
twice, dc in next 10 dc, 2 dc in next ch-2
sp; repeat from ★ 11 times **more**, (dc in
next dc, ch 2) 3 times, skip next 2 dc, dc
in last dc, add on 3 dc: 235 sts.

Row 6: Ch 5, turn; dc in fourth ch from
hook and in next ch, dc in next dc, ch 2,
skip next 2 dc, dc in next dc, (ch 2, dc in
next dc) twice, 2 dc in next ch-2 sp, dc
in next 10 dc, ch 2, ★ skip next 2 dc, dc
in next dc, ch 2, dc in next dc, 2 dc in
next ch-2 sp, dc in next 10 dc, ch 2;
repeat from ★ 10 times **more**, skip next
2 dc, (dc in next dc, ch 2) 4 times, skip
next 2 dc, dc in last dc, add on 3 dc: 241
sts.

Row 7: Turn; slip st in first 4 dc, ch 3
**(counts as first dc, now and
throughout)**, 2 dc in next ch-2 sp, dc
in next dc, (ch 2, dc in next dc) 3 times,
2 dc in next ch-2 sp, dc in next 10 dc,
ch 2, skip next 2 dc, dc in next dc,
★ ch 2, dc in next dc, 2 dc in next ch-2
sp, dc in next 10 dc, ch 2, skip next 2
dc, dc in next dc; repeat from ★ 10
times **more**, (ch 2, dc in next dc) twice,
2 dc in next ch-2 sp, dc in next dc, leave
remaining 3 dc unworked: 235 sts.

Row 8: Turn; slip st in first 4 dc, ch 3,
2 dc in next ch-2 sp, dc in next dc, (ch 2,
dc in next dc) twice, ★ ch 2, skip next 2
dc, dc in next 10 dc, (ch 2, dc in next dc)
twice; repeat from ★ 11 times **more**, 2
dc in next ch-2 sp, dc in next dc, leave
remaining 3 dc unworked: 229 sts.

Row 9: Turn; slip st in first 4 dc, ch 3,
2 dc in next ch-2 sp, (dc in next dc, ch 2)
twice, skip next 2 dc, dc in next 4 dc,
ch 2, skip next 2 dc, dc in next dc,
★ ch 2, (dc in next dc, ch 2) 3 times, skip
next 2 dc, dc in next 4 dc, ch 2, skip
next 2 dc, dc in next dc; repeat from ★
10 times **more**, (ch 2, dc in next dc)
twice, 2 dc in next ch-2 sp, dc in next
dc, leave remaining 3 dc unworked: 223
sts.

Row 10: Turn; slip st in first 4 dc, ch 3,
2 dc in next ch-2 sp, (dc in next dc, ch 2)
3 times, ★ skip next 2 dc, (dc in next dc,
ch 2) 6 times; repeat from ★ 10 times
more, skip next 2 dc, dc in next dc,
ch 2, dc in next dc, 2 dc in next ch-2 sp,
dc in next dc, leave remaining 3 dc
unworked: 217 sts.

Row 11: Turn; slip st in first 4 dc, ch 3,
(2 dc in next ch-2 sp, dc in next dc)
across to last 3 dc, leave remaining dc
unworked: 211 dc.

Rows 12-91: Repeat Rows 2-11, 8
times.

Finish off.

Design by Terry Kimbrough.

BREEZY DIAMONDS AFGHAN

This soft and inviting cover-up is quite a gem! Cluster stitches form diamonds, which are surrounded by open chain spaces. Beautiful in its simplicity, the afghan is an ideal companion for a sofa or chair.

■■□□ **EASY**

Finished Size:
49" x 65" (124.5 cm x 165 cm)

MATERIALS
Medium/Worsted Weight Yarn
[5 ounces, 328 yards
(140 grams, 300 meters)
per skein]: 6 skeins
Crochet hook, size I (5.5 mm) **or** size needed for gauge

GAUGE: In pattern,
sc, (work Cluster, sc) 3 times
and Rows 1-6 = 3¹/₄" (8.25 cm)

To work Cluster, ch 3, YO, insert hook in third ch from hook, YO and pull up a loop, YO and draw through 2 loops on hook, YO, insert hook in **same** ch, YO and pull up a loop, YO and draw through 2 loops on hook, YO and draw through all 3 loops on hook.

AFGHAN
Ch 198.

Row 1: Sc in second ch from hook, ★ work Cluster, skip next 3 chs, sc in next ch; repeat from ★ across: 49 Clusters.

To work treble crochet (abbreviated tr), YO twice, insert hook in sc indicated, YO and pull up a loop (4 loops on hook), (YO and draw through 2 loops on hook) 3 times.

Row 2 (Right side)**:** Ch 5 **(counts as first tr plus ch 1, now and throughout unless otherwise indicated)**, turn; sc in next Cluster (ch-3 sp), work Cluster, sc in next Cluster, ch 4, sc in next Cluster, ★ (work Cluster, sc in next Cluster) twice, ch 4, sc in next Cluster; repeat from ★ across to last Cluster, work Cluster, sc in last Cluster, ch 1, tr in last sc: 32 Clusters.

Row 3: Ch 1, turn; sc in first tr, work Cluster, ★ sc in next Cluster, ch 4, sc in next ch-4 sp, ch 4, sc in next Cluster, work Cluster; repeat from ★ across to last tr, sc in last tr: 17 Clusters.

Row 4: Ch 5, turn; sc in next Cluster, ★ ch 4, (sc in next ch-4 sp, ch 4) twice, sc in next Cluster; repeat from ★ across to last sc, ch 1, tr in last sc: 48 ch-4 sps.

Row 5: Ch 1, turn; sc in first tr, work Cluster, ★ sc in next ch-4 sp, (ch 4, sc in next ch-4 sp) twice, work Cluster; repeat from ★ across to last tr, sc in last tr: 17 Clusters.

Row 6: Ch 5, turn; sc in next Cluster, ★ work Cluster, sc in next ch-4 sp, ch 4, sc in next ch-4 sp, work Cluster, sc in next Cluster; repeat from ★ across to last sc, ch 1, tr in last sc: 32 Clusters.

Row 7: Ch 1, turn; sc in first tr, work Cluster, sc in next Cluster, work Cluster, sc in next ch-4 sp, work Cluster, ★ (sc in next Cluster, work Cluster) twice, sc in next ch-4 sp, work Cluster; repeat from ★ across to last Cluster, sc in last Cluster, work Cluster, sc in last tr: 49 Clusters.

Row 8: Ch 5, turn; sc in next Cluster, work Cluster, sc in next Cluster, ch 4, sc in next Cluster, ★ (work Cluster, sc in next Cluster) twice, ch 4, sc in next Cluster; repeat from ★ across to last Cluster, work Cluster, sc in last Cluster, ch 1, tr in last sc: 32 Clusters.

Rows 9-127: Repeat Rows 3-8, 19 times; then repeat Rows 3-7 once **more**.

Row 128: Ch 5 **(counts as first hdc plus ch 3)**, turn; skip first Cluster, hdc in next sc, ★ ch 3, skip next Cluster, hdc in next sc; repeat from ★ across, do **not** finish off.

To work Scallop, ch 3, dc in third ch from hook.

Edging: Do **not** turn; work Scallop; working in end of rows, skip first 2 rows, ★ slip st around tr on next row, work Scallop, skip next row; repeat from ★ across; working in free loops *(Fig. 3b, page 205)* and in sps across beginning ch, slip st in ch at base of first sc, work Scallop, (slip st in next sp, work Scallop) across to last ch, slip st in last ch, work Scallop; working in end of rows, skip first row, slip st around tr on next row, work Scallop, † skip next row, slip st around tr on next row, work Scallop †, repeat from † to † across to last 2 rows, skip last 2 rows; working across Row 128, slip st in first hdc, work Scallop, (slip st in next ch-3 sp, work Scallop) across to last hdc, slip st in last hdc; finish off.

Design by Anne Halliday.

SERENITY

Hexagons crocheted in soft white and spruce create a serene wrap for summer lounging. Lush tassels accent the dramatic edges.

■■□□ EASY

Finished Size:
46" x 62" (117 cm x 157.5 cm)

MATERIALS
Medium/Worsted Weight Yarn
[8 ounces, 452 yards (230 grams, 413 meters) per skein]:
MC (Soft White) - 4 skeins
CC (Spruce) - 3 skeins
Crochet hook, size I (5.5 mm) **or** size needed for gauge
Yarn needle

GAUGE: Each Motif = 7¹/₂" (19 cm) (from straight edge to straight edge)

MOTIF A (Make 25)
With CC, ch 8; join with slip st to form a ring.

Rnd 1 (Right side)**:** Ch 1, 18 sc in ring; join with slip st to first sc.

Note: Mark Rnd 1 as **right** *side.*

Rnd 2: Ch 1, sc in same st, ch 5, skip next 2 sc, ★ sc in next sc, ch 5, skip next 2 sc; repeat from ★ around; join with slip st to first sc: 6 ch-5 sps.

To work treble crochet (abbreviated tr), YO twice, insert hook in sp indicated, YO and pull up a loop (4 loops on hook), (YO and draw through 2 loops on hook) 3 times.

Rnd 3: Slip st in first ch-5 sp, ch 4 **(counts as first tr, now and throughout)**, 7 tr in same sp, 8 tr in each ch-5 sp around; join with slip st to first tr: 48 tr.

Rnd 4: Ch 1, sc in same st and in next 3 tr, ch 3, (sc in next 4 tr, ch 3) around; join with slip st to first sc, finish off: 12 ch-3 sps.

To work beginning Cluster, ch 3, ★ YO twice, insert hook in sp indicated, YO and pull up a loop, (YO and draw through 2 loops on hook) twice; repeat from ★ once **more**, YO and draw through all 3 loops on hook.

To work Cluster, ★ YO twice, insert hook in sp indicated, YO and pull up a loop, (YO and draw through 2 loops on hook) twice; repeat from ★ 2 times **more**, YO and draw through all 4 loops on hook.

Rnd 5: With **right** side facing, join MC with slip st in last ch-3 sp (before joining); work (beginning Cluster, ch 4, Cluster) in same sp, ch 3, work (Cluster, ch 5, Cluster) in next ch-3 sp, ch 3, ★ work (Cluster, ch 4, Cluster) in next ch-3 sp, ch 3, work (Cluster, ch 5, Cluster) in next ch-3 sp, ch 3; repeat from ★ around; join with slip st to top of beginning Cluster, finish off: 24 sps.

Rnd 6: With **right** side facing, join CC with sc in any corner ch-5 sp *(see Joining With Sc, page 205)*; (2 sc, ch 3, 3 sc) in same sp, 3 sc in each of next 3 sps, ★ (3 sc, ch 3, 3 sc) in next ch-5 sp, 3 sc in each of next 3 sps; repeat from ★ around; join with slip st to first sc: 90 sc and 6 ch-3 sps.

Rnd 7: Ch 1, sc in same st and in each sc around working 3 sc in each ch-3 sp; join with slip st to first sc, finish off: 108 sc.

MOTIF B (Make 24)
With MC, work same as Motif A through Rnd 4: 12 ch-3 sps.

Rnd 5: With CC, work same as Motif A: 24 sps.

Rnds 6 and 7: With MC, work same as Motif A: 108 sc.

ASSEMBLY
With corresponding color and using diagram as a guide, whipstitch Motifs together **(Fig. 9c, page 206)** forming 5 horizontal strips of 5 Motifs each and 4 horizontal strips of 6 Motifs each, beginning in center sc of first corner 3-sc group and ending in center sc of next corner 3-sc group; then whipstitch strips together in same manner.

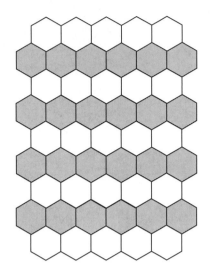

KEY
⬡ Motif A
⬢ Motif B

EDGING
Rnd 1: With **right** side facing, join MC with sc in any st; sc evenly around entire Afghan working an even number of sc; join with slip st to first sc.

Rnd 2: Ch 2, hdc in same st, skip next sc, ★ slip st in next sc, ch 2, hdc in same st, skip next sc; repeat from ★ around; join with slip st to first slip st, finish off.

With MC, add tassels at points across short edges of Afghan **(Figs. 11a & b, page 207)**.

Design by Eleanor Albano.

SPIDER LACE AFGHAN

Our unique cover-up is as splendid as a beautifully spun spider web. The delicate pattern is nicely complemented by a lovely shell edging.

■■□□ **EASY**

Finished Size:
52" x 70" (132 cm x 178 cm)

MATERIALS
Medium/Worsted Weight Yarn
[3 ounces, 170 yards **MEDIUM 4**
(90 grams, 155 meters)
per skein]: 14 skeins
Crochet hook, size I (5.5 mm) **or** size
needed for gauge

GAUGE: One repeat and
6 rows = 2¼" (5.75 cm)

AFGHAN

Ch 156.

Row 1 (Right side): Sc in second ch from hook and in each ch across: 155 sc.

Note: Mark Row 1 as **right** side.

Row 2: Ch 1, turn; sc in first 3 sc, ch 5, (skip next 2 sc, sc in next 5 sc, ch 5) across to last 5 sc, skip next 2 sc, sc in last 3 sc: 22 ch-5 sps.

Row 3: Ch 1, turn; sc in first 2 sc, ch 3, sc in next ch-5 sp, ch 3, ★ skip next sc, sc in next 3 sc, ch 3, sc in next ch-5 sp, ch 3; repeat from ★ across to last 3 sc, skip next sc, sc in last 2 sc: 44 ch-3 sps.

Row 4: Ch 1, turn; sc in first sc, ch 3, sc in next ch-3 sp, sc in next sc and in next ch-3 sp, ch 3, ★ skip next sc, sc in next sc, ch 3, sc in next ch-3 sp, sc in next sc and in next ch-3 sp, ch 3; repeat from ★ across to last 2 sc, skip next sc, sc in last sc.

Row 5: Ch 5 (**counts as first dc plus ch 2**), turn; sc in next ch-3 sp, sc in next 3 sc and in next ch-3 sp, ★ ch 5, sc in next ch-3 sp, sc in next 3 sc and in next ch-3 sp; repeat from ★ across to last sc, ch 2, dc in last sc: 21 ch-5 sps.

Row 6: Ch 1, turn; sc in first dc, ch 3, skip next sc, sc in next 3 sc, ch 3, ★ sc in next ch-5 sp, ch 3, skip next sc, sc in next 3 sc, ch 3; repeat from ★ across to last dc, sc in last dc: 44 ch-3 sps.

Row 7: Ch 1, turn; sc in first sc and in next ch-3 sp, ch 3, skip next sc, sc in next sc, ch 3, sc in next ch-3 sp, ★ sc in next sc and in next ch-3 sp, ch 3, skip next sc, sc in next sc, ch 3, sc in next ch-3 sp; repeat from ★ across to last sc, sc in last sc.

Row 8: Ch 1, turn; sc in first 2 sc and in next ch-3 sp, ch 5, sc in next ch-3 sp, ★ sc in next 3 sc and in next ch-3 sp, ch 5, sc in next ch-3 sp; repeat from ★ across to last 2 sc, sc in last 2 sc.

Rows 9-169: Repeat Rows 3-8, 26 times; then repeat Rows 3-7 once **more**.

Row 170: Ch 1, turn; sc in first 2 sc and in next ch-3 sp, ch 2, sc in next ch-3 sp, ★ sc in next 3 sc and in next ch-3 sp, ch 2, sc in next ch-3 sp; repeat from ★ across to last 2 sc, sc in last 2 sc: 21 ch-2 sps.

Row 171: Ch 1, turn; sc in each sc and in each ch across; do **not** finish off: 155 sc.

EDGING

Rnd 1: Ch 1, do **not** turn; work 173 sc evenly spaced across end of rows; ch 2, working in free loops of beginning ch (**Fig. 3b, page 205**), 2 sc in first ch, sc in next 153 chs, 2 sc in next ch, ch 2; work 173 sc evenly spaced across end of rows, ch 2; working across Row 171, 2 sc in first sc, sc in each sc across to last sc, 2 sc in last sc, ch 2; join with slip st to first sc: 660 sc and 4 ch-2 sps.

Rnd 2: Ch 1, sc in same st and in each sc across to next corner ch-2 sp, (sc, ch 2, sc) in corner ch-2 sp, ★ sc in each sc across to next corner ch-2 sp, (sc, ch 2, sc) in corner ch-2 sp; repeat from ★ 2 times **more**; join with slip st to first sc: 668 sc and 4 ch-2 sps.

Rnd 3: Ch 1, skip next sc, † (dc, ch 1, dc) in next sc, ch 1, skip next sc, slip st in next sc, ch 1, skip next sc †, repeat from † to † across to next corner ch-2 sp, (dc, ch 1) 4 times in corner ch-2 sp, skip next sc, ★ slip st in next sc, ch 1, skip next sc, repeat from † to † across to next corner ch-2 sp, (dc, ch 1) 4 times in corner ch-2 sp, skip next sc; repeat from ★ 2 times **more**; join with slip st to joining slip st: 344 dc and 512 ch-1 sps.

Rnd 4: Slip st in next ch, slip st in next dc and in next ch-1 sp, ch 3 (**counts as first dc**), 2 dc in same sp, ch 1, skip next 2 ch-1 sps, (3 dc in next ch-1 sp, ch 1, skip next 2 ch-1 sps) 42 times, † (3 dc in next ch-1 sp, ch 1) 3 times, skip next 2 ch-1 sps, (3 dc in next ch-1 sp, ch 1, skip next 2 ch-1 sps) 39 times, (3 dc in next ch-1 sp, ch 1) 3 times, skip next 2 ch-1 sps †, (3 dc in next ch-1 sp, ch 1, skip next 2 ch-1 sps) 43 times, repeat from † to † once; join with slip st to first dc: 528 dc.

Rnd 5: Slip st in next dc, ch 4, dc in same st, ch 1, slip st in next ch-1 sp, ch 1, skip next dc, ★ (dc, ch 1) twice in next dc, slip st in next ch-1 sp, ch 1, skip next st; repeat from ★ around; join with slip st to third ch of beginning ch-4, finish off.

Design by Anne Halliday.

CAPTIVATING CRESCENTS AFGHAN

*Believe it or not — this stunning afghan is surprisingly easy to make! The lacy spaces
above and below each crescent make the pretty shapes appear to be formed
in strips, but the cover-up is actually crocheted all in one piece.*

■■□□ EASY

Finished Size:
48" x 62" (122 cm x 157.5 cm)

MATERIALS
Medium/Worsted Weight Yarn
  [6 ounces, 325 yards
  (170 grams, 297 meters) **4** MEDIUM
  per skein]: 9 skeins
Crochet hook, size I (5.5 mm) **or** size
  needed for gauge

GAUGE: In pattern, one repeat
and 8 rows = 5" (12.75 cm)

AFGHAN
Ch 151.

Row 1: Dc in fourth ch from hook **(3
skipped chs count as first dc)** and in
next 3 chs, ★ ch 4, skip next 4 chs, sc
in next ch, ch 3, skip next ch, sc in next
ch, ch 4, skip next 4 chs, dc in next 5
chs; repeat from ★ across: 50 dc and 27
sps.

Row 2 (Right side): Ch 3 **(counts as
first dc, now and throughout)**, turn;
dc in next 4 dc, ★ ch 2, sc in next ch-4
sp, ch 1, 7 dc in next ch-3 sp, ch 1, sc
in next ch-4 sp, ch 2, dc in next 5 dc;
repeat from ★ across: 113 dc.

Note: Mark Row 2 as **right** side.

To work Bobble, ★ YO, insert hook in
dc indicated, YO and pull up a loop, YO
and draw through 2 loops on hook;
repeat from ★ 3 times **more**, YO and
draw through all 5 loops on hook.

Row 3: Ch 3, turn; dc in next 4 dc,
★ ch 1, work Bobble in next dc, (ch 3,
skip next dc, work Bobble in next dc) 3
times, ch 1, dc in next 5 dc; repeat from
★ across: 50 dc and 36 Bobbles.

Row 4: Ch 3, turn; dc in next 4 dc,
★ ch 2, skip next ch-1 sp, sc in next
ch-3 sp, (ch 3, sc in next ch-3 sp) twice,
ch 2, dc in next 5 dc; repeat from ★
across: 36 sps.

Row 5: Ch 3, turn; dc in next 4 dc,
★ ch 4, skip next ch-2 sp, sc in next
ch-3 sp, ch 3, sc in next ch-3 sp, ch 4,
dc in next 5 dc; repeat from ★ across:
27 sps.

Row 6: Ch 3, turn; dc in next 4 dc,
★ ch 2, sc in next ch-4 sp, ch 1, 7 dc in
next ch-3 sp, ch 1, sc in next ch-4 sp,
ch 2, dc in next 5 dc; repeat from ★
across: 113 dc.

Rows 7-97: Repeat Rows 3-6, 22
times; then repeat Rows 3-5 once
more; do **not** finish off.

EDGING
Rnd 1: Ch 1, do **not** turn; sc evenly
around entire Afghan working 3 sc in
each corner; join with slip st to first sc.

Rnd 2: Ch 1, **turn**; sc in same st and in
each sc around working 3 sc in center sc
of each corner 3-sc group; join with slip
st to first sc, finish off.

Holding three 16" (40.5 cm) strands of
yarn together for each fringe, add fringe
across short edges of Afghan (*Figs. 12a
& b, page 207*).

*Design by Brenda Stratton and
Carol Alexander.*

MILE-A-MINUTE VIOLETS

Add luxurious violets to any room with this mile-a-minute beauty!
The dimensional flowers brighten every other diamond-shaped motif.

⬤⬤⬤◻ INTERMEDIATE

Finished Size:
49" x 64" (124.5 cm x 162.5 cm)

MATERIALS

Medium/Worsted Weight Yarn
[3½ ounces, 198 yards
(100 grams, 181 meters)
per skein]:
Eggshell - 8 skeins
Medium Spruce - 5 skeins
Light Plum - 2 skeins
Cornmeal - 1 skein
Crochet hook, size G (4 mm) **or** size
   needed for gauge

GAUGE:

Each Motif = 2" (5 cm) square;
Each Strip = 3¾" (9.5 cm) wide

STRIP A (Make 7)
FIRST MOTIF

Rnd 1 (Right side): With Cornmeal,
ch 2, 8 sc in second ch from hook; join
with slip st to first sc, finish off.

Note: Mark Rnd 1 as **right** side.

Rnd 2: With **right** side facing and
working in Front Loops Only *(Fig. 2,
page 205)*, join Light Plum with sc in
any sc *(see Joining With Sc,
page 205)*; ch 5, sc in same st, (sc,
ch 5, sc) in each sc around; join with slip
st to **both** loops of first sc, finish off: 8
Petals.

Rnd 3: With **right** side facing and
working in free loops on Rnd 1 (**behind**
Petals) *(Fig. 3a, page 205)*, join
Medium Spruce with sc in any sc; ch 3,
(sc in next sc, ch 3) around; join with slip
st to first sc, do **not** finish off: 8 ch-3
sps.

Rnd 4: Slip st in first ch-3 sp, ch 1, sc
in same sp, (2 hdc, ch 3, 2 hdc) in next
ch-3 sp, ★ sc in next ch-3 sp, (2 hdc,
ch 3, 2 hdc) in next ch-3 sp; repeat from
★ 2 times **more**; join with slip st to first
sc, finish off: 20 sts and 4 ch-3 sps.

SECOND MOTIF

Rnd 1 (Right side): With Medium
Spruce, ch 2, 8 sc in second ch from
hook; join with slip st to first sc.

Note: Mark Rnd 1 as **right** side.

Rnd 2: Ch 1, sc in same st, ch 3, (sc in
next sc, ch 3) around; join with slip st to
first sc: 8 ch-3 sps.

Rnd 3 (Joining rnd): Slip st in first ch-3
sp, ch 1, sc in same sp, ★ (2 hdc, ch 3,
2 hdc) in next ch-3 sp, sc in next ch-3
sp; repeat from ★ 2 times **more**, 2 hdc
in last ch-3 sp, ch 1; holding Motifs with
wrong sides together, sc in
corresponding corner ch-3 sp on
previous Motif, ch 1, 2 hdc in same sp
on **new** Motif; join with slip st to first sc,
finish off.

THIRD MOTIF

Rnds 1-3: Work same as First Motif: 8
ch-3 sps.

Rnd 4 (Joining rnd): Slip st in first ch-3
sp, ch 1, sc in same sp, ★ (2 hdc, ch 3,
2 hdc) in next ch-3 sp, sc in next ch-3
sp; repeat from ★ 2 times **more**, 2 hdc
in last ch-3 sp, ch 1; holding Motifs with
wrong sides together, sc in
corresponding corner ch-3 sp on
previous Motif, ch 1, 2 hdc in same sp
on **new** Motif; join with slip st to first sc,
finish off.

REMAINING 16 MOTIFS

Repeat Second and Third Motifs, 8
times.

STRIP B (Make 6)
FIRST MOTIF

Rnd 1 (Right side): With Medium
Spruce, ch 2, 8 sc in second ch from
hook; join with slip st to first sc.

Note: Mark Rnd 1 as **right** side.

Rnd 2: Ch 1, sc in same st, ch 3, (sc in
next sc, ch 3) around; join with slip st to
first sc: 8 ch-3 sps.

Rnd 3: Slip st in first ch-3 sp, ch 1, sc
in same sp, (2 hdc, ch 3, 2 hdc) in next
ch-3 sp, ★ sc in next ch-3 sp, (2 hdc,
ch 3, 2 hdc) in next ch-3 sp; repeat from
★ 2 times **more**; join with slip st to first
sc, finish off: 20 sts and 4 ch-3 sps.

Instructions continued on page 18.

Continued from page 16.

SECOND MOTIF

Rnd 1 (Right side): With Cornmeal, ch 2, 8 sc in second ch from hook; join with slip st to first sc, finish off.

Note: Mark Rnd 1 as **right** side.

Rnd 2: With **right** side facing and working in Front Loops Only, join Light Plum with sc in any sc; ch 5, sc in same st, (sc, ch 5, sc) in each sc around; join with slip st to **both** loops of first sc, finish off: 8 Petals.

Rnd 3: With **right** side facing and working in free loops on Rnd 1 (**behind** Petals), join Medium Spruce with sc in any sc; ch 3, (sc in next sc, ch 3) around; join with slip st to first sc, do **not** finish off: 8 ch-3 sps.

Rnd 4 (Joining rnd): Slip st in first ch-3 sp, ch 1, sc in same sp, ★ (2 hdc, ch 3, 2 hdc) in next ch-3 sp, sc in next ch-3 sp; repeat from ★ 2 times **more**, 2 hdc in last ch-3 sp, ch 1; holding Motifs with **wrong** sides together, sc in corresponding corner ch-3 sp on **previous** Motif, ch 1, 2 hdc in same sp on **new** Motif; join with slip st to first sc, finish off.

THIRD MOTIF

Rnds 1 and 2: Work same as First Motif: 8 ch-3 sps.

Rnd 3 (Joining rnd): Slip st in first ch-3 sp, ch 1, sc in same sp, ★ (2 hdc, ch 3, 2 hdc) in next ch-3 sp, sc in next ch-3 sp; repeat from ★ 2 times **more**, 2 hdc in last ch-3 sp, ch 1; holding Motifs with **wrong** sides together, sc in corresponding corner ch-3 sp on **previous** Motif, ch 1, 2 hdc in same sp on **new** Motif; join with slip st to first sc, finish off.

REMAINING 16 MOTIFS

Repeat Second and Third Motifs, 8 times.

EDGING

Note: Beginning and ending with Strip A, alternately add Edging to Strips A and B for assembly.

FIRST STRIP

To work 3-dc Cluster, † YO, insert hook in **next** sp, YO and pull up a loop, YO and draw through 2 loops on hook †, YO, insert hook in side of joining sc, YO and pull up a loop, YO and draw through 2 loops on hook, repeat from † to † once, YO and draw through all 4 loops on hook (**counts as one dc**).

Rnd 1: With **right** side facing, join Eggshell with sc in end ch-3 sp; 2 sc in same sp, sc in next 5 sts, 3 sc in next ch-3 sp, † sc in next hdc, hdc in next hdc, dc in next 3 sts, work 3-dc Cluster, dc in next 3 sts, hdc in next hdc, sc in next hdc, 3 sc in next ch-3 sp †, repeat from † to † 17 times **more**, (sc in next 5 sts, 3 sc in next ch-3 sp) twice, repeat from † to † across to last 5 sts, sc in last 5 sts; join with slip st to first sc: 536 sts.

To work treble crochet (abbreviated *tr*), YO twice, insert hook in dc indicated, YO and pull up a loop (4 loops on hook), (YO and draw through 2 loops on hook) 3 times.

To work 5-tr Cluster (uses next 5 dc), ★ YO twice, insert hook in **next** dc, YO and pull up a loop, (YO and draw through 2 loops on hook) twice; repeat from ★ 4 times **more**, YO and draw through all 6 loops on hook.

Rnd 2: Ch 1, (sc, ch 3, sc) in same st, † ch 5, (sc, ch 7, sc) in next sc, ch 5, (sc, ch 3, sc) in next sc, (ch 3, sc in next sc) 6 times, (sc, ch 3, sc) in next sc, ★ sc in next sc, hdc in next sc, dc in next hdc, ch 3, tr in next dc, ch 1, work 5-tr Cluster, ch 1, tr in next dc, ch 3, dc in next hdc, hdc in next sc, sc in next sc, (sc, ch 3, sc) in next sc; repeat from ★ 17 times **more**, (sc in next sc, ch 3) 6 times †, (sc, ch 3, sc) in next sc, repeat from † to † once; join with slip st to first sc, finish off: 436 sts and 216 sps.

REMAINING 12 STRIPS

Rnd 1: Work same as First Strip: 536 sts.

Rnd 2 (Joining rnd): Ch 1, (sc, ch 3, sc) in same st, ch 5, (sc, ch 7, sc) in next sc, ch 5, (sc, ch 3, sc) in next sc, (ch 3, sc in next sc) 6 times, (sc, ch 3, sc) in next sc, ★ sc in next sc, hdc in next sc, dc in next hdc, ch 3, tr in next dc, ch 1, work 5-tr Cluster, ch 1, tr in next dc, ch 3, dc in next hdc, hdc in next sc, sc in next sc, (sc ch 3, sc) in next sc; repeat from ★ 17 times **more**, (sc in next sc, ch 3) 6 times, (sc, ch 3, sc) in next sc, ch 5, (sc, ch 7, sc) in next sc, ch 5, (sc, ch 3) twice in next sc, (sc in next sc, ch 3) 5 times, sc in next 2 sc, ch 1; holding Strips with **wrong** sides together, sc in corresponding ch-3 sp on **previous** Strip, ch 1, † sc in same st and in next sc on **new** Strip, hdc in next sc, dc in next hdc, ch 1, sc in next ch-3 sp on **previous** Strip, ch 1, tr in next dc on **new** Strip, ch 1, work 5-tr Cluster, ch 1, tr in next dc, ch 1, sc in next ch-3 sp on **previous** Strip, ch 1, dc in next hdc on **new** Strip, hdc in next sc, sc in next 2 sc, ch 1, sc in next ch-3 sp on **previous** Strip, ch 1 †, repeat from † to † 17 times **more**, sc in same st on **new** Strip, (sc in next sc, ch 3) 6 times; join with slip st to first sc, finish off.

Design by Katherine Satterfield.

LUXURIOUS LACE COVER-UP

Surround yourself in a lacy latticework of luxury. We finished off this mellow wrap with a cascade of extra-long fringe.

◼◼◻◻ **EASY**

Finished Size:
49" x 68" (124.5 cm x 172.5 cm)

MATERIALS
Medium/Worsted Weight Yarn
[5 ounces, 328 yards
(140 grams, 300 meters)
per skein]: 9 skeins

MEDIUM 4

Crochet hook, size I (5.5 mm) **or** size
needed for gauge

GAUGE: In pattern, [sc, ch 1,
(dc, ch 1) 3 times] = $1^1/_2$" (3.75 cm);
8 rows = 3" (7.5 cm)

COVER-UP
Row 1 (Right side): Ch 258, sc in
second ch from hook, ★ ch 1, skip next
3 chs, (dc, ch 1) 3 times in next ch, skip
next 3 chs, sc in next ch; repeat from ★
across: 96 dc, 33 sc, and 128 ch-1 sps.

Note: Mark Row 1 as **right** side.

Row 2: Ch 6 **(counts as first dc plus
ch 3)**, turn; skip next dc, sc in next dc,
ch 3, skip next dc, dc in next sc, ★ ch 3,
skip next dc, sc in next dc, ch 3, skip
next dc, dc in next sc; repeat from ★
across: 33 dc, 32 sc, and 64 ch-3 sps.

Row 3: Ch 1, turn; sc in first dc,
★ ch 1, (dc, ch 1) 3 times in next sc, sc
in next dc; repeat from ★ across: 96 dc,
33 sc, and 128 ch-1 sps.

Repeat Rows 2 and 3 until Cover-up
measures approximately 68" (172.5 cm)
from beginning ch, ending by working
Row 2; finish off.

Trim: With **right** side of one long edge
facing and working in end of rows, join
yarn with sc in first row **(see Joining
With Sc, page 205)**; sc evenly across;
finish off.

Repeat for Trim on opposite long edge.

Holding six 17" (43 cm) strands of yarn
together for each fringe, add fringe
across short edges of Cover-up **(Figs.
12a & b, page 207)**.

Design by Melissa Leapman.

LIGHT & AIRY AFGHAN

The simplicity of this airy afghan makes it a perfect project for beginners. Picots provide interest throughout the pattern and edging.

■■□□ **EASY**

Finished Size:
47" x 65" (119.5 cm x 165 cm)

MATERIALS
Medium/Worsted Weight Yarn
[3¹/₂ ounces, 198 yards (100 grams, 181 meters) per skein]:
Medium Spruce - 8 skeins
Off-White - 4 skeins
Crochet hook, size I (5.5 mm) **or** size needed for gauge

GAUGE: In pattern,
2 repeats 4¹/₄" (10.75 cm);
8 rows = 4¹/₂" (11.5 cm)

To work Picot, ch 6, slip st in top of last dc made.

AFGHAN
With Medium Spruce, ch 159.

Row 1 (Right side)**:** Dc in fourth ch from hook **(3 skipped chs count as first dc)** and in next 2 chs, ch 2, skip next 2 chs, dc in next ch, work Picot, ch 2, ★ skip next 2 chs, dc in next 3 chs, ch 2, skip next 2 chs, dc in next ch, work Picot, ch 2; repeat from ★ across to last 6 chs, skip next 2 chs, dc in last 4 chs: 19 Picots.

Note: Mark Row 1 as **right** side.

Row 2: Ch 3 **(counts as first dc, now and throughout)**, turn; ★ dc in next 3 dc, ch 2, sc in next Picot, ch 2; repeat from ★ across to last 4 dc, dc in last 4 dc.

Row 3: Ch 3, turn; ★ dc in next 3 dc, ch 2, dc in next sc, ch 2; repeat from ★ across to last 4 dc, dc in last 4 dc; finish off.

Row 4: With **wrong** side facing and working in Front Loops Only **(Fig. 2, page 205)**, join Off-White with slip st in first dc; ch 3, dc in next dc and in each st across; finish off: 157 dc.

Row 5: With **right** side facing and working in both loops, join Medium Spruce with slip st in first dc; ch 3, dc in next 3 dc, ch 2, skip next 2 dc, dc in next dc, work Picot, ch 2, ★ skip next 2 dc, dc in next 3 dc, ch 2, skip next 2 dc, dc in next dc, work Picot, ch 2; repeat from ★ across to last 6 dc, skip next 2 dc, dc in last 4 dc; do **not** finish off.

Rows 6-107: Repeat Rows 2-5, 25 times; then repeat Rows 2 and 3 once **more**.

EDGING
Rnd 1: With **wrong** side facing and working in Front Loops Only, join Off-White with slip st in first dc on last row; ch 3, 2 dc in same st, dc in each st across to last dc, 5 dc in last dc; work 215 dc evenly spaced across end of rows; working in free loops of beginning ch **(Fig. 3b, page 205)**, 5 dc in ch at base of first dc, dc in each ch across to last ch, 5 dc in last ch; work 215 dc evenly spaced across end of rows, 2 dc in same st as first dc; join with slip st to first dc, finish off: 760 dc.

Rnd 2: With **right** side facing and working in both loops, join Medium Spruce with slip st in same st as joining; ch 3, 2 dc in same st, dc in each dc around working 5 dc in center dc of each corner 5-dc group, 2 dc in same st as first dc; join with slip st to first dc: 776 dc.

Rnd 3: Ch 4, do **not** turn; (dc, work Picot, ch 1, dc) in same st, ch 1, skip next dc, dc in next dc, work Picot, ch 1, skip next dc, † dc in next dc, ch 1, skip next dc, dc in next dc, work Picot, ch 1, skip next dc †, repeat from † to † across to center dc of next corner 5-dc group, ★ (dc, ch 1, dc, work Picot, ch 1, dc) in center dc, ch 1, skip next dc, dc in next dc, work Picot, ch 1, skip next dc, repeat from † to † across to center dc of next corner 5-dc group; repeat from ★ around; join with slip st to third ch of beginning ch-4, finish off.

Design by Janet L. Akins.

CHECKMATE COVER-UP

You'll feel like a winner after crocheting this throw! The design was whimsically constructed with a game of checkers in mind.

◼◼◻◻ EASY

Finished Size:
48" x 66" (122 cm x 167.5 cm)

MATERIALS
Medium/Worsted Weight Yarn
[8 ounces, 452 yards
(230 grams, 413 meters)
per skein]: **MEDIUM 4**
Cherry Red - 5 skeins
Black - 3 skeins
White - 2 skeins
Crochet hook, size I (5.5 mm) **or** size
 needed for gauge
Yarn needle

GAUGE: Each Square = 6" (15.25 cm)

SQUARE (Make 88)
To work Cluster, ★ YO, insert hook in ring, YO and pull up a loop, YO and draw through 2 loops on hook; repeat from ★ once **more**, YO and draw through all 3 loops on hook.

With Black, ch 5; join with slip st to form a ring.

Rnd 1 (Right side)**:** Ch 2, dc in ring, (ch 1, work Cluster) twice, ch 2, ★ work Cluster, (ch 1, work Cluster) twice, ch 2; repeat from ★ 2 times **more**; join with slip st to first dc, finish off: 8 ch-1 sps and 4 ch-2 sps.

Note: Mark Rnd 1 as **right** side.

To work beginning Popcorn, ch 3 **(counts as first dc, now and throughout)**, 2 dc in st or sp indicated, drop loop from hook, insert hook in first dc of 3-dc group, hook dropped loop and draw through st.

To work Popcorn, 3 dc in st or sp indicated, drop loop from hook, insert hook in first dc of 3-dc group, hook dropped loop and draw through st.

Rnd 2: With **right** side facing, join Cherry Red with slip st in any corner ch-2 sp; work (beginning Popcorn, ch 2, slip st, ch 2, Popcorn) in same sp, ch 1, (work Popcorn in next ch-1 sp, ch 1) twice, ★ work (Popcorn, ch 2, slip st, ch 2, Popcorn) in next corner ch-2 sp, ch 1, (work Popcorn in next ch-1 sp, ch 1) twice; repeat from ★ 2 times **more**; join with slip st to top of beginning Popcorn, finish off: 12 ch-1 sps and 8 ch-2 sps.

Rnd 3: With **right** side facing, join White with slip st in any corner slip st (between ch-2 sps); work (beginning Popcorn, ch 3, Popcorn) in same st, 2 sc in each of next 5 sps, ★ work (Popcorn, ch 3, Popcorn) in next corner slip st, 2 sc in each of next 5 sps; repeat from ★ 2 times **more**; join with slip st to top of beginning Popcorn, do **not** finish off: 40 sc, 8 Popcorns, and 4 ch-3 sps.

Rnd 4: Ch 1, sc in same st, 3 sc in next ch-3 sp, ★ sc in each Popcorn and in each sc across to next ch-3 sp, 3 sc in ch-3 sp; repeat from ★ 2 times **more**, sc in next Popcorn and in each sc across; join with slip st to first sc, finish off: 60 sc.

To decrease, pull up a loop in next 2 sc, YO and draw through all 3 loops on hook.

Rnd 5: With **right** side facing, join Cherry Red with sc in center sc of any corner 3-sc group **(see Joining With Sc, page 205)**; ch 3, sc in same st, ch 1, (decrease, ch 1) across to center sc of next corner 3-sc group, ★ (sc, ch 3, sc) in center sc, ch 1, (decrease, ch 1) across to center sc of next corner 3-sc group; repeat from ★ 2 times **more**; join with slip st to first sc, finish off: 32 ch-1 sps and 4 ch-3 sps.

Rnd 6: With **right** side facing, join Black with sc in any corner ch-3 sp; † ch 3, slip st in ch-3 sp 2 rnds **below** (between first and second sc of corner 3-sc group), ch 3, sc in same sp on Rnd 5, ch 3, slip st in same sp 2 rnds **below**, ch 3, sc in same sp on Rnd 5 †, 2 sc in each of next 8 ch-1 sps, ★ sc in next corner ch-3 sp, repeat from † to † once, 2 sc in each of next 8 ch-1 sps; repeat from ★ 2 times **more**; join with slip st to first sc, finish off: 76 sc and 16 ch-3 sps.

Rnd 7: With **right** side facing, join Cherry Red with slip st in any corner ch-3 sp one rnd **below** (between first and second sc of corner 3-sc group); ch 3, 2 dc in same sp, ★ † skip next ch-3 sp on Rnd 6, skip next sc and next ch-3 sp, 2 dc in same sp one rnd **below** (between second and third sc of corner 3-sc group), skip next ch-3 sp and next sc on Rnd 6, sc in next 16 sc, skip next sc and next ch-3 sp †, 3 dc in corner ch-3 sp one rnd **below** (between first and second sc of corner 3-sc group); repeat from ★ 2 times **more**, then repeat from † to † once; join with slip st to first dc, finish off: 84 sts.

ASSEMBLY
With Cherry Red and working through **inside** loops, whipstitch Squares together **(Fig. 9c, page 206)** to form 8 vertical strips of 11 Squares each, beginning in center dc of first corner 5-dc group and ending in center dc of next corner 5-dc group; then whipstitch strips together in same manner.

EDGING
With **right** side of short edge facing and working in Back Loops Only **(Fig. 2, page 205)**, join Cherry Red with sc in center dc of corner 5-dc group; 2 sc in same st, ★ ♥ sc in next 20 sts, † hdc in same st as joining on same Square, dc in joining, hdc in same st as joining on next Square, sc in next 20 sts †; repeat from † to † across to center dc of next corner 5-dc group ♥, 3 sc in center dc; repeat from ★ 2 times **more**, then repeat from ♥ to ♥ once; join with slip st to first sc, finish off.

Design by Jennine Korejko.

BLUE BREEZE AFGHAN

Shades of periwinkle contrasted with soft white give definition to the pretty shell stitches in this granny-strip afghan. The wrap is a breeze to make because it features the quick "join-as-you-go" method.

■■■□ INTERMEDIATE

Finished Size:
45" x 61" (114.5 cm x 155 cm)

MATERIALS
Medium/Worsted Weight Yarn
 [8 ounces, 452 yards
 (230 grams, 413 meters)
 per skein]:
 Color A (Light Periwinkle) - 2 skeins
 Color B (Periwinkle) - 2 skeins
 Color C (Soft White) - 3 skeins
Crochet hook, size H (5 mm) **or** size
 needed for gauge

GAUGE: In pattern,
2 repeats = 3¹/₄" (8.25 cm)
Each Strip = 5" (12.75 cm) wide

FIRST STRIP

To work Shell, (3 dc, ch 2, 3 dc) in st or sp indicated.

With Color A, ch 208.

Rnd 1 (Right side)**:** (2 Dc, ch 2, 3 dc) in fourth ch from hook, (skip next 2 chs, sc in next ch, skip next 2 chs, work Shell in next ch) across, ch 2; working in free loops of beginning ch **(Fig. 3b, page 205)**, work Shell in same st as last Shell made, (skip next 2 chs, sc in next ch, skip next 2 chs, work Shell in next ch) 34 times, ch 2; join with slip st to top of beginning ch, finish off: 70 Shells.

Note: Mark Rnd 1 as **right** side.

Rnd 2: With **right** side facing, join Color B with slip st in ch-2 sp at either end; ch 3 **(counts as first dc, now and throughout)**, (2 dc, ch 2, 3 dc) in same sp, † ch 1, work Shell in next Shell (ch-2 sp), (dc in next sc, work Shell in next Shell) across to ch-2 sp at opposite end, ch 1 †, work Shell in end ch-2 sp, repeat from † to † once; join with slip st to first dc, finish off: 76 sps.

Rnd 3: With **right** side facing, join Color C with slip st in ch-2 sp at either end; ch 3, (2 dc, ch 2, 3 dc) in same sp, † ch 1, 3 dc in next ch-1 sp, ch 1, work Shell in next Shell, (skip next 3 dc, dc in next dc, work Shell in next Shell) across to next ch-1 sp, ch 1, 3 dc in next ch-1 sp, ch 1 †, work Shell in end ch-2 sp, repeat from † to † once; join with slip st to first dc, do **not** finish off: 80 sps.

To work Picot, ch 4, slip st in top of dc just made.

Rnd 4: Slip st in next 2 dc and in next ch-2 sp, ch 1, (sc in same sp, ch 4) twice, † (sc, ch 4) twice in each of next 2 ch-1 sps, (sc, ch 4, sc) in next Shell, ★ ch 2, skip next 3 dc, dc in next dc, work Picot, ch 2, (sc, ch 4, sc) in next Shell; repeat from ★ across to next ch-1 sp, ch 4, (sc, ch 4) twice in each of next 2 ch-1 sps †, (sc, ch 4) twice in next Shell, repeat from † to † once; join with slip st to first sc, finish off: 228 sps and 68 Picots.

REMAINING 8 STRIPS

Work same as First Strip through Rnd 3: 80 sps.

Rnd 4 (Joining rnd)**:** Slip st in next 2 dc and in next ch-2 sp, ch 1, (sc, ch 4) twice in same sp and in each of next 2 ch-1 sps, (sc, ch 4, sc) in next Shell, ★ ch 2, skip next 3 dc, dc in next dc, work Picot, ch 2, (sc, ch 4, sc) in next Shell; repeat from ★ across to next ch-1 sp, ch 4, (sc, ch 4) twice in each of next 2 ch-1 sps, (sc, ch 4) twice in next Shell and in each of next 2 ch-1 sps, sc in next Shell, ch 2, holding Strips with **wrong** sides together, slip st in corresponding ch-4 sp on **previous** Strip, ch 2, sc in same Shell on **new** Strip, † ch 2, skip next 3 dc, dc in next dc, ch 2, slip st in next Picot on **previous** Strip, ch 2, slip st in dc just made on **new** Strip, ch 2, sc in next Shell, ch 2, slip st in next ch-4 sp on **previous** Strip, ch 2, sc in same Shell on **new** Strip †, repeat from † to † across to next ch-1 sp, ch 4, (sc, ch 4) twice in each of last 2 ch-1 sps; join with slip st to first sc, finish off.

Design by Maggie Weldon.

STAR-SPANGLED AFGHAN

Oh, say, can you see the all-American inspiration in our star-spangled afghan? This red, white, and blue salute will make a bold accent to enjoy on all the patriotic days of the year!

◼◼◻◻ **EASY**

Finished Size:
56" x 67" (142 cm x 170 cm)

MATERIALS
Medium/Worsted Weight Yarn
 [8 ounces, 452 yards
 (230 grams, 413 meters) **4** MEDIUM
 per skein]:
 Color A (White) - 2 skeins
 Color B (Royal) - 2 skeins
 Color C (Cherry Red) - 4 skeins
Crochet hook, size J (6 mm) **or** size
 needed for gauge
Yarn needle

GAUGE: Each Square = 7³/₄"
(19.75 cm)

SQUARE (Make 50)
To work Puff St, ★ YO, insert hook in sp indicated, YO and pull up a loop even with loop on hook; repeat from ★ 2 times **more**, YO and draw through all 7 loops on hook.

With Color A, ch 6; join with slip st to form a ring.

Rnd 1 (Right side)**:** Pull up a 1¹/₄" (3 cm) loop, (work Puff St in ring, ch 5) 5 times; join with slip st to top of first Puff St, finish off: 5 ch-5 sps.

Note: Mark Rnd 1 as **right** side.

Rnd 2: With **right** side facing, join Color B with sc in any ch-5 sp *(see Joining With Sc, page 205)*; 5 sc in same sp, 6 sc in each ch-5 sp around; join with slip st to first sc: 30 sc.

Rnd 3: Ch 1, sc in same st and in next 3 sc, 2 sc in next sc, (sc in next 4 sc, 2 sc in next sc) around; join with slip st to first sc: 36 sc.

To work treble crochet (abbreviated *tr*), YO twice, insert hook in sc indicated, YO and pull up a loop (4 loops on hook), (YO and draw through 2 loops on hook) 3 times.

Rnd 4: Ch 1, sc in same st and in next 3 sc, hdc in next sc, dc in next sc, 3 tr in next sc, dc in next sc, hdc in next sc, ★ sc in next 4 sc, hdc in next sc, dc in next sc, 3 tr in next sc, dc in next sc, hdc in next sc; repeat from ★ around; join with slip st to first sc, finish off: 44 sts.

Rnd 5: With **right** side facing and working in Back Loops Only *(Fig. 2, page 205)*, join Color C with slip st in any st; ch 3 **(counts as first dc, now and throughout)**, dc in each st around working 5 dc in center tr of each corner 3-tr group; join with slip st to first dc, finish off: 60 dc.

Rnd 6: With **right** side facing and working in Back Loops Only, join Color A with slip st in any dc; ch 3, dc in each dc around working 5 dc in center dc of each corner 5-dc group; join with slip st to first dc, finish off: 76 dc.

Rnd 7: With **right** side facing and working in Back Loops Only, join Color C with slip st in any dc; ch 2 **(counts as first hdc, now and throughout)**, hdc in each dc around working 5 hdc in center dc of each corner 5-dc group; join with slip st to first hdc, finish off: 92 hdc.

ASSEMBLY
With Color C, using diagram as a guide, and working through **inside** loops, whipstitch Squares together *(Fig. 9c, page 206)*, beginning in center hdc of first corner 5-hdc group and ending in center hdc of next corner 5-hdc group.

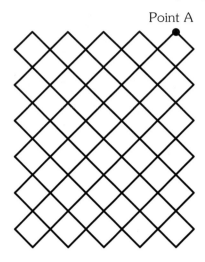
Point A

EDGING
To decrease, YO, insert hook in same st as joining on **same** Square, YO and pull up a loop, YO, insert hook in same st as joining on **next** Square, YO and pull up a loop, YO and draw through all 5 loops on hook.

Rnd 1: With **right** side facing and working in both loops, join Color C with slip st in first hdc to **left** of center hdc of top right corner 5-hdc group (Point A on diagram); ch 2, ★ † hdc in each hdc across to next joining, decrease, hdc in each hdc across to center hdc of next corner 5-hdc group, 3 hdc in center hdc †, repeat from † to † 3 times **more**, hdc in each hdc across to center hdc of next corner 5-hdc group, 3 hdc in center hdc, repeat from † to † 5 times, hdc in each hdc across to center hdc of next corner 5-hdc group, 3 hdc in center hdc; repeat from ★ once **more**; join with slip st to first hdc, finish off.

CHEVRON COMFORTER

Symbolic of rippling waves of grain, this chevron comforter with flowing fringe makes a homey, relaxing wrap.

■■□□ **EASY**

Finished Size:
52" x 65" (132 cm x 165 cm)

MATERIALS
Medium/Worsted Weight Yarn
  [5 ounces, 328 yards
  (140 grams, 300 meters) **MEDIUM 4**
  per skein]: 9 skeins
Crochet hook, size I (5.5 mm) **or** size
  needed for gauge

GAUGE: Each repeat
(from point to point) = $6^1/2$" (16.5 cm);
Rows 1-8 = 4" (10 cm)

COMFORTER

To decrease (uses next 5 chs or sc),
★ YO, insert hook in **next** ch or sc, YO and pull up a loop, YO and draw through 2 loops on hook; repeat from ★ 4 times **more**, YO and draw through all 6 loops on hook **(counts as one dc)**.

Ch 212.

Row 1 (Right side): 2 Dc in fourth ch from hook **(3 skipped chs count as first dc)**, ch 2, skip next 2 chs, dc in next 8 chs, decrease, dc in next 8 chs, ch 2, ★ skip next 2 chs, 5 dc in next ch, ch 2, skip next 2 chs, dc in next 8 chs, decrease, dc in next 8 chs, ch 2; repeat from ★ across to last 3 chs, skip next 2 chs, 3 dc in last ch: 177 dc and 16 ch-2 sps.

Note: Mark Row 1 as **right** side.

Row 2: Ch 1, turn; sc in first 3 dc, 2 sc in next ch-2 sp, (sc in each dc across to next ch-2 sp, 2 sc in ch-2 sp) across to last 3 dc, sc in last 3 dc: 209 sc.

Row 3: Ch 3 **(counts as first dc, now and throughout)**, turn; 2 dc in same st, dc in next 2 sc, ch 2, skip next 2 sc, dc in next 6 sc, decrease, dc in next 6 sc, ch 2, ★ skip next 2 sc, dc in next 2 sc, 5 dc in next sc, dc in next 2 sc, ch 2, skip next 2 sc, dc in next 6 sc, decrease, dc in next 6 sc, ch 2; repeat from ★ across to last 5 sc, skip next 2 sc, dc in next 2 sc, 3 dc in last sc: 177 dc and 16 ch-2 sps.

Row 4: Ch 1, turn; sc in first 5 dc, 2 sc in next ch-2 sp, (sc in each dc across to next ch-2 sp, 2 sc in ch-2 sp) across to last 5 dc, sc in last 5 dc: 209 sc.

Row 5: Ch 3, turn; 2 dc in same st, dc in next 4 sc, ch 2, skip next 2 sc, dc in next 4 sc, decrease, dc in next 4 sc, ch 2, ★ skip next 2 sc, dc in next 4 sc, 5 dc in next sc, dc in next 4 sc, ch 2, skip next 2 sc, dc in next 4 sc, decrease, dc in next 4 sc, ch 2; repeat from ★ across to last 7 sc, skip next 2 sc, dc in next 4 sc, 3 dc in last sc: 177 dc and 16 ch-2 sps.

Row 6: Ch 1, turn; sc in first 7 dc, 2 sc in next ch-2 sp, (sc in each dc across to next ch-2 sp, 2 sc in ch-2 sp) across to last 7 dc, sc in last 7 dc: 209 sc.

Row 7: Ch 3, turn; 2 dc in same st, dc in next 6 sc, ch 2, skip next 2 sc, dc in next 2 sc, decrease, dc in next 2 sc, ch 2, ★ skip next 2 sc, dc in next 6 sc, 5 dc in next sc, dc in next 6 sc, ch 2, skip next 2 sc, dc in next 2 sc, decrease, dc in next 2 sc, ch 2; repeat from ★ across to last 9 sc, skip next 2 sc, dc in next 6 sc, 3 dc in last sc: 177 dc and 16 ch-2 sps.

Row 8: Ch 1, turn; sc in first 9 dc, 2 sc in next ch-2 sp, (sc in each dc across to next ch-2 sp, 2 sc in ch-2 sp) across to last 9 dc, sc in last 9 dc: 209 sc.

Row 9: Ch 3, turn; 2 dc in same st, dc in next 8 sc, ch 2, skip next 2 sc, decrease, ch 2, ★ skip next 2 sc, dc in next 8 sc, 5 dc in next sc, dc in next 8 sc, ch 2, skip next 2 sc, decrease, ch 2; repeat from ★ across to last 11 sc, skip next 2 sc, dc in next 8 sc, 3 dc in last sc: 177 dc and 16 ch-2 sps.

Row 10: Ch 1, turn; sc in first 11 dc, 2 sc in next ch-2 sp, (sc in each dc across to next ch-2 sp, 2 sc in ch-2 sp) across to last 11 dc, sc in last 11 dc: 209 sc.

Row 11: Ch 3, turn; 2 dc in same st, ch 2, skip next 2 sc, dc in next 8 sc, decrease, dc in next 8 sc, ch 2, ★ skip next 2 sc, 5 dc in next sc, ch 2, skip next 2 sc, dc in next 8 sc, decrease, dc in next 8 sc, ch 2; repeat from ★ across to last 3 sc, skip next 2 sc, 3 dc in last sc: 177 dc and 16 ch-2 sps.

Rows 12-130: Repeat Rows 2-11, 11 times; then repeat Rows 2-10 once **more**; finish off.

Holding fourteen 17" (43 cm) strands of yarn together for each fringe, add fringe **(Figs. 12a & b, page 207)** to each point across short edges of Comforter.

Design by Melissa Leapman.

HARVEST WRAP

This earthy afghan resembles a neatly cultivated field ready for harvest. Rows of popcorn and post stitches yield abundant texture.

■■□□ EASY

Finished Size:
44" x 74" (112 cm x 188 cm)

MATERIALS
Medium/Worsted Weight Yarn
[3 ounces, 170 yards
(90 grams, 155 meters)
per skein]:
Cornmeal - 5 skeins
Brown - 2 skeins
Medium Coral Rose - 2 skeins
Crochet hook, size G (4 mm) **or** size needed for gauge

GAUGE: In pattern,
(2 dc, Popcorn) 4 times and
one repeat (9 rows) = 3¹⁄₂" (9 cm)

Note: Each row is worked across length of Wrap.

WRAP

With Brown, ch 251.

Row 1: Sc in second ch from hook and in each ch across: 250 sc.

Note: When changing colors, work over unused color, holding it with normal tension and keeping yarn to **wrong** side *(Fig. A)*.

Fig. A

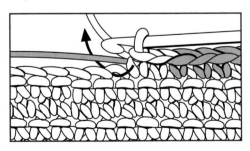

To work Popcorn, 4 dc in next sc changing to Brown in last dc made, drop loop from hook, insert hook in first dc of 4-dc group, hook dropped loop and draw through st.

Row 2 (Right side)**:** Ch 3 **(counts as first dc)**, turn; ★ dc in next 2 sc changing to Medium Coral Rose in last dc made, work Popcorn; repeat from ★ across to last 3 sc, cut Medium Coral Rose, dc in last 3 sc: 82 Popcorns.

Note: Mark Row 2 as **right** side.

Row 3: Ch 1, turn; sc in each dc and in each Popcorn across; finish off: 250 sc.

Row 4: With **right** side facing and working in Back Loops Only *(Fig. 2, page 205)*, join Cornmeal with sc in first sc *(see Joining With Sc, page 205)*; sc in each sc across.

Row 5: Ch 2 **(counts as first hdc, now and throughout)**, turn; working in both loops, dc in next sc and in each sc across to last sc, hdc in last sc.

To work Front Post treble crochet (abbreviated FPtr), YO twice, working in **front** of last 2 dc made, insert hook from **front** to **back** around post of dc indicated *(Fig. 4, page 205)*, YO and pull up a loop (4 loops on hook), (YO and draw through 2 loops on hook) 3 times.

Row 6: Ch 3 **(counts as first hdc plus ch 1)**, turn; ★ skip next dc, dc in next 2 dc, work FPtr around skipped dc, ch 1; repeat from ★ across to last 3 sts, skip next dc, dc in next dc, hdc in last hdc.

To work Back Post treble crochet (abbreviated BPtr), YO twice, working **behind** last 2 dc made, insert hook from **back** to **front** around post of FPtr indicated *(Fig. 4, page 205)*, YO and pull up a loop (4 loops on hook), (YO and draw through 2 loops on hook) 3 times.

Row 7: Ch 2, turn; dc in next dc, ch 1, ★ skip next ch and next FPtr, dc in next 2 dc, work BPtr around skipped FPtr, ch 1; repeat from ★ across to last 2 sts, skip next ch, hdc in last hdc.

Row 8: Ch 1, turn; sc in first hdc, (skip next ch-1 sp, sc in next 3 sts) across to last ch-1 sp, sc in last ch-1 sp and in last 2 sts; finish off: 250 sc.

Row 9: With **right** side facing and working in Front Loops Only, join Brown with sc in first sc; sc in each sc across.

Row 10: Ch 1, turn; sc in both loops of each sc across.

Rows 11-110: Repeat Rows 2-10, 11 times; then repeat Row 2 once **more**.

Row 111: Ch 1, turn; sc in each dc and in each Popcorn across; do **not** finish off: 250 sc.

To work Picot, ch 4, dc in fourth ch from hook.

Edging: Ch 1, turn; sc in first sc, work Picot, (skip next 2 sc, sc in next sc, work Picot) across; working in end of rows, skip first row, (sc in next row, work Picot, skip next row) across; working in free loops of beginning ch *(Fig. 3b, page 205)*, sc in ch at base of first sc, work Picot, (skip next 2 chs, sc in next ch, work Picot) across; working in end of rows, skip first row, (sc in next row, work Picot, skip next row) across; join with slip st to first sc, finish off.

Design by Dot Drake.

AUTUMN LEAVES AFGHAN SET

Echoing the brilliance of autumn, this richly hued afghan and pillow set is a comfy way to welcome the season.

■■■□ INTERMEDIATE

Finished Sizes:
Afghan - 49" x 63"
  (124.5 cm x 160 cm)
Pillow - 14¹/₂" (37 cm) square

MATERIALS
Medium/Worsted Weight Yarn
  [8 ounces, 452 yards
  (230 grams, 413 meters)
  per skein]:
  Medium Sage - 5 skeins
  Gold - 2 skeins
  Cherry Red - 2 skeins
  Warm Brown - 1 skein
Crochet hook, size H (5 mm) **or** size
  needed for gauge
Pillow finishing materials: 14" (35.5
  cm) square purchased pillow form,
  two 14¹/₂" (37 cm) fabric squares for
  pillow form cover, sewing machine,
  sewing needle and thread

GAUGE:
Each Square = 6³/₄" (17.25 cm)

SQUARE (Make 63 for Afghan; Make 8 for Pillow)

With Medium Sage, ch 6; join with slip st to form a ring.

Rnd 1 (Right side): Ch 3, dc in ring, ch 3, ★ slip st in ring, ch 3, dc in ring, ch 3; repeat from ★ 6 times **more**; join with slip st to joining slip st, finish off: 8 dc.

Note: Mark Rnd 1 as **right** side.

To work Leaf, ch 2, (hdc, ch 2, slip st, ch 3, dc, ch 3, slip st, ch 2, hdc, ch 2, slip st) in st or sp indicated.

Rnd 2: With **right** side facing, join Gold with slip st in any dc; work Leaf in same st, ch 2, sc in next dc, ch 2, ★ (slip st, work Leaf) in next dc, ch 2, sc in next dc, ch 2; repeat from ★ 2 times **more**; join with slip st to joining slip st, finish off: 4 Leaves and 4 sc.

Rnd 3: With **right** side facing, join Warm Brown with slip st in any dc; work Leaf in same st, ch 3, (dc, ch 3) twice in next sc, ★ (slip st, work Leaf) in next dc, ch 3, (dc, ch 3) twice in next sc; repeat from ★ 2 times **more**; join with slip st to joining slip st, finish off: 4 Leaves and 12 ch-3 sps.

Rnd 4: With **right** side facing, join Cherry Red with slip st in dc at tip of any Leaf; work Leaf in same st, ★ † ch 4, (slip st, work Leaf) in ch-3 sp **between** next 2 dc, ch 4 †, (slip st, work Leaf) in dc at tip of next Leaf; repeat from ★ 2 times **more**, then repeat from † to † once; join with slip st to joining slip st, finish off: 8 Leaves and 8 ch-4 sps.

To work treble crochet (abbreviated tr), YO twice, insert hook in sp indicated, YO and pull up a loop (4 loops on hook), (YO and draw through 2 loops on hook) 3 times.

Rnd 5: With **right** side facing, join Medium Sage with sc in dc at tip of any corner Leaf *(see Joining With Sc, page 205)*; 2 sc in same st, ★ † ch 3, (tr, ch 2) twice in next ch-4 sp, sc in next dc, (ch 2, tr) twice in next ch-4 sp, ch 3 †, 3 sc in next dc; repeat from ★ 2 times **more**, then repeat from † to † once; join with slip st to first sc, do **not** finish off: 32 sts and 24 sps.

Rnd 6: Ch 1, sc in same st, ★ † 3 sc in next sc, sc in next sc, 3 sc in next ch-3 sp, (sc in next tr, 2 sc in next ch-2 sp) twice, sc in next sc, (2 sc in next ch-2 sp, sc in next tr) twice, 3 sc in next ch-3 sp †, sc in next sc; repeat from ★ 2 times **more**, then repeat from † to † once; join with slip st to first sc: 96 sc.

Rnd 7: Ch 3 **(counts as first dc)**, dc in next sc and in each sc around working 3 dc in center sc of each corner 3-sc group; join with slip st to first dc, finish off: 104 dc.

AFGHAN FINISHING
ASSEMBLY
Place two Squares with **wrong** sides together. Working through **inside** loop of each st on **both** pieces, join Gold with slip st in center dc of first corner 3-dc group; (ch 1, slip st in next dc) across working last st in center dc of next corner 3-dc group; finish off. Join remaining Squares in same manner, forming 7 vertical strips of 9 Squares each; then join strips in same manner.

EDGING
Rnd 1: With **right** side facing and working in Back Loops Only *(Fig. 2, page 205)*, join Gold with sc in any dc; sc in each dc around working hdc in each joining dc and 3 sc in center dc of each corner 3-dc group; join with slip st to **both** loops of first sc.

Rnd 2: Ch 1, sc in both loops of same st and each st around working 3 sc in center sc of each corner 3-sc group; join with slip st to first sc, finish off.

PILLOW FINISHING
PILLOW FORM
Matching right sides and raw edges, use a ¹/₄" (7 mm) seam allowance to sew fabric squares together, leaving bottom edge open. Clip seam allowances at corners. Turn cover right side out, carefully pushing corners outward. Insert pillow form and sew final closure by hand.

FRONT/BACK ASSEMBLY
Place two Squares with **wrong** sides together. Working through **inside** loop of each st on **both** pieces, join Gold with slip st in center dc of first corner 3-dc group; (ch 1, slip st in next dc) across working last st in center dc of next corner 3-dc group; finish off. Join remaining Squares in same manner, forming 4 vertical strips of 2 Squares each; then join strips in same manner to form one block of 4 Squares for Front and another block of 4 Squares for Back.

EDGING

Back: With **right** side facing and working in Back Loops Only, join Gold with sc in any dc; sc in each dc around working hdc in each joining dc and 3 sc in center dc of each corner 3-dc group; join with slip st to **both** loops of first sc, finish off: 216 sc.

Front: Work same as Back; do **not** finish off.

Joining Rnd: Place Front and Back with **wrong** sides together. With Front facing and working in **both** loops of each st on **both** pieces, slip st in same st, ch 1, (slip st in next st, ch 1) around inserting pillow form before closing; join with slip st to first slip st, finish off.

Designs by Sue Galucki.

DOUBLE-COZY COVER-UP

Quickly worked holding two strands of yarn together, our extra-cozy afghan features rows of open V-stitches and a sprinkling of bobbles.

◼◼◻◻ **EASY**

Finished Size:
48" x 70" (122 cm x 178 cm)

MATERIALS
Medium/Worsted Weight Yarn
[8 ounces, 452 yards
(230 grams, 413 meters) **MEDIUM 4**
per skein]: 11 skeins
Crochet hook, size K (6.5 mm) **or** size
needed for gauge

GAUGE: In pattern,
2 repeats and 5 rows = 4$^1/_2$" (11.5 cm)

PATTERN STITCHES
Decrease *(uses next 2 sts)*
★ YO, insert hook in **next** st, YO and pull up a loop, YO and draw through 2 loops on hook; repeat from ★ once **more**, YO and draw through all 3 loops on hook **(counts as one dc)**.
Double Decrease
YO, † insert hook in **next** dc or ch-2 sp, YO and pull up a loop, YO and draw through 2 loops on hook †, YO, skip next st, repeat from † to † once, YO and draw through all 3 loops on hook **(counts as one dc)**.
V-St
(Dc, ch 2, dc) in dc indicated.
Cluster
★ YO, insert hook in sp indicated, YO and pull up a loop, YO and draw through 2 loops on hook; repeat from ★ once **more**, YO and draw through all 3 loops on hook **(counts as one dc)**.
Bobble
★ YO, insert hook in dc indicated, YO and pull up a loop, YO and draw through 2 loops on hook; repeat from ★ 3 times **more**, YO and draw through all 5 loops on hook. Push Bobble to **right** side.

Note: Entire Afghan is worked holding two strands of yarn together.

AFGHAN
Ch 151.

Row 1 (Right side): YO, insert hook in fourth ch from hook **(3 skipped chs count as first dc)**, YO and pull up a loop, YO and draw through 2 loops on hook, YO, insert hook in **next** ch, YO and pull up a loop, YO and draw through 2 loops on hook, YO and draw through all 3 loops on hook, dc in next ch, 3 dc in next ch, dc in next ch, ★ YO, † insert hook in **next** ch, YO and pull up a loop, YO and draw through 2 loops on hook †, YO, skip next 2 chs, repeat from † to † once, YO and draw through all 3 loops on hook, dc in next ch, 3 dc in next ch, dc in next ch; repeat from ★ across to last 3 chs, decrease, dc in last ch: 129 sts.

Row 2: Ch 3 **(counts as first dc, now and throughout)**, turn; working in Front Loops Only **(Fig. 2, page 205)**, decrease, dc in next dc, 3 dc in next dc, dc in next dc, ★ double decrease, dc in next dc, 3 dc in next dc, dc in next dc; repeat from ★ across to last 3 sts, decrease, dc in last dc.

Row 3: Ch 3, turn; skip next dc, working in Back Loops Only, dc in next dc, ★ ch 2, skip next dc, work V-St in next dc, ch 2, skip next dc, double decrease; repeat from ★ across: 63 ch-2 sps.

Row 4: Ch 3, turn; work Cluster in next ch-2 sp, working in both loops, dc in next dc, 3 dc in next ch-2 sp, dc in next dc, ★ double decrease, dc in next dc, 3 dc in next ch-2 sp, dc in next dc; repeat from ★ across to last ch-2 sp, work Cluster in last ch-2 sp, dc in next dc, leave remaining dc unworked: 129 dc.

Row 5: Ch 3, turn; working in Back Loops Only, decrease, dc in next dc, 3 dc in next dc, dc in next dc, ★ double decrease, dc in next dc, 3 dc in next dc, dc in next dc; repeat from ★ across to last 3 dc, decrease, dc in last dc.

Row 6: Ch 3, turn; working in Front Loops Only, decrease, dc in next dc, ch 1, work Bobble in next dc, ch 1, dc in next dc, ★ double decrease, dc in next dc, ch 1, work Bobble in next dc, ch 1, dc in next dc; repeat from ★ across to last 3 dc, decrease, dc in last dc.

Row 7: Ch 3, turn; working in Back Loops Only of dc and in **both** loops of Bobbles, decrease, dc in next ch, 3 dc in next Bobble, dc in next ch, ★ double decrease, dc in next ch, 3 dc in next Bobble, dc in next ch; repeat from ★ across to last 3 dc, decrease, dc in last dc.

Row 8: Ch 3, turn; working in Front Loops Only, decrease, dc in next dc, 3 dc in next dc, dc in next dc, ★ double decrease, dc in next dc, 3 dc in next dc, dc in next dc; repeat from ★ across to last 3 dc, decrease, dc in last dc.

Rows 9-77: Repeat Rows 3-8, 11 times; then repeat Rows 3-5 once **more**.

Finish off.

Holding ten 18" (45.5 cm) lengths of yarn together for each fringe, add fringe **(Figs. 12a & b, page 207)** at points across short edges of Afghan.

Design by Sarah J. Green.

BIG ON RIPPLES

This thick and cozy wrap is big on ripples! Made with variegated worsted weight yarn, the afghan works up fast because you hold four strands of yarn together as you crochet with a large Q hook.

◼◼◻◻ **EASY**

Finished Size:
54" x 68" (137 cm x 172.5 cm)

MATERIALS
Medium/Worsted Weight Yarn
[6 ounces, 348 yards
(170 grams, 318 meters)
per skein]: 20 skeins
Crochet hook, size Q (15 mm) **or** size
  needed for gauge

GAUGE: One repeat
(from point to point) = 9" (23 cm)
and Rows 1-4 = 4" (10 cm)

Note: Entire Afghan is worked holding
four strands of yarn together.

AFGHAN
Ch 113.

Row 1 (Right side)**:** Working in back ridge of each ch **(Fig. 1, page 205)**, sc in second ch from hook and in next 7 chs, 3 sc in next ch, sc in next 8 chs, ★ skip next 2 chs, sc in next 8 chs, 3 sc in next ch, sc in next 8 chs; repeat from ★ across: 114 sc.

Row 2: Ch 1, turn; sc in first sc, skip next sc, sc in next 7 sc, 3 sc in next sc, ★ sc in next 8 sc, skip next 2 sc, sc in next 8 sc, 3 sc in next sc; repeat from ★ 4 times **more**, sc in next 7 sc, skip next sc, sc in last sc.

To decrease (uses next 4 sc), YO, insert hook in **next** sc, YO and pull up a loop, YO and draw through 2 loops on hook, YO, skip **next** 2 sc, insert hook in **next** sc, YO and pull up a loop, YO and draw through 2 loops on hook, YO and draw through all 3 loops on hook **(counts as one dc)**.

To work ending decrease (uses last 2 sc), ★ YO, insert hook in **next** sc, YO and pull up a loop, YO and draw through 2 loops on hook; repeat from ★ once **more**, YO and draw through all 3 loops on hook **(counts as one dc)**.

Row 3: Ch 2, turn; dc in next sc, ★ † skip next sc, (dc, ch 1, dc) in next sc, skip next 2 sc, (dc, ch 1, dc) in next sc, skip next sc, dc in next sc, ch 1, (dc, ch 1) twice in next sc, dc in next sc, skip next sc, (dc, ch 1, dc) in next sc, skip next 2 sc, (dc, ch 1, dc) in next sc, skip next sc †, decrease; repeat from ★ 4 times **more**, then repeat from † to † once, work ending decrease: 79 dc and 42 ch-1 sps.

Row 4: Ch 1, turn; sc in first dc, skip next dc, ★ † (sc in next ch-1 sp and in next 2 dc) twice, skip next ch-1 sp, sc in next dc, 3 sc in next ch-1 sp, sc in next dc, skip next ch-1 sp, (sc in next 2 dc and in next ch-1 sp) twice †, sc in next dc, skip next dc, sc in next dc; repeat from ★ 4 times **more**, then repeat from † to † once, skip next dc, sc in last dc, leave remaining ch-2 unworked: 114 sc.

Repeat Rows 2-4 until Afghan measures approximately 68" (172.5 cm) from beginning ch, ending by working Row 2; finish off.

Design by Sue Galucki.

BRAIDED ILLUSION AFGHAN

Capture the colors of Christmas in this warm mile-a-minute wrap! It makes a festive addition to your decor — or a great gift for a family.

◼◼◼◻ INTERMEDIATE

Finished Size:
46" x 63" (117 cm x 160 cm)

MATERIALS
Medium/Worsted Weight Yarn
[8 ounces, 452 yards
(230 grams, 413 meters)
per skein]:
Cherry Red - 3 skeins
Hunter Green - 3 skeins
Soft White - 2 skeins
Crochet hook, size I (5.5 mm) **or** size needed for gauge
Yarn needle

GAUGE: Center = $2^1/4$" (5.75 cm) wide and 8 rows = 5" (12.75 cm); Each Strip = $3^1/2$" (9 cm) wide

STRIP (Make 13)
CENTER
With Cherry Red, ch 10.

Row 1: Dc in fourth ch from hook **(3 skipped chs count as first dc)** and in each ch across: 8 dc.

To change colors, work stitch indicated to within one step of completion, hook new yarn and draw through all loops on hook **(Fig. 7b, page 206)**. Carry unused colors loosely on **wrong** side of work; do not cut yarn unless instructed.

To work Front Post treble crochet (abbreviated FPtr), YO twice, insert hook from **front** to **back** around post of st indicated **(Fig. 4, page 205)**, YO and pull up a loop (4 loops on hook), (YO and draw through 2 loops on hook) 3 times. Skip st behind FPtr.

Row 2 (Right side)**:** Ch 3 **(counts as first dc, now and throughout)**, turn; dc in next 2 dc changing to Hunter Green in last dc made, skip next 2 dc, work FPtr around each of next 2 dc changing to Soft White in last FPtr made, working in **front** of last 2 FPtr made, work FPtr around first skipped dc and around next skipped dc, dc in last dc.

Note: Mark Row 2 as **right** side and bottom edge.

To work Back Post treble crochet (abbreviated BPtr), YO twice, insert hook from **back** to **front** around post of st indicated **(Fig. 4, page 205)**, YO and pull up a loop (4 loops on hook), (YO and draw through 2 loops on hook) 3 times. Skip st in front of BPtr.

Row 3: Ch 3, turn; dc in next 2 FPtr changing to Cherry Red in last dc made, skip next 2 FPtr, work BPtr around each of next 2 dc changing to Hunter Green in last BPtr made, working **behind** last 2 BPtr made, work BPtr around first skipped FPtr and around next skipped FPtr, dc in last dc.

Row 4: Ch 3, turn; dc in next 2 BPtr changing to Soft White in last dc made, skip next 2 BPtr, work FPtr around each of next 2 dc changing to Cherry Red in last FPtr made, working in **front** of last 2 FPtr made, work FPtr around first skipped BPtr and around next skipped BPtr, dc in last dc.

Row 5: Ch 3, turn; dc in next 2 FPtr changing to Hunter Green in last dc made, skip next 2 FPtr, work BPtr around each of next 2 dc changing to Soft White in last BPtr made, working **behind** last 2 BPtr made, work BPtr around first skipped FPtr and around next skipped FPtr, dc in last dc.

Row 6: Ch 3, turn; dc in next 2 BPtr changing to Cherry Red in last dc made, skip next 2 BPtr, work FPtr around each of next 2 dc changing to Hunter Green in last FPtr made, working in **front** of last 2 FPtr made, work FPtr around first skipped BPtr and around next skipped BPtr, dc in last dc.

Row 7: Ch 3, turn; dc in next 2 FPtr changing to Soft White in last dc made, skip next 2 FPtr, work BPtr around each of next 2 dc changing to Cherry Red in last BPtr made, working **behind** last 2 BPtr made, work BPtr around first skipped FPtr and around next skipped FPtr, dc in last dc.

Row 8: Ch 3, turn; dc in next 2 BPtr changing to Hunter Green in last dc made, skip next 2 BPtr, work FPtr around each of next 2 dc changing to Soft White in last FPtr made, working in **front** of last 2 FPtr made, work FPtr around first skipped BPtr and around next skipped BPtr, dc in last dc.

Rows 9-97: Repeat Rows 3-8, 14 times; then repeat Rows 3-7 once **more**; cut Hunter Green and Soft White.

Row 98: Ch 1, turn; sc in each st across; do **not** finish off.

BORDER
Rnd 1: Ch 3, do **not** turn; working in end of rows, skip first row, 2 dc in next row and in each row across; working in free loops of beginning ch **(Fig. 3b, page 205)**, 5 dc in ch at base of first dc, dc in each ch across to last ch, 5 dc in last ch; working in end of rows, 2 dc in first row and in each row across to last row, dc in last row; working across Row 98, 5 dc in first sc, dc in each sc across to last sc, 5 dc in last sc; join with slip st to first dc changing to Hunter Green **(Fig. 7c, page 206)**, cut Cherry Red: 422 dc.

Rnd 2: Ch 1, sc in same st and in each dc around working 3 sc in center dc of each corner 5-dc group; join with slip st to first sc, finish off: 430 sc.

ASSEMBLY

Place two Strips with **wrong** sides together and bottom edges at the same end. With Hunter Green and working through **inside** loops, whipstitch Strips together **(Fig. 9d, page 206)**, beginning in center sc of first corner 3-sc group and ending in center sc of next corner 3-sc group.

Join remaining Strips in same manner, always working in the same direction.

EDGING

Rnd 1: With **right** side facing, join Soft White with slip st in any sc; ch 1, (slip st in next st, ch 1) around; join with slip st to joining slip st, finish off.

Design by Joan Beebe.

BABY'S BED OF ROSES

When you snuggle a little one in this winsome wrap, you'll be providing the tender, loving care that Baby needs to blossom! Rows of rosebuds work up quickly in this join-as-you-go blanket.

■■■□ INTERMEDIATE

Finished Size:
35" x 44" (89 cm x 112 cm)

MATERIALS
Light/Worsted Weight Yarn
[6 ounces, 480 yards
(170 grams, 439 meters)
per skein]:
White - 2 skeins
Pastel Green - 2 skeins
Light Pink - 1 skein
Crochet hook, size G (4 mm) **or** size
needed for gauge

GAUGE: 18 dc = 4" (10 cm);
Each Strip = 5" (12.75 cm) wide

FIRST STRIP
With White, ch 149.

Foundation Row (Right side)**:** Dc in fourth ch from hook **(3 skipped chs count as first dc)** and in each ch across; finish off: 147 dc.

Note: Mark first dc on Foundation Row as **right** side and bottom edge.

To work Back Post double crochet (abbreviated BPdc), YO, insert hook from **back** to **front** around post of dc indicated *(Fig. 4, page 205)*, YO and pull up a loop even with last st made (3 loops on hook), (YO and draw through 2 loops on hook) twice. Skip st in front of BPdc.

Rnd 1: With **wrong** side facing and working in end of Foundation Row, join Pastel Green with sc *(see Joining With Sc, page 205)* around post of marked dc (do **not** remove marker); working across beginning ch, sc in ch at base of same dc, work BPdc around dc **below** next ch, (sc in free loop of next 5 chs, work BPdc around dc **below** next ch) across to last ch, sc in free loop of last ch; working across end of Foundation Row, sc around post of dc **above** same ch, working **behind** same post, work BPdc around next dc on Foundation Row, sc around post of dc at end of Foundation Row (same dc as last sc made); working across opposite side of Foundation Row, sc in first dc, work BPdc around next dc (same dc as corresponding BPdc on opposite side), (sc in next 5 dc, work BPdc around next dc) across to last dc, sc in last dc; working across end of Foundation Row, sc around post of same dc, working **behind** same post, work BPdc around next dc on Foundation Row; join with slip st to first sc, do **not** finish off: 248 sc and 52 BPdc.

To work Front Post double crochet (abbreviated FPdc), YO, insert hook from **front** to **back** around post of st indicated *(Fig. 4, page 205)*, YO and pull up a loop even with last st made (3 loops on hook), (YO and draw through 2 loops on hook) twice. Skip st behind FPdc unless otherwise specified.

Rnd 2: **Turn**; slip st in next BPdc, ch 3 **(counts as first dc, now and throughout)**, dc in same st, † ch 2, work FPdc around same st, ch 2, 2 dc in same st, ch 1, skip next 2 sc, 2 dc in next BPdc, ch 2, work FPdc around same st, ch 2, 2 dc in same st, ch 1, skip next 2 sc, ★ sc in next sc, ch 1, skip next 2 sc, 2 dc in next BPdc, ch 2, work FPdc around same st, ch 2, 2 dc in same st, ch 1, skip next 2 sts; repeat from ★ 23 times **more** †, 2 dc in next BPdc, repeat from † to † once; join with slip st to first dc, finish off: 204 sps.

Rnd 3: With **right** side facing, join Light Pink with slip st in first ch-2 sp to **left** of joining; † work 3 FPdc around next FPdc, slip st in next ch-2 sp, ch 7, skip next ch-1 sp, slip st in next ch-2 sp, work 3 FPdc around next FPdc, slip st in next ch-2 sp, ★ ch 5, skip next 2 ch-1 sps, slip st in next ch-2 sp, work 3 FPdc around next FPdc, slip st in next ch-2 sp; repeat from ★ 23 times **more**, ch 7, skip next ch-1 sp †, slip st in next ch-2 sp, repeat from † to † once; join with slip st to joining slip st, finish off: 52 3-FPdc groups and 52 sps.

To dc decrease (uses next 2 dc), ★ YO, insert hook in **next** dc, YO and pull up a loop, YO and draw through 2 loops on hook; repeat from ★ once **more**, YO and draw through all 3 loops on hook.

Note: Work in both loops of each stitch unless otherwise specified.

Rnd 4: With **right** side facing and working in sts and in sps on Rnd 2 in **front** of Rnd 3 ch-5 and ch-7 sps, join Pastel Green with slip st in same st as joining on Rnd 2; ch 2, dc in next dc, † sc in next ch-2 sp **(over Rnd 3 slip st, now and throughout)**, ch 3, sc in Back Loop Only *(Fig. 2, page 205)* of next FPdc **(behind Rnd 3 3-FPdc group, now and throughout)**, ch 3, sc in next ch-2 sp, dc decrease, ch 3, dc decrease, sc in next ch-2 sp, ch 3, sc in Back Loop Only of next FPdc, ch 3, sc in next ch-2 sp, dc decrease, ★ ch 1, dc decrease, sc in next ch-2 sp, ch 3, sc in Back Loop Only of next FPdc, ch 3, sc in next ch-2 sp, dc decrease; repeat from ★ 23 times **more**, ch 3 †, dc decrease, repeat from † to † once; join with slip st to first dc, finish off: 108 ch-3 sps and 48 ch-1 sps.

Instructions continued on page 47.

HIS & HERS BABY AFGHANS

Crocheted in blue for him and pink for her, these wraps will offer a warm welcome to new arrivals. The boy's coverlet has a wavy shell pattern, while the girl's has a faux picot design.

■■□□ EASY

GIRL'S AFGHAN

Finished Size:
34" x 45" (86.5 cm x 114.5 cm)

MATERIALS

Light/Worsted Weight Yarn
  [6 ounces, 480 yards
  (170 grams, 439 meters)
  per skein]: 4 skeins
Crochet hook, size H (5 mm) **or** size
  needed for gauge

GAUGE: In pattern,
10 dc = 3" (7.5 cm);
8 rows = 3¹/₄" (8.25 cm)

Ch 108.

Row 1 (Right side): Dc in fourth ch from hook **(3 skipped chs count as first dc)** and in each ch across: 106 dc.

Row 2: Ch 1, turn; skip first dc, (sc, ch 3, hdc) in next dc, ★ skip next dc, (sc, ch 3, hdc) in next dc; repeat from ★ across to last 2 dc, skip next dc, sc in last dc: 53 sc.

Row 3: Ch 3 **(counts as first dc, now and throughout)**, turn; dc in same st, 2 dc in next sc and in each sc across: 106 dc.

Rows 4-105: Repeat Rows 2 and 3, 51 times; do **not** finish off.

EDGING

Rnd 1: Ch 3, do **not** turn; † working in end of rows, 2 dc in first row, (dc in next row, 2 dc in next row) across †; working in free loops of beginning ch **(Fig. 3b, page 205)**, 4 dc in first ch, dc in next 104 chs, 4 dc in next ch, repeat from † to † once; working across Row 93, 4 dc in first dc, dc in next dc and in each dc across, 3 dc in same st as first dc; join with slip st to first dc: 540 dc.

Rnd 2: Ch 1, sc in same st, ch 4, skip next dc, ★ sc in next dc, ch 4, skip next dc; repeat from ★ around; join with slip st to first sc.

Rnd 3: Slip st in first ch-4 sp, ch 1, (sc, ch 3, hdc) in same sp and in each ch-4 sp around; join with slip st to first sc, finish off.

Design by Jennine Korejko.

BOY'S AFGHAN

Finished Size:
34" x 45¹/₂" (86.5 cm x 115.5 cm)

MATERIALS

Light/Worsted Weight Yarn
  [6 ounces, 480 yards
  (170 grams, 439 meters)
  per skein]: 4 skeins
Crochet hook, size G (4 mm) **or** size
  needed for gauge

GAUGE: In pattern, 2 repeats and
9 rows = 3¹/₄" (8.25 cm)

Ch 156.

Row 1: 2 Dc in fourth ch from hook **(3 skipped chs count as first dc)**, skip next 2 chs, sc in next 3 chs, ★ skip next 2 chs, 5 dc in next ch, skip next 2 chs, sc in next 3 chs; repeat from ★ across to last 3 chs, skip next 2 chs, 3 dc in last ch: 153 sts.

Row 2 (Right side): Ch 1, turn; working in Back Loops Only **(Fig. 2, page 205)**, sc in first 2 dc, ch 1, skip next 2 sts, (dc, ch 1) twice in next sc, ★ skip next 2 sts, sc in next 3 dc, ch 1, skip next 2 sts, (dc, ch 1) twice in next sc; repeat from ★ across to last 4 sts, skip next 2 sts, sc in last 2 dc: 96 sts and 57 ch-1 sps.

Row 3: Ch 1, turn; working in both loops, sc in first 2 sc, skip next ch-1 sp, 5 dc in next ch-1 sp, ★ sc in next 3 sc, skip next ch-1 sp, 5 dc in next ch-1 sp; repeat from ★ across to last ch-1 sp, skip last ch-1 sp, sc in last 2 sc: 153 sts.

Row 4: Ch 4 **(counts as first dc plus ch 1)**, turn; working in Back Loops Only, dc in same st, ch 1, skip next 2 sts, sc in next 3 dc, ch 1, ★ skip next 2 sts, (dc, ch 1) twice in next sc, skip next 2 sts, sc in next 3 dc, ch 1; repeat from ★ across to last 3 sts, skip next 2 sts, (dc, ch 1, dc) in last sc: 97 sts and 58 ch-1 sps.

Row 5: Ch 3 **(counts as first dc)**, turn; working in both loops, 2 dc in same st, sc in next 3 sc, ★ skip next ch-1 sp, 5 dc in next ch-1 sp, sc in next 3 sc; repeat from ★ across to last 2 ch-1 sps, skip last 2 ch-1 sps, 3 dc in last dc: 153 sts.

Row 6: Ch 1, turn; working in Back Loops Only, sc in first 2 dc, ch 1, skip next 2 sts, (dc, ch 1) twice in next sc, ★ skip next 2 sts, sc in next 3 dc, ch 1, skip next 2 sts, (dc, ch 1) twice in next sc; repeat from ★ across to last 4 sts, skip next 2 sts, sc in last 2 dc: 96 sts and 57 ch-1 sps.

Rows 7-118: Repeat Rows 3-6, 28 times; do **not** finish off.

Instructions continued on page 47.

BABY'S "FAN-CY" AFGHAN

You're sure to strike Baby's "fan-cy" with this pretty patterned coverlet. The downy blanket is enhanced with a beribboned edging.

■■□□ **EASY**

Finished Size:
38" x 41" (96.5 cm x 104 cm)

MATERIALS
Medium/Worsted Weight Yarn
[8 ounces, 452 yards
(230 grams, 413 meters)
per skein]: 3 skeins
MEDIUM 4
Crochet hook, size H (5 mm) **or** size
needed for gauge
¼" (7 mm) wide Ribbon - 7 yards
(6.5 meters)

GAUGE: In pattern, one repeat
and 9 rows = 3½" (9 cm)

CENTER
Ch 110.

Row 1: Sc in second ch from hook, ★ ch 3, skip next 2 chs, sc in next ch; repeat from ★ across: 37 sc and 36 ch-3 sps.

Row 2 (Right side): Ch 4 **(counts as first dc plus ch 1, now and throughout)**, turn; sc in next ch-3 sp, ch 3, sc in next ch-3 sp, 3 dc in next sc, sc in next ch-3 sp, ★ (ch 3, sc in next ch-3 sp) 3 times, 3 dc in next sc, sc in next ch-3 sp; repeat from ★ across to last ch-3 sp, ch 3, sc in last ch-3 sp, ch 1, dc in last sc: 29 dc and 28 sps.

Row 3: Ch 1, turn; sc in first dc, ch 3, sc in next ch-3 sp, 2 dc in each of next 3 dc, sc in next ch-3 sp, ★ (ch 3, sc in next ch-3 sp) twice, 2 dc in each of next 3 dc, sc in next ch-3 sp; repeat from ★ across to last ch-1 sp, ch 3, skip last ch-1 sp, sc in last dc: 54 dc and 18 ch-3 sps.

Row 4: Ch 4, turn; sc in next ch-3 sp, 2 dc in each of next 6 dc, sc in next ch-3 sp, ★ ch 3, sc in next ch-3 sp, 2 dc in each of next 6 dc, sc in next ch-3 sp; repeat from ★ across to last sc, ch 1, dc in last sc: 110 dc and 10 sps.

Row 5: Ch 1, turn; sc in first dc, ch 3, skip next sc and next 3 dc, sc in sp **before** next dc *(Fig. 5, page 205)*, ch 3, (skip next 3 dc, sc in sp **before** next dc, ch 3) twice, ★ sc in next ch-3 sp, ch 3, skip next 4 sts, sc in sp **before** next dc, ch 3, (skip next 3 dc, sc in sp **before** next dc, ch 3) twice; repeat from ★ across to last ch-1 sp, skip last ch-1 sp, sc in last dc: 37 sc and 36 ch-3 sps.

Row 6: Ch 3 **(counts as first dc, now and throughout)**, turn; dc in same st, sc in next ch-3 sp, (ch 3, sc in next ch-3 sp) 3 times, ★ 3 dc in next sc, sc in next ch-3 sp, (ch 3, sc in next ch-3 sp) 3 times; repeat from ★ across to last sc, 2 dc in last sc: 28 dc and 27 ch-3 sps.

Row 7: Ch 3, turn; 2 dc in next dc, sc in next ch-3 sp, (ch 3, sc in next ch-3 sp) twice, ★ 2 dc in each of next 3 dc, sc in next ch-3 sp, (ch 3, sc in next ch-3 sp) twice; repeat from ★ across to last 3 sts, skip next sc, 2 dc in next dc, dc in last dc: 54 dc and 18 ch-3 sps.

Row 8: Ch 3, turn; dc in same st, 2 dc in each of next 2 dc, sc in next ch-3 sp, ch 3, sc in next ch-3 sp, ★ 2 dc in each of next 6 dc, sc in next ch-3 sp, ch 3, sc in next ch-3 sp; repeat from ★ across to last 4 sts, skip next sc, 2 dc in each of last 3 dc: 108 dc and 9 ch-3 sps.

Row 9: Ch 1, turn; sc in first dc, ch 3, skip next 2 dc, sc in sp **before** next dc, ch 3, sc in next ch-3 sp, ch 3, skip next 4 sts, sc in sp **before** next dc, ch 3, ★ (skip next 3 dc, sc in sp **before** next dc, ch 3) twice, sc in next ch-3 sp, ch 3, skip next 4 sts, sc in sp **before** next dc, ch 3; repeat from ★ across to last 3 dc, skip next 2 dc, sc in last dc: 37 sc and 36 ch-3 sps.

Row 10: Ch 4, turn; sc in next ch-3 sp, ch 3, sc in next ch-3 sp, 3 dc in next sc, sc in next ch-3 sp, ★ (ch 3, sc in next ch-3 sp) 3 times, 3 dc in next sc, sc in next ch-3 sp; repeat from ★ across to last ch-3 sp, ch 3, sc in last ch-3 sp, ch 1, dc in last sc: 29 dc and 28 sps.

Rows 11-89: Repeat Rows 3-10, 9 times; then repeat Rows 3-9 once **more**; do **not** finish off.

EDGING
Rnd 1: Ch 1, turn; 2 sc in first sc, work 95 sc evenly spaced across to last sc, 3 sc in last sc; work 119 sc evenly spaced across end of rows; working in free loops *(Fig. 3b, page 205)* and in sps across beginning ch, 3 sc in ch at base of first sc, work 95 sc evenly spaced across to last ch, 3 sc in free loop of last ch; work 119 sc evenly spaced across end of rows, sc in same st as first sc; join with slip st to first sc: 440 sc.

Rnd 2 (Eyelet rnd): Ch 6 **(counts as first dc plus ch 3)**, do **not** turn; dc in same st, ★ † ch 1, skip next sc, (dc in next sc, ch 1, skip next sc) across to center sc of next corner 3-sc group †, (dc, ch 3, dc) in center sc; repeat from ★ 2 times **more**, then repeat from † to † once; join with slip st to first dc: 224 dc and 224 sps.

Rnd 3: Slip st in first ch-3 sp, ch 1, 2 sc in same sp, (sc in each dc and in each ch-1 sp across to next ch-3 sp, 3 sc in ch-3 sp) 3 times, sc in each dc and in each ch-1 sp across, sc in same sp as first sc; join with slip st to first sc: 456 sc.

Instructions continued on page 46.

Continued from page 44.

Rnd 4: Ch 1, (sc in same st, ch 3) twice, ★ † skip next 2 sc, (sc in next sc, ch 3, skip next 2 sc) across to center sc of next corner 3-sc group †, (sc, ch 3) 3 times in center sc; repeat from ★ 2 times **more**, then repeat from † to † once, sc in same st as first sc, ch 3; join with slip st to first sc: 160 sc and 160 ch-3 sps.

Rnd 5: Ch 3, 5 dc in same st, sc in next ch-3 sp, (ch 3, sc in next ch-3 sp) 3 times, † 3 dc in next sc, sc in next ch-3 sp, (ch 3, sc in next ch-3 sp) 3 times †; repeat from † to † across to center sc of next corner 3-sc group, ★ 6 dc in center sc, sc in next ch-3 sp, (ch 3, sc in next ch-3 sp) 3 times, repeat from † to † across to center sc of next corner 3-sc group; repeat from ★ 2 times **more**; join with slip st to first dc.

Rnd 6: Ch 3, dc in same st, 2 dc in each of next 5 dc, sc in next ch-3 sp, (ch 3, sc in next ch-3 sp) twice, † 2 dc in each of next 3 dc, sc in next ch-3 sp, (ch 3, sc in next ch-3 sp) twice †; repeat from † to † across to next corner 6-dc group, ★ 2 dc in each of next 6 dc, sc in next ch-3 sp, (ch 3, sc in next ch-3 sp) twice, repeat from † to † across to next corner 6-dc group; repeat from ★ 2 times **more**; join with slip st to first dc.

Rnd 7: Ch 3, dc in same st, 2 dc in each of next 11 dc, sc in next ch 3 sp, ch 3, sc in next ch-3 sp, † 2 dc in each of next 6 dc, sc in next ch-3 sp, ch 3, sc in next ch-3 sp †; repeat from † to † across to next corner 12-dc group, ★ 2 dc in each of next 12 dc, sc in next ch-3 sp, ch 3, sc in next ch-3 sp, repeat from † to † across to next corner 12-dc group; repeat from ★ 2 times **more**; join with slip st to first dc.

Rnd 8: Slip st in sp **before** next dc, ch 1, sc in same sp, (ch 4, skip next 2 dc, sc in sp **before** next dc) 11 times, sc in next ch-3 sp, † skip next 2 sts, sc in sp **before** next dc, (ch 4, skip next 2 dc, sc in sp **before** next dc) 5 times, sc in next ch-3 sp †; repeat from † to † across to next corner 24-dc group, ★ skip next 2 sts, sc in sp **before** next dc, (ch 4, skip next 2 dc, sc in sp **before** next dc) 11 times, sc in next ch-3 sp, repeat from † to † across to next corner 24-dc group; repeat from ★ 2 times **more**; join with slip st to first sc, finish off.

Cut ribbon into two 66" (167.5 cm) lengths and two 60" (152.5 cm) lengths.

Using photo as a guide for placement:

Working across **length** of Afghan, weave one 66" (167.5 cm) length of ribbon through Eyelet rnd on one side; repeat across opposite side.

Working across **width** of Afghan, weave one 60" (152.5 cm) length of ribbon through Eyelet rnd on one side; repeat across opposite side.

Tie ribbon ends in a bow at each corner.

Design by Sandra Abbate.

BABY'S BED OF ROSES
Continued from page 40.

Rnd 5: With **right** side facing and working around ch-7 one rnd **below**, join White with sc in first ch-3 sp to **right** of joining; 2 sc in same sp, † ch 5, sc in next ch-3 sp, sc in next sc and in next ch-3 sp, ch 5, working around ch-7 one rnd **below**, 3 sc in next ch-3 sp, ch 5, sc in next ch-3 sp, sc in next sc and in next ch-3 sp, ★ ch 3, working around ch-5 one rnd **below**, sc in next ch-1 sp, ch 3, sc in next ch-3 sp, sc in next sc and in next ch-3 sp; repeat from ★ 23 times **more**, ch 5 †, working around ch-7 one rnd **below**, 3 sc in next ch-3 sp, repeat from † to † once; join with slip st to first sc, do **not** finish off: 216 sc and 104 sps.

To work Cluster, ★ YO, insert hook in sp indicated, YO and pull up a loop, YO and draw through 2 loops on hook; repeat from ★ once **more**, YO and draw through all 3 loops on hook.

To sp decrease (uses next 2 ch-3 sps), ★ YO, insert hook in **next** ch-3 sp, YO and pull up a loop, YO and draw through 2 loops on hook; repeat from ★ once **more**, YO and draw through all 3 loops on hook.

Rnd 6: Ch 3, dc in next 2 sc, ch 3, (work Cluster in next ch-5 sp, ch 3, dc in next 3 sc, ch 3) 3 times, † (sp decrease, ch 3, dc in next 3 sc, ch 3) 24 times †, (work Cluster in next ch-5 sp, ch 3, dc in next 3 sc, ch 3) 4 times, repeat from † to † once, work Cluster in last ch-5 sp, ch 3; join with slip st to first dc, finish off: 112 ch-3 sps.

REMAINING 6 STRIPS
Work same as First Strip through Rnd 5: 216 sc and 104 sps.

Rnd 6 (Joining rnd)**:** Ch 3, dc in next 2 sc, ch 3, (work Cluster in next ch-5 sp, ch 3, dc in next 3 sc, ch 3) 3 times, (sp decrease, ch 3, dc in next 3 sc, ch 3) 24 times, work Cluster in next ch-5 sp, ch 3, dc in next 3 sc, (ch 3, work Cluster in next ch-5 sp, ch 3, dc in next 3 sc) 3 times, ch 1, holding Strips with **wrong** sides together and bottom edges at same end, slip st in corresponding ch-3 sp on **previous Strip**, ch 1, sp decrease on **new Strip**, ch 1, slip st in next ch-3 sp on **previous Strip**, ch 1, dc in next 3 sc on **new Strip**, ★ ch 1, slip st in next ch-3 sp on **previous Strip**, ch 1, sp decrease on **new Strip**, ch 1, slip st in next ch-3 sp on **previous Strip**, ch 1, dc in next 3 sc on **new Strip**; repeat from ★ 22 times **more**, ch 3, work Cluster in last ch-5 sp, ch 3; join with slip st to first dc, finish off.

Design by Tammy Kreimeyer.

HIS & HERS BABY AFGHANS
Continued from page 42.

EDGING
Rnd 1: Ch 1, do **not** turn; working in both loops, 2 sc in same st, work 189 sc evenly spaced across end of rows; 3 sc in ch at base of first dc, working in sps and in free loops across beginning ch *(Fig. 3b, page 205)*, work 149 sc evenly spaced across to last ch, 3 sc in last ch; work 189 sc evenly spaced across end of rows; 3 sc in first sc, work 149 sc evenly spaced across Row 118, sc in same st as first sc; join with slip st to first sc: 688 sc.

Rnd 2: Ch 1, turn; 2 sc in same st, ★ † sc in next 2 sc, skip next sc, 5 dc in next sc, ♥ skip next 2 sc, sc in next 3 sc, skip next 2 sc, 5 dc in next sc ♥, repeat from ♥ to ♥ across to within 2 sc of next corner 3-sc group, skip next sc, sc in next 2 sc †, 3 sc in center sc of corner 3-sc group; repeat from ★ 2 times **more**, then repeat from † to † once, sc in same st as first sc; join with slip st to Front Loop Only of first sc: 86 5-dc groups.

Rnd 3: Ch 1, turn; working in Back Loops Only, sc in same st, ★ † skip next sc, 5 dc in next sc, ♥ skip next 2 sts, sc in next 3 dc, skip next 2 sts, 5 dc in next sc ♥, repeat from ♥ to ♥ across to next corner 3-sc group, skip next sc †, sc in center sc of corner 3-sc group; repeat from ★ 2 times **more**, then repeat from † to † once; join with slip st to **both** loops of first sc: 90 5-dc groups.

To work Picot, ch 3, slip st in top of last sc made.

Rnd 4: Ch 1, do **not** turn; working in both loops, sc in same st, work Picot, ★ † dc in next 2 dc, (dc, ch 1, dc) in next dc, dc in next 2 dc, ♥ sc in next 2 sc, work Picot, sc in next sc, dc in next 2 dc, (dc, ch 1, dc) in next dc, dc in next 2 dc ♥, repeat from ♥ to ♥ across to next corner sc †, sc in corner sc, work Picot; repeat from ★ 2 times **more**, then repeat from † to † once; join with slip st to first sc, finish off.

Design by Teresa Smith.

DAISY BLANKET

With picturesque petals and a snuggly texture, this little blanket will captivate wee ones and wrap them in warmth.

◼◼◻◻ **EASY**

Finished Size:
32¹/₂" x 45" (82.5 cm x 114.5 cm)

MATERIALS
Light/Worsted Weight Yarn
[6 ounces, 480 yards
(170 grams, 439 meters)
per skein]:
Baby Yellow - 2 skeins
Baby Blue - 1 skein
Pastel Green - 1 skein
Light Pink - 1 skein
White - 1 skein
Crochet hook, size G (4 mm) **or** size
   needed for gauge
Yarn needle

GAUGE:
Each Square = 4¹/₄" (10.75 cm)

SQUARE (Make 70)
With Baby Yellow, ch 5; join with slip st to form a ring.

Rnd 1 (Right side): Ch 1, 12 sc in ring; join with slip st to first sc, finish off: 12 sc.

Note #1: Mark Rnd 1 as **right** side.

Note #2: Using the following colors for Rnd 2, make 24 flowers with White, 23 flowers **each** with Light Pink and Baby Blue.

Rnd 2: With **right** side facing, join next color with slip st in same st as joining; ★ ch 6 **loosely**, working in top loop only of each ch, dc in third ch from hook and in last 3 chs **(Petal made)**, slip st in next sc; repeat from ★ around working last slip st in same st as joining; finish off: 12 Petals.

Rnd 3: With **right** side facing, join Pastel Green with slip st in ch-2 sp at tip of any Petal; ch 3 **(counts as first dc, now and throughout)**, (2 dc, ch 3, 3 dc) in same sp, ch 1, sc in ch-2 sp at tip of next Petal, ch 2, sc in ch-2 sp at tip of next Petal, ch 1, ★ (3 dc, ch 3, 3 dc) in ch-2 sp at tip of next Petal, ch 1, sc in ch-2 sp at tip of next Petal, ch 2, sc in ch-2 sp at tip of next Petal, ch 1; repeat from ★ 2 times **more**; join with slip st to first dc, finish off: 16 sps.

Rnd 4: With **right** side facing, join Baby Yellow with slip st in any ch-3 sp; ch 3, (2 dc, ch 3, 3 dc) in same sp, ch 1, 2 dc in next ch-1 sp, hdc in next sc, ch 1, 2 hdc in next ch-2 sp, ch 1, hdc in next sc, 2 dc in next ch-1 sp, ch 1, ★ (3 dc, ch 3, 3 dc) in next ch-3 sp, ch 1, 2 dc in next ch-1 sp, hdc in next sc, ch 1, 2 hdc in next ch-2 sp, ch 1, hdc in next sc, 2 dc in next ch-1 sp, ch 1; repeat from ★ 2 times **more**; join with slip st to first dc, finish off: 56 sts and 20 sps.

ASSEMBLY
Using diagram as a guide for placement, with Baby Yellow, and working through **both** loops of each stitch on **both** pieces, whipstitch Squares together **(Fig. 9a, page 206)**, beginning in center ch of first corner ch-3 and ending in center ch of next corner ch-3; then whipstitch strips together in same manner.

EDGING
Rnd 1: With **right** side facing, join Light Pink with slip st in top right corner ch-3 sp; ch 3, (2 dc, ch 3, 3 dc) in same sp, ch 2, (dc in next sp, ch 2) across to next corner ch-3 sp, ★ (3 dc, ch 3, 3 dc) in corner ch-3 sp, ch 2, (dc in next sp, ch 2) across to next corner ch-3 sp; repeat from ★ 2 times **more**; join with slip st to first dc, finish off: 220 dc and 204 sps.

Rnd 2: With **right** side facing, join Pastel Green with slip st in top right corner ch-3 sp; ch 3, (2 dc, ch 3, 3 dc) in same sp, ★ 3 dc in each ch-2 sp across to next corner ch-3 sp, (3 dc, ch 3, 3 dc) in corner ch-3 sp; repeat from ★ 2 times **more**, 3 dc in each ch-2 sp across; join with slip st to first dc, finish off: 624 dc and 4 ch-3 sps.

To work Picot, ch 3, sc in third ch from hook.

Rnd 3: With **right** side facing, join Baby Blue with sc in top right corner ch-3 sp *(see Joining With Sc, page 205)*; work Picot, (sc in same sp, work Picot) twice, ★ † skip next 3 dc, sc in sp **before** next dc, work Picot †, repeat from † to † across to within 3 dc of next corner ch-3 sp, skip next 3 dc, (sc, work Picot) 3 times in corner ch-3 sp; repeat from ★ 2 times **more**, then repeat from † to † across to last 3 dc, skip last 3 dc; join with slip st to first sc, finish off.

Design by Jane Pearson.

MILES OF LOVE BABY BLANKET

Mom will get lots of mileage out of this cuddle-'em, bounce-'em, bundle-'em blanket for Baby. And with the mile-a-minute method, she'll also find the lightweight wrap speedy to crochet.

■■□□ EASY

Finished Size:
36" x 46" (91.5 cm x 117 cm)

MATERIALS
Light/Worsted Weight Yarn
[2½ ounces, 250 yards
(70 grams, 229 meters)
per skein]:
Blue Jewel - 6 skeins
White - 4 skeins
Crochet hook, size G (4 mm) **or** size
 needed for gauge
Yarn needle

GAUGE: Center = 1⅞" (4.75 cm) wide
and 8 rows = 4" (10 cm);
Each Strip = 3¾" (9.5 cm)

STRIP (Make 9)
CENTER
With Blue Jewel, ch 11.

Row 1 (Right side)**:** Dc in fourth ch
from hook **(3 skipped chs count as
first dc)**, ch 1, skip next 3 chs, dc in
next ch, ch 1, working **around** last dc
made, dc in second skipped ch, ch 1,
skip next ch, dc in last 2 chs: 6 dc and 3
ch-1 sps.

Note: Mark Row 1 as **right** side and
bottom edge.

Row 2: Ch 3 **(counts as first dc,
now and throughout)**, turn; dc in next
dc, ch 1, skip next ch-1 sp, (dc, ch 1) 3
times in next ch-1 sp, skip next dc, dc in
last 2 dc: 7 dc and 4 ch-1 sps.

Row 3: Ch 3, turn; dc in next dc, ch 1,
skip next 2 ch-1 sps, dc in next ch-1 sp,
ch 1, working **around** last dc made, dc
in second skipped ch-1 sp, ch 1, skip
next dc, dc in last 2 dc: 6 dc and 3 ch-1
sps.

Row 4: Ch 3, turn; dc in next dc, ch 1,
skip next ch-1 sp, (dc, ch 1) 3 times in
next ch-1 sp, skip next dc, dc in last 2
dc: 7 dc and 4 ch-1 sps.

Rows 5-89: Repeat Rows 3 and 4, 42
times; then repeat Row 3 once **more**;
finish off.

BORDER
Rnd 1: With **right** side facing and
working across Row 89, skip first dc and
join White with sc in sp **before** next dc
(see Joining With Sc, page 205);
ch 2, sc in same sp, ch 2, sc in next ch-1
sp, ch 2, skip next ch-1 sp, sc in next
ch-1 sp, ch 2, skip next dc, (sc, ch 2)
twice in sp **before** last dc; working in
end of rows (around posts of dc), skip
first row, (sc in next row, ch 2) across to
last row, skip last row; working in sps
across beginning ch, (sc, ch 2) twice in
first sp (between last 2 dc on Row 1), sc
in next sp, ch 2, skip next sp (between
crossed dc), sc in next sp, ch 2, (sc, ch 2)
twice in last sp (between first 2 dc on
Row 1); working in end of rows (around
posts of dc), skip first row, (sc in next
row, ch 2) across to last row, skip last
row; join with slip st to first sc: 186 ch-2
sps.

To work Cross St, hdc in next ch-2 sp,
working **around** hdc just made, hdc in
previous ch-2 sp (same sp as slip st
before hdc just made **or** same sp as first
leg of last Cross St made).

Rnd 2: Ch 1, slip st in first ch-2 sp,
ch 3, place marker around ch-3 just
made for st placement, † work Cross St
4 times, ch 3, slip st in same sp as first
leg of last Cross St made (corner ch-2
sp), ch 3, work Cross St 89 times,
ch 3 †, slip st in same sp as first leg of
last Cross St made (corner ch-2 sp),
ch 3, repeat from † to † once; skip first
ch; join with slip st to next slip st, finish
off: 372 hdc and 8 ch-3 sps.

Rnd 3: With **right** side facing, join
Blue Jewel with slip st in marked ch-3
sp; ch 3, † (skip next hdc, 2 hdc in next
hdc) across to next ch-3 sp, ch 3, (slip st
in next ch-3 sp, ch 3) twice, skip next
hdc, hdc in next hdc, place marker
around hdc just made for joining
placement, hdc in same st, (skip next
hdc, 2 hdc in next hdc) across to next
ch-3 sp, ch 1, place marker in ch just
made for joining placement, ch 2 †, (slip
st in next ch-3 sp, ch 3) twice, repeat
from † to † once, slip st in last ch-3 sp,
ch 3; join with slip st to joining slip st,
finish off.

ASSEMBLY
Place two Strips with **wrong** sides
together and bottom edges at the same
end. With Blue Jewel, matching
corresponding marked stitches, and
working through **inside** loops,
whipstitch Strips together **(Fig. 9d,
page 206)**, beginning in first marked
stitch and ending in next marked stitch.

Join remaining Strips in same manner,
always working in the same direction.

Design by Ruth G. Shepherd.

BABY BLOCKS AFGHAN

A palette of pleasing pastels, this cuddly coverlet will fascinate Baby with its soft pattern of alternating stripes. A round of reverse single crochet tops off the classic edging.

 EASY

Finished Size:
36¹/₂" x 42" (92.5 cm x 106.5 cm)

MATERIALS
Medium/Worsted Weight Yarn
[5 ounces, 253 yards
(140 grams, 231 meters) **MEDIUM 4**
per skein]:
White - 5 skeins
Mint - 1 skein
Light Blue - 1 skein
Light Yellow - 1 skein
Light Pink - 1 skein
Crochet hook, size I (5.50 mm) **or**
size needed for gauge
Yarn needle

GAUGE:
Each Block = 5¹/₂" (14 cm) square

Note: Referring to table below, make the number of Blocks specified in the colors indicated.

Block	A	B	C	D	E	F	G	H
Make	6	5	4	6	4	6	6	5
Rows								
1&2	W	W	W	W	Y	B	P	M
3&4	Y	B	P	M	W	W	W	W
5&6	W	W	W	W	Y	B	P	M
7&8	Y	B	P	M	W	W	W	W
9&10	W	W	W	W	Y	B	P	M
11&12	Y	B	P	M	W	W	W	W
13&14	W	W	W	W	Y	B	P	M

BLOCK
With color indicated, ch 16.

Row 1 (Right side): Insert hook in second ch from hook, YO and pull up a loop, insert hook in next ch, YO and pull up a loop, YO and draw through all 3 loops on hook **(Cluster made)**, ch 1, ★ (insert hook in **next** ch, YO and pull up a loop) twice, YO and draw through all 3 loops on hook **(Cluster made)**, ch 1; repeat from ★ across to last ch, sc in last ch: 8 sts and 7 ch-1 sps.

Note: Mark Row 1 as **right** side.

To work beginning Cluster, insert hook in first sc, YO and pull up a loop, insert hook in next ch-1 sp, YO and pull up a loop, YO and draw through all 3 loops on hook.

To work Cluster, insert hook in next Cluster, YO and pull up a loop, insert hook in next ch-1 sp, YO and pull up a loop, YO and draw through all 3 loops on hook.

Row 2: Ch 1, turn; work beginning Cluster, ch 1, (work Cluster, ch 1) across to last Cluster, sc in last Cluster changing to next color.

Row 3: Ch 1, turn; work beginning Cluster, ch 1, (work Cluster, ch 1) across to last Cluster, sc in last Cluster; do **not** finish off.

BLOCKS A, B, C, AND D ONLY
Rows 4-14: Repeat Rows 2 and 3, 5 times; then repeat Row 3 once **more**; do **not** finish off.

BLOCKS E, F, G, AND H ONLY
Rows 4-14: Repeat Rows 2 and 3, 5 times; then repeat Row 2 once **more**; do **not** finish off.

ALL BLOCKS
Trim: Ch 3 **(counts as first dc)**, turn; 2 dc in same st, dc in next ch, (dc in next Cluster and in next ch) 6 times, 3 dc in last Cluster; working in end of rows, skip first row, dc in next 13 rows; working in free loops of beginning ch **(Fig. 3b, page 205)**, 3 dc in first ch, dc in next 13 chs, 3 dc in next ch; working in end of rows, dc in first 13 rows, leave last row unworked; join with slip st to first dc, finish off: 64 dc.

ASSEMBLY
With White, using diagram as a guide and working through **both** loops, whipstitch Blocks together forming 6 vertical strips of 7 Blocks each **(Fig. 9a, page 206)**, beginning in center dc of first corner 3-dc group and ending in center dc of next corner 3-dc group; then whipstitch strips together in same manner.

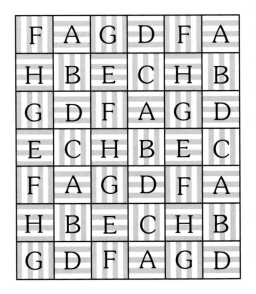

EDGING
Rnd 1: With **right** side facing and working in Back Loops Only **(Fig. 2, page 205)**, join White with sc in center dc of any corner 3-dc group **(see Joining With Sc, page 205)**; sc in each dc and in each joining around working 3 sc in center dc of each corner 3-dc group; join with slip st to Back Loop Only of first sc: 424 sc.

Rnds 2-4: Ch 1, sc in Back Loop Only of same st and each sc around working 3 sc in center sc of each corner 3-sc group; join with slip st to Back Loop Only of first sc.

Rnd 5: Ch 1, sc in Back Loop Only of same st and in each sc around working 3 sc in center sc of each corner 3-sc group; join with slip st to **both** loops of first sc.

Rnd 6: Ch 1, working from **left** to **right** and in **both** loops, work reverse sc *(Figs. 8a-d, page 206)* in each sc around; join with slip st to first st, finish off.

Design by C. A. Riley.

"BOOTIE-FUL" AFGHAN

Light as a summer breeze, our softly textured set for Baby is just right for afternoon naps. Accent with blue for him or pink for her.

■■□□ EASY

Finished Sizes:
Afghan - 35" x 49" (89 cm x 124.5 cm)
Booties - 6 months

MATERIALS
Light/Worsted Weight Yarn
[6 ounces, 480 yards
(170 grams, 439 meters)
per skein]:
White - 4 skeins
Baby Blue **or** Light Pink - 2 skeins
Crochet hook, size F (3.75 mm) **or** size
   needed for gauge
Tapestry needle
1/4" (7 mm) wide Ribbon - two 14"
   (35.5 cm) lengths (for Booties)

GAUGE:
Afghan Square = 4 3/4" (12 cm);
Bootie Sole = 4"l x 1 1/2"w
(10 cm x 4 cm)

AFGHAN
SQUARE (Make 70)
With White, ch 4; join with slip st to form a ring.

Rnd 1 (Right side): Ch 3 **(counts as first dc, now and throughout)**, 2 dc in ring, ch 3, (3 dc in ring, ch 3) 3 times; join with slip st to first dc, finish off: 12 dc and 4 ch-3 sps.

Note: Mark Rnd 1 as **right** side.

To work treble crochet (abbreviated tr), YO twice, insert hook in st indicated, YO and pull up a loop (4 loops on hook), (YO and draw through 2 loops on hook) 3 times.

Rnd 2: With **wrong** side facing, working in Front Loops Only *(Fig. 2, page 205)* and pushing tr to **right** side, join Baby Blue or Light Pink with sc in center ch of any corner ch-3 *(see Joining With Sc, page 205)*; (tr, sc) in same st, tr in next ch, (sc in next dc, tr in next st) across to center ch of next corner ch-3, ★ (sc, tr, sc) in center ch, tr in next ch, (sc in next dc, tr in next st) across to center ch of next corner ch-3; repeat from ★ 2 times **more**; join with slip st to first sc, finish off: 32 sts.

Rnd 3: With **right** side facing and working in Back Loops Only, join White with slip st in center tr of any corner 3-st group; ch 6 **(counts as first dc plus ch 3)**, dc in same st and in each st across to center tr of next corner 3-st group, ★ (dc, ch 3, dc) in center tr, dc in each st across to center tr of next corner 3-st group; repeat from ★ 2 times **more**; join with slip st to first dc, finish off: 36 dc and 4 ch-3 sps.

Rnds 4 and 5: Repeat Rnds 2 and 3; at end of Rnd 5, do **not** finish off: 60 dc and 4 ch-3 sps.

Rnd 6: Working in Back Loops Only, ch 4 **(counts as first dc plus ch 1, now and throughout)**, skip next ch, (dc, ch 1) 3 times in next ch, ★ (dc in next dc, ch 1, skip next st) across to center ch of next corner ch-3, (dc, ch 1) 3 times in center ch; repeat from ★ 2 times **more**, (dc in next dc, ch 1, skip next st) across; join with slip st to first dc, finish off: 44 dc and 44 ch-1 sps.

ASSEMBLY
SQUARE JOINING
With **right** sides of two Squares facing, join White with slip st in center dc of any corner 3-dc group on **first Square**; ch 1, slip st in corresponding dc on **second Square**, ch 1, ★ slip st in next ch-1 sp on **first Square**, ch 1, slip st in next ch-1 sp on **second Square**, ch 1; repeat from ★ across to center dc of next corner 3-dc group on **first Square**, slip st in center dc, ch 1, slip st in center dc of next corner 3-dc group on **second Square**; finish off.

Repeat to join remaining Squares, forming 7 vertical strips of 10 Squares each.

STRIP JOINING
With **right** sides of two Strips facing, join White with slip st in center dc of first corner 3-dc group on **first Strip**; ch 1, slip st in corresponding dc on **second Strip**, ch 1, ★ † slip st in next ch-1 sp on **first Strip**, ch 1, slip st in next ch-1 sp on **second Strip**, ch 1 †; repeat from † to † across to next joining, slip st in same dc as joining on **first Strip**, ch 1, slip st in same dc as joining on **second Strip**, ch 1, slip st in same dc as joining on next Square of **first Strip**, ch 1, slip st in same dc as joining on next Square of **second Strip**, ch 1; repeat from ★ 8 times **more**, then repeat from † to † across to center dc of last corner 3-dc group on **first Strip**, slip st in center dc, ch 1, slip st in center dc of last corner 3-dc group on **second Strip**; finish off.

Repeat to join remaining Strips.

Instructions continued on page 56.

Continued from page 54.

EDGING

Rnd 1: With **right** side facing and working in Back Loops Only, join White with slip st in center dc of any corner 3-dc group; ch 4, (dc in same st, ch 1) 3 times, † (dc in next dc, ch 1) across to next joining, dc in same st as joining on **same** Square, ch 1, dc in same st as joining on **next** Square, ch 1 †; repeat from † to † across to last Square on same side, (dc in next dc, ch 1) across to center dc of next corner 3-dc group, ★ (dc, ch 1) 4 times in center dc, repeat from † to † across to last Square on same side, (dc in next dc, ch 1) across to center dc of next corner 3-dc group; repeat from ★ 2 times **more**; join with slip st to first dc, finish off.

Rnd 2: With **wrong** side facing, working in Front Loops Only and pushing tr to **right** side, join Baby Blue or Light Pink with sc in center ch of any corner; (tr, sc) in same st, (tr in next dc, sc in next ch) across to center ch of next corner, ★ (sc, tr, sc) in center ch, (tr in next dc, sc in next ch) across to center ch of next corner; repeat from ★ 2 times **more**; join with slip st to **both** loops of first sc, finish off.

BOOTIES
SOLE

With Baby Blue or Light Pink, ch 16.

Rnd 1 (Right side)**:** 3 Dc in fourth ch from hook **(3 skipped chs count as first dc)**, hdc in next 3 chs, sc in next 3 chs, hdc in next 3 chs, dc in next 2 chs, 7 dc in last ch; working in free loops of beginning ch **(Fig. 3b, page 205)**, dc in next 2 chs, hdc in next 3 chs, sc in next 3 chs, hdc in next 3 chs, 3 dc in same ch as first dc; join with slip st to first dc: 36 sts.

Rnd 2: Ch 3 **(counts as first dc)**, dc in same st, working in Back Loops Only, 2 dc in each of next 3 dc, dc in next 3 hdc, hdc in next 3 sc, dc in next 5 sts, 2 dc in each of next 7 dc, dc in next 5 sts, hdc in next 3 sc, dc in next 3 hdc, 2 dc in each of next 3 dc; join with slip st to first dc, finish off: 50 sts.

SIDES

Rnd 1: With **right** side facing and working in Back Loops Only, join White with sc in same st as joining; sc in each st around; join with slip st to **both** loops of first sc.

Rnd 2: Ch 3 **(counts as first dc)**, dc in next sc and in each sc around; join with slip st to first dc.

Rnd 3: Ch 1, sc in same st and in each dc around; join with slip st to first sc, finish off.

To dc decrease (uses next 2 sts), ★ YO, insert hook in **next** st, YO and pull up a loop, YO and draw through 2 loops on hook; repeat from ★ once **more**, YO and draw through all 3 loops on hook **(counts as one dc)**.

To tr decrease (uses next 2 sc), ★ YO twice, insert hook in **next** sc, YO and pull up a loop, (YO and draw through 2 loops on hook) twice; repeat from ★ once **more**, YO and draw through all 3 loops on hook **(counts as one tr)**.

Rnd 4: With **right** side facing and working in Back Loops Only, join Baby Blue or Light Pink with sc in same st as joining; sc in next 15 sc, dc decrease twice, tr decrease 5 times, dc decrease twice, sc in last 16 sc; join with slip st to **both** loops of first sc: 41 sts.

To sc decrease, pull up a loop in next 2 sts, YO and draw through all 3 loops on hook **(counts as one sc)**.

Rnd 5: Ch 1, working in both loops, sc in same st and in next 14 sc, dc decrease twice, dc in next 3 tr, dc decrease twice, sc in next 13 sc, sc decrease; join with slip st to first sc, do **not** finish off: 36 sts.

CUFF

Rnd 1 (Eyelet rnd)**:** Ch 3 **(counts as first hdc plus ch 1)**, skip next sc, ★ hdc in next st, ch 1, skip next st; repeat from ★ around; join with slip st to first hdc, finish off: 18 hdc and 18 ch-1 sps.

Rnd 2: With **right** side facing, join White with slip st in first ch-1 sp; ch 3 **(counts as first dc, now and throughout)**, dc in same sp, 2 dc in each ch-1 sp around; join with slip st to first dc, finish off: 36 dc.

Rnd 3: With **wrong** side facing, working in Front Loops Only and pushing tr to **right** side, skip joining and join Baby Blue or Light Pink with sc in next dc; tr in next dc, (sc in next dc, tr in next st) around; join with slip st to **both** loops of first sc, finish off.

Rnd 4: With **right** side facing and working in Back Loops Only, skip joining and join White with slip st in next tr; ch 3, dc in next sc and in each st around; join with slip st to first dc, finish off.

Rnd 5: With **wrong** side facing, working in Front Loops Only and pushing tr to **right** side, skip joining and join Baby Blue or Light Pink with sc in next dc; tr in next dc, (sc in next dc, tr in next st) around; join with slip st to **both** loops of first sc, finish off.

Weave a 14" (35.5 cm) length of ribbon through Eyelet round.

Designs by Mary Ann Sipes.

CLOUD-SOFT LAYETTE

This beribboned bubble-look layette will wrap Baby in clouds of softness!
It includes a blanket, a sacque, a bonnet, and booties.

Instructions begin on page 58.

CLOUD-SOFT LAYETTE
Shown on page 57.

◼◼▢▢▢ **EASY**

Finished Size: 3 months

MATERIALS
Light/Worsted Weight Yarn
[5 ounces, 500 yards
(140 grams, 457 meters)
per skein]:
Complete set - 6 skeins
Sacque only - 1 skein
Bonnet **and** Booties only - 1 skein
Blanket only - 4 skeins
Crochet hook, size I (5.5 mm) **or** size
needed for gauge
Yarn needle
1/4" (7 mm) wide Ribbon:
Complete set - 9 1/2 yards (8.75 meters)
Sacque only - 1 1/4 yards (1.15 meters)
Bonnet only - 1 3/4 yards (1.6 meters)
Booties only - 1 yard (.9 meters)
Blanket only - 5 1/2 yards (5 meters)
Ribbon roses - 2 each for Sacque **and**
Bonnet; 4 for Blanket
Sewing needle and thread

GAUGE: In pattern, (sc, ch 2, hdc) 5
times and 9 rows = 3" (7.5 cm)

SACQUE
BODY
Ch 54.

Row 1 (Right side)**:** Dc in fourth ch
from hook **(3 skipped chs count as
first dc, now and throughout)** and in
each ch across: 52 dc.

Note: Mark Row 1 as **right** side.

Row 2: Ch 1, turn; skip first dc, (sc,
ch 2, hdc) in next dc, ★ skip next dc, (sc,
ch 2, hdc) in next dc; repeat from ★
across to last 2 dc, skip next dc, sc in last
dc: 26 sc and 25 ch-2 sps.

Row 3 (Increase row)**:** Ch 1, turn; 2 sc
in first sc, working **behind** ch-2 sps, 3
sc in each sc across to last sc, 2 sc in last
sc: 76 sc.

Row 4: Ch 1, turn; skip first sc, (sc,
ch 2, hdc) in next sc, ★ skip next sc, (sc,
ch 2, hdc) in next sc; repeat from ★
across to last 2 sc, skip next sc, sc in last
sc: 38 sc and 37 ch-2 sps.

Row 5: Ch 1, turn; working **behind**
ch-2 sps, 2 sc in each sc across: 76 sc.

Row 6: Ch 1, turn; skip first sc, (sc,
ch 2, hdc) in next sc, ★ skip next sc, (sc,
ch 2, hdc) in next sc; repeat from ★
across to last 2 sc, skip next sc, sc in last
sc: 38 sc and 37 ch-2 sps.

Rows 7-10: Repeat Rows 3-6: 56 sc
and 55 ch-2 sps.

Row 11: Ch 1, turn; working **behind**
ch-2 sps, 2 sc in each of first 9 sc, skip
next 11 ch-2 sps (armhole), 2 sc in each
of next 18 sc, skip next 11 ch-2 sps
(armhole), 2 sc in each of last 9 sc: 72
sc.

Row 12: Ch 1, turn; skip first sc, (sc,
ch 2, hdc) in next sc, ★ skip next sc, (sc,
ch 2, hdc) in next sc; repeat from ★
across to last 2 sc, skip next sc, sc in last
sc: 36 sc and 35 ch-2 sps.

Rows 13 and 14: Repeat Rows 3
and 4: 53 sc and 52 ch-2 sps.

Rows 15-26: Repeat Rows 5 and 6,
6 times; do **not** finish off.

EDGING
Rnd 1: Ch 1, turn; 3 sc in first sc,
working **behind** ch-2 sps, sc in next sc,
2 sc in each sc across to last sc, 3 sc in
last sc; work 27 sc evenly spaced across
end of rows; working in free loops of
beginning ch **(Fig. 3b, page 205)**, 3 sc
in first ch, place marker around last sc
made for st placement, sc in next 50
chs, 3 sc in next ch; work 27 sc evenly
spaced across end of rows; join with slip
st to first sc: 217 sc.

Rnd 2: Ch 1, do **not** turn; (sc, ch 2,
hdc) in same st, ★ skip next sc, (sc, ch 2,
hdc) in next sc; repeat from ★ around to
neck edge working last (sc, ch 2, hdc) in
marked sc, [skip next 2 sc, (sc, ch 2, hdc)
in next sc] 17 times, skip next sc, † (sc,
ch 2, hdc) in next sc, skip next sc †,
repeat from † to † around; join with slip
st to first sc, finish off.

SLEEVE
Rnd 1: With **right** side facing, join
yarn with sc in side of first sc at
underarm **(see Joining With Sc, page
205)**; sc in same st, 2 sc in side of next
sc; working **behind** ch-2 sps and in
unworked sc on armhole, 2 sc in each sc
around; join with slip st to first sc: 24 sc.

Rnd 2: Ch 1, turn; (sc, ch 2, hdc) in
same st, skip next sc, ★ (sc, ch 2, hdc) in
next sc, skip next sc; repeat from ★
around; join with slip st to first sc: 12 sc
and 12 ch-2 sps.

Rnd 3: Ch 1, turn; working **behind**
ch-2 sps, 2 sc in same st and in each sc
around; join with slip st to first sc: 24 sc.

Rnds 4-12: Repeat Rnds 2 and 3, 4
times; then repeat Rnd 2 once **more**.

Finish off.

Repeat for second Sleeve.

Weave ribbon through Row 1 on Body,
working over and under two dc.

Sew a ribbon rose to each corner at
neck.

BONNET

Ch 34.

Row 1 (Right side): Dc in fourth ch from hook and in each ch across: 32 dc.

Note: Mark Row 1 as **right** side.

Row 2: Ch 1, turn; skip first dc, (sc, ch 2, hdc) in next dc, ★ skip next dc, (sc, ch 2, hdc) in next dc; repeat from ★ across to last 2 dc, skip next dc, sc in last dc: 16 sc and 15 ch-2 sps.

Row 3: Ch 1, turn; working **behind** ch-2 sps, 2 sc in each sc across: 32 sc.

Row 4: Ch 1, turn; skip first sc, (sc, ch 2, hdc) in next sc, ★ skip next sc, (sc, ch 2, hdc) in next sc; repeat from ★ across to last 2 sc, skip next sc, sc in last sc: 16 sc and 15 ch-2 sps.

Rows 5 and 6: Repeat Rows 3 and 4.

Row 7: Ch 1, turn; 2 sc in first sc, working **behind** ch-2 sps, 3 sc in each sc across to last sc, 2 sc in last sc: 46 sc.

Row 8: Ch 1, turn; skip first sc, (sc, ch 2, hdc) in next sc, ★ skip next sc, (sc, ch 2, hdc) in next sc; repeat from ★ across to last 2 sc, skip next sc, sc in last sc: 23 sc and 22 ch-2 sps.

Rows 9-14: Repeat Rows 3 and 4, 3 times.

Row 15: Ch 3 **(counts as first dc, now and throughout)**, turn; dc in same st, working **behind** ch-2 sps, 2 dc in next sc and in each sc across: 46 dc.

Row 16: Ch 1, turn; skip first dc, (sc, ch 2, hdc) in next dc, ★ skip next dc, (sc, ch 2, hdc) in next dc; repeat from ★ across to last 2 dc, skip next dc, sc in last dc: 23 sc and 22 ch-2 sps.

Row 17: Ch 1, turn; working **behind** ch-2 sps, 2 sc in first sc and in next sc, 3 sc in each sc across to last sc, 2 sc in last sc: 66 sc.

Row 18: Ch 1, turn; skip first sc, (sc, ch 2, hdc) in next sc, ★ skip next sc, (sc, ch 2, hdc) in next sc; repeat from ★ across to last 2 sc, skip next sc, sc in last sc; do **not** finish off: 33 sc and 32 ch-2 sps.

EDGING

To decrease, pull up a loop in next 2 chs, YO and draw through all 3 loops on hook.

Ch 3, turn; (slip st in next ch-2 sp, ch 3) across to last sc, slip st in last sc; work 14 sc evenly spaced across end of rows; working in free loops of beginning ch **(Fig. 3b, page 205)**, 2 sc in first ch, sc in next ch, decrease 14 times, sc in next ch, 2 sc in next ch; work 14 sc evenly spaced across end of rows; join with slip st to base of beginning ch-3, finish off.

Weave a 20" (51 cm) length of ribbon through Row 1, working over and under two dc. Pull ribbon ends to gather back of Bonnet slightly and tie ends in a bow.

Weave remaining ribbon through Row 15, working over and under two dc.

Sew a ribbon rose to each end of Row 15.

BOOTIES
SOLE AND SIDES

Ch 10.

Rnd 1 (Right side): 2 Hdc in third ch from hook, hdc in next 6 chs, 5 hdc in last ch; working in free loops of beginning ch **(Fig. 3b, page 205)**, hdc in next 6 chs, 2 hdc in next ch; join with slip st to top of beginning ch: 22 sts.

Note: Mark Rnd 1 as **right** side.

Rnd 2: Ch 3, 2 dc in each of next 2 hdc, dc in next 6 hdc, 2 dc in each of next 5 hdc, dc in next 6 hdc, 2 dc in each of last 2 hdc, dc in same st as first dc; join with slip st to first dc: 32 dc.

Rnd 3: Ch 1, sc in Back Loop Only **(Fig. 2, page 205)** of same st and each dc around; join with slip st to **both** loops of first sc.

Rnd 4: Ch 1, **turn**; working in both loops, (sc, ch 2, hdc) in same st, skip next sc, ★ (sc, ch 2, hdc) in next sc, skip next sc; repeat from ★ around; join with slip st to first sc: 16 sc and 16 ch-2 sps.

Rnd 5: Ch 1, turn; working **behind** ch-2 sps, 2 sc in same st and in each sc around; join with slip st to first sc, finish off: 32 sc.

Instructions continued on page 60.

INSTEP

Row 1: With **wrong** side facing, skip joining and next 6 sc and join yarn with sc in next sc *(see Joining With Sc, page 205)*; ch 2, hdc in same st, ★ skip next sc, (sc, ch 2, hdc) in next sc; repeat from ★ 6 times **more**, skip next sc, sc in next sc, leave remaining 8 sc unworked: 9 sc and 8 ch-2 sps.

Row 2: Ch 1, turn; working **behind** ch-2 sps, 2 sc in first sc and in next sc, sc in next 5 sc, 2 sc in each of last 2 sc; finish off leaving a long end for sewing: 13 sc.

Fold Row 2 in half; working through **both** loops of each stitch on **both** thicknesses, sew seam.

CUFF

Rnd 1: With **right** side facing, join yarn with slip st in same st as joining on Rnd 5 of Sides; ch 3, dc in next sc and in each sc around to Instep, dc in same st as last sc on Row 1 of Instep; working in end of rows, dc in next 2 rows, dc in seam and in next 2 rows, dc in same st as Instep joining and in each sc around; join with slip st to first dc: 22 dc.

Rnd 2: Ch 1, turn; (sc, ch 2, hdc) in same st, skip next dc, ★ (sc, ch 2, hdc) in next dc, skip next dc; repeat from ★ around; join with slip st to first sc: 11 sc and 11 ch-2 sps.

Rnd 3: Ch 1, turn; working **behind** ch-2 sps, 2 sc in same st and in each sc around; join with slip st to first sc: 22 sc.

Rnd 4: Ch 1, turn; (sc, ch 2, hdc) in same st, skip next sc, ★ (sc, ch 2, hdc) in next sc, skip next sc; repeat from ★ around; join with slip st to first sc: 11 sc and 11 ch-2 sps.

Rnd 5: Turn; slip st in next hdc and in next ch-2 sp, ch 3, (slip st in next ch-2 sp, ch 3) around; join with slip st to slip st at base of beginning ch-3, finish off.

Beginning and ending at center front of Cuff, weave an 18" (45.5 cm) length of ribbon through Rnd 1 on each Bootie, working over and under two dc; tie ends in a bow.

BLANKET
Finished Size: 39" (99 cm) square

Ch 123.

Row 1 (Right side)**:** Sc in back ridge *(Fig. 1, page 205)* of second ch from hook and each ch across: 122 sc.

Row 2: Ch 1, turn; skip first sc, (sc, ch 2, hdc) in next sc, ★ skip next sc, (sc, ch 2, hdc) in next sc; repeat from ★ across to last 2 sc, skip next sc, sc in last sc: 61 sc and 60 ch-2 sps.

Row 3: Ch 1, turn; working **behind** ch-2 sps, 2 sc in each sc across: 122 sc.

Rows 4-109: Repeat Rows 2 and 3, 53 times; do **not** finish off.

EDGING

Rnd 1: Ch 3, do **not** turn; work 120 dc evenly spaced across end of rows; working in free loops of beginning ch *(Fig. 3b, page 205)*, 3 dc in first ch, 2 dc in next ch, dc in next 119 chs, 3 dc in next ch; work 121 dc evenly spaced across end of rows; working across last row, 3 dc in first sc, 2 dc in next sc, dc in each sc across to last sc, 3 dc in last sc; join with slip st to first dc: 496 dc.

Rnd 2: Ch 1, (sc, ch 2, hdc) in same st, skip next dc, ★ (sc, ch 2, hdc) in next dc, skip next dc; repeat from ★ around; join with slip st to first sc: 248 ch-2 sps.

Rnd 3: Slip st in first ch and in same sp, ch 3, (slip st in next ch-2 sp, ch 3) around; join with slip st to slip st at base of beginning ch-3, finish off.

Using photo as a guide for placement:

Cut ribbon into four equal lengths. Weave each length through Rnd 1 along one side of Blanket, working over and under two dc; tie ribbon ends at each corner in a bow.

Sew a ribbon rose to each corner of Blanket.

Designs by Ruth G. Shepherd.

FANCY FRENCH KNOTS LAYETTE

Dress Baby in a rainbow of pastels from head to toe! The look of French knots is created by alternating single and treble crochets.

Shown on page 63.

 ◼◼☐☐☐ **EASY**

Finished Size: 6 months

MATERIALS
Baby Fingering Weight Yarn
[1³/₄ ounces, 270 yards
(50 grams, 247 meters)
per skein]:
Complete set
White - 7 skeins
Light Pink - 2 skeins
Baby Blue - 2 skeins
Baby Yellow - 2 skeins
Pastel Green - 2 skeins
Peach - 2 skeins
Bonnet, Booties, & Sacque only
White - 3 skeins
Light Pink - 1 skein
Baby Blue - 1 skein
Baby Yellow - 1 skein
Pastel Green - 1 skein
Peach - 1 skein
Blanket only
White - 4 skeins
Light Pink - 1 skein
Baby Blue - 1 skein
Baby Yellow - 1 skein
Pastel Green - 1 skein
Peach - 1 skein
Crochet hooks, sizes F (3.75 mm) **and**
H (5 mm) **or** sizes needed for gauge
Tapestry needle
³/₈" (10 mm) wide Ribbon
Complete set - 3 yards (2.75 meters)
Sacque only - 1 yard (.9 meter)
Bonnet only - 1 yard (.9 meter)
Booties only - 1 yard (.9 meter)

Note: Use larger size hook for Blanket only; use smaller size hook for all other layette pieces.

SACQUE
GAUGE: 15 hdc and
11 rows = 3" (7.5 cm)

BODICE
With White, ch 78.

Row 1: Hdc in third ch from hook **(2 skipped chs count as first hdc)** and in next 11 chs, 3 hdc in next ch, hdc in next 11 chs, 3 hdc in next ch, hdc in next 25 chs, 3 hdc in next ch, hdc in next 11 chs, 3 hdc in next ch, hdc in last 13 chs: 85 hdc.

Row 2 (Right side)**:** Ch 2 **(counts as first hdc, now and throughout)**, turn; hdc in next hdc and in each hdc across working 3 hdc in center hdc of each corner 3-hdc group: 93 hdc.

Note: Mark Row 2 as **right** side.

Rows 3-12: Ch 2, turn; hdc in next hdc and in each hdc across working 3 hdc in center hdc of each corner 3-hdc group; do **not** finish off: 173 hdc.

BODY
Row 1: Ch 1, turn; sc in first 2 hdc, (2 sc in next hdc, sc in next 5 hdc) 4 times, skip next 35 hdc (armhole), 2 sc in next hdc, sc in next 2 hdc, (2 sc in next hdc, sc in next 5 hdc) 8 times, skip next 35 hdc (armhole), sc in next 2 hdc, (2 sc in next hdc, sc in next 5 hdc) 4 times; finish off: 120 sc.

To work treble crochet *(abbreviated tr)*, YO twice, insert hook in st indicated, YO and pull up a loop (4 loops on hook), (YO and draw through 2 loops on hook) 3 times.

Row 2: With **right** side facing, join Light Pink with sc in first sc *(see Joining With Sc, page 205)*; tr in next sc, (sc in next sc, tr in next sc) across.

Row 3: Ch 1, turn; sc in first tr, tr in next sc, (sc in next tr, tr in next sc) across; finish off.

Row 4: With **right** side facing, join White with slip st in first tr; ch 2, hdc in next sc and in each st across.

Row 5: Ch 2, turn; hdc in next hdc and in each hdc across; finish off.

Row 6: With **right** side facing, join Baby Blue with sc in first hdc; tr in next hdc, (sc in next hdc, tr in next hdc) across.

Rows 7-9: Repeat Rows 3-5.

Row 10: With **right** side facing, join Baby Yellow with sc in first hdc; tr in next hdc, (sc in next hdc, tr in next hdc) across.

Rows 11-13: Repeat Rows 3-5.

Row 14: With **right** side facing, join Peach with sc in first hdc; tr in next hdc, (sc in next hdc, tr in next hdc) across.

Rows 15-17: Repeat Rows 3-5.

Row 18: With **right** side facing, join Pastel Green with sc in first hdc; tr in next hdc, (sc in next hdc, tr in next hdc) across.

Rows 19-21: Repeat Rows 3-5.

Row 22: With **right** side facing, join Light Pink with sc in first hdc; tr in next hdc, (sc in next hdc, tr in next hdc) across.

Rows 23 and 24: Repeat Rows 3 and 4.

Row 25: Ch 2, turn; hdc in next hdc and in each hdc across; do **not** finish off.

Instructions continued on page 62.

EDGING

Rnd 1: Ch 2, turn; hdc in next hdc and in each hdc across to last hdc, 3 hdc in last hdc; hdc evenly across right front edge; working in free loops of beginning ch **(Fig. 3b, page 205)**, ch 4, skip next ch, dc in next ch, (ch 1, skip next ch, dc in next ch) across to last 2 chs, ch 4, skip next ch, slip st in last ch; hdc evenly across left front edge, 2 hdc in same st as first hdc; join with slip st to first hdc: 38 sps at neck edge.

Rnd 2: Ch 1, do **not** turn; sc in same st and in each hdc across to center hdc of next corner 3-hdc group, 3 sc in center hdc, sc in each hdc across to first sp, 5 sc in sp, sc in next dc, (sc in next ch-1 sp and in next dc) across to last sp, 5 sc in sp, sc in each hdc across to last hdc, 3 sc in last hdc; join with slip st to first sc, finish off.

SLEEVE

Rnd 1: With **right** side facing and working in skipped hdc on Row 12 of Bodice, join Light Pink with slip st in last hdc of armhole; ch 1, pull up a loop in same st and in first hdc of armhole, YO and draw through all 3 loops on hook, tr in next hdc, (sc in next hdc, tr in next hdc) around; join with slip st to first st: 34 sts.

Rnd 2: Ch 4 **(counts as first tr)**, turn; sc in next tr, (tr in next sc, sc in next tr) around; join with slip st to first tr, finish off.

Rnd 3: With **right** side facing, join White with slip st in same st as joining; ch 2, hdc in next sc and in each st around; join with slip st to first hdc.

Rnd 4: Ch 2, turn; hdc in next hdc and in each hdc around; join with slip st to first hdc, finish off.

Rnd 5: With **right** side facing, join Baby Blue with sc in same st as joining; tr in next hdc, (sc in next hdc, tr in next hdc) around; join with slip st to first sc.

Rnds 6-8: Repeat Rnds 2-4.

Rnd 9: With **right** side facing, join Baby Yellow with sc in same st as joining; tr in next hdc, (sc in next hdc, tr in next hdc) around; join with slip st to first sc.

Rnds 10-12: Repeat Rnds 2-4.

Rnd 13: With **right** side facing, join Peach with sc in same st as joining; tr in next hdc, (sc in next hdc, tr in next hdc) around; join with slip st to first sc.

Rnds 14-16: Repeat Rnds 2-4.

Rnd 17: With **right** side facing, join Pastel Green with sc in same st as joining; tr in next hdc, (sc in next hdc, tr in next hdc) around; join with slip st to first sc.

Rnds 18 and 19: Repeat Rnds 2 and 3.

Rnd 20: Ch 2, turn; hdc in next hdc and in each hdc around; join with slip st to first hdc.

To hdc decrease (uses next 2 sts), ★ YO, insert hook in **next** st, YO and pull up a loop; repeat from ★ once **more**, YO and draw through all 5 loops on hook **(counts as one hdc)**.

Rnd 21: Ch 2, turn; (hdc decrease, hdc in next hdc) around; join with slip st to first hdc: 23 hdc.

Rnd 22: Ch 1, turn; sc in same st and in each hdc around; join with slip st to first sc, finish off.

Repeat for second Sleeve.

Weave ribbon through spaces along neck edge.

With White tack underarm opening closed.

BONNET
GAUGE: Rnds 1-6 = 3½" (9 cm)

BACK

With White, ch 3; join with slip st to form a ring.

Rnd 1 (Right side): Ch 2, 7 hdc in ring; join with slip st to first hdc: 8 hdc.

Note: Mark Rnd 1 as **right** side.

Rnd 2: Ch 2, hdc in same st, 2 hdc in each hdc around; join with slip st to first hdc: 16 hdc.

Rnd 3: Ch 2, 2 hdc in next hdc, (hdc in next hdc, 2 hdc in next hdc) around; join with slip st to first hdc: 24 hdc.

Rnd 4: Ch 2, hdc in next hdc, 2 hdc in next hdc, (hdc in next 2 hdc, 2 hdc in next hdc) around; join with slip st to first hdc: 32 hdc.

Rnd 5: Ch 2, hdc in next 2 hdc, 2 hdc in next hdc, (hdc in next 3 hdc, 2 hdc in next hdc) around; join with slip st to first hdc: 40 hdc.

Rnd 6: Ch 2, hdc in next 3 hdc, 2 hdc in next hdc, (hdc in next 4 hdc, 2 hdc in next hdc) around; join with slip st to first hdc: 48 hdc.

Rnd 7: Ch 2, hdc in next 4 hdc, 2 hdc in next hdc, (hdc in next 5 hdc, 2 hdc in next hdc) around; join with slip st to first hdc: 56 hdc.

Rnd 8: Ch 2, hdc in next 5 hdc, 2 hdc in next hdc, (hdc in next 6 hdc, 2 hdc in next hdc) around; join with slip st to first hdc: 64 hdc.

Rnd 9: Ch 2, hdc in next 6 hdc, (2 hdc in next hdc, hdc in next 7 hdc) 5 times, 2 dc in next hdc, dc in next hdc, (tr, ch 3, sc) in next hdc, sc in next 11 hdc, (sc, ch 3, tr) in next hdc, dc in next hdc, 2 dc in last hdc; join with slip st to first hdc, finish off: 73 sts and 2 ch-3 sps.

Instructions continued on page 64.

Continued from page 62.

CROWN

Row 1: With **wrong** side facing, join Light Pink with sc in second ch-3 sp to **left** of joining *(see Joining With Sc, page 205)*; tr in next tr, sc in next dc, tr in next dc, sc in next dc, tr in next hdc, (sc in next hdc, tr in next hdc) 5 times, (sc, tr) in next hdc, ★ (sc in next hdc, tr in next hdc) twice, (sc, tr) in next hdc; repeat from ★ 5 times **more**, (sc in next hdc, tr in next hdc) 5 times, sc in next dc, tr in next dc, sc in next dc, tr in next tr, sc in next ch-3 sp, leave remaining 13 sc unworked: 69 sts.

To sc decrease, pull up a loop in next 2 sts, YO and draw through all 3 loops on hook **(counts as one sc).**

Row 2: Ch 1, turn; sc decrease, tr in next sc, (sc in next tr, tr in next sc) across to last 2 sts, sc decrease; finish off: 67 sts.

Row 3: With **wrong** side facing, join White with slip st in first sc; ch 2, hdc in next tr and in each st across.

Row 4: Ch 2, turn; hdc in next hdc and in each hdc across; finish off.

Row 5: With **wrong** side facing, join Baby Blue with sc in first hdc; (tr in next hdc, sc in next hdc) across.

Row 6: Ch 4 **(counts as first tr)**, turn; (sc in next tr, tr in next sc) across; finish off.

Row 7: With **wrong** side facing, join White with slip st in first tr; ch 2, hdc in next sc and in each st across.

Row 8: Ch 2, turn; hdc in next hdc and in each hdc across; finish off.

Row 9: With **wrong** side facing, join Baby Yellow with sc in first hdc; (tr in next hdc, sc in next hdc) across.

Rows 10-12: Repeat Rows 6-8.

Row 13: With **wrong** side facing, join Peach with sc in first hdc, (tr in next hdc, sc in next hdc) across.

Rows 14 and 15: Repeat Rows 6 and 7.

Row 16: Ch 2, turn; hdc in next hdc and in each hdc across; do **not** finish off.

Edging: Ch 1, do **not** turn; 2 sc in same st; work 13 sc evenly spaced across end of rows to Back; working across Back, 2 sc in first sp, sc in next 13 sc, 2 sc in last sp; work 13 sc evenly spaced across end of rows; working across last row on Crown, 3 sc in first hdc, sc in each hdc across, sc in same st as first sc; join with slip st to first sc, do **not** finish off: 114 sc.

NECKBAND

Row 1: Ch 1, sc in same st and in each sc across neck edge working last sc in center sc of next corner 3-sc group, leave remaining 67 sc unworked: 47 sc.

Row 2 (Eyelet row): Ch 4 **(counts as first dc plus ch 1)**, turn; skip next sc, dc in next sc, ★ ch 1, skip next sc, dc in next sc; repeat from ★ across: 23 sps.

Row 3: Ch 1, turn; sc in first dc and in each ch-1 sp and each dc across; finish off.

Weave ribbon through Eyelet row.

BOOTIES
GAUGE: Sole = 3³/₄" (9.5 cm)

SOLE
With White, ch 12.

Rnd 1 (Right side): 2 Sc in second ch from hook, sc in next 9 chs, 4 sc in last ch; working in free loops of beginning ch *(Fig. 3b, page 205)*, sc in next 9 chs, 2 sc in next ch; join with slip st to first sc: 26 sc.

Note: Mark Rnd 1 as **right** side.

Rnd 2: Ch 1, sc in same st, 2 sc in next sc, sc in next 9 sc, 2 sc in next sc, sc in next 2 sc, 2 sc in next sc, sc in next 9 sc, 2 sc in next sc, sc in last sc; join with slip st to first sc: 30 sc.

Rnd 3: Ch 1, 2 sc in same st and in next sc, sc in next 11 sc, 2 sc in each of next 4 sc, sc in next 11 sc, 2 sc in each of last 2 sc; join with slip st to first sc: 38 sc.

Rnd 4: Ch 1, 2 sc in same st, (sc in next sc, 2 sc in next sc) twice, sc in next 10 sc, 2 sc in next sc, (sc in next sc, 2 sc in next sc) 4 times, sc in next 10 sc, (2 sc in next sc, sc in next sc) twice; join with slip st to first sc: 48 sc.

Rnd 5: Ch 1, sc in same st and in next 2 sc, 2 sc in next sc, sc in next sc, 2 sc in next sc, sc in next 13 sc, 2 sc in next sc, sc in next sc, 2 sc in next sc, sc in next 5 sc, 2 sc in next sc, sc in next sc, 2 sc in next sc, sc in next 13 sc, 2 sc in next sc, sc in next sc, 2 sc in next sc, sc in last 2 sc; join with slip st to first sc, do **not** finish off: 56 sc.

SIDES
Rnd 1: Ch 2, hdc in Back Loop Only *(Fig. 2, page 205)* of next sc and each sc around; join with slip st to first hdc, finish off.

Rnd 2: With **wrong** side facing and working in both loops, join Light Pink with sc in same st as joining *(see Joining With Sc, page 205)*; tr in next hdc, (sc in next hdc, tr in next hdc) around; join with slip st to first sc, finish off.

Rnd 3: With **right** side facing, join White with slip st in same st as joining; ch 2, hdc in next tr and in each st around; join with slip st to first hdc, finish off.

Rnd 4: With **wrong** side facing, join Baby Blue with sc in same st as joining; tr in next hdc, (sc in next hdc, tr in next hdc) around; join with slip st to first sc, finish off.

Rnd 5: With **right** side facing, join White with slip st in same st as joining; ch 2, hdc in next 2 sts, place marker around last hdc made for Cuff placement, hdc in next 21 sts, hdc decrease, place marker around hdc just made for Instep placement, hdc decrease 5 times, hdc in last 20 sts; join with slip st to first hdc, finish off: 50 hdc.

INSTEP

Row 1: With **right** side facing, join White with slip st in marked hdc on Sides; ch 2, hdc in next 5 hdc, leave remaining hdc unworked: 6 hdc.

Rows 2-6: Ch 2, turn; hdc in next hdc and in each hdc across.

Finish off.

Sew Instep to Sides using 7 hdc on each side of Bootie.

CUFF

Rnd 1 (Eyelet rnd): With **right** side facing, join White with slip st in marked hdc on Sides; ch 4 **(counts as first dc plus ch 1)**, (skip next hdc, dc in next hdc, ch 1) 7 times, skip Instep seam, (dc in next hdc, ch 1, skip next hdc) 3 times, dc in next Instep seam, ch 1, skip next hdc on Sides, (dc in next hdc, ch 1, skip next hdc) 7 times; join with slip st to third ch of beginning ch-4: 19 ch-1 sps.

Rnd 2: Ch 2, hdc in next ch-1 sp and in each dc and each ch-1 sp around; join with slip st to first hdc, finish off: 38 hdc.

Rnd 3: With **wrong** side facing, join Baby Yellow with sc in same st as joining; tr in next hdc, (sc in next hdc, tr in next hdc) around; join with slip st to first sc, finish off.

Rnd 4: With **right** side facing, join White with slip st in same st as joining; ch 2, hdc in next tr and in each st around; join with slip st to first hdc, finish off.

Rnd 5: With **wrong** side facing, join Peach with sc in same st as joining; tr in next hdc, (sc in next hdc, tr in next hdc) around; join with slip st to first sc, finish off.

Rnd 6: Repeat Rnd 4.

Beginning and ending at center front, weave an 18" (45.5 cm) length of ribbon through Eyelet rnd.

BLANKET
Finished Size:
35" x 44¹/₂" (89 cm x 113 cm)

GAUGE: In pattern,
16 sts and 14 rows = 4" (10 cm)

Note: Each row is worked across length of Blanket.

With White, ch 179.

Row 1 (Right side): Hdc in back ridge **(Fig. 1, page 205)** of third ch from hook **(2 skipped chs count as first hdc)** and each ch across: 178 hdc.

Note: Mark Row 1 as **right** side.

Row 2: Ch 2 **(counts as first hdc, now and throughout)**, turn; hdc in next hdc and in each hdc across; finish off.

Row 3: With **right** side facing, join Light Pink with sc in first hdc **(see Joining With Sc, page 205)**; tr in next hdc, (sc in next hdc, tr in next hdc) across.

Row 4: Ch 1, turn; sc in first tr, tr in next sc, (sc in next tr, tr in next sc) across; finish off.

Row 5: With **right** side facing, join White with slip st in first tr; ch 2, hdc in next sc and in each st across.

Row 6: Ch 2, turn; hdc in next hdc and in each hdc across; finish off.

Row 7: With **right** side facing, join Baby Blue with sc in first hdc; tr in next hdc, (sc in next hdc, tr in next hdc) across.

Rows 8-10: Repeat Rows 4-6.

Row 11: With **right** side facing, join Baby Yellow with sc in first hdc; tr in next hdc, (sc in next hdc, tr in next hdc) across.

Rows 12-14: Repeat Rows 4-6.

Row 15: With **right** side facing, join Peach with sc in first hdc; tr in next hdc, (sc in next hdc, tr in next hdc) across.

Rows 16-18: Repeat Rows 4-6.

Row 19: With **right** side facing, join Pastel Green with sc in first hdc; tr in next hdc, (sc in next hdc, tr in next hdc) across.

Rows 20-22: Repeat Rows 4-6.

Rows 23-122: Repeat Rows 3-22, 5 times.

Holding five 12" (30.5 cm) strands of corresponding color yarn together for each fringe, add fringe across short edges of Blanket **(Figs. 12c & d, page 207)**.

Designs by Sarah Anne Phillips.

CUTIE-PIE BUBBLE SUITS

Our bubble suits for Baby are cool, comfortable, and downright adorable. Each romper features simple embroidery on the yoke.

⬤⬤◻◻ **EASY**

Finished Sizes:
3 months - 16" (40.5 cm) long
6 months – 18¹/₂" (47 cm) long
12 months - 21" (53.5 cm) long

Size Note: Instructions are written for size 3 months with sizes 6 and 12 months in braces { }. Instructions will be easier to read if you circle all the numbers pertaining to your baby's size. If only one number is given, it applies to all sizes. If a zero is given, it means to do nothing.

MATERIALS
Light/Worsted Weight Yarn
 7 ounces, 700 yards
 (200 grams, 640 meters)
 per skein]:
 Boy's version
 White - 1 skein
 Baby Yellow - 1 skein
 Pastel Green, Baby Blue, and Silver - small amount of **each** color
 Girl's version
 White - 1 skein
 Pastel Green - 1 skein
 Baby Yellow - small amount
Crochet hook, size D (3.25 mm) **or** size needed for gauge
Yarn needle
Snap tape - 6" (15 cm) length for each Suit
¹/₂" (12 mm) Buttons - 3 for each Suit
Sulky® Solvy stabilizer
Sewing needle and thread

GAUGE:
20 dc and 10 rows = 4" (10 cm)
In pattern, (Cluster, ch 2) 7 times and 19 rows = 4" (10 cm)

YOKE
With White, ch 53{58-60}.

Row 1 (Right side): Sc in second ch from hook and in each ch across: 52{57-59} sc.

Note: Mark Row 1 as **right** side.

Row 2: Ch 3 **(counts as first dc, now and throughout)**, turn; dc in next 2{2-3} sc, 2 dc in next sc, (dc in next 4 sc, 2 dc in next sc) across to last 3{3-4} sc, dc in last 3{3-4} sc: 62{68-70} dc.

Row 3: Ch 3, turn; dc in next 2{0-1} dc, 2 dc in next dc, (dc in next 4 dc, 2 dc in next dc) across to last 3{1-2} dc, dc in last 3{1-2} dc: 74{82-84} dc.

Row 4: Ch 3, turn; dc in next 3{1-2} dc, 2 dc in next dc, (dc in next 5 dc, 2 dc in next dc) across to last 3{1-2} dc, dc in last 3{1-2} dc: 86{96-98} dc.

Row 5: Ch 3, turn; dc in next 3{1-2} dc, 2 dc in next dc, (dc in next 6 dc, 2 dc in next dc) across to last 4{2-3} dc, dc in last 4{2-3} dc: 98{110-112} dc.

Row 6: Ch 3, turn; dc in next 4{2-3} dc, 2 dc in next dc, (dc in next 7 dc, 2 dc in next dc) across to last 4{2-3} dc, dc in last 4{2-3} dc: 110{124-126} dc.

Row 7: Ch 3, turn; dc in next 4{2-3} dc, 2 dc in next dc, (dc in next 8 dc, 2 dc in next dc) across to last 5{3-4} dc, dc in last 5{3-4} dc: 122{138-140} dc.

Row 8: Ch 3, turn; dc in next 5{3-4} dc, 2 dc in next dc, (dc in next 9 dc, 2 dc in next dc) across to last 5{3-4} dc, dc in last 5{3-4} dc: 134{152-154} dc.

Row 9: Ch 3, turn; dc in next 5{3-4} dc, 2 dc in next dc, (dc in next 10 dc, 2 dc in next dc) across to last 6{4-5} dc, dc in last 6{4-5} dc: 146{166-168} dc.

Row 10: Ch 3, turn; dc in next 6{4-5} dc, 2 dc in next dc, (dc in next 11 dc, 2 dc in next dc) across to last 6{4-5} dc, dc in last 6{4-5} dc; do **not** finish off: 158{180-182} dc.

SIZES 3 AND 6 MONTHS ONLY
Row 11: Ch 3, turn; dc in next 6{4} dc, 2 dc in next dc, (dc in next 12 dc, 2 dc in next dc) across to last 7{5} dc, dc in last 7{5} dc; finish off: 170{194} dc.

SIZE 12 MONTHS ONLY
Row 11: Ch 3, turn; dc in next 5 dc, 2 dc in next dc, (dc in next 12 dc, 2 dc in next dc) across to last 6 dc, dc in last 6 dc: 196 dc.

Row 12: Ch 3, turn; dc in next 6 dc, 2 dc in next dc, (dc in next 13 dc, 2 dc in next dc) across to last 6 dc, dc in last 6 dc; finish off: 210 dc.

BODY
Boy's only - Rnd 1: With **right** side facing, skip first 58{67-72} dc and join Baby Yellow with sc in next dc **(see Joining With Sc, page 205)**; sc in next 53{59-65} dc, skip next 32{38-40} dc (armhole), 2 sc in next dc, sc in next 25{28-31} dc; working across dc on right back, 2 sc in next dc, sc in next 25{28-31} dc, leave remaining 32{38-40} dc unworked (armhole); join with slip st to first sc, do **not** finish off: 108{120-132} sc.

Girl's only - Rnd 1: With **wrong** side facing, skip first 58{67-72} dc and join Pastel Green with sc in next dc **(see Joining With Sc, page 205)**; sc in next 53{59-65} dc, skip next 32{38-40} dc (armhole), 2 sc in next dc, sc in next 25{28-31} dc; working across dc on left back, 2 sc in next dc, sc in next 25{28-31} dc, leave remaining 32{38-40} dc unworked (armhole); join with slip st to first sc, do **not** finish off: 108{120-132} sc.

Instructions continued on page 68.

Continued from page 66.

BOTH VERSIONS

To work beginning Cluster, pull up a loop in same st and in next 2 sc, YO and draw through all 4 loops on hook.

To work Cluster, pull up a loop in next 3 sc, YO and draw through all 4 loops on hook.

Rnd 2: Ch 1, turn; work beginning Cluster, ch 2, (work Cluster, ch 2) around; join with slip st to top of beginning Cluster: 36{40-44} Clusters and 36{40-44} ch-2 sps.

Rnd 3: Ch 1, turn; (2 sc in next ch-2 sp, sc in next Cluster) around working last sc in same Cluster as joining; join with slip st to first sc: 108{120-132} sc.

Rnd 4: Ch 1, turn; work beginning Cluster, ch 2, (work Cluster, ch 2) around; join with slip st to top of beginning Cluster.

Rnd 5: Ch 1, turn; sc in same st, 2 sc in next ch-2 sp, (sc in next Cluster, 2 sc in next ch-2 sp) around; join with slip st to first sc.

Repeat Rnds 2-5 until piece measures approximately 11{13-15}"/28{33-38} cm from beginning ch, ending by working Rnd 4; do **not** finish off: 36{40-44} Clusters and 36{40-44} ch-2 sps.

FRONT LEG SHAPING

Row 1: Turn; slip st in next ch-2 sp and in next Cluster, ch 1, sc in same st, (sc in next ch-2 sp and in next Cluster) twice, (2 sc in next ch-2 sp, sc in next Cluster) 11{13-15} times, (sc in next ch-2 sp and in next Cluster) twice, leave remaining 20{22-24} ch-2 sps unworked: 42{48-54} sc.

Row 2: Ch 1, turn; work Cluster, (ch 2, work Cluster) across: 14{16-18} Clusters and 13{15-17} ch-2 sps.

Row 3: Ch 1, turn; sc in first Cluster, (sc in next ch-2 sp and in next Cluster) twice, (2 sc in next ch-2 sp, sc in next Cluster) across to last 2 ch-2 sps, (sc in next ch-2 sp and in next Cluster) twice: 36{42-48} sc.

Rows 4-10: Repeat Rows 2 and 3, 3 times; then repeat Row 2 once **more**: 6{8-10} Clusters and 5{7-9} ch-2 sps.

Row 11: Ch 1, turn; 2 sc in first Cluster and in next ch-2 sp, (sc in next Cluster, 2 sc in next ch-2 sp) across to last Cluster, 2 sc in last Cluster: 18{24-30} sc.

Row 12: Ch 1, turn; work Cluster, (ch 2, work Cluster) across: 6{8-10} Clusters and 5{7-9} ch-2 sps.

Rows 13 thru 18{20-22}: Repeat Rows 11 and 12, 3{4-5} times.

Row 19{21-23}: Ch 1, turn; 2 sc in first Cluster, sc in next ch-2 sp, (sc in next Cluster and in next ch-2 sp) across to last Cluster, 2 sc in last Cluster; do **not** finish off: 13{17-21} sc.

LOWER BAND
Rows 1-5: Ch 1, turn; sc in each sc across: 13{17-21} sc.

Finish off.

BACK LEG SHAPING
Boy's only - Row 1: With **right** side facing, skip next ch-2 sp and next Cluster from Front Leg Shaping and join Baby Yellow with sc in next ch-2 sp; sc in next Cluster, sc in next ch-2 sp and in next Cluster, (2 sc in next ch-2 sp, sc in next Cluster) 15{17-19} times, sc in next ch-2 sp and in next Cluster, leave remaining ch-2 sp and joining unworked; do **not** finish off: 51{57-63} sc.

Girl's only - Row 1: With **wrong** side facing, skip next ch-2 sp and next Cluster from Front Leg Shaping and join Pastel Green with sc in next ch-2 sp; sc in next Cluster, sc in next ch-2 sp and in next Cluster, (2 sc in next ch-2 sp, sc in next Cluster) 15{17-19} times, sc in next ch-2 sp and in next Cluster, leave remaining ch-2 sp and joining unworked; do **not** finish off: 51{57-63} sc.

BOTH VERSIONS
Row 2: Ch 1, turn; work Cluster, (ch 2, work Cluster) across: 17{19-21} Clusters and 16{18-20} ch-2 sps.

Row 3: Ch 1, turn; sc in first Cluster, (sc in next ch-2 sp and in next Cluster) twice, (2 sc in next ch-2 sp, sc in next Cluster) across to last 2 ch-2 sps, (sc in next ch-2 sp and in next Cluster) twice: 45{51-57} sc.

Rows 4-12: Repeat Rows 2 and 3, 4 times; then repeat Row 2 once **more**: 7{9-11} Clusters and 6{8-10} ch-2 sps.

Row 13: Ch 1, turn; 2 sc in first Cluster and in next ch-2 sp, (sc in next Cluster, 2 sc in next ch-2 sp) across to last Cluster, 2 sc in last Cluster: 21{27-33} sc.

Row 14: Ch 1, turn; work Cluster, (ch 2, work Cluster) across: 7{9-11} Clusters and 6{8-10} ch-2 sps.

Rows 15 thru 18{20-22}: Repeat Rows 13 and 14, 2{3-4} times.

Row 19{21-23}: Ch 1, turn; sc in each Cluster and in each ch-2 sp across; do **not** finish off: 13{17-21} sc.

LOWER BAND
Rows 1-5: Ch 1, turn; sc in each sc across: 13{17-21} sc.

Finish off.

SLEEVE
BOY'S VERSION
SIZES 3 AND 6 MONTHS ONLY
Rnd 1: With **right** side facing, join Baby Yellow with sc at underarm; working in skipped dc on Yoke, sc in next dc and in each dc around; join with slip st to first sc: 33{39} sc.

Rnd 2: Ch 1, turn; work beginning Cluster, ch 2, (work Cluster, ch 2) around; join with slip st to top of beginning Cluster: 11{13} Clusters and 11{13} ch-2 sps.

Rnd 3: Ch 1, turn; (2 sc in next ch-2 sp, sc in next Cluster) around working last sc in same Cluster as joining; join with slip st to first sc: 33{39} sc.

Rnd 4: Ch 1, turn; work beginning Cluster, ch 2, (work Cluster, ch 2) around; join with slip st to top of beginning Cluster.

Rnd 5: Ch 1, turn; sc in same st, 2 sc in next ch-2 sp, (sc in next Cluster, 2 sc in next ch-2 sp) around; join with slip st to first sc.

Rnds 6 and 7: Repeat Rnds 2 and 3.

Rnd 8: Ch 1, do **not** turn; sc in same st and in each sc around; join with slip st to first sc, finish off.

Repeat for second Sleeve.

SIZE 12 MONTHS ONLY
Rnd 1: With **right** side facing, join Baby Yellow with sc at underarm; working in skipped dc on Yoke, 2 sc in next dc, sc in each dc around; join with slip st to first sc: 42 sc.

Rnd 2: Ch 1, turn; work beginning Cluster, ch 2, (work Cluster, ch 2) around; join with slip st to top of beginning Cluster: 14 Clusters and 14 ch-2 sps.

Rnd 3: Ch 1, turn; (2 sc in next ch-2 sp, sc in next Cluster) around working last sc in same Cluster as joining; join with slip st to first sc: 42 sc.

Rnd 4: Ch 1, turn; work beginning Cluster, ch 2, (work Cluster, ch 2) around; join with slip st to top of beginning Cluster.

Rnd 5: Ch 1, turn; sc in same st, 2 sc in next ch-2 sp, (sc in next Cluster, 2 sc in next ch-2 sp) around; join with slip st to first sc.

Rnds 6-9: Repeat Rnds 2-5.

Rnd 10: Ch 1, do **not** turn; sc in same st and in each sc around; join with slip st to first sc, finish off.

Repeat for second Sleeve.

GIRL'S VERSION
SIZES 3 AND 6 MONTHS ONLY
Rnd 1: With **wrong** side facing, join Pastel Green with sc at underarm; working in skipped dc on Yoke, sc in next dc and in each dc around; join with slip st to first sc: 33{39} sc.

Rnds 2-7: Work same as Boy's version.

Rnd 8: Ch 1, turn; sc in same st and in each sc around; join with slip st to first sc, finish off.

Repeat for second Sleeve.

SIZE 12 MONTHS ONLY
Rnd 1: With **wrong** side facing, join Pastel Green with sc at underarm; working in skipped dc on Yoke, 2 sc in next dc, sc in each dc around; join with slip st to first sc: 42 sc.

Rnds 2-9: Work same as Boy's version.

Rnd 10: Ch 1, turn; sc in same st and in each sc around; join with slip st to first sc, finish off.

Repeat for second Sleeve.

FINISHING
LEG EDGING
Row 1: With **right** side facing, join Baby Yellow for Boy's or Pastel Green for Girl's with sc in end of first row on either Lower Band; work 59{69-74} sc evenly spaced across Leg opening: 60{70-75} sc.

To decrease, pull up a loop in next 2 sc, YO and draw through all 3 loops on hook **(counts as one sc).**

Row 2: Ch 1, turn; sc in first 2 sc, decrease, (sc in next 3 sc, decrease) across to last sc, sc in last sc: 48{56-60} sc.

Row 3: Ch 1, turn; sc in each sc across; finish off.

Repeat for second Leg opening.

BACK EDGING
Row 1: With **wrong** side facing, join White with slip st in corner at left back neck edge; ch 1, work 21{21-23} sc evenly spaced across end of rows, work 21{21-23} sc evenly spaced across end of rows on right back; do **not** finish off: 42{42-46} sc.

Boy's only - Row 2 (Buttonhole row): Ch 1, turn; sc in first sc, ch 3, skip next 2 sc, ★ sc in next 6{6-7} sc, ch 3, skip next 2 sc; repeat from ★ once **more**, sc in next sc, decrease, sc in each sc across; finish off.

Girl's only - Row 2 (Buttonhole row): Ch 1, turn; sc in first 20{20-22} sc, decrease, sc in next sc, ch 3, skip next 2 sc, ★ sc in next 6{6-7} sc, ch 3, skip next 2 sc; repeat from ★ once **more**, sc in last sc; finish off.

BOTH VERSIONS
Add buttons.

Sew snap tape to each Lower Band, lapping Front over Back.

Following manufacturer's instructions, trace embroidery diagram from page 208 onto stabilizer. Center design on front of Yoke and baste in place. Embroider design on stabilizer, then remove stabilizer by taking out basting stitches and tearing or cutting away large areas of stabilizer. To remove remaining stabilizer, submerge Bubble Suit in water for 30 seconds to 2 minutes, then shape Suit and air dry.

ENDEARING EASTER OUTFIT

Dolled up in this darling ensemble, your little girl will be as pretty as a pansy! Satin ribbon embellishes the lightweight dress and hat.

■■□□ EASY

Finished Chest Measurements:
3 months - 19¹/₂" (49.5 cm)
6 months - 21" (53.5 cm)
12 months - 22¹/₂" (57 cm)

Size Note: Instructions are written for size 3 months with sizes 6 and 12 months in braces { }. Instructions will be easier to read if you circle all the numbers pertaining to your child's size. If only one number is given, it applies to all sizes. If a zero is given, it means to do nothing.

MATERIALS
Light/Worsted Weight Yarn
2¹/₂ ounces, 250 yards (70 grams, 229 meters) per skein:
Lilac - 4 skeins
Maize - 1 skein
Crochet hook, size D (3.25 mm) **or** size needed for gauge
Yarn needle
³/₈" (10 mm) Buttons - 4
³/₈" (10 mm) wide Ribbon - 3 yards (2.75 meters)
Sewing needle and thread

GAUGE: In pattern, 2 repeats = 3¹/₄{3¹/₂-3³/₄}"/8.25{9-9.5} cm; 6 rows = 2¹/₂" (6.25 cm)

DRESS
BODICE

With Lilac, ch 108{121-132}; being careful not to twist ch, join with slip st to form a ring.

Rnd 1 (Right side)**:** Ch 3 **(counts as first dc, now and throughout)**, dc in next 1{2-2} ch(s), skip next 2 chs, (2 dc, ch 1, 2 dc) in next ch, ★ skip next 2 chs, dc in next 4{5-6} chs, skip next 2 chs, (2 dc, ch 1, 2 dc) in next ch; repeat from ★ around to last 4{5-5} chs, skip next 2 chs, dc in last 2{3-3} chs; join with slip st to first dc: 96{109-120} dc and 12 ch-1 sps.

Note: Mark Rnd 1 as **right** side.

Rnds 2 thru 4{6-7}: Ch 3, dc in next 1{2-2} dc, (2 dc, ch 1, 2 dc) in next ch-1 sp, ★ skip next 2 dc, dc in next 4{5-6} dc, (2 dc, ch 1, 2 dc) in next ch-1 sp; repeat from ★ around to last 4{5-5} dc, skip next 2 dc, dc in last 2{3-3} dc; join with slip st to first dc.

Note: Begin working in rows.

Row 1: Do **not** turn; slip st in next dc, ch 3, dc in next 0{1-1} dc, (2 dc, ch 1, 2 dc) in next ch-1 sp, ★ skip next 2 dc, dc in next 4{5-6} dc, (2 dc, ch 1, 2 dc) in next ch-1 sp; repeat from ★ across to last 4{5-5} dc, skip next 2 dc, dc in next 1{2-2} dc, leave remaining dc unworked: 94{107-118} dc.

Row 2: Ch 3, **turn;** dc in next 0{1-1} dc, (2 dc, ch 1, 2 dc) in next ch-1 sp, ★ skip next 2 dc, dc in next 4{5-6} dc, (2 dc, ch 1, 2 dc) in next ch-1 sp; repeat from ★ across to last 3{4-4} dc, skip next 2 dc, dc in last 1{2-2} dc; do **not** finish off.

LEFT BACK
Row 1: Ch 3, turn; dc in next 0{1-1} dc, (2 dc, ch 1, 2 dc) in next ch-1 sp, skip next 2 dc, dc in next 4{5-6} dc, (2 dc, ch 1, 2 dc) in next ch-1 sp, skip next 2 dc, dc in next 6{7-8} dc, leave remaining 75{85-94} dc unworked: 19{22-24} dc and 2 ch-1 sps.

Row 2: Ch 3, turn; dc in next 5{6-7} dc, (2 dc, ch 1, 2 dc) in next ch-1 sp, skip next 2 dc, dc in next 4{5-6} dc, (2 dc, ch 1, 2 dc) in next ch-1 sp, skip next 2 dc, dc in last 1{2-2} dc.

Row 3: Ch 3, turn; dc in next 0{1-1} dc, (2 dc, ch 1, 2 dc) in next ch-1 sp, skip next 2 dc, dc in next 4{5-6} dc, (2 dc, ch 1, 2 dc) in next ch-1 sp, skip next 2 dc, dc in last 6{7-8} dc.

Rows 4-7: Repeat Rows 2 and 3 twice; do **not** finish off.

NECK SHAPING
Row 1: Ch 3, turn; dc in next 5{6-7} dc, (2 dc, ch 1, 2 dc) in next ch-1 sp, skip next 2 dc, dc in next 2{1-2} dc, leave remaining 7{10-10} dc unworked: 12{12-14} dc and one ch-1 sp.

Row 2: Ch 3, turn; dc in next 1{0-1} dc, (2 dc, ch 1, 2 dc) in next ch-1 sp, skip next 2 dc, dc in last 6{7-8} dc.

Row 3: Ch 3, turn; dc in next 5{6-7} dc, (2 dc, ch 1, 2 dc) in next ch-1 sp, skip next 2 dc, dc in last 2{1-2} dc.

Sizes 3 and 6 months only
Finish off.

Size 12 months only
Row 4: Repeat Row 2; finish off.

FRONT
Row 1: With **right** side facing, skip next 8{9-10} dc from Left Back and join Lilac with slip st in next dc; ch 3, dc in next 5{6-7} dc, (2 dc, ch 1, 2 dc) in next ch-1 sp, ★ skip next 2 dc, dc in next 4{5-6} dc, (2 dc, ch 1, 2 dc) in next ch-1 sp; repeat from ★ 2 times **more**, skip next 2 dc, dc in next 6{7-8} dc, leave remaining 27{31-34} dc unworked: 40{45-50} dc and 4 ch-1 sps.

Rows 2-7: Ch 3, turn; dc in next 5{6-7} dc, (2 dc, ch 1, 2 dc) in next ch-1 sp, ★ skip next 2 dc, dc in next 4{5-6} dc, (2 dc, ch 1, 2 dc) in next ch-1 sp; repeat from ★ 2 times **more**, skip next 2 dc, dc in last 6{7-8} dc; at end of Row 7, do **not** finish off.

RIGHT NECK SHAPING

Row 1: Ch 3, turn; dc in next 5{6-7} dc, (2 dc, ch 1, 2 dc) in next ch-1 sp, skip next 2 dc, dc in next 2{1-2} dc, leave remaining 28{33-36} dc unworked: 12{12-14} dc and one ch-1 sp.

Row 2: Ch 3, turn; dc in next 1{0-1} dc, (2 dc, ch 1, 2 dc) in next ch-1 sp, skip next 2 dc, dc in last 6{7-8} dc.

Row 3: Ch 3, turn; dc in next 5{6-7} dc, (2 dc, ch 1, 2 dc) in next ch-1 sp, skip next 2 dc, dc in last 2{1-2} dc.

Sizes 3 and 6 months only
Finish off, leaving a long end for sewing.

Size 12 months only
Row 4: Repeat Row 2; finish off leaving a long end for sewing.

LEFT NECK SHAPING

Row 1: With **wrong** side facing, skip next 16{21-22} dc from Right Neck Shaping and join Lilac with slip st in next dc; ch 3, dc in next 1{0-1} dc, (2 dc, ch 1, 2 dc) in next ch-1 sp, skip next 2 dc, dc in last 6{7-8} dc: 12{12-14} dc and one ch-1 sp.

Row 2: Ch 3, turn; dc in next 5{6-7} dc, (2 dc, ch 1, 2 dc) in next ch-1 sp, skip next 2 dc, dc in last 2{1-2} dc.

Row 3: Ch 3, turn; dc in next 1{0-1} dc, (2 dc, ch 1, 2 dc) in next ch-1 sp, skip next 2 dc, dc in last 6{7-8} dc.

Sizes 3 and 6 months only
Finish off, leaving a long end for sewing.

Size 12 months only
Row 4: Repeat Row 2; finish off leaving a long end for sewing.

RIGHT BACK

Row 1: With **right** side facing, skip next 8{9-10} dc from Front and join Lilac with slip st in next dc; ch 3, dc in next 5{6-7} dc, (2 dc, ch 1, 2 dc) in next ch-1 sp, skip next 2 dc, dc in next 4{5-6} dc, (2 dc, ch 1, 2 dc) in next ch-1 sp, skip next 2 dc, dc in last 1{2-2} dc: 19{22-24} dc and 2 ch-1 sps.

Instructions continued on page 72.

Row 2: Ch 3, turn; dc in next 0{1-1} dc, (2 dc, ch 1, 2 dc) in next ch-1 sp, skip next 2 dc, dc in next 4{5-6} dc, (2 dc, ch 1, 2 dc) in next ch-1 sp, skip next 2 dc, dc in last 6{7-8} dc.

Row 3: Ch 3, turn; dc in next 5{6-7} dc, (2 dc, ch 1, 2 dc) in next ch-1 sp, skip next 2 dc, dc in next 4{5-6} dc, (2 dc, ch 1, 2 dc) in next ch-1 sp, skip next 2 dc, dc in last 1{2-2} dc.

Rows 4-7: Repeat Rows 2 and 3 twice; do **not** finish off.

NECK SHAPING

Row 1: Turn, slip st in first 8{11-11} sts, ch 3, dc in next 1{0-1} dc, (2 dc, ch 1, 2 dc) in next ch-1 sp, skip next 2 dc, dc in last 6{7-8} dc: 12{12-14} dc and one ch-1 sp.

Row 2: Ch 3, turn; dc in next 5{6-7} dc, (2 dc, ch 1, 2 dc) in next ch-1 sp, skip next 2 dc, dc in last 2{1-2} dc.

Row 3: Ch 3, turn; dc in next 1{0-1} dc, (2 dc, ch 1, 2 dc) in next ch-1 sp, skip next 2 dc, dc in last 6{7-8} dc.

Sizes 3 and 6 months only
Finish off.

Sew shoulder seams.

Size 12 months only
Row 4: Repeat Row 2; finish off.

Sew shoulder seams.

BUTTONHOLE BAND

Row 1: With **right** side facing and working in end of rows across Right Back, join Lilac with sc in first row *(see Joining With Sc, page 205)*; work 19 sc evenly spaced across: 20 sc.

Row 2 (Buttonhole row): Ch 1, turn; sc in first 3 sc, ch 1, skip next sc **(buttonhole made)**, ★ sc in next 4 sc, ch 1, skip next sc **(buttonhole made)**; repeat from ★ 2 times **more**, sc in last sc.

Row 3: Ch 1, turn; sc in each sc and in each ch-1 sp across; finish off leaving a long end for sewing.

BUTTON BAND

Row 1: With **right** side facing and working in end of rows across Left Back, join Lilac with sc in first row; work 19 sc evenly spaced across to Neck Shaping: 20 sc.

Rows 2 and 3: Ch 1, turn; sc in each sc across; do **not** finish off.

NECK EDGING

Row 1: Ch 1, do **not** turn; sc evenly across neck edge; finish off.

ARMHOLE EDGING

Rnd 1: With **right** side facing, skip next 3{4-5} dc from first unworked ch-1 sp at armhole and join Lilac with sc in next dc; 1{2-1} sc in next dc, sc in next 3 dc and in next ch-1 sp; 2 sc in end of each row across; sc in next ch-1 sp and in last 3{4-5} dc; join with slip st to first sc: 50{52-56} sc.

Rnd 2: Ch 1, sc in same st, ch 3, skip next sc, ★ sc in next sc, ch 3, skip next sc; repeat from ★ around; join with slip st to first sc, finish off.

Repeat for second armhole.

SKIRT

Rnd 1: With **right** side facing and working in free loops *(Fig. 3b, page 205)* and in sps across beginning ch, join Lilac with sc in ch at base of first dc; sc in next 2{3-3} chs, 2{1-2} sc in next sp, sc in next ch, 2 sc in next sp, ★ sc in next 4{5-6} chs, 2 sc in next sp, sc in next ch, 2 sc in next sp; repeat from ★ around to last 1{2-2} ch(s), sc in last 1{2-2} ch(s); join with slip st to first sc: 108{120-132} sc.

To work treble crochet (abbreviated tr), YO twice, insert hook in sc or sp indicated, YO and pull up a loop (4 loops on hook), (YO and draw through 2 loops on hook) 3 times.

Rnd 2 (Eyelet rnd): Ch 5 **(counts as first tr plus ch 1, now and throughout)**, skip next sc, ★ tr in next sc, ch 1, skip next sc; repeat from ★ around; join with slip st to first tr: 54{60-66} tr and 54{60-66} ch-1 sps.

Rnd 3: Ch 1, sc in same st and in each ch-1 sp and each tr around; join with slip st to first sc: 108{120-132} sc.

Rnd 4: Ch 1, (sc, ch 1) in same st and in each sc around; join with slip st to first sc changing to Maize *(Fig. 7c, page 206)*, do **not** cut Lilac: 108{120-132} sc and 108{120-132} ch-1 sps.

Note: Carry yarn not being used **loosely** along wrong side of Skirt.

Rnd 5: Slip st in first ch-1 sp, ch 1, sc in same sp, ch 1, (sc in next ch-1 sp, ch 1) around; join with slip st to first sc changing to Lilac.

Rnd 6: Slip st in first ch-1 sp, ch 1, sc in same sp, ch 1, (sc in next ch-1 sp, ch 1) around; join with slip st to first sc.

Rnd 7: Slip st in first ch-1 sp, ch 1, sc in same sp, ch 1, (sc in next ch-1 sp, ch 1) around; join with slip st to first sc changing to Maize.

Rnds 8 thru 25{31-37}: Repeat Rnds 5-7, 6{8-10} times; at end of Rnd 25{31-37}, do **not** change colors, cut Maize.

Rnd 26{32-38} (Eyelet rnd): Slip st in first ch-1 sp, ch 5, (tr in next ch-1 sp, ch 1) around; join with slip st to first tr: 108{120-132} tr and 108{120-132} ch-1 sps.

Rnd 27{33-39}: Slip st in first ch-1 sp, ch 1, sc in same sp, ch 1, (sc in next ch-1 sp, ch 1) around; join with slip st to first sc.

Rnd 28{34-40}: Slip st in first ch-1 sp, ch 1, sc in same sp, ch 3, (sc in next ch-1 sp, ch 3) around; join with slip st to first sc, finish off.

PANSY

With Lilac, ch 4; join with slip st to form a ring.

Rnd 1 (Right side): Ch 1, (sc in ring, ch 3) 5 times; join with slip st to first sc, finish off: 5 ch-3 sps.

Note: Mark Rnd 1 as **right** side.

Rnd 2: With **right** side facing, join Maize with slip st in any ch-3 sp; (ch 2, 6 dc, ch 2, slip st) in same sp, (slip st, ch 2, 6 dc, ch 2, slip st) in each of next 2 ch-3 sps, (slip st, ch 3, 8 tr, ch 3, slip st) in each of last 2 ch-3 sps; join with slip st to joining slip st, finish off.

Rnd 3: With **right** side facing, join Lilac with sc in top of beginning ch-2; ch 3, ★ † (sc in next dc, ch 3) 6 times, sc in next ch, ch 3, skip next 2 slip sts †, sc in top of next ch-2, ch 3; repeat from ★ once **more**, then repeat from † to † once, ♥ sc in top of next ch-3, ch 3, (sc in next tr, ch 3) 8 times, sc in next ch, ch 3, skip next 2 slip sts ♥, repeat from ♥ to ♥ once **more**; join with slip st to first sc, finish off.

FINISHING

Thread yarn needle with long end, place Buttonhole Band over Button Band and sew to wrong side of Bodice.

Sew buttons to Button Band opposite buttonholes.

Using photo as a guide for placement:

Weave a 48" (122 cm) length of ribbon through bottom Eyelet rnd; tie in a bow at front.

Weave a 44" (112 cm) length of ribbon through top Eyelet rnd and tie in a bow at back.

Sew Pansy to top Eyelet rnd diagonally across from bow on bottom Eyelet rnd.

HAT

Head Measurements:
3 months - 16¼" (41.5 cm)
6 months - 16¼" (41.5 cm)
12 months - 17¾" (45 cm)

CROWN

With Lilac, ch 90{90-99}; being careful not to twist ch, join with slip st to form a ring.

Rnd 1 (Right side)**:** Ch 3 **(counts as first dc, now and throughout)**, dc in next 3 chs, skip next 2 chs, (2 dc, ch 1, 2 dc) in next ch, skip next 2 chs, ★ dc in next 4 chs, skip next 2 chs, (2 dc, ch 1, 2 dc) in next ch, skip next 2 chs; repeat from ★ around; join with slip st to first dc: 80{80-88} dc and 10{10-11} ch-1 sps.

Note: Mark Rnd 1 as **right** side.

Rnds 2 thru 8{8-10}: Ch 3, dc in next 3 dc, (2 dc, ch 1, 2 dc) in next ch-1 sp, skip next 2 dc, ★ dc in next 4 dc, (2 dc, ch 1, 2 dc) in next ch-1 sp, skip next 2 dc; repeat from ★ around; join with slip st to first dc.

To decrease (uses next 2 dc), ★ YO, insert hook in **next** dc, YO and pull up a loop, YO and draw through 2 loops on hook; repeat from ★ once **more**, YO and draw through all 3 loops on hook **(counts as one dc)**.

Rnd 9{9-11}: Ch 2, dc in next dc, decrease, (2 dc, ch 1, 2 dc) in next ch-1 sp, skip next 2 dc, ★ decrease twice, (2 dc, ch 1, 2 dc) in next ch-1 sp, skip next 2 dc; repeat from ★ around; join with slip st to first dc: 60{60-66} dc and 10{10-11} ch-1 sps.

Rnd 10{10-12}: Ch 2, dc in next dc, (2 dc, ch 1, 2 dc) in next ch-1 sp, skip next 2 dc, ★ decrease, (2 dc, ch 1, 2 dc) in next ch-1 sp, skip next 2 dc; repeat from ★ around; join with slip st to first dc: 50{50-55} dc.

Rnd 11{11-13}: Ch 3, 2 dc in next ch-1 sp, skip next 2 dc, ★ dc in next dc, 2 dc in next ch-1 sp, skip next 2 dc; repeat from ★ around; join with slip st to first dc: 30{30-33} dc.

Rnd 12{12-14}: Ch 3, decrease, (dc in next dc, decrease) around; join with slip st to first dc, finish off leaving a long end for sewing.

BRIM

Rnd 1: With **right** side facing and working in free loops *(Fig. 3b, page 205)* and in sps across beginning ch, join Lilac with sc in ch at base of first dc *(see Joining With Sc, page 205)*; 2 sc in next sp, sc in next ch, 2 sc in next sp, ★ sc in next 4 chs, 2 sc in next sp, sc in next ch, 2 sc in next sp; repeat from ★ around to last 3 chs, sc in last 3 chs; join with slip st to first sc: 90{90-99} sc.

Rnd 2: Ch 1, (sc, ch 1) in same st and in each sc around; join with slip st to first sc, finish off: 90{90-99} sc and 90{90-99} ch-1 sps.

Rnd 3: With **right** side facing, join Maize with sc in first ch-1 sp; ch 1, (sc in next ch-1 sp, ch 1) around; join with slip st to first sc, finish off.

Rnd 4: With **right** side facing, join Lilac with sc in first ch-1 sp; ch 1, (sc in next ch-1 sp, ch 1) around; join with slip st to first sc, do **not** finish off.

Rnd 5: Slip st in first ch-1 sp, ch 1, sc in same sp, ch 1, (sc in next ch-1 sp, ch 1) around; join with slip st to first sc, finish off.

Rnds 6-8: Repeat Rnds 3-5; at end of Rnd 8, do **not** finish off.

Rnd 9: Slip st in first ch-1 sp, ch 1, sc in same sp, ch 3, (sc in next ch-1 sp, ch 3) around; join with slip st to first sc, finish off.

PANSY

Work same as Dress Pansy.

FINISHING

Thread yarn needle with long end on Crown and weave through stitches on Rnd 12{12-14}; gather tightly and secure end.

Tie a 16" (40.5 cm) length of ribbon in a bow.

Using photo as a guide for placement, turn Brim up; sew bow and Pansy to Hat.

Designs by Sandra Abbate.

BUNDLE-UP BUNTING

Everyone will love this sweet little baby bunting! The cozy set has button-on thumbless mittens and a cute tie-on cap.

■■□□ EASY

Finished Chest Measurements:
0-3 months - 24" (61 cm)
3-6 months - 28¹/₂" (72.5 cm)

Size Note: Instructions are written for size 0-3 months with size 6-9 months in braces { }. Instructions will be easier to read if you circle all the numbers pertaining to your child's size. If only one number is given, it applies to both sizes.

MATERIALS
Medium/Worsted Weight Yarn
4 ounces, 242 yards
(110 grams, 221 meters)
per skein (Nursery) or
5 ounces, 328 yards
(140 grams, 300 meters)
per skein (White):
Nursery - 4{6} skeins
White - 1 skein
Crochet hooks, sizes G (4 mm) **and**
I (5.5 mm) **or** sizes needed for gauge
Yarn needle

GAUGE: With two strands of yarn and larger size hook, in pattern, (sc, ch 1) 7 times and 13 rows = 4" (10 cm);
With one strand of yarn and smaller size hook, 10 sc = 3" (7.5 cm)

Note: Bunting and Cap are worked holding two strands of yarn together, unless otherwise instructed.

BUNTING
BODY
With Nursery and larger size hook, ch 82{98}.

Row 1 (Wrong side)**:** Sc in second ch from hook, ★ ch 1, skip next ch, sc in next ch; repeat from ★ across: 41{49} sc and 40{48} ch-1 sps.

Note: Mark **back** of any stitch on Row 1 as **right** side.

Rows 2 thru 42{48}: Ch 1, turn; sc in first sc, (ch 1, sc in next sc) across; do **not** finish off.

LEFT FRONT
Row 1: Ch 1, turn; sc in first sc, (ch 1, sc in next sc) 8{10} times, leave remaining 32{38} sc unworked: 9{11} sc and 8{10} ch-1 sps.

Rows 2 thru 10{18}: Ch 1, turn; sc in first sc, (ch 1, sc in next sc) across; do **not** finish off.

Neck Shaping
Row 1: Turn; slip st in first sc, (slip st in next ch-1 sp and in next sc) 1{2} time(s), ch 1, sc in same st, (ch 1, sc in next sc) across: 8{9} sc and 7{8} ch-1 sps.

To work ending decrease, insert hook in next sc, YO and pull up a loop, skip next ch-1 sp, insert hook in last sc, YO and pull up a loop, YO and draw through all 3 loops on hook **(counts as one sc)**.

Row 2: Ch 1, turn; sc in first sc, ch 1, (sc in next sc, ch 1) across to last 2 sc, work ending decrease: 7{8} sc and 6{7} ch-1 sps.

To work beginning decrease, insert hook in first sc, YO and pull up a loop, skip next ch-1 sp, insert hook in next sc, YO and pull up a loop, YO and draw through all 3 loops on hook **(counts as one sc)**.

Row 3: Ch 1, turn; work beginning decrease, (ch 1, sc in next sc) across: 6{7} sc and 5{6} ch-1 sps.

Rows 4-6: Ch 1, turn; sc in first sc, (ch 1, sc in next sc) across.

Finish off, leaving long ends for sewing.

BACK
Row 1: With **wrong** side facing and larger size hook, skip next ch-1 sp on last row of Body from Left Front and join Nursery with sc in next sc *(see Joining With Sc, page 205)*; (ch 1, sc in next sc) 22{26} times, leave remaining 9{11} sc unworked: 23{27} sc and 22{26} ch-1 sps.

Rows 2 thru 14{22}: Ch 1, turn; sc in first sc, (ch 1, sc in next sc) across; do **not** finish off.

Left Neck Shaping
Row 1: Ch 1, turn; sc in first sc, (ch 1, sc in next sc) 5{6} times, leave remaining 17{20} sc unworked: 6{7} sc and 5{6} ch-1 sps.

Row 2: Ch 1, turn; sc in first sc, (ch 1, sc in next sc) across; finish off.

Right Neck Shaping
Row 1: With **wrong** side facing and larger size hook, skip next 11{13} sc on last row of Back from Left Neck Shaping and join Nursery with sc in next sc; (ch 1, sc in next sc) across: 6{7} sc and 5{6} ch-1 sps.

Row 2: Ch 1, turn; sc in first sc, (ch 1, sc in next sc) across; finish off.

RIGHT FRONT
Row 1: With **wrong** side facing and larger size hook, skip next ch-1 sp on last row of Body from Back and join Nursery with sc in next sc; (ch 1, sc in next sc) across: 9{11} sc and 8{10} ch-1 sps.

Rows 2 thru 10{18}: Ch 1, turn; sc in first sc, (ch 1, sc in next sc) across; do **not** finish off.

Instructions continued on page 76.

Continued from page 74.

NECK SHAPING

Row 1: Ch 1, turn; sc in first sc, (ch 1, sc in next sc) 7{8} times, leave remaining 1{2} sc unworked: 8{9} sc and 7{8} ch-1 sps.

Row 2: Ch 1, turn; work beginning decrease, (ch 1, sc in next sc) across: 7{8} sc and 6{7} ch-1 sps.

Row 3: Ch 1, turn; sc in first sc, ch 1, (sc in next sc, ch 1) 4{5} times, work ending decrease: 6{7} sc and 5{6} ch-1 sps.

Rows 4-6: Ch 1, turn; sc in first sc, (ch 1, sc in next sc) across.

Finish off, leaving long ends for sewing.

Sew shoulder seams.

SLEEVE (Make 2)

With Nursery and larger size hook, ch 22{26}; being careful not to twist ch, join with slip st to form a ring.

Rnd 1 (Wrong side)**:** Ch 1, sc in same st, ch 1, skip next ch, ★ sc in next ch, ch 1, skip next ch; repeat from ★ around; join with slip st to first sc: 11{13} sc and 11{13} ch-1 sps.

Note: Mark **back** of any stitch on Rnd 1 as **right** side.

Rnd 2 (Increase rnd)**:** Ch 1, turn; 2 sc in same st, ch 1, (sc in next sc, ch 1) around, sc in same st as first sc; join with slip st to first sc: 13{15} sc and 11{13} ch-1 sps.

Rnds 3 and 4: Ch 1, turn; sc in same st, ch 1, (sc in next sc, ch 1) around; join with slip st to first sc: 13{15} sc and 13{15} ch-1 sps.

Rnds 5-11: Repeat Rnds 2-4 twice, then repeat Rnd 2 once **more**: 19{21} sc and 17{19} ch-1 sps.

Rnds 12 thru 14{16}: Ch 1, turn; sc in same st, ch 1, (sc in next sc, ch 1) around; join with slip st to first sc: 19{21} sc and 19{21} ch-1 sps.

Finish off, leaving long ends for sewing.

CUFF

Rnd 1: With **right** side facing, smaller size hook, and working in free loops *(Fig. 3b, page 205)* and in sps across beginning ch, join one strand of White with sc in same st as joining; sc in each ch and in each sp around; join with slip st to first sc: 22{26} sc.

Rnds 2 and 3: Ch 1, do **not** turn; sc in same st and in each sc around; join with slip st to first sc.

Finish off.

Sew each Sleeve to Bunting, matching center of last round on Sleeve to shoulder seam.

NECK EDGING

Row 1: With **right** side facing, smaller size hook, and working in end of rows and in sts across neck opening, join one strand of White with sc in first unworked sc on Row 10{18} of Right Front; sc evenly across.

Rows 2 and 3: Ch 1, turn; sc in each sc across.

Finish off.

BUTTONHOLE BAND

Row 1: With **right** side facing, smaller size hook, and working in end of rows across left side of Bunting and Neck Edging, join one strand of White with sc in first row; work 57{66} sc evenly spaced across: 58{67} sc.

Rows 2 and 3: Ch 1, turn; sc in each sc across.

Row 4 (Buttonhole row)**:** Ch 1, turn; sc in first 12{14} sc, ch 2, skip next 2 sc **(buttonhole made)**, ★ sc in next 12{14} sc, ch 2, skip next 2 sc **(buttonhole made)**; repeat from ★ across to last 2{3} sc, sc in last 2{3} sc: 50 sc and 4 ch-2 sps.

Row 5: Ch 1, turn; sc in each sc and in each ch across: 58{67} sc.

Rows 6 and 7: Ch 1, turn; sc in each sc across.

Finish off.

BUTTON BAND

Row 1: With **right** side facing, smaller size hook, and working in end of rows across right side of Bunting and Neck Edging, join one strand of White with sc in first row; work 57{66} sc evenly spaced across: 58{67} sc.

Rows 2-7: Ch 1, turn; sc in each sc across.

Finish off.

NECK TRIM

With **right** side facing, smaller size hook, and working in end of rows on Bands and in sc on Neck Edging, join one strand of White with sc in first row of Button Band; sc evenly across; finish off.

BOTTOM TRIM

With **right** side facing, lap Buttonhole Band over Button Band. Using larger size hook and working through **both** thicknesses, join Nursery with sc in end of first row on Buttonhole Band; (skip next row, sc in end of next row) 3 times; working in sps across beginning ch of Body, sc in each sp around; join with slip st to first sc, finish off: 44{52} sc.

BOTTOM PANEL

With Nursery and larger size hook, ch 21{25}.

Rnd 1 (Right side)**:** 2 Sc in second ch from hook, sc in each ch across to last ch, 3 sc in last ch; working in free loops of beginning ch, sc in next 18{22} chs and in same ch as first sc; join with slip st to first sc: 42{50} sc.

Note: Mark Rnd 1 as **right** side.

Rnd 2: Ch 1, 2 sc in same st, sc in next 20{24} sc, 2 sc in next sc, sc in each sc around; join with slip st to first sc: 44{52} sc.

Rnd 3: Ch 1, sc in same st and in each sc around; join with slip st to first sc, finish off leaving a long end for sewing.

Using photo as a guide for placement, with **wrong** sides together, and working through **both** loops of each stitch, whipstitch Bottom Panel to Bottom Trim **(Fig. 9b, page 206)**.

BUTTON (Make 6)
Note: Buttons will measure 1¼" (3 cm) in diameter.

With Nursery and smaller size hook, ch 3; join with slip st to form a ring.

Rnd 1 (Wrong side)**:** Ch 1, 6 sc in ring; join with slip st to first sc.

Note: Mark **back** of any stitch on Rnd 1 as **right** side.

Rnd 2: Ch 1, working over sc on Rnd 1, work 12 sc in beginning ring; join with slip st to first sc.

Rnd 3: Ch 1, sc in same st, skip next sc, (sc in next sc, skip next sc) around; join with slip st to first sc, finish off leaving long ends for sewing.

Thread needle with ends and weave through sc on Rnd 3; gather tightly and secure ends; do **not** cut yarn.

Using photo as a guide for placement, sew one Button to each Cuff; then sew remaining Buttons to Button Band.

THUMBLESS MITTEN
(Make 2)
With one strand of White and smaller size hook, ch 24{28}; being careful not to twist ch, join with slip st to form a ring.

Rnd 1 (Right side)**:** Ch 1, sc in same st and in each ch around; join with slip st to first sc: 24{28} sc.

Note: Mark any stitch on Rnd 1 as **right** side.

Rnd 2 (Buttonhole rnd)**:** Ch 1, sc in same st and in next sc, ch 2, skip next 2 sc **(buttonhole made)**, sc in each sc around; join with slip st to first sc: 22{26} sc and one ch-2 sp.

Rnd 3: Ch 1, sc in same st and in each sc and each ch around; join with slip st to first sc, finish off: 24{28} sc.

Rnd 4: With **right** side facing and smaller size hook, join one strand of Nursery with sc in same st as joining; sc in each sc around; join with slip st to first sc.

Rnds 5 thru 11{15}: Ch 1, sc in same st and in each sc around; join with slip st to first sc.

To decrease, pull up a loop in next 2 sc, YO and draw through all 3 loops on hook **(counts as one sc)**.

Rnd 12{16}: Ch 1, sc in same st and in next sc, decrease, (sc in next 2 sc, decrease) around; join with slip st to first sc: 18{21} sc.

Rnd 13{17}: Ch 1, sc in same st, decrease, (sc in next sc, decrease) around; join with slip st to first sc: 12{14} sc.

Rnd 14{18}: Ch 1, pull up a loop in same st and in next sc, YO and draw through all 3 loops on hook **(counts as first sc)**, decrease around; join with slip st to first sc, finish off leaving a long end for sewing.

Thread needle with long end and weave through stitches on last round; gather tightly and secure end.

Using photo as a guide for placement, button one Mitten to each Cuff.

CAP
CROWN
With Nursery and larger size hook, ch 34{42}.

Row 1 (Wrong side)**:** Sc in second ch from hook, ★ ch 1, skip next ch, sc in next ch; repeat from ★ across: 17{21} sc and 16{20} ch-1 sps.

Note: Mark **back** of any stitch on Row 1 as **right** side.

Rows 2 thru 18{22}: Ch 1, turn; sc in first sc, (ch 1, sc in next sc) across.

Finish off, leaving long ends for sewing.

Fold last row in half with **wrong** sides together and matching stitches; using long ends, whipstitch back seam **(Fig. 9b, page 206)**.

BRIM
Row 1: With **wrong** side facing, smaller size hook, and working in free loops **(Fig. 3b, page 205)** and in sps across beginning ch, join one strand of White with sc in first ch **(see Joining With Sc, page 205)**; sc in each ch and in each sp across: 33{41} sc.

Rows 2-7: Ch 1, turn; sc in each sc across.

Finish off.

Fold Brim to **right** side of Crown.

NECK TRIM
Row 1: With **right** side facing, smaller size hook, and working in end of rows, and through **both** thicknesses on Brim and Crown, join one strand of White with sc in first row; work 36{44} sc evenly spaced across: 37{45} sc.

Row 2 (Eyelet row)**:** Ch 4 **(counts as first dc plus ch 1)**, turn; skip next sc, dc in next sc, ★ ch 1, skip next sc, dc in next sc; repeat from ★ across: 19{23} dc and 18{22} ch-1 sps.

Row 3: Ch 1, turn; sc in each dc and in each ch-1 sp across; finish off.

Tie: With Nursery and larger size hook, make a chain 28{30}"/71{76} cm long; finish off.

Weave Tie through ch-1 sps on Eyelet row.

With White, make a pom-pom **(Figs. 10a & b, page 207)** and sew to top of Cap.

Designs by Sandra Abbate.

WEE BIBS & BOTTLE COVERS

*Wee ones will be fashionably accessorized with these matching
bibs and bottle covers for baby girls and boys.*

▰▰▱▱ **EASY**

MATERIALS
Medium/Worsted Weight Yarn
  8 ounces, 452 yards
  (230 grams, 413 meters)
  per skein:
  Boy's Set
  Light Blue - 1 skein
  White - 1 skein
  Girl's Set
  Baby Pink - 1 skein
  White - 1 skein
Crochet hook, size F (3.75 mm) **or** size
  needed for gauge
Ribbon for Boy's set:
  5/8" (16 mm) wide - 12" (30.5 cm)
  for Bib
  1/8" (3 mm) wide - 12" (30.5 cm)
  for Bottle Cover
Ribbon for Girl's set:
  1/4" (7 mm) wide - 12" (30.5 cm)
  for Bib
  1/8" (3 mm) wide - 12" (30.5 cm)
  for Bottle Cover

GAUGE: 17 sc and
19 rows = 4" (10 cm)

GIRL'S SET
BIB
Finished Size:
8 1/4" x 9 1/2" (21 cm x 24 cm)

BODY
With White, ch 3.

Row 1: Sc in second ch from hook and
in last ch: 2 sc.

Row 2 (Right side): Ch 1, turn; 2 sc in
each sc across: 4 sc.

Note: Mark Row 1 as **right** side.

Rows 3-15: Ch 1, turn; 2 sc in first sc,
sc in each sc across to last sc, 2 sc in last
sc: 30 sc.

Rows 16-20: Ch 1, turn; sc in each sc
across.

To work beginning decrease, pull up
a loop in first 2 sc, YO and draw
through all 3 loops on hook **(counts as
one sc).**

To work ending decrease, pull up a
loop in last 2 sc, YO and draw through
all 3 loops on hook **(counts as one
sc).**

Rows 21-23: Ch 1, turn; work
beginning decrease, sc in each sc across
to last 2 sc, work ending decrease: 24
sc.

Rows 24-31: Ch 1, turn; sc in each sc
across.

Row 32: Ch 1, turn; work beginning
decrease, sc in each sc across to last 2
sc, work ending decrease; do **not** finish
off: 22 sc.

RIGHT SIDE
Row 1: Ch 1, turn; sc in first 7 sc, leave
remaining 15 sc unworked: 7 sc.

Row 2: Ch 1, turn; work beginning
decrease, sc in each sc across: 6 sc.

Row 3: Ch 1, turn; sc in each sc across
to last 2 sc, work ending decrease: 5 sc.

Rows 4 and 5: Repeat Rows 2 and 3:
3 sc.

Row 6: Ch 1, turn; work beginning
decrease, sc in last sc; finish off: 2 sc.

LEFT SIDE
Row 1: With **wrong** side facing, skip
next 8 sc from Right Side on Row 32 of
Body and join White with sc in next sc
(see Joining With Sc, page 205); sc
in each sc across: 7 sc.

Row 2: Ch 1, turn; sc in each sc across
to last 2 sc, work ending decrease: 6 sc.

Row 3: Ch 1, turn; work
decrease, sc in each sc across: 5 sc.

Rows 4 and 5: Repeat Rows 2 and 3:
3 sc.

Row 6: Ch 1, turn; sc in first sc, work
ending decrease; finish off: 2 sc.

EDGING
With **right** side facing, join Baby Pink
with sc in first sc on Row 6 of Right
Side; sc in same st, 2 sc in next sc; work
40 sc evenly spaced across end of rows;
working in free loops of beginning ch
(Fig. 3b, page 205), 2 sc in ch at base
of first sc and in last ch; work 39 sc
evenly spaced across end of rows; sc in
first sc on Row 6 of Left Side, place
marker around sc just made for Left Tie
placement, sc in same st, 2 sc in last sc;
sc in end of first 6 rows; sc in next 8
skipped sc on Body; sc in end of first 6
rows on Right Side; join with slip st to
first sc, do **not** finish off: 111 sc.

Right Tie
To decrease, pull up a loop in next 2
sc, YO and draw through all 3 loops on
hook **(counts as one sc).**

Row 1: Ch 1, do **not** turn; pull up a
loop in same st and in next sc, YO and
draw through all 3 loops on hook
(counts as one sc), decrease, leave
remaining sc unworked: 2 sc.

Row 2: Ch 1, turn; work beginning
decrease, chain a 12" (30.5 cm) length;
finish off.

Instructions continued on page 80.

Continued from page 78.

Left Tie

Row 1: With **right** side facing, join Baby Pink with slip st in marked sc on Left Side; ch 1, pull up a loop in same st and in next sc, YO and draw through all 3 loops on hook **(counts as one sc)**, decrease, leave remaining sc unworked: 2 sc.

Row 2: Ch 1, turn; work beginning decrease, chain a 12" (30.5 cm) length; finish off.

TRIM

With **right** side facing, join Baby Pink with slip st in end of Row 1 on Right Tie; working in sc on Edging, skip first sc, 3 dc in next sc, skip next sc, ★ sc in next sc, skip next sc, 3 dc in next sc, skip next sc; repeat from ★ around to Left Tie, slip st in end of Row 1 on Left Tie, finish off.

Using photo as a guide for placement, tie ribbon in a bow; then sew bow to Bib.

BOTTLE COVER

Finished Size:
Fits an 8 ounce (236.6 milliliter) bottle

BOTTOM

Rnd 1 (Right side): With Baby Pink, ch 2, 6 sc in second ch from hook; join with slip st to first sc.

Note: Mark Rnd 1 as **right** side.

Rnd 2: Ch 1, 2 sc in same st and in each sc around; join with slip st to first sc: 12 sc.

Rnd 3: Ch 1, sc in same st, 2 sc in next sc, (sc in next sc, 2 sc in next sc) around; join with slip st to first sc: 18 sc.

Rnd 4: Ch 1, sc in same st and in next sc, 2 sc in next sc, (sc in next 2 sc, 2 sc in next sc) around; join with slip st to Back Loop Only of first sc *(Fig. 2, page 205)*, do **not** finish off: 24 sc.

SIDES

Rnd 1: Ch 1, working in Back Loops Only, 2 sc in same st, sc in next 5 sc, (2 sc in next sc, sc in next 5 sc) around; join with slip st to **both** loops of first sc: 28 sc.

Rnd 2: Ch 1, sc in both loops of same st and each sc around; join with slip st to first sc.

Rnd 3: Ch 1, sc in same st, skip next sc, 3 dc in next sc, skip next sc, ★ sc in next sc, skip next sc, 3 dc in next sc, skip next sc; repeat from ★ around; join with slip st to first sc: 7 sc and 21 dc.

Rnds 4 and 5: Slip st in next 2 dc, ch 1, sc in same st, 3 dc in next dc, skip next dc, ★ sc in next dc, 3 dc in next dc, skip next st; repeat from ★ around; at end of Rnd 5 change to White in last dc *(Fig. 7b, page 206)*; join with slip st to first sc.

Rnds 6-11: Ch 1, sc in same st and in each st around; join with slip st to first sc; at end of Rnd 11 change to Baby Pink in last sc: 28 sc.

Rnds 12-20: Repeat Rnds 3-11.

Rnd 21 (Eyelet rnd): Ch 1, sc in same st, ch 1, skip next sc, ★ sc in next sc, ch 1, skip next sc; repeat from ★ around; join with slip st to first sc: 14 ch-1 sps.

Rnd 22: Slip st in first ch-1 sp, ch 1, sc in same sp, (ch 3, sc in next ch-1 sp) around, ch 1, hdc in first sc to form last ch-3 sp: 14 ch-3 sps.

Rnd 23: Ch 1, sc in same sp, ch 3, (sc in next ch-3 sp, ch 3) around; join with slip st to first sc, finish off.

Weave ribbon through ch-1 sps on Eyelet round; tie ends in a bow.

BOY'S SET
BIB
Finished Size:
7³/₄" x 10" (19.5 cm x 25.5 cm)

BODY

With White, ch 29.

Row 1 (Wrong side): Sc in second ch from hook and in each ch across: 28 sc.

Note: Mark **back** of any stitch on Row 1 as **right** side.

Rows 2-32: Ch 1, turn; sc in each sc across; do **not** finish off.

RIGHT SIDE

Row 1: Ch 1, turn; sc in first 8 sc, leave remaining 20 sc unworked: 8 sc.

To work beginning decrease, pull up a loop in first 2 sc, YO and draw through all 3 loops on hook **(counts as one sc)**.

Row 2: Ch 1, turn; work beginning decrease, sc in each sc across: 7 sc.

To work ending decrease, pull up a loop in last 2 sc, YO and draw through all 3 loops on hook **(counts as one sc)**.

Row 3: Ch 1, turn; sc in each sc across to last 2 sc, work ending decrease: 6 sc.

Rows 4 and 5: Repeat Rows 2 and 3: 4 sc.

Finish off.

LEFT SIDE

Row 1: With **wrong** side facing, skip next 12 sc from Right Side on last row of Body and join White with sc in next sc *(see Joining With Sc, page 205)*; sc in each sc across: 8 sc.

Row 2: Ch 1, turn; sc in each sc across to last 2 sc, work ending decrease: 7 sc.

Row 3: Ch 1, turn; work beginning decrease, sc in each sc across: 6 sc.

Rows 4 and 5: Repeat Rows 2 and 3; do **not** finish off: 4 sc.

EDGING

Rnd 1: Ch 1, turn; sc in first 3 sc, 2 sc in last sc; sc in end of first 5 rows; sc in next 12 skipped sc on Body; sc in end of first 5 rows; working across Row 5 on Right Side, 2 sc in first sc, sc in next 2 sc, 2 sc in last sc; sc in end of each row across; working in free loops of beginning ch *(Fig. 3b, page 205)*, 3 sc in ch at base of first sc, sc in each ch across to last ch, 3 sc in last ch; sc in end of each row across, sc in same st as first sc; join with slip st to first sc, finish off: 140 sc.

Rnd 2: With **right** side facing and working in Back Loops Only *(Fig. 2, page 205)*, join Light Blue with sc in same st as joining; sc in same st and in next 2 sc, 2 sc in next sc, sc in next 25 sc, place marker around last sc made for Right Tie placement, sc in same st and in next 2 sc, 2 sc in next sc, sc in next 39 sc, 3 sc in next sc, sc in next 28 sc, 3 sc in next sc, sc in last 39 sc; join with slip st to Back Loop Only of first sc, do **not** finish off.

Left Tie

To decrease, pull up a loop in next 2 sc, YO and draw through all 3 loops on hook **(counts as one sc)**.

Row 1: Ch 1, do **not** turn; working in Back Loops Only, sc in same st and in next 3 sc, decrease, leave remaining sc unworked: 5 sc.

Row 2: Ch 1, turn; working in both loops, work beginning decrease, sc in last 3 sc: 4 sc.

Row 3: Ch 1, turn; sc in first 2 sc, work ending decrease: 3 sc.

Row 4: Ch 1, turn; work beginning decrease, sc in last sc: 2 sc.

Row 5: Ch 1, turn; work beginning decrease, chain a 12" (30.5 cm) length; finish off.

Right Tie

Row 1: With **right** side facing and working in Back Loops Only, join Light Blue with slip st in marked sc; pull up a loop in same st and in next sc, YO and draw through all 3 loops on hook **(counts as one sc)**, sc in next 4 sc, leave remaining sc unworked: 5 sc.

Row 2: Ch 1, turn; working in both loops, sc in first 3 sc, work ending decrease: 4 sc.

Row 3: Ch 1, turn; work beginning decrease, sc in last 2 sc: 3 sc.

Row 4: Ch 1, turn; sc in first sc, work ending decrease: 2 sc.

Row 5: Ch 1, turn; work beginning decrease, chain a 12" (30.5 cm) length; finish off.

Using photo as a guide for placement, make a bow tie with ribbon; then sew bow tie to Bib.

BOTTLE COVER

Finished Size:
Fits an 8 ounce (236.6 milliliter) bottle

With Light Blue, work same as Girl's Bottle Cover through Rnd 2 of Sides: 28 sc.

To work beginning Popcorn, ch 3 **(counts as first dc, now and throughout)**, 2 dc in st indicated, drop loop from hook, insert hook in first dc of 3-dc group, hook dropped loop and draw through st.

To work Popcorn, 3 dc in sc indicated, drop loop from hook, insert hook in first dc of 3-dc group, hook dropped loop and draw through st.

Rnd 3: Work beginning Popcorn in same st, ch 1, skip next sc, ★ work Popcorn in next sc, ch 1, skip next sc; repeat from ★ around; join with slip st to top of beginning Popcorn, finish off: 14 Popcorns and 14 chs.

Rnd 4: With **right** side facing, join White with sc in same st as joining; sc in each ch and in each Popcorn around; join with slip st to first sc: 28 sc.

Rnds 5-9: Ch 1, sc in same st and in each sc around; at end Rnd 9 change to Light Blue in last sc *(Fig. 7a, page 206)*; join with slip st to first sc.

Rnd 10: Work beginning Popcorn in same st, ch 1, skip next sc, ★ work Popcorn in next sc, ch 1, skip next sc; repeat from ★ around; join with slip st to top of beginning Popcorn: 14 Popcorns and 14 chs.

Rnd 11: Ch 1, sc in same st and in each ch and each Popcorn around; join with slip st to first sc.

Rnds 12-14: Ch 1, sc in same st and in each sc around; at end of Rnd 14 change to White in last sc; join with slip st to first sc.

Rnds 15-20: Ch 1, sc in same st and in each sc around; at end of Rnd 20 change to Light Blue in last sc; join with slip st to first sc.

Rnd 21: Ch 1, sc in same st and in each sc around; join with slip st to first sc.

Rnd 22 (Eyelet rnd): Ch 1, sc in same st, ch 1, skip next sc, ★ sc in next sc, ch 1, skip next sc; repeat from ★ around; join with slip st to first sc: 14 sc and 14 ch-1 sps.

Rnd 23: Ch 3, 2 dc in next ch-1 sp, (dc in next sc, 2 dc in next ch-1 sp) around; join with slip st to first dc, finish off.

Weave ribbon through ch-1 sps on Eyelet round; tie ends in a bow.

Designs by Jan Hatfield.

THIRSTY BABY BIBS

Cut from washcloths, our thirsty bibs make darling baby gifts! They're edged with crochet cotton and tied with dainty ribbons.

■■□□ **EASY**

MATERIALS

Bedspread Weight Cotton Thread (size 10) [225 yards (206 meters) per ball]: 1 ball (sufficient for two Bibs)
Steel crochet hook, size 6 (1.8 mm)
$10^1/_2$" x $11^1/_2$" (26.5 cm x 29 cm) piece of tracing paper
Liquid fray preventative
Washcloth - $11^1/_2$" (29 cm) square **minimum**
$^1/_8$" (3 mm) wide Ribbon - two 12" (30.5 cm) lengths for each Bib
Sewing needle and thread

PREPARING BIB

Fold tracing paper in half matching long edges. Place tracing paper over pattern with fold on solid line and trace pattern; cut out pattern along dashed lines. Unfold pattern and pin pattern to washcloth. Apply liquid fray preventative to washcloth along edges of pattern (**before** cutting) and allow to dry. Cut out Bib.

EDGING #1

Rnd 1 (Right side): With **right** side facing, join thread with sc in top left corner of outside edge **(see Joining With Sc, page 205)**; 2 sc in same corner, sc evenly around working 3 sc in each corner; join with slip st to first sc.

Note: The total number of stitches worked on Rnd 2 counting from center dc of top left corner of outside edge to center dc of top right corner of outside edge must be an odd number.

Rnd 2: Ch 3, 3 dc in next sc, dc in each sc around working 3 dc in center sc of each corner 3-sc group **and** increasing and decreasing as necessary to keep piece lying flat; join with slip st to top of beginning ch-3.

Rnd 3: Slip st in next 2 dc, (sc, hdc, 3 dc) around post of **same** st as last slip st made, ★ skip next dc, slip st in next dc, (sc, hdc, 3 dc) around post of **same** st as slip st just made; repeat from ★ around to top right corner of outside edge, leave remaining sts unworked; finish off.

Add ribbon ties.

EDGING #2

Rnd 1 (Right side): With **right** side facing, join thread with sc in top left corner of outside edge **(see Joining With Sc, page 205)**; 2 sc in same corner, sc evenly around working 3 sc in each corner; join with slip st to first sc.

Note: The total number of stitches worked on Rnd 2 counting from center sc of top left corner of outside edge to center sc of top right corner of outside edge must be divisible by 6 with 1 left over. (For example, 181 is divisible by 6, 30 times, with 1 left over.)

Rnd 2: Slip st in next sc, ch 1, 3 sc in same st, sc in each sc around working 3 sc in center sc of each corner 3-sc group **and** increasing and decreasing as necessary to keep piece lying flat; join with slip st to first sc.

To work Picot, (ch 3, slip st, ch 5, slip st, ch 3, slip st) in last sc made.

Rnd 3: Ch 1, sc in same st and in next sc, work Picot, (sc in next 6 sc, work Picot) around to top right corner of outside edge, sc in each sc around neck opening; join with slip st to first sc, finish off.

Add ribbon ties.

EDGING #3

Rnd 1 (Right side): With **right** side facing, join thread with sc in top left corner of outside edge **(see Joining With Sc, page 205)**; 2 sc in same corner, sc evenly around working 3 sc in each corner; join with slip st to first sc.

Note: The total number of stitches worked on Rnd 2 counting from center sc of top left corner of outside edge to center sc of top right corner of outside edge must be divisible by 5 with 1 left over. (For example, 201 is divisible by 5, 40 times, with 1 left over.)

Rnd 2: Slip st in next sc, ch 1, 3 sc in same st, sc in each sc around working 3 sc in center sc of each corner 3-sc group **and** increasing and decreasing as necessary to keep piece lying flat; join with slip st to first sc.

Rnd 3: Slip st in next sc, ch 1, sc in same st, ch 5, skip next 4 sc, ★ sc in next sc, ch 5, skip next 4 sc; repeat from ★ around to center sc of 3-sc group at top right corner of outside edge, sc in center sc, ch 1, (slip st in next sc, ch 1) around; join with slip st to first sc.

Rnd 4: Ch 3, 2 dc in same st, sc in next loop, (5 dc in next sc, sc in next loop) around to sc at corner of top right outside edge (sc following last loop), 3 dc in corner sc, leave remaining sts unworked; finish off.

Add ribbon ties.

Designs by Jackie Mooneyham.

BABY BLANKET BORDERS

Five different edgings crocheted with bedspread weight cotton thread adorn these soft receiving blankets made of flannel.

▮▮▯▯ **EASY**

Finished Size: 37" (94 cm) square

MATERIALS
Bedspread Weight Cotton Thread
 (size 10) [400 yards (366 meters) per
 ball (White), 300 yards (274 cm)
 per ball (Shaded Pinks), or 350 yards
 (320 meters) per ball (all other colors)]:
 Border #1 (Dusty Rose) - 1 ball
 Border #2 (White) - 1 ball
 Border #3 (White) - 1 ball
 Border #4 (Shaded Pinks) - 1 ball
 Border #5 (Iris Blue) - 1 ball
Steel crochet hook, size 7 (1.65 mm) **or**
 size needed to obtain specified
 number of sc per inch
1 1/8 yards (1 meter) of cotton flannel
 [44/45" (112/114.5 cm) wide] for
 each blanket
6" (15 cm) diameter cardboard circle
Fabric marking pen
Sewing needle and thread

PREPARING BLANKET
Wash, dry, and press flannel. Trim flannel to a 36" (91.5 cm) square. Place cardboard circle on one corner of fabric with edge of circle even with edges of fabric. Use fabric marking pen to draw along edge of circle in corner, then cut along drawn line. Repeat for remaining corners. Press all edges of blanket 1/4" (7 mm) to wrong side and hand baste in place. Remove basting stitches after first round of Border has been added.

Note: When working sc on first round of each Border, insert hook through blanket 1/4" (7 mm) from pressed edge.

BORDER #1
Rnd 1 (Right side): With **right** side of blanket facing, join thread with slip st in center of any rounded corner; ch 1, ★ work 216 sc evenly spaced across to center of next rounded corner **(there should be approximately 6 sc per inch)**; repeat from ★ around; join with slip st to first sc: 864 sc.

Rnd 2: Ch 1, sc in same st, ch 1, skip next 2 sc, (dc, ch 1) 5 times in next sc, skip next 2 sc, ★ sc in next sc, ch 1, skip next 2 sc, (dc, ch 1) 5 times in next sc, skip next 2 sc; repeat from ★ around; join with slip st to first sc.

Rnd 3: Ch 1, sc in same st, ch 1, sc in next dc, (ch 3, sc in next dc) 4 times, ch 1, ★ sc in next sc, ch 1, sc in next dc, (ch 3, sc in next dc) 4 times, ch 1; repeat from ★ around; join with slip st to first sc, finish off.

BORDER #2
Rnd 1 (Right side): With **right** side of blanket facing, join thread with slip st in center of any rounded corner; ch 1, ★ work 270 sc evenly spaced across to center of next rounded corner **(there should be approximately 7 1/2 sc per inch)**; repeat from ★ around; join with slip st to first sc: 1080 sc.

Rnd 2: Ch 1, sc in same st and in each sc around; join with slip st to first sc.

Rnds 3 and 4: Ch 1, (sc, 2 dc) in same st, skip next 2 sts, ★ (sc, 2 dc) in next sc, skip next 2 sts; repeat from ★ around; join with slip st to first sc.

Finish off.

BORDER #3
Rnd 1 (Right side): With **right** side of blanket facing, join thread with slip st in center of any rounded corner; ch 1, ★ work 216 sc evenly spaced across to center of next rounded corner **(there should be approximately 6 sc per inch)**; repeat from ★ around; join with slip st to first sc: 864 sc.

Rnd 2: Ch 3 **(counts as first dc, now and throughout)**, (dc, ch 1, 2 dc) in same st, skip next 2 sc, ★ (2 dc, ch 1, 2 dc) in next sc, skip next 2 sc; repeat from ★ around; join with slip st to first dc.

To work Picot, ch 3, slip st in third ch from hook.

Rnd 3: Slip st in next dc and in next ch-1 sp, ch 3, (dc, work Picot, 2 dc) in same sp, (2 dc, work Picot, 2 dc) in each ch-1 sp around; join with slip st to first dc, finish off.

BORDER #4
Rnd 1 (Right side): With **right** side of blanket facing, join thread with slip st in center of any rounded corner; ch 1, ★ work 216 sc evenly spaced across to center of next rounded corner **(there should be approximately 6 sc per inch)**; repeat from ★ around; join with slip st to first sc: 864 sc.

Rnd 2: Ch 3 **(counts as first dc)**, working **around** dc just made, dc in sc to **right** of dc just made, ★ skip next sc, dc in next sc, working **around** dc just made, dc in skipped sc; repeat from ★ around; join with slip st to first dc.

Rnd 3: Ch 1, (sc, ch 3, 2 dc) in same st, skip next 2 dc, ★ (sc, ch 3, 2 dc) in next dc, skip next 2 dc; repeat from ★ around; join with slip st to first sc, finish off.

BORDER #5
Rnd 1 (Right side): With **right** side of blanket facing, join thread with slip st in center of any rounded corner; ch 1, ★ work 280 sc evenly spaced across to center of next rounded corner **(there should be approximately 7 3/4 sc per inch)**; repeat from ★ around; join with slip st to first sc: 1120 sc.

To work Cluster, ★ YO twice, insert hook in st indicated, YO and pull up a loop, (YO and draw through 2 loops on hook) twice; repeat from ★ once **more**, YO and draw through all 3 loops on hook.

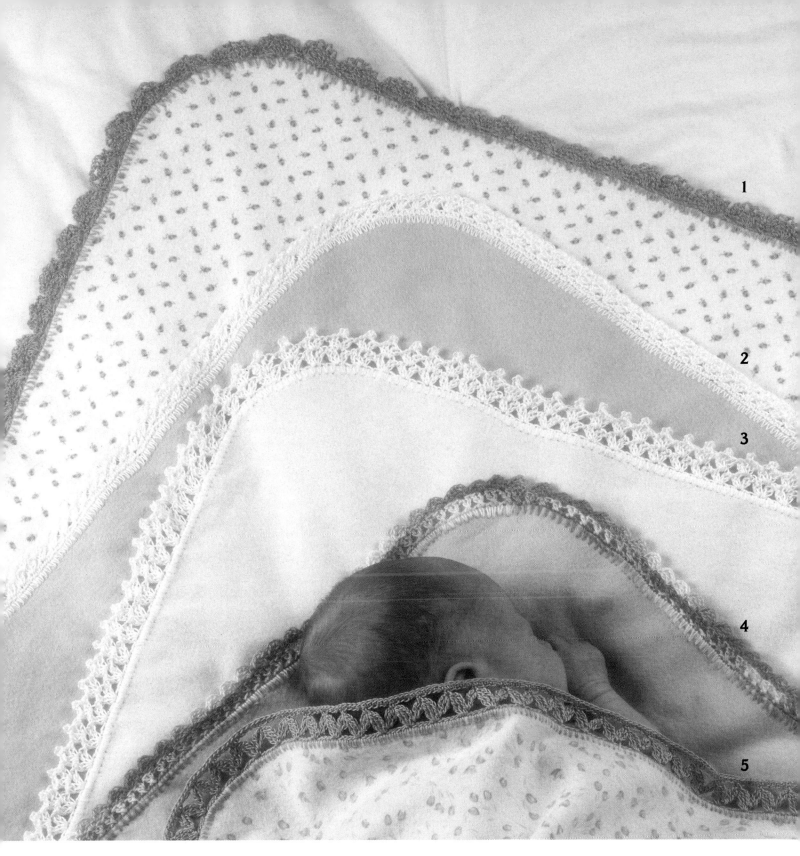

Rnd 2: Ch 1, (sc, ch 4, work Cluster) in same st, ch 4, work Cluster in top of Cluster just made, skip next 4 sc, ★ (sc, ch 4, work Cluster) in next sc, ch 4, work Cluster in top of Cluster just made, skip next 4 sc; repeat from ★ around; join with slip st to first sc.

Rnd 3: Slip st in next 4 chs and in top of next Cluster, ch 1, sc in same st, ch 4, skip next Cluster, ★ sc in top of next Cluster, ch 4, skip next Cluster; repeat from ★ around; join with slip st to first sc.

Rnd 4: Ch 1, sc in same st, 4 sc in next ch-4 sp, (sc in next sc, 4 sc in next ch-4 sp) around; join with slip st to first sc, finish off.

Designs by Lorraine White.

FRILLY BABY SOCKS

Give a precious pair of feet the frills they deserve. Just crochet our flirty edgings onto the cuffs of little dress crew socks.

■■□□ **EASY**

MATERIALS
Bedspread Weight Cotton Thread
   (size 10) [225 yards (206 meters) per
   ball (White) or 150 yards (137 meters)
   per ball (Orchid Pink and Mint Green)]:
   Edging #1
   White - 1 ball
   Edging #2
   White - 1 ball
   Orchid Pink - 1 ball
   Edging #3
   White - 1 ball
   Orchid Pink - 1 ball
   Mint Green - 1 ball
Steel crochet hook, size 7 (1.65 mm)
Dress crew socks with fold-down cuff
Tapestry needle
For Edging #2 only - 66 beads

EDGING #1
Rnd 1 (Right side): With **wrong** side of cuff facing, join thread with sc at center back *(see Joining With Sc, page 205)*; work 67 sc evenly spaced around; join with slip st to first sc: 68 sc.

Rnd 2: Ch 1, sc in same st and in next sc, ch 2, skip next 2 sc, ★ sc in next 2 sc, ch 2, skip next 2 sc; repeat from ★ around; join with slip st to first sc: 17 ch-2 sps.

Rnds 3 and 4: Slip st in next sc and in next ch-2 sp, ch 1, 2 sc in same sp, ch 2, (2 sc in next ch-2 sp, ch 2) around; join with slip st to first sc.

To work Picot, ch 3, slip st in third ch from hook.

Rnd 5: Slip st in next sc and in next ch-2 sp, ch 1, (sc, work Picot, sc) in same sp, ch 2, ★ (sc, work Picot, sc) in next ch-2 sp, ch 2; repeat from ★ around; join with slip st to first sc, finish off.

EDGING #2
Rnd 1 (Right side): With **wrong** side of cuff facing, join White with sc at center back *(see Joining With Sc, page 205)*; work 65 sc evenly spaced around; join with slip st to first sc: 66 sc.

Rnd 2: Ch 1, sc in same st, ★ ch 3, skip next sc, sc in next sc; repeat from ★ around to last sc, ch 1, skip last sc, hdc in first sc to form last ch-3 sp: 33 ch-3 sps.

Rnd 3: Ch 1, sc in same sp, (ch 3, sc in next ch-3 sp) around, ch 1, hdc in first sc to form last ch-3 sp.

Rnd 4: Ch 1, sc in same sp, ch 3, (sc in next ch-3 sp, ch 3) around; join with slip st to first sc, finish off.

Thread tapestry needle with end of Orchid Pink; string 33 beads onto thread.

Rnd 5: With **wrong** side of Edging facing, join Orchid Pink with slip st in any ch-3 sp; ch 1, (sc, ch 1, slide one bead up, ch 1, sc) in same sp and in each ch-3 sp around; join with slip st to first sc, finish off.

EDGING #3
Rnd 1 (Right side): With **wrong** side of cuff facing, join White with sc at center back *(see Joining With Sc, page 205)*; work 65 sc evenly spaced around; join with slip st to first sc: 66 sc.

Rnd 2: Ch 5 (**counts as first dc plus ch 2, now and throughout**), skip next sc, ★ dc in next sc, ch 2, skip next sc; repeat from ★ around; join with slip st to first dc: 33 ch-2 sps.

Rnd 3: Ch 5, (dc in next dc, ch 2) around; join with slip st to first dc; do **not** finish off.

RIGHT SOCK
Rnd 4: Ch 5, dc in next dc, (ch 2, dc in next dc) 8 times, ch 3, sc in next dc, 2 sc in next ch-2 sp, sc in next dc, ch 3, (dc in next dc, ch 2) around; join with slip st to first dc, finish off.

To work Picot, ch 3, slip st in third ch from hook.

To work Flower, working **over** sc on Rnd 4 **and** in next ch-2 sp on Rnd 3, (hdc, 4 dc, hdc) in ch-2 sp (**Petal made**), rotate piece clockwise, (hdc, 4 dc, hdc) around post of next dc on Rnd 3, rotate piece clockwise, (hdc, 4 dc, hdc) in next ch-2 sp on Rnd 2, rotate piece clockwise, (hdc, 4 dc, hdc) around post of next dc on Rnd 3.

Rnd 5: With **right** side facing, join Orchid Pink with slip st in first ch-2 sp; ch 1, 3 sc in same sp, work Picot, (3 sc in next ch-2 sp, work Picot) 8 times, 3 sc in next ch-3 sp, work Flower, working in sts on first Petal, slip st in first hdc, sc in next 5 sts, working in sps on Rnd 4, 3 sc in next ch-3 sp, work Picot, (3 sc in next ch-2 sp, work Picot) around; join with slip st to first sc, finish off.

Leaves: With **right** side facing, join Mint Green with slip st in same dc as second Petal; ★ ch 5, sc in second ch from hook, hdc in last 3 chs, sc in same st as joining; repeat from ★ once **more**; finish off.

LEFT SOCK
Rnd 4: Ch 5, dc in next dc, (ch 2, dc in next dc) 18 times, ch 3, sc in next dc, 2 sc in next ch-2 sp, sc in next dc, ch 3, (dc in next dc, ch 2) around; join with slip st to first dc, finish off.

Rnd 5: With **right** side facing, join Orchid Pink with slip st in first ch-2 sp; ch 1, 3 sc in same sp, work Picot, (3 sc in next ch-2 sp, work Picot) 18 times, 3 sc in next ch-3 sp, work Flower, working in sts on first Petal, slip st in first hdc, sc in next 5 sts, working in sps on Rnd 4, 3 sc in next ch-3 sp, work Picot, (3 sc in next ch-2 sp, work Picot) around; join with slip st to first sc, finish off.

Leaves: With **right** side facing, join Mint Green with slip st in same dc as fourth Petal; ★ ch 5, sc in second ch from hook, hdc in last 3 chs, sc in same st as joining; repeat from ★ once **more**; finish off.

Designs by Nair Carswell.

SASSY SHRUG

Even a fashion diva can be as snug as a bug in our shrug! The sassy accessory is a stylish way to warm up bare shoulders and arms.

■■■□ **INTERMEDIATE**

Finished Size: Small/Medium
Cuff to Cuff Measurement:
54" (137 cm)

MATERIALS
Medium/Worsted Weight Yarn
  [8 ounces, 452 yards
  (230 grams, 413 meters)
  per skein]: **MEDIUM 4**
  Cherry Red - 2 skeins
  Cornmeal, Royal, and Black - 5 yards
  (4.5 meters) of **each** color
Crochet hook, size I (5.5 mm) **or** size
  needed for gauge
Yarn needle

GAUGE:
6 sts and Rows 1-6 = 2" (5 mm)

RIGHT SLEEVE
With Cherry Red and leaving a long end for sewing, ch 37.

Row 1: Sc in second ch from hook and in each ch across: 36 sc.

Row 2 (Right side)**:** Ch 2, turn; hdc in first sc, hdc **between** legs of next sc *(Fig. A)* and each sc across to last sc, hdc in last sc.

Note: Mark Row 2 as **right** side.

Fig. A

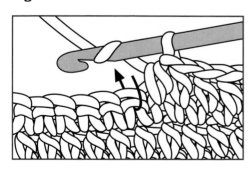

Row 3: Ch 1, turn; sc in first hdc, sc in sp **before** next hdc *(Fig. 5, page 205)* across to sp **before** last hdc, skip sp, sc in last hdc.

Row 4: Ch 2, turn; hdc in first sc, hdc **between** legs of next sc and each sc across to last sc, hdc in last sc.

Row 5: Ch 1, turn; sc in first hdc, skip sp **before** next hdc, sc in sp **before** next hdc across, sc in last hdc.

Row 6 (Increase row)**:** Ch 2, turn; 2 hdc in first sc, hdc **between** legs of next sc and each sc across to last sc, 2 hdc in last sc: 38 hdc.

Rows 7-14: Repeat Rows 3-6 twice: 42 hdc.

Row 15: Ch 1, turn; sc in first hdc, sc in sp **before** next hdc across to sp **before** last hdc, skip sp, sc in last hdc.

Row 16: Ch 2, turn; hdc in first sc, hdc **between** legs of next sc and each sc across to last sc, hdc in last sc.

Row 17: Ch 1, turn; sc in first hdc, skip sp **before** next hdc, sc in sp **before** next hdc across, sc in last hdc.

Row 18: Ch 2, turn; hdc in first sc, hdc **between** legs of next sc and each sc across to last sc, hdc in last sc.

Rows 19-33: Repeat Rows 15-18, 3 times; then repeat Rows 15-17 once **more**.

Row 34: Repeat Row 6: 44 hdc.

Rows 35-42: Repeat Rows 3-6 twice: 48 hdc.

Row 43: Ch 1, turn; sc in first hdc, sc in sp **before** next hdc across to sp **before** last hdc, skip sp, sc in last hdc.

Row 44: Repeat Row 6: 50 hdc.

Rows 45 and 46: Repeat Rows 5 and 6: 52 hdc.

Rows 47 and 48: Repeat Rows 43 and 44: 54 hdc.

Row 49: Repeat Row 17.

Row 50 (Decrease row)**:** Ch 2, turn; hdc in first sc, hdc **between** legs of next sc and each sc across to last 2 sc, skip next sc, hdc in last sc: 53 hdc.

Row 51: Repeat Row 15.

Row 52 (Decrease row)**:** Ch 2, turn; hdc in first sc, hdc **between** legs of next sc and each sc across to last 2 sc, skip next sc, hdc in last sc: 53 hdc.

Rows 53-76: Repeat Rows 49-52, 6 times: 40 sc.

Rows 77 and 78: Repeat Rows 17 and 18.

Rows 79-85: Repeat Rows 15-18 once, then repeat Rows 15-17 once **more**.

Finish off, leaving a long end for sewing.

Instructions continued on page 90.

Continued from page 88.

LEFT SLEEVE

Work same as Right Sleeve, page 88, through Row 48: 54 hdc.

Row 49: Repeat Row 17.

Row 50 (Decrease row)**:** Ch 2, turn; skip first sc, hdc in next sc, hdc **between** legs of next sc and each sc across to last sc, hdc in last sc: 53 hdc.

Row 51: Repeat Row 15.

Row 52 (Decrease row)**:** Ch 2, turn; skip first sc, hdc in next sc, hdc **between** legs of next sc and each sc across to last sc, hdc in last sc: 53 hdc.

Rows 53-76: Repeat Rows 49-52, 6 times: 40 sc.

Rows 77 and 78: Repeat Rows 17 and 18.

Rows 79-85: Repeat Rows 15-18 once, then repeat Rows 15-17 once **more**.

Finish off, leaving a long end for sewing.

FINISHING

With **right** sides together and matching rows, thread needle with long end and sew underarm seam on one Sleeve from Row 1 to Row 50.

Repeat for second Sleeve.

CUFF

Rnd 1: With **right** side facing and working in free loops of beginning ch on one Sleeve *(Fig. 3b, page 205)*, join Cherry Red with sc in underarm seam *(see Joining With Sc, page 205)*; work 35 sc evenly spaced around; join with slip st to first sc, finish off: 36 sc.

Rnd 2: With **right** side facing, join Cornmeal with sc in same st as joining; ch 1, skip next sc, ★ sc in next sc, ch 1, skip next sc; repeat from ★ around; join with slip st to first sc, finish off: 18 ch-1 sps.

Rnd 3: With **right** side facing, join Royal with sc in first ch-1 sp; ch 1, (sc in next ch-1 sp, ch 1) around; join with slip st to first sc, finish off.

Rnd 4: With **right** side facing, join Cherry Red with sc in first ch-1 sp; ch 1, (sc in next ch-1 sp, ch 1) around; join with slip st to first sc, finish off.

Rnd 5: With **right** side facing, join Black with sc in first ch-1 sp; ch 1, (sc in next ch-1 sp, ch 1) around; join with slip st to first sc, finish off.

Rnd 6: With **right** side facing, join Cherry Red with slip st in first ch-1 sp; ch 2, (slip st in next ch-1 sp, ch 2) around; join with slip st to joining slip st, finish off.

Repeat for second Sleeve.

With **right** sides together and matching stitches on Row 85 of each Sleeve, thread needle with long end and whipstitch center seam *(Fig. 9b, page 206)*.

TRIM

With **right** side facing, join Cherry Red with sc in any seam; sc evenly around; join with slip st to first sc, finish off.

Design by Ruth Shepherd.

FOR GIRLS ON THE GO

*In-the-groove gals will flip over this awesome ensemble! The
headband, purse, and cell phone case are a must for girls on the go.*

Instructions begin on page 92.

FOR GIRLS ON THE GO

Shown on page 91.

■■□□ **EASY**

MATERIALS
HEADBAND AND CELL PHONE HOLDER only
Bedspread Weight Cotton Thread (size 10) [350 yards (320 meters) per ball]:
  Headband
  Black - 1 ball
  Victory Red - 1 ball
  Goldenrod - 1 ball
  Cell Phone Holder
  Black - 1 ball
  Victory Red - 1 ball
Steel crochet hook, size 5 (1.9 mm) **or** size needed for gauge
Tapestry needle
Medium braided elastic hairband for Headband
9" x 12" (23 cm x 30.5 cm) Black self-adhesive felt for Cell Phone Holder
Hook and loop self-adhesive fastener for Cell Phone Holder
PURSE only
Crochet Nylon [150 yards (137 meters) per tube]:
  Black - 2 tubes
  Red - 1 tube
Crochet hook, size F (3.75 mm) **or** size needed for gauge
Yarn needle
18" x 5¼" (45.5 cm x 13.5 cm) Fabric for lining
Sewing needle and thread

HEADBAND
Finished Measurement:
17½" (44.5 cm)

GAUGE:
Each Square = 2¼" (5.75 cm)

SQUARE A (Make 3)
To work treble crochet (abbreviated tr), YO twice, insert hook in sp or st indicated, YO and pull up a loop (4 loops on hook), (YO and draw through 2 loops on hook) 3 times.

With Black indicated, ch 4; join with slip st to form a ring.

Rnd 1 (Right side): Ch 4 **(counts as first tr, now and throughout)**, 2 tr in ring, ch 2, (3 tr in ring, ch 2) 3 times; join with slip st to first tr, finish off: 12 tr and 4 ch-2 sps.

Note: Mark Rnd 1 as **right** side.

To work Front Post treble crochet (abbreviated FPtr), YO twice, insert hook from **front** to **back** around post of tr indicated **(Fig. 4, page 205)**, YO and pull up a loop (4 loops on hook), (YO and draw through 2 loops on hook) 3 times. Skip st behind FPtr.

To work triple treble crochet (abbreviated tr tr), YO 4 times, insert hook in sp indicated, YO and pull up a loop (6 loops on hook), (YO and draw through 2 loops on hook) 5 times.

Rnd 2: With **right** side facing, join Goldenrod with slip st in any ch-2 sp; ch 4, 2 tr in same sp, ch 1, skip next tr, work FPtr around next tr, ch 1, ★ 3 tr in next ch-2 sp, † ch 1, working in **front** of last rnd, tr tr in beginning ring, ch 1 †, 3 tr in same sp as last tr made, ch 1, skip next tr, work FPtr around next tr, ch 1; repeat from ★ 2 times **more**, 3 tr in same sp as first tr, repeat from † to † once; join with slip st to first tr, finish off: 32 sts and 16 ch-1 sps.

To work Front Post double crochet (abbreviated FPdc), YO, insert hook from **front** to **back** around post of st indicated **(Fig. 4, page 205)**, YO and pull up a loop (3 loops on hook), (YO and draw through 2 loops on hook) twice. Skip st behind FPdc.

Rnd 3: With **right** side facing, join Victory Red with slip st in any tr tr; ch 4, 4 tr in same st, ch 1, skip next tr, work FPdc around next tr, ch 1, dc in next ch-1 sp, work FPdc around next FPtr, dc in next ch-1 sp, ch 1, skip next tr, work FPdc around next tr, ch 1, skip next tr, ★ 5 tr in next tr tr, ch 1, skip next tr, work FPdc around next tr, ch 1, dc in next ch-1 sp, work FPdc around next FPtr, dc in next ch-1 sp, ch 1, skip next tr, work FPdc around next tr, ch 1, skip next tr; repeat from ★ 2 times **more**; join with slip st to first tr, finish off: 40 sts and 16 ch-1 sps.

Rnd 4: With **right** side facing, join Black with sc in center tr of any corner 5-tr group *(see Joining With Sc, page 205)*; 2 sc in same st, sc in each st and in each sp around working 3 sc in center tr of each corner 5-tr group; join with slip st to first sc, finish off: 64 sc.

SQUARE B (Make 3)
With Black indicated, ch 4; join with slip st to form a ring.

Rnd 1 (Right side): Ch 4, 2 tr in ring, ch 2, (3 tr in ring, ch 2) 3 times; join with slip st to first tr, finish off: 12 tr and 4 ch-2 sps.

Note: Mark Rnd 1 as **right** side.

Rnd 2: With **right** side facing, join Victory Red with slip st in any ch-2 sp; ch 4, 2 tr in same sp, ch 1, skip next tr, work FPtr around next tr, ch 1, ★ 3 tr in next ch-2 sp, † ch 1, working in **front** of last rnd, tr tr in beginning ring, ch 1 †, 3 tr in same sp as last tr made, ch 1, skip next tr, work FPtr around next tr, ch 1; repeat from ★ 2 times **more**, 3 tr in same sp as first tr, repeat from † to † once; join with slip st to first tr, finish off: 32 sts and 16 ch-1 sps.

Rnd 3: With **right** side facing, join Goldenrod with slip st in any tr tr; ch 4, 4 tr in same st, ch 1, skip next tr, work FPdc around next tr, ch 1, dc in next ch-1 sp, work FPdc around next FPtr, dc in next ch-1 sp, ch 1, skip next tr, work FPdc around next tr, ch 1, skip next tr, ★ 5 tr in next tr tr, ch 1, skip next tr, work FPdc around next tr, ch 1, dc in next ch-1 sp, work FPdc around next FPtr, dc in next ch-1 sp, ch 1, skip next tr, work FPdc around next tr, ch 1, skip next tr; repeat from ★ 2 times **more**; join with slip st to first tr, finish off: 40 sts and 16 ch-1 sps.

Rnd 4: With **right** side facing, join Black with sc in center tr of any corner 5-tr group; 2 sc in same st, sc in each st and in each sp around working 3 sc in center tr of each corner 5-tr group; join with slip st to first sc, finish off: 64 sc.

ASSEMBLY

Place one Square A and one Square B together. With Black and working through **both** loops, whipstitch Squares together *(Fig. 9a, page 206)*, beginning in center sc of first corner 3-sc group and ending in center sc of next 3-sc group. Alternating Square A and Square B, join remaining Squares in same manner to form a strip.

EDGING

Rnd 1: With **right** side facing and working across one short end, join Black with dc in center sc of any corner 3-sc group *(see Joining With Dc, page 205)*; dc in same st and in each st and joining around working 3 dc in center sc of each corner 3-sc group, dc in same st as first dc; join with slip st to first dc, do **not** finish off.

FIRST END

Row 1: Ch 3 **(counts as first dc, now and throughout)**, dc in next 18 dc, leave remaining dc unworked.

Rows 2-8: Ch 3, turn; dc in next dc and in each dc across.

Finish off, leaving a long end for sewing.

SECOND END

Row 1: With **right** side facing, join Black with dc in center dc of first corner 3-dc group on opposite end; dc in next 18 dc, leave remaining dc unworked.

Complete same as First End.

Fold Row 8 of either End to wrong side along Row 7 and around braided elastic hairband. Thread tapestry needle with long end and sew top of Row 8 to bottom of Row 7.

Repeat for opposite End.

CELL PHONE HOLDER

Finished Size: Fits a phone 5¹/₄" (13.5 cm) long (excluding antenna) x 6³/₄" (17 cm) around

GAUGE: Each Square = 2¹/₄" (5.75 cm)

SQUARE (Make 3)

To work treble crochet (abbreviated tr), YO twice, insert hook in sp or st indicated, YO and pull up a loop (4 loops on hook), (YO and draw through 2 loops on hook) 3 times.

With Victory Red, ch 4; join with slip st to form a ring.

Rnd 1 (Right side)**:** Ch 4 **(counts as first tr, now and throughout)**, 2 tr in ring, ch 2, (3 tr in ring, ch 2) 3 times; join with slip st to first tr, finish off: 12 tr and 4 ch-2 sps.

Note: Mark Rnd 1 as **right** side.

To work Front Post treble crochet (abbreviated FPtr), YO twice, insert hook from **front** to **back** around post of tr indicated *(Fig. 4, page 205)*, YO and pull up a loop (4 loops on hook), (YO and draw through 2 loops on hook) 3 times. Skip st behind FPtr.

To work triple treble crochet (abbreviated tr tr), YO 4 times, insert hook in sp indicated, YO and pull up a loop (6 loops on hook), (YO and draw through 2 loops on hook) 5 times.

Rnd 2: With **right** side facing, join Black with slip st in any ch-2 sp; ch 4, 2 tr in same sp, ch 1, skip next tr, work FPtr around next tr, ch 1, ★ 3 tr in next ch-2 sp, † ch 1, working in **front** of last rnd, tr tr in beginning ring, ch 1 †, 3 tr in same sp as last tr made, ch 1, skip next tr, work FPtr around next tr, ch 1; repeat from ★ 2 times **more**, 3 tr in same sp as first tr, repeat from † to † once; join with slip st to first tr, finish off: 32 sts and 16 ch-1 sps.

To work Front Post double crochet (abbreviated FPdc), YO, insert hook from **front** to **back** around post of st indicated *(Fig. 4, page 205)*, YO and pull up a loop (3 loops on hook), (YO and draw through 2 loops on hook) twice. Skip st behind FPdc.

Rnd 3: With **right** side facing, join Victory Red with slip st in any tr tr; ch 4, 4 tr in same st, ch 1, skip next tr, work FPdc around next tr, ch 1, dc in next ch-1 sp, work FPdc around next FPtr, dc in next ch-1 sp, ch 1, skip next tr, work FPdc around next tr, ch 1, skip next tr, ★ 5 tr in next tr tr, ch 1, skip next tr, work FPdc around next tr, ch 1, dc in next ch-1 sp, work FPdc around next FPtr, dc in next ch-1 sp, ch 1, skip next tr, work FPdc around next tr, ch 1, skip next tr; repeat from ★ 2 times **more**; join with slip st to first tr, finish off: 40 sts and 16 ch-1 sps.

Rnd 4: With **right** side facing, join Black with sc in center tr of any corner 5-tr group *(see Joining With Sc, page 205)*; 2 sc in same st, sc in each st and in each sp around working 3 sc in center tr of each corner 5-tr group; join with slip st to first sc, finish off: 64 sc.

Instructions continued on page 94.

FRONT

With Black and working through **both** loops, whipstitch two Squares together **(Fig. 9a, page 206)**, beginning in center sc of first corner 3-sc group and ending in center sc of next corner 3-sc group.

Edging: With **right** side of one short edge facing, join Black with dc in center sc of first corner 3-sc group **(see Joining With Dc, page 205)**; dc in each sc across to center sc of next corner 3-sc group, 3 dc in center sc, † dc in each sc across to joining, dc in same sc as joining on same Square, dc in joining and in same sc as joining on next Square †, (dc in each sc across to center sc of next corner 3-sc group, 3 dc in center sc) twice, repeat from † to † once; 2 dc in same st as first dc; join with slip st to first dc, do **not** finish off: 108 dc.

TOP

Row 1: Ch 3 **(counts as first dc, now and throughout)**, turn; dc in next 16 dc, leave remaining dc unworked: 17 dc.

Rows 2 and 3: Ch 3, turn; dc in next dc and in each dc across.

Finish off.

BOTTOM

Row 1: With **right** side of opposite short edge facing, skip center dc of first corner 3-dc group and join Black with dc in next dc; dc in next 16 dc, leave remaining dc unworked: 17 dc.

Row 2: Ch 3, turn; dc in next dc and in each dc across; do **not** finish off.

BACK

Row 1: Ch 9, turn; dc in fourth ch from hook **(3 skipped chs count as first dc)** and in each ch and each dc across, add on 7 dc **(Fig. 6, page 205)**: 31 dc.

Rows 2-20: Ch 3, turn; dc in next dc and in each dc across.

Finish off.

FINISHING

Flap: With **wrong** sides together, center one edge of remaining Square on top edge of Row 20 on Back. With Black, working through **both** loops, and beginning in third dc of first corner 3-sc group on Square and ninth dc on Row 20 of Back, whipstitch Square and Back together, ending in first sc of next corner 3-sc group on Square and leaving remaining 8 dc on Back unworked.

Using crocheted piece as a pattern, cut self-adhesive felt for lining $1/8$" (3 mm) smaller than Holder on all sides. Attach felt to **wrong** side of Holder.

Beginning on Row 1 of Back, sew beginning chs or added on dc to end of Rows 1 and 2 of Bottom, then sew end of rows of Back to dc on Front, easing to fit when needed.

Attach loop side of fastener to **right** side of Front and hook side of fastener to **wrong** side of Flap.

Note: If a longer holder is desired, before sewing Flap onto Back, work as follows:

Rnd 1: With **right** side facing, join Black with dc in any joining; dc in next dc and in each dc and each joining around; join with slip st to first dc.

Rnd 2: Ch 3, dc in next dc and in each dc around; join with slip st to first dc.

Repeat Rnd 2 until desired length; finish off.

Sew Flap to center Back.

PURSE

Finished Measurement:
$7^1/2$" (19 cm) high

GAUGE:
Each Square = $4^1/4$" (10.75 cm); 4 sc and 5 rows = 1" (2.5 cm)

To work treble crochet (abbreviated **tr**), YO twice, insert hook in sp or st indicated, YO and pull up a loop (4 loops on hook), (YO and draw through 2 loops on hook) 3 times.

With Red, ch 4; join with slip st to form a ring.

Rnd 1 (Right side): Ch 4 **(counts as first tr, now and throughout)**, 2 tr in ring, ch 2, (3 tr in ring, ch 2) 3 times; join with slip st to first tr, finish off: 12 tr and 4 ch-2 sps.

Note: Mark Rnd 1 as **right** side.

To work Front Post treble crochet (abbreviated **FPtr**), YO twice, insert hook from **front** to **back** around post of tr indicated **(Fig. 4, page 205)**, YO and pull up a loop (4 loops on hook), (YO and draw through 2 loops on hook) 3 times. Skip st behind FPtr.

To work triple treble crochet (abbreviated **tr tr**), YO 4 times, insert hook in sp indicated, YO and pull up a loop (6 loops on hook), (YO and draw through 2 loops on hook) 5 times.

Rnd 2: With **right** side facing, join Black with slip st in any ch-2 sp; ch 4, 2 tr in same sp, ch 1, skip next tr, work FPtr around next tr, ch 1, ★ 3 tr in next ch-2 sp, † ch 1, working in **front** of last rnd, tr tr in beginning ring, ch 1 †, 3 tr in same sp as last tr made, ch 1, skip next tr, work FPtr around next tr, ch 1; repeat from ★ 2 times **more**, 3 tr in same sp as first tr, repeat from † to † once; join with slip st to first tr, finish off: 32 sts and 16 ch-1 sps.

To work Front Post double crochet (abbreviated FPdc), YO, insert hook from **front** to **back** around post of st indicated *(Fig. 4, page 205)*, YO and pull up a loop (3 loops on hook), (YO and draw through 2 loops on hook) twice. Skip st behind FPdc.

Rnd 3: With **right** side facing, join Red with slip st in any tr tr; ch 4, 4 tr in same st, ch 1, skip next tr, work FPdc around next tr, ch 1, dc in next ch-1 sp, work FPdc around next FPtr, dc in next ch-1 sp, ch 1, skip next tr, work FPdc around next tr, ch 1, skip next tr, ★ 5 tr in next tr tr, ch 1, skip next tr, work FPdc around next tr, ch 1, dc in next ch-1 sp, work FPdc around next FPtr, dc in next ch-1 sp, ch 1, skip next tr, work FPdc around next tr, ch 1, skip next tr; repeat from ★ 2 times **more**; join with slip st to first tr, finish off: 40 sts and 16 ch-1 sps.

Rnd 4: With **right** side facing, join Black with sc in center tr of any corner 5-tr group *(see Joining With Sc, page 205)*; 2 sc in same st, sc in each st and in each sp around working 3 sc in center tr of each corner 5-tr group; join with slip st to first sc, finish off: 64 sc.

ASSEMBLY

With Black and working through **both** loops, whipstitch Squares together *(Fig. 9a, page 206)*, beginning in center sc of first corner 3-sc group and ending in center sc of next corner 3-sc group. Join remaining Squares in same manner to form a ring of four Squares.

BOTTOM

Rnd 1: With **right** side of either edge of ring facing, join Black with sc in any seam; work 65 sc evenly spaced around; do **not** join, place marker *(see Markers, page 205)*: 66 sc.

Rnds 2-5: Sc in each sc around.

Rnd 6: Sc in Back Loop Only of each sc around *(Fig. 2, page 205)*.

To decrease, pull up a loop in each of next 2 sc, YO and draw through all 3 loops on hook **(counts as one sc)**.

Rnd 7: Working in both loops, (sc in next 9 sc, decrease) around: 60 sc.

Rnd 8: (Sc in next 8 sc, decrease) around: 54 sc.

Rnd 9: (Sc in next 7 sc, decrease) around: 48 sc.

Rnd 10: (Sc in next 6 sc, decrease) around: 42 sc.

Rnd 11: (Sc in next 5 sc, decrease) around: 36 sc.

Rnd 12: (Sc in next 4 sc, decrease) around: 30 sc.

Rnd 13: (Sc in next 3 sc, decrease) around: 24 sc.

Rnd 14: (Sc in next 2 sc, decrease) around: 18 sc.

Rnd 15: (Sc in next sc, decrease) around: 12 sc.

Rnd 16: Decrease around: 6 sc.

Rnd 17: Decrease around; slip st in next sc, finish off: 3 sc.

TOP

Rnd 1: With **right** side facing, join Black with sc in any joining; work 65 sc evenly spaced around; do **not** join, place marker: 66 sc.

Rnds 2-4: Sc in each sc around.

Rnd 5: Sc in each sc around; slip st in next sc.

Rnd 6 (Eyelet rnd): Ch 4 **(counts as first dc plus ch 1)**, skip next sc, ★ dc in next sc, ch 1, skip next sc; repeat from ★ around; join with slip st to first dc: 33 dc and 33 ch-1 sps.

Rnd 7: Ch 1, sc in same st and in each ch-1 sp and each dc around; join with slip st to first sc: 66 sc.

Rnds 8 and 9: Ch 1, sc in same st and in each sc around; join with slip st to first sc.

Finish off.

LINING

Matching right sides and short edges of fabric, use a 1/4" (7 mm) seam allowance to sew short edges together; press seam open.

Press one long edge of fabric 1/4" (7 mm) to wrong side; press 1/4" (7 mm) to wrong side again and hem. Repeat for opposite long edge. With wrong sides together, sew in place behind Motifs.

TIES (Make 2)

Cut two 4 yard (3.75 meter) strands of Black. Holding both strands together, fasten one end to a stationary object or have another person hold it; twist until tight. Fold in half and let it twist itself.

Beginning on opposite sides, weave ties through Eyelet rnd. Tie ends in a knot.

COZY CABLED PULLOVER

Cool temperatures don't have to put the freeze on personal style!
Bulky yarn makes this cabled pullover a cozy seasonal favorite.

■■■□ INTERMEDIATE

Finished Chest Measurements:
Small - 37^1/$_2$" (95.5 cm)
Medium - 43^1/$_2$" (110.5 cm)
Large - 49^1/$_2$" (125.5 cm)

Size Note: Instructions are written for size Small with sizes Medium and Large in braces { }. Instructions will be easier to read if you circle all the numbers pertaining to your size. If only one number is given, it applies to all sizes.

MATERIALS
Bulky Weight Yarn
[5 ounces, 196 yards
(140 grams, 179 meters)
per skein]: 5{6-7} skeins
Crochet hook, size I (5.5 mm) **or** size needed for gauge
Yarn needle

GAUGE:
8 sc and 9 rows = 3" (7.5 cm)

Note: Pullover is worked in one piece to armholes.

BOTTOM RIBBING
Ch 7.

Row 1 (Right side)**:** Sc in back ridge of second ch from hook *(Fig. 1, page 205)* and each ch across: 6 sc.

Rows 2 thru 99{115-131}: Ch 1, turn; sc in Back Loop Only of each sc across *(Fig. 2, page 205)*; do **not** finish off.

Joining: Ch 1, turn; with **right** side together, working in Back Loops Only of sc and in free loops of beginning ch *(Fig. 3b, page 205)*, slip st in each st across, do **not** finish off.

BODY
Rnd 1 (Right side)**:** Ch 1, turn; sc in joining row and in end of each row around; join with slip st to first sc: 100{116-132} sc.

Note: Mark Rnd 1 as **right** side.

Rnd 2: Ch 1, do **not** turn; slip st **loosely** in Front Loop Only of each sc around; join with slip st to **both** loops of joining slip st.

Rnd 3: Ch 1, turn; working in free loops of sc on Rnd 1 *(Fig. 3a, page 205)*, sc in each sc around; join with slip st to first sc.

To work Front Post double crochet (abbreviated FPdc), YO, insert hook from **front** to **back** around post of st indicated *(Fig. 4, page 205)*, YO and pull up a loop (3 loops on hook), (YO and draw through 2 loops on hook) twice. Skip st behind FPdc.

To work Twist, skip next st, work FPdc around next st, working in **front** of FPdc just made, work FPdc around skipped st.

To work Front Post treble crochet (abbreviated FPtr), YO twice, insert hook from **front** to **back** around post of st indicated *(Fig. 4, page 205)*, YO and pull up a loop (4 loops on hook), (YO and draw through 2 loops on hook) 3 times. Skip st behind FPdc.

To work Back Cable (uses next 4 sts), skip next 2 sts, work FPtr around each of next 2 sts, working **behind** last 2 FPtr made, work FPtr around first skipped st and around next skipped st.

To work Front Cable (uses next 4 sts), skip next 2 sts, work FPtr around each of next 2 sts, working in **front** of last 2 FPtr made, work FPtr around first skipped st and around next skipped st.

Rnd 4: Ch 3 **(counts as first dc, now and throughout)**, turn; dc in next sc, † (work FPdc around each of next 2 sc, dc in next 2 sc) 1{2-3} times, work Twist, dc in next 2 sc, work FPdc around each of next 2 sc, dc in next 2 sc, work Back Cable, work Front Cable, dc in next 2 sc, work FPdc around each of next 2 sc, dc in next 2 sc, work Back Cable, work Front Cable, dc in next 2 sc, work FPdc around each of next 2 sc, dc in next 2 sc, work Twist, (dc in next 2 sc, work FPdc around each of next 2 sc) 1{2-3} times †, dc in next 4 sc, repeat from † to † once, dc in last 2 sc; join with slip st to first dc.

Instructions continued on page 98.

Continued from page 96.

To work Back Post double crochet (abbreviated BPdc), YO, insert hook from **back** to **front** around post of st indicated *(Fig. 4, page 205)*, YO and pull up a loop (3 loops on hook), (YO and draw through 2 loops on hook) twice. Skip st in front of BPdc.

Rnd 5: Ch 3, turn; dc in next 2 dc, † (work BPdc around each of next 2 FPdc, dc in next 2 dc) 3{4-5} times, work BPdc around each of next 8 FPtr, dc in next 2 dc, work BPdc around each of next 2 FPdc, dc in next 2 dc, work BPdc around each of next 8 FPtr, (dc in next 2 dc, work BPdc around each of next 2 FPdc) 3{4-5} times †, dc in next 4 dc, repeat from † to † once, dc in last dc; join with slip st to first dc.

Rnd 6: Ch 3, turn; dc in next dc, † (work FPdc around each of next 2 BPdc, dc in next 2 dc) 1{2-3} times, work Twist, dc in next 2 dc, work FPdc around each of next 2 BPdc, dc in next 2 dc, work Back Cable, work Front Cable, dc in next 2 dc, work FPdc around each of next 2 BPdc, dc in next 2 dc, work Back Cable, work Front Cable, dc in next 2 dc, work FPdc around each of next 2 BPdc, dc in next 2 dc, work Twist, (dc in next 2 dc, work FPdc around each of next 2 BPdc) 1{2-3} times †, dc in next 4 dc, repeat from † to † once, dc in last 2 dc; join with slip st to first dc.

Rnds 7 thru 17{19-21}: Repeat Rnds 5 and 6, 5{6-7} times; then repeat Rnd 5 once **more**.

FRONT

Row 1: Ch 1, turn; sc in Back Loop Only of next 50{58-66} sts, leave remaining 50{58-66} sts unworked: 50{58-66} sc.

Rows 2 thru 21{23-25}: Ch 1, turn; sc in each sc across; do **not** finish off.

RIGHT NECK SHAPING

To decrease, pull up a loop in each of next 2 sc, YO and draw through all 3 loops on hook **(counts as one sc)**.

Row 1: Ch 1, turn; sc in first 17{21-25} sc, decrease, leave remaining 31{35-39} sc unworked: 18{22-26} sc.

Row 2: Ch 1, turn; sc in each sc across.

To work ending decrease, pull up a loop in each of last 2 sc, YO and draw through all 3 loops on hook **(counts as one sc)**.

Row 3: Ch 1, turn; sc in each sc across to last 2 sc, work ending decrease: 17{21-25} sc.

Rows 4 and 5: Repeat Rows 2 and 3: 16{20-24} sc.

Row 6: Ch 1, turn; sc in each sc across; finish off leaving a long end for sewing.

LEFT NECK SHAPING

To work beginning decrease, pull up a loop in same st and in next sc, YO and draw through all 3 loops on hook **(counts as one sc)**.

Row 1: With **wrong** side facing, skip 12 sc on Row 21{23-25} of Front from Right Neck Shaping and join yarn with slip st in next sc; ch 1, work beginning decrease, sc in each sc across: 18{22-26} sc.

Row 2: Ch 1, turn; sc in each sc across.

Row 3: Ch 1, turn; pull up a loop in each of first 2 sc, YO and draw through all 3 loops on hook **(counts as one sc)**, sc in next sc and in each sc across: 17{21-25} sc.

Rows 4 and 5: Repeat Rows 2 and 3: 16{20-24} sc.

Row 6: Ch 1, turn; sc in each sc across; finish off leaving a long end for sewing.

BACK

Row 1: With **right** side facing and working in Back Loops Only of unworked sts on Rnd 17{19-21} of Body, join yarn with sc in first sc from Front *(see Joining With Sc, page 205)*; sc in next st and in each st across: 50{58-66} sc.

Rows 2 thru 27{29-31}: Ch 1, turn; sc in each sc across.

Finish off.

Sew shoulder seams.

SLEEVE

Rnd 1: With **right** facing and working in end of rows on Body, join yarn with sc in Row 1 of Back **or** Front; work 23{25-26} sc evenly spaced across to shoulder seam, work 24{26-27} sc evenly spaced across; join with slip st to first sc: 48{52-54} sc.

Rnds 2-4: Ch 1, turn; sc in each sc around; join with slip st to first sc.

Rnd 5 (Decrease rnd)**:** Ch 1, turn; work beginning decrease, sc in each sc across to last 2 sc, work ending decrease; join with slip st to first sc: 46{50-52} sc.

Rnds 6-8: Ch 1, turn; sc in same st and in each sc around; join with slip st to first sc.

Rnds 9 thru 52{44-40}: Repeat Rnds 5-8, 11{9-8} times: 24{32-36} sc.

Rnd 53{45-41} (Decrease rnd)**:** Ch 1, turn; work beginning decrease, sc in each sc across to last 2 sc, work ending decrease; join with slip st to first sc: 22{30-34} sc.

Rnd 54{46-42}: Ch 1, turn; sc in same st and in each sc around; join with slip st to first sc.

Rnds 55{47-43} thru 56: Repeat Rnds 53{45-41} and 54{46-42}, 1{5-7} time(s): 20 sc.

Rnd 57: Ch 1, do **not** turn; slip st **loosely** in Back Loop Only of next sc and each sc around; join with slip st to **both** loops of joining slip st, do **not** finish off.

RIBBING

Foundation Rnd: Ch 1, turn; working in free loops of sc on Rnd 56, sc in each sc around; join with slip st to first sc.

Row 1: Ch 6, sc in second ch from hook and in each ch across, skip first sc on Foundation Rnd, slip st in next 2 sc: 7 sts.

Row 2: Turn; skip first 2 slip sts, sc in Back Loop Only of each sc across: 5 sc.

Row 3: Ch 1, turn; sc in Back Loop Only of each sc across, slip st in **both** loops of next 2 sc on Foundation Rnd: 7 sts.

Rows 4-19: Repeat Rows 2 and 3, 8 times; then repeat Row 2 once **more**: 5 sc.

Row 20: Ch 1, turn; sc in Back Loop Only of each sc across, slip st in **both** loops of last sc on Foundation Rnd; finish off leaving a long end for sewing.

Sew Ribbing seam.

Repeat for second Sleeve.

NECK RIBBING

Foundation Rnd: With **right** side facing, join yarn with sc in first unworked sc on Back; sc in next 17 sc and in next shoulder seam; sc in end of next 6 rows on Neck Shaping; sc in next 12 skipped sc; sc in end of next 6 rows on Neck Shaping; sc in next shoulder seam; join with slip st to first sc: 44 sc.

Rnd 1: Ch 1, turn; slip st **loosely** in Back Loop Only of each sc around; join with slip st to **both** loops of first slip st.

Note: Begin working in rows.

Row 1: Ch 8, sc in second ch from hook and in each ch across, skip first sc on Foundation Rnd, slip st in free loops of next 2 sc: 9 sts.

Row 2: Turn; skip first 2 slip sts, sc in Back Loop Only of each sc across: 7 sc.

Row 3: Ch 1, turn; sc in Back Loop Only of each sc across, slip st in free loops of next 2 sc on Foundation Rnd: 9 sts.

Rows 4-42: Repeat Rows 2 and 3, 19 times; then repeat Row 2 once **more**: 7 sc.

Row 43: Ch 1, turn; sc in Back Loop Only of each sc across, slip st in free loop of last sc on Foundation Rnd; finish off leaving a long end for sewing.

Sew Neck Ribbing seam.

Design by Marilyn Buys.

CAPTIVATING CABLES TEE

Cables give this sweater its captivating appeal. Crocheted in cotton thread for cool comfort, the pullover can be made in three sizes.

■■□□ EASY

Finished Chest Measurements:
Small - 36" (91.5 cm)
Medium - 42" (106.5 cm)
Large - 48" (122 cm)

Size Note: Instructions are written for size Small with sizes Medium and Large in braces { }. Instructions will be easier to read if you circle all the numbers pertaining to your size. If only one number is given, it applies to all sizes. If a zero is given, it means to do nothing.

MATERIALS
Bedspread Weight Cotton Thread
  (size 10) [400 yards (366 meters)
  per ball]: 4{5-6} balls
Steel crochet hook, size 5 (1.9 mm) **or**
  size needed for gauge
Tapestry needle

GAUGE: 16 dc and 8 rows = 2" (5 cm)

BACK
BODY
Ch 146{170-194}.

Row 1: Dc in fourth ch from hook **(3 skipped chs count as first dc, now and throughout)** and in each ch across: 144{168-192} dc.

Row 2 (Right side)**:** Ch 3 **(counts as first dc, now and throughout)**, turn; dc in next dc and in each dc across.

Note: Mark Row 2 as **right** side.

Rows 3 thru 48{54-60}: Ch 3, turn; dc in next dc and in each dc across; do **not** finish off.

SLEEVES
Row 1: Ch 26{26-28}, turn; dc in fourth ch from hook and in each ch and each dc across, add on 24{24-26} dc *(Fig. 6, page 205)*: 192{216-244} dc.

Rows 2 thru 37{39-42}: Ch 3, turn; dc in next dc and in each dc across.

Finish off.

FRONT
BODY
Ch 146{170-194}.

Row 1 (Wrong side)**:** Dc in fourth ch from hook and in each ch across: 144{168-192} dc.

Note: Mark **back** of any dc on Row 1 as **right** side.

To work Front Post treble crochet (abbreviated FPtr), YO twice, insert hook from **front** to **back** around post of st indicated *(Fig. 4, page 205)*, YO and pull up a loop (4 loops on hook), (YO and draw through 2 loops on hook) 3 times. Skip st behind FPtr.

Row 2: Ch 3, turn; dc in next 40{48-56} dc, work FPtr around each of next 2 sts, dc in next 2 dc, work FPtr around each of next 2 sts, ★ dc in next 8{10-12} dc, work FPtr around each of next 2 sts, dc in next 2 dc, work FPtr around each of next 2 sts; repeat from ★ 3 times **more**, dc in next dc and in each dc across.

To work Back Post treble crochet (abbreviated BPtr), YO twice, insert hook from **back** to **front** around post of st indicated *(Fig. 4, page 205)*, YO and pull up a loop (4 loops on hook), (YO and draw through 2 loops on hook) 3 times. Skip st in front of BPtr.

Row 3: Ch 3, turn; dc in next 40{48-56} dc, work BPtr around each of next 2 FPtr, dc in next 2 dc, work BPtr around each of next 2 FPtr, ★ dc in next 8{10-12} dc, work BPtr around each of next 2 FPtr, dc in next 2 dc, work BPtr around each of next 2 FPtr; repeat from ★ 3 times **more**, dc in next dc and in each dc across.

Rows 4 and 5: Repeat Rows 2 and 3.

Instructions continued on page 102.

Continued from page 100.

To work Front Post double treble crochet *(abbreviated FPdtr)*, YO 3 times, insert hook from **front** to **back** around post of BPtr indicated *(Fig. 4, page 205)*, YO and pull up a loop (5 loops on hook), (YO and draw through 2 loops on hook) 4 times. Skip st behind FPdtr.

To work Twist *(uses next 6 sts)*, skip next 4 sts, work FPdtr around each of next 2 BPtr, working **behind** last 2 FPdtr made, dc in next 2 skipped dc, working in **front** of last 2 FPdtr made, work FPdtr around first skipped BPtr and next skipped BPtr.

Row 6: Ch 3, turn; dc in next 40{48-56} dc, work Twist, [dc in next 8{10-12} dc, work Twist] 4 times, dc in next dc and in each dc across.

Row 7: Ch 3, turn; dc in next 40{48-56} dc, work BPtr around each of next 2 FPdtr, dc in next 2 dc, work BPtr around each of next 2 FPdtr, ★ dc in next 8{10-12} dc, work BPtr around each of next 2 FPdtr, dc in next 2 dc, work BPtr around each of next 2 FPdtr; repeat from ★ 3 times **more**, dc in next dc and in each dc across.

Rows 8 thru 48{54-60}: Repeat Rows 2-7, 6{7-8} times; then repeat Rows 2-6 once **more**; do **not** finish off.

SLEEVES

Row 1: Ch 26{26-28}, turn; dc in fourth ch from hook and in each ch across, dc in next 41{49-57} dc, work BPtr around each of next 2 FPdtr, dc in next 2 dc, work BPtr around each of next 2 FPdtr, ★ dc in next 8{10-12} dc, work BPtr around each of next 2 FPdtr, dc in next 2 dc, work BPtr around each of next 2 FPdtr; repeat from ★ 3 times **more**, dc in last 41{49-57} dc, add on 24{24-26} dc: 192{216-244} sts.

Row 2: Ch 3, turn; dc in next dc and in each dc across to next BPtr, work FPtr around each of next 2 BPtr, dc in next 2 dc, work FPtr around each of next 2 BPtr, ★ dc in next 8{10-12} dc, work FPtr around each of next 2 BPtr, dc in next 2 dc, work FPtr around each of next 2 BPtr; repeat from ★ 3 times **more**, dc in next dc and in each dc across.

Row 3: Ch 3, turn; dc in next dc and in each dc across to next FPtr, work BPtr around each of next 2 FPtr, dc in next 2 dc, work BPtr around each of next 2 FPtr, ★ dc in next 8{10-12} dc, work BPtr around each of next 2 FPtr, dc in next 2 dc, work BPtr around each of next 2 FPtr; repeat from ★ 3 times **more**, dc in next dc and in each dc across.

Rows 4 and 5: Repeat Rows 2 and 3.

Row 6: Ch 3, turn; dc in next dc and in each dc across to next BPtr, [work Twist, dc in next 8{10-12} dc] twice, skip next 4 sts, work FPdtr around each of next 2 BPtr, working **behind** last 2 FPdtr made, dc in first skipped dc, dc in sp **before** next skipped dc and in skipped dc, working in **front** of last 2 FPdtr made, work FPdtr around first skipped BPtr and next skipped BPtr, [dc in next 8{10-12} dc, work Twist] twice, dc in next dc and in each dc across: 193{217-245} sts.

To work Front Post double crochet *(abbreviated FPdc)*, YO, insert hook from **front** to **back** around post of st indicated *(Fig. 4, page 205)*, YO and pull up a loop (3 loops on hook), (YO and draw through 2 loops on hook) twice. Skip st behind FPdc.

To work Back Post double crochet *(abbreviated BPdc)*, YO, insert hook from **back** to **front** around post of st indicated *(Fig. 4, page 205)*, YO and pull up a loop (3 loops on hook), (YO and draw through 2 loops on hook) twice. Skip st in front of BPdc.

Row 7: Ch 3, turn; work BPdc around next st, (work FPdc around next st, work BPdc around next st) across to last dc, dc in last dc.

Row 8: Ch 3, turn; work FPdc around next BPdc, (work BPdc around next FPdc, work FPdc around next BPdc) across to last dc, dc in last dc.

Rows 9-13: Repeat Rows 7 and 8 twice; then repeat Row 7 once **more**; do **not** finish off.

LEFT NECK SHAPING

To work neck decrease (uses next 2 sts), YO, insert hook from **front** to **back** around post of next BPdc, † YO and pull up a loop, YO and draw through 2 loops on hook †, YO and insert hook from **back** to **front** around post of next FPdc, repeat from † to † once, YO and draw through all 3 loops on hook.

Row 1: Ch 3, turn; dc in next 86{98-112} sts, (work FPdc around next BPdc, work BPdc around next FPdc) 4 times, work neck decrease, leave remaining 96{108-122} sts unworked: 96{108-122} sts.

Row 2: Ch 2, turn; work FPdc around next BPdc, (work BPdc around next FPdc, work FPdc around next st) 4 times, dc in next dc and in each dc across: 95{107-121} sts.

Row 3: Ch 3, turn; dc in next dc and in each dc across to last 10 sts, (work FPdc around next st, work BPdc around next FPdc) 4 times, work neck decrease: 94{106-120} sts.

Rows 4 thru 24{26-29}: Repeat Rows 2 and 3, 10{11-13} times; then repeat Row 2, 1{1-0} time(s) **more**: 73{83-94} sts.

Finish off, leaving a long end for sewing.

RIGHT NECK SHAPING

Row 1: With **right** side facing, join thread with slip st from **back** to **front** around post of same st as last leg of neck decrease at end of Row 1 of Left Neck Shaping, ch 2; work FPdc around next BPdc, (work BPdc around next FPdc, work FPdc around next BPdc) 4 times, dc in next FPdc and in each st across: 96{108-122} sts.

Row 2: Ch 3, turn; dc in next dc and in each dc across to last 10 sts, (work FPdc around next st, work BPdc around next FPdc) 4 times, work neck decrease: 95{107-121} sts.

Row 3: Ch 2, turn; work FPdc around next BPdc, (work BPdc around next FPdc, work FPdc around next st) 4 times, dc in next dc and in each dc across: 94{106-120} sts.

Rows 4 thru 24{26-29}: Repeat Rows 2 and 3, 10{11-13} times; then repeat Row 2, 1{1-0} time(s) **more**: 73{83-94} sts.

Finish off, leaving a long end for sewing.

FINISHING

On each side of Tee, match stitches and whipstitch shoulder and top of Sleeve seam *(Fig. 9b, page 206)*.

Sew each underarm and side in one continuous seam.

NECK EDGING

With **right** side facing, join thread with sc in right shoulder seam *(see Joining With Sc, page 205)*; sc in each dc across Back, sc in next seam; working in end of rows across Left Neck Shaping, [sc, (ch 2, sc) twice] in each row across to last row, 3 sc in last row, sc in next st (same st as last leg of neck decrease); working in end of rows across Right Neck Shaping, 3 sc in first row, [sc, (ch 2, sc) twice] in each row across; join with slip st to first sc, finish off.

SLEEVE EDGING

To work treble crochet (abbreviated tr), YO twice, insert hook in sp indicated, YO and pull up a loop (4 loops on hook), (YO and draw through 2 loops on hook) 3 times.

Rnd 1: With **right** side facing, join thread with slip st in seam at underarm; ch 3, dc in same sp, 2 dc in end of each row across to next seam, tr in seam, 2 dc in end of each row across; join with slip st to first dc.

Rnds 2 and 3: Ch 3, (work FPdc around next st, work BPdc around next st) around; join with slip st to first dc.

Rnd 4: Ch 1, sc in same st, ch 2, (sc in next st, ch 2) around; join with slip st to first sc, finish off.

Repeat for second Sleeve.

Design by Leana Moon.

CHIC SHAWL

Here's vintage apparel that reflects today's sense of style! Our timeless triangular shawl will enhance any outfit.

◼◼◼◻ INTERMEDIATE

Finished Size: 47$\frac{1}{2}$" x 47$\frac{1}{2}$" x 67" (120.5 cm x 120.5 cm x 170 cm)

MATERIALS
Medium/Worsted Weight Yarn [8 ounces, 452 yards (230 grams, 413 meters) per skein]: 2 skeins
Crochet hook, size G (4 mm) **or** size needed for gauge

GAUGE: Each Square = 3$\frac{1}{2}$" (9 cm)

FIRST SQUARE
Ch 4; join with slip st to form a ring.

Rnd 1 (Right side)**:** Ch 4, dc in ring, (ch 2, dc in ring, ch 1, dc in ring) 3 times, hdc in third ch of beginning ch-4 to form last ch-2 sp: 8 sps.

Note: Mark Rnd 1 as **right** side.

Rnd 2: Ch 7, dc in same sp, ch 2, dc in next ch-1 sp, ch 2, ★ (dc, ch 4, dc) in next ch-2 sp, ch 2, dc in next ch-1 sp, ch 2; repeat from ★ 2 times **more**; join with slip st to third ch of beginning ch-7: 12 sps.

To work Picot, ch 3, slip st in third ch from hook.

To work corner Picot, ch 5, slip st in fifth ch from hook.

Rnd 3: Slip st in first ch-4 sp, ch 1, (2 sc, work corner Picot, 2 sc) in same sp, work Picot, (2 sc in next ch-2 sp, work Picot) twice, ★ (2 sc, work corner Picot, 2 sc) in next ch-4 sp, work Picot, (2 sc in next ch-2 sp, work Picot) twice; repeat from ★ 2 times **more**; join with slip st to first sc, finish off.

Note: Join Squares and Triangles following diagram for placement.

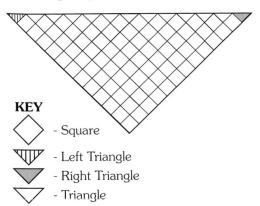

KEY

◇ - Square

▽ (striped) - Left Triangle

▽ (shaded) - Right Triangle

▽ - Triangle

ADDITIONAL SQUARES
ONE SIDE JOINING

Rnds 1 and 2: Work same as First Square: 12 sps.

Rnd 3 (Joining rnd): Slip st in first ch-4 sp, ch 1, 2 sc in same sp, ch 2; holding Squares with **wrong** sides together, sc in corresponding corner Picot on **adjacent** Square, ch 2, slip st in first ch (before sc joining), 2 sc in same ch-4 sp on **new** Square, ch 1, sc in next Picot on **adjacent** Square, ch 1, slip st in first ch, † 2 sc in next ch-2 sp on **new** Square, ch 1, sc in next Picot on **adjacent** Square, ch 1, slip st in first ch †, repeat from † to † once **more**, 2 sc in next corner ch-4 sp on **new** Square, ch 2, sc in next corner Picot on **adjacent** Square, ch 2, slip st in first ch, 2 sc in same sp on **new** Square, work Picot, (2 sc in next ch-2 sp, work Picot) twice, ★ (2 sc, work corner Picot, 2 sc) in next corner ch-4 sp, work Picot, (2 sc in next ch-2 sp, work Picot) twice; repeat from ★ once **more**; join with slip st to first sc, finish off.

TWO SIDE JOINING

Rnds 1 and 2: Work same as First Square: 12 sps.

Rnd 3 (Joining rnd): Slip st in first ch-4 sp, ch 1, 2 sc in same sp, ch 2; holding Squares with **wrong** sides together, sc in corresponding corner Picot on **adjacent** Square, ch 2, slip st in first ch (before sc joining), 2 sc in same ch-4 sp on **new** Square, ★ † ch 1, sc in next Picot on **adjacent** Square, ch 1, slip st in first ch, 2 sc in next ch-2 sp on **new** Square †, repeat from † to † once

more, ch 1, sc in next Picot on **adjacent** Square, ch 1, slip st in first ch, 2 sc in next corner ch-4 sp on **new** Square, ch 2, sc in next corner Picot on **adjacent** Square, ch 2, slip st in first ch, 2 sc in same sp on **new** Square; repeat from ★ once **more**, work Picot, (2 sc in next ch-2 sp, work Picot) twice, (2 sc, work corner Picot, 2 sc) in next corner ch-4 sp, work Picot, (2 sc in next ch-2 sp, work Picot) twice; join with slip st to first sc, finish off.

RIGHT TRIANGLE

To work treble crochet (abbreviated **tr**), YO twice, insert hook in sp indicated, YO and pull up a loop (4 loops on hook), (YO and draw through 2 loops on hook) 3 times.

Ch 4; join with slip st to form a ring.

Row 1 (Right side): Ch 5, (dc in ring, ch 1, dc in ring, ch 2) twice, tr in ring: 5 sps.

Note: Mark Row 1 as **right** side.

Row 2: Ch 6, turn; dc in first ch-2 sp, ch 2, dc in next ch-1 sp, ch 2, (dc, ch 4, dc) in next ch-2 sp, ch 2, dc in next ch-1 sp, ch 2, (dc, ch 2, tr) in last sp: 7 sps.

Row 3 (Joining row): Ch 4, turn; holding Triangle and Shawl with **wrong** sides together and working in Picots on top right Square of Shawl, sc in corresponding corner Picot on Square, ch 3, slip st in second ch (before sc joining), 2 sc in first ch-2 sp on **Right** Triangle, ★ ch 1, sc in next Picot on **adjacent** Square, ch 1, slip st in first ch, 2 sc in next sp on **Right** Triangle; repeat from ★ 2 times **more**, ch 2, sc in next corner Picot on **adjacent** Square, ch 2, slip st in first ch, 2 sc in same sp on **Right** Triangle, (work Picot, 2 sc in next sp) 3 times, ch 5, slip st in fifth ch from hook, slip st in same sp as last sc on **Right** Triangle; finish off.

LEFT TRIANGLE

Work same as Right Triangle through Row 2: 7 sps.

Row 3 (Joining row): Ch 5, turn; slip st in fifth ch from hook, 2 sc in first sp, (work Picot, 2 sc in next sp) 3 times, ch 4; holding Triangle and Shawl with **wrong** sides together and working in Picots on top left Square of Shawl, sc in corresponding corner Picot on **adjacent** Square, ch 3, slip st in second ch (before sc joining), 2 sc in same sp on **Left** Triangle, ★ ch 1, sc in next Picot on **adjacent** Square, ch 1, slip st in first ch, 2 sc in next sp on **Left** Triangle; repeat from ★ 2 times **more**, ch 2, sc in next corner Picot on **adjacent** Square, ch 2, slip st in first ch, ch 1, slip st in same sp as last sc on **Left** Triangle; finish off.

NEXT 11 TRIANGLES

Work same as Right Triangle through Row 2: 7 sps.

Row 3 (Joining row): Ch 4, turn; holding Triangle and Shawl with **wrong** sides together and working in Picots of next 2 Squares, sc in corresponding corner Picot on **adjacent** Square, ch 3, slip st in second ch (before sc joining), 2 sc in first ch-2 sp on **new** Triangle, † ch 1, sc in next Picot on **adjacent** Square, ch 1, slip st in first ch, 2 sc in next sp on **new** Triangle †; repeat from † to † 2 times **more**, ch 2, sc in joining of next corner Picot on **adjacent** Square, ch 2, slip st in first ch, 2 sc in same sp on **new** Triangle, repeat from † to † 3 times, ch 3, sc in next corner Picot on **adjacent** Square, ch 3, slip st in second ch (before sc joining), ch 1, slip st in same sp as last sc on **new** Triangle; finish off.

EDGING

With **right** side facing and working across top edge of Shawl only, join yarn with sc in top right corner **(see Joining With Sc, page 205)**; sc evenly across ending in left corner; finish off.

Holding three 16" (40.5 cm) strands of yarn together for each fringe, add fringe in Picots across short edges of Shawl **(Figs. 12a & b, page 207)**.

Design by Nancy Fuller.

EASY EVENING BAG

Whether fashioned using two strands of black thread or a blend of black and white, our sophisticated bag will hold your necessities while giving a polished look to your evening wardrobe.

■■□□ EASY

Finished Size: 7¼"w x 7¾"h (18.5 cm x 19.5 cm)

MATERIALS
Bedspread Weight Cotton Thread (size 10) [225 yards (206 meters) per ball (White) or 150 yards (137 meters) per ball (Black)]:
Solid - 5 balls
Variegated
White - 2 balls
Black - 3 balls
Steel crochet hook, size 0 (3.25 mm) **or** size needed for gauge
Tapestry needle
3" x 12" (7.5 cm x 30.5 cm) Piece of cardboard
Pins

GAUGE: 16 sc = 3" (7.5 cm)
In pattern, (sc, 2 dc) 4 times = 2¼" (5.75 cm); 9 rows = 2" (5 cm)

Note: Solid Bag is worked holding two strands of Black together. Variegated Bag is worked holding one strand of White and one strand of Black together.

BODY
Ch 37.

Rnd 1 (Right side): 3 Sc in second ch from hook, sc in each ch across to last ch, 5 sc in last ch; working in free loops of beginning ch (*Fig. 3b, page 205*), sc in next 34 chs, 2 sc in same st as first sc; join with slip st to first sc: 78 sc.

Rnds 2-8: Ch 1, sc in same st and in each sc around; join with slip st to first sc.

Rnd 9: Ch 1, (sc, 2 dc) in same st, skip next 2 sc, ★ (sc, 2 dc) in next sc, skip next 2 sc; repeat from ★ around; join with slip st to first sc: 26 sc and 52 dc.

Rnd 10: Ch 1, sc in same st, skip next 2 dc, ★ (2 dc, sc) in next sc, skip next 2 dc; repeat from ★ around, 2 dc in same st as first sc; join with slip st to first sc.

Rnd 11: Ch 1, (sc, 2 dc) in same st, skip next 2 dc, ★ (sc, 2 dc) in next sc, skip next 2 dc; repeat from ★ around; join with slip st to first sc.

Rnds 12-37: Repeat Rnds 10 and 11, 13 times; do **not** finish off.

FLAP
Row 1: Slip st in next 3 sts, ch 2, **turn**; 2 dc in same st, skip next 2 sts, ★ (sc, 2 dc) in next st, skip next 2 dc; repeat from ★ 11 times **more**, sc in next sc, leave remaining 38 sts unworked: 13 sc and 26 dc.

Rows 2-30: Ch 2, turn; 2 dc in first sc, skip next 2 dc, ★ (sc, 2 dc) in next sc, skip next 2 dc; repeat from ★ 11 times **more**, sc in top of turning ch.

Edging: Ch 1, do **not** turn; sc evenly around entire Flap and in each unworked st on Rnd 37 of Body working 3 sc in each corner of Flap; join with slip st to first sc, finish off.

STRAP
For Solid Bag: Cut thirty-two 56" (142 cm) strands of Black.

For Variegated Bag: Cut sixteen 56" (142 cm) strands **each** of Black and White.

For both Bags: Tie strands together in a knot at one end and pin knot to cardboard. To work braid, divide strands into 4 groups of 8 strands each. Beginning with group at far left, number each group of thread from 1 through 4. Starting with groups 3 and 4, bring 3 over 4, 4 over 2, 1 over 4, 2 over 1, then bring 1 over 3, 3 over 2, 4 over 3, 2 over 4 (*Fig. A*); repeat same movements for braid, beginning with thread group at far right; knot strands together at opposite end.

Fig. A

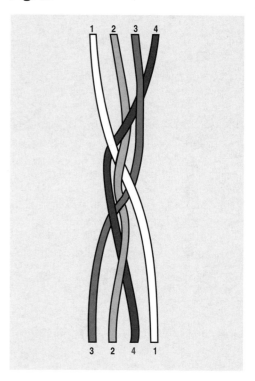

Using photo as a guide for placement, sew ends of Strap to inside of Body.

LOVELY LINEN VEST

The lustrous linen color and floral motifs of our classy vest will complement any outfit. By choosing different hook sizes, you can tailor the pattern to fit six adult sizes.

■■■□ INTERMEDIATE

Finished Chest Measurement:
X-Small - 33" (84 cm)
Small - 36" (91.5 cm)
Medium - 39" (99 cm)
Large - 44" (112 cm)
X-Large - 48" (122 cm)
XX-Large - 52" (132 cm)

Size Note: Instructions are written with sizes X-Small, Small, and Medium in first set of braces { } and sizes Large, X-Large, and XX-Large in second set. If only one number is given, it applies to all sizes. Using a different size hook for each gauge as recommended under Materials, work Small Motif for sizes X-Small and Large, Medium Motif for sizes Small and X-Large, and Large Motif for sizes Medium and XX-Large. Finished chest measurement is obtained by the size and number of Motifs specified for each size. Once gauge is obtained, use the same hook throughout.

MATERIALS
Light/Worsted Weight Yarn
[1³/₄ ounces, 150 yards (50 grams, 137 meters) per ball]: {13-14-15}{17-18-19} balls
Steel crochet hook, size indicated below
  or size needed for gauge
  Small Motif: 2 (2.25 mm)
  Medium Motif: 0 (3.25 mm)
  Large Motif: 00 (3.5 mm)
³/₄" (19 mm) Buttons - 3
Sewing needle and thread

GAUGE: Small Motif = 2³/₄" (7 cm)
Medium Motif = 3" (7.5 cm)
Large Motif = 3¹/₄" (8.25 cm)

MOTIF
[Make {68-68-68}{114-114-114}]
Ch 4; join with slip st to form a ring.

Rnd 1 (Right side)**:** Ch 1, 8 sc in ring; join with slip st to first sc.

Note: Mark Rnd 1 as **right** side.

Rnd 2: Ch 1, sc in same st, (ch 2, sc in next sc) around, ch 1, sc in first sc to form last ch-2 sp: 8 ch-2 sps.

Rnd 3: Ch 3 **(counts as first dc, now and throughout),** (dc, slip st) in same sp, (slip st, 3 dc, slip st) in next ch-2 sp and in each ch-2 sp around, (slip st, dc) in same sp as first dc; join with slip st to first dc.

To work treble crochet (abbreviated tr), YO twice, insert hook in st, sp, or loop indicated, YO and pull up a loop (4 loops on hook), (YO and draw through 2 loops on hook) 3 times.

Rnd 4: Ch 6, slip st in center dc of next 3-dc group, ★ ch 8, slip st in center dc of next 3-dc group, ch 6, slip st in center dc of next 3-dc group; repeat from ★ 2 times **more**, ch 4, tr in joining slip st to form last loop.

Rnd 5: Ch 4 **(counts as first tr)**, 3 tr in same loop, ch 1, 4 dc in next loop, ch 1, ★ (4 tr, ch 3, 4 tr) in next corner loop, ch 1, 4 dc in next loop, ch 1; repeat from ★ 2 times **more**, 4 tr in same loop as first tr, dc in first tr to form last ch-3 sp: 48 sts and 12 sps.

Rnd 6: (Slip st in same sp, ch 5) twice, (slip st in next ch-1 sp, ch 5) twice, ★ (slip st, ch 5) twice in next corner ch-3 sp, (slip st in next ch-1 sp, ch 5) twice; repeat from ★ 2 times **more**; join with slip st to first slip st, finish off: 16 ch-5 sps.

HALF MOTIF (Make 6)
Ch 4; join with slip st to form a ring.

Row 1 (Right side)**:** Ch 1, 5 sc in ring.

Note: Mark Row 1 as **right** side.

Row 2: Ch 1, turn; sc in first sc, (ch 2, sc in next sc) across: 4 ch-2 sps.

Row 3: Ch 3, turn; dc in same st, (slip st, 3 dc, slip st) in each of next 4 ch-2 sps, 2 dc in last sc: 4 3-dc groups.

Row 4: Ch 4, turn; † slip st in center dc of next 3-dc group, ch 6, slip st in center dc of next 3-dc group †, ch 8, repeat from † to † once, ch 4, slip st in last dc: 2 ch-4 sps and 3 loops.

Row 5: Ch 4 **(counts as first tr)**, turn; 3 tr in next ch-4 sp, ch 1, 4 dc in next loop, ch 1, (4 tr, ch 3, 4 tr) in next loop, ch 1, 4 dc in next loop, ch 1, 3 tr in last ch-4 sp, tr in st at base of last ch-4; do **not** finish off.

Edging: Turn; (slip st, ch 5) twice in first tr, (slip st in next ch-1 sp, ch 5) twice, (slip st, ch 5) twice in next ch-3 sp, (slip st in next ch-1 sp, ch 5) twice, (slip st, ch 5) twice in last tr; working in end of rows, skip first 2 rows, slip st in next dc row (Row 3), ch 5, slip st in beginning ring, ch 5, skip next 2 rows, slip st in next row, ch 5; join with slip st to first slip st, finish off: 13 ch-5 sps.

Instructions continued on page 110.

Continued from page 108.

ASSEMBLY

Using diagram indicated as a guide for placement and following instructions given below, join Motifs and Half Motifs together to form strips, then join strips; leaving edges of Motifs along dotted lines unworked.

Join Motifs as follows:
With **right** sides together and working through **both** pieces, join yarn with slip st in center ch of first corner ch-5; ch 5, (slip st in next ch-5 sp, ch 5) across to next corner ch-5, slip st in center ch of corner ch-5; finish off.

Join strips in same manner, skipping corner ch-5 sp at previously joined corners and working slip st in joining slip st **between** those corner ch-5 sps.

Join sides in same manner.

BODY EDGING

For Sizes X-Small, Small, and Medium Only - Rnd 1: With **right** side facing, join yarn with sc in ch-5 sp at Point A on Diagram A *(see Joining With Sc, page 205)*; 2 sc in same sp, 6 sc in each of next 3 ch-5 sps, ★ 2 sc in next sp, sc in next joining, 2 sc in next sp, 5 sc in each sp across to next joining sp; repeat from ★ around, 3 sc in same sp as first sc; join with slip st to first sc; do **not** finish off: 594 sc.

For Sizes Large, X-Large, and XX-Large Only - Rnd 1: With **right** side facing, join yarn with sc in ch-5 sp at Point A on Diagram B *(see Joining With Sc, page 205)*; 2 sc in same sp, 6 sc in each of next 3 ch-5 sps, ★ 2 sc in next sp, sc in next joining, 2 sc in next sp, 5 sc in each sp across to next joining sp; repeat from ★ around, 3 sc in same sp as first sc; join with slip st to first sc: 714 sc.

For All Sizes - Rnd 2: Ch 4, 7 tr in same st, skip next 2 sc, sc in next sc, skip next 2 sc, ★ 8 tr in next sc, skip next 2 sc, sc in next sc, skip next 2 sc; repeat from ★ around; join with slip st to first tr, finish off.

ARMHOLE EDGING

Rnd 1: With **right** side facing, join yarn with sc in joining of Half Motifs; 2 sc in next sp, 5 sc in each of next 4 ch-5 sps, 2 sc in next sp, sc in next joining, 2 sc in next sp, ★ 5 sc in each of next 3 ch-5 sps, 2 sc in next sp, sc in next joining, 2 sc in next sp; repeat from ★ 4 times **more**, 5 sc in each of next 4 ch-5 sps, 2 sc in last sp; join with slip st to first sc: 150 sc.

Rnd 2: Ch 1, sc in same st and in next 6 sc, skip next 2 sc, 8 tr in next sc, ★ skip next 2 sc, sc in next sc, skip next 2 sc, 8 tr in next sc; repeat from ★ around to last 8 sc, skip next 2 sc, sc in last 6 sc; join with slip st to first sc, finish off.

Repeat for second armhole.

Using photo as a guide for placement, sew one button to each of top three 8-tr groups on Rnd 2 of left front Edging; use spaces between tr on right front for buttonholes.

Design by Leana Moon.

DIAGRAM A
X-Small - Small - Medium

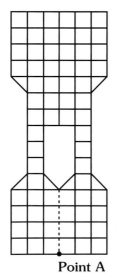

Point A

DIAGRAM B
Large - X-Large - XX-Large

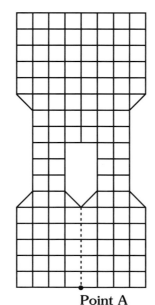

Point A

RICH RAGLAN

In a hue as rich as the deepest fall foliage, our cozy cardigan is embellished with bobble stitches along the shoulders and edges.

■■■□ INTERMEDIATE

Finished Chest Measurements:
Small - 39" (99 cm)
Medium - 43" (109 cm)
Large - 47" (119.5 cm)

Size Note: Instructions are written for size Small with sizes Medium and Large in braces { }. Instructions will be easier to read if you circle all the numbers pertaining to your size. If only one number is given, it applies to all sizes. If a zero is given, it means to do nothing.

MATERIALS
Medium/Worsted Weight Yarn [6 ounces, 348 yards (170 grams, 318 meters) per skein]: 4{5-5} skeins

MEDIUM 4

Crochet hook, size J (6 mm) **or** size needed for gauge
³/₄" Button
Sewing needle and thread
Yarn needle

GAUGE:
13 hdc and 10 rows = 4" (10 cm)

BODY
Ch 123{137-151}.

Row 1 (Right side): Sc in second ch from hook and in each ch across: 122{136-150} sc.

Note: Mark Row 1 as **right** side.

Instructions continued on page 112.

Row 2: Ch 2 **(counts as first hdc, now and throughout)**, turn; hdc in next sc and in each sc across.

Rows 3 thru 29{31-33}: Ch 2, turn; hdc in next hdc and in each hdc across; do **not** finish off.

LEFT FRONT
SIZES SMALL AND MEDIUM ONLY

Row 1: Ch 2, turn; hdc in next 27{31} hdc, leave remaining 94{104} hdc unworked: 28{32} hdc.

Row 2: Turn; slip st in next hdc, ch 2, hdc in next hdc and in each hdc across: 27{31} hdc.

Row 3: Ch 2, turn; hdc in next hdc and in each hdc across to last hdc, leave last hdc unworked: 26{30} hdc.

Rows 4 thru 11{12}: Repeat Rows 2 and 3, 4 times; then repeat Row 2, 0{1} time(s): 18{21} hdc.

Row 12{13}: Ch 2, turn; hdc in next hdc and in each hdc across.

Rows 13{14} thru 23{25}: Repeat Rows 2 thru 12{13}: 8{10} hdc.

Finish off.

SIZE LARGE ONLY

Row 1: Ch 2, turn; hdc in next 35 hdc, leave remaining 114 hdc unworked: 36 hdc.

Row 2: Turn; slip st in next hdc, ch 2, hdc in next hdc and in each hdc across: 35 hdc.

Row 3: Ch 2, turn; hdc in next hdc and in each hdc across to last hdc, leave last hdc unworked: 34 hdc.

Rows 4-27: Repeat Rows 2 and 3, 12 times: 10 hdc.

Finish off.

BACK
Row 1: With **wrong** side facing, skip next 2 hdc from Left Front and join yarn with slip st in next hdc on Row 29{31-33} of Body; ch 2, hdc in next 61{67-73} hdc, leave remaining 30{34-38} hdc unworked: 62{68-74} hdc.

Rows 2 thru 23{24-27}: Turn; slip st in next hdc, ch 2, hdc in next hdc and in each hdc across to last hdc, leave last hdc unworked: 18{22-22} hdc.

SIZES SMALL AND LARGE ONLY
Finish off.

SIZE MEDIUM ONLY
Row 25: Ch 2, turn; hdc in next hdc and in each hdc across.

Finish off.

RIGHT FRONT
SIZES SMALL AND MEDIUM ONLY

Row 1: With **wrong** side facing, skip next 2 hdc from Back and join yarn with slip st in next hdc on Row 29{31} of Body; ch 2, hdc in next hdc and in each hdc across: 28{32} hdc.

Row 2: Ch 2, turn; hdc in next hdc and in each hdc across to last hdc, leave last hdc unworked: 27{31} hdc.

Row 3: Turn; slip st in next hdc, ch 2, hdc in next hdc and in each hdc across: 26{30} hdc.

Rows 4 thru 11{12}: Repeat Rows 2 and 3, 4 times; then repeat Row 2, 0{1} time(s): 18{21} hdc.

Row 12{13}: Ch 2, turn; hdc in next hdc and in each hdc across.

Rows 13{14} thru 23{25}: Repeat Rows 2 thru 12{13}: 8{10} hdc.

Finish off.

SIZE LARGE ONLY
Row 1: With **wrong** side facing, skip next 2 hdc from Back and join yarn with slip st in next hdc on Row 33 of Body; ch 2, hdc in next hdc and in each hdc across: 36 hdc.

Row 2: Ch 2, turn; hdc in next hdc and in each hdc across to last hdc, leave last hdc unworked: 35 hdc.

Row 3: Turn; slip st in next hdc, ch 2, hdc in next hdc and in each hdc across: 34 hdc.

Rows 4-27: Repeat Rows 2 and 3, 12 times: 10 hdc.

Finish off.

SLEEVE (Make 2)
BODY
Ch 28{30-32}.

Row 1 (Right side)**:** Sc in second ch from hook and in each ch across: 27{29-31} sc.

Note: Mark Row 1 as **right** side.

Row 2: Ch 2, turn; hdc in next sc and in each sc across.

Row 3: Ch 2, turn; hdc in next hdc and in each hdc across.

Row 4: Ch 2, turn; hdc in next 5{6-5} hdc, 2 hdc in next hdc, ★ hdc in next 4{5-5} hdc, 2 hdc in next hdc; repeat from ★ 2{1-2} time(s) **more**, hdc in each hdc across: 31{32-35} hdc.

Row 5: Ch 2, turn; hdc in next hdc and in each hdc across.

Row 6 (Increase row)**:** Ch 2, turn; hdc in same st and in each hdc across: 32{33-36} hdc.

Row 7: Ch 2, turn; hdc in next hdc and in each hdc across.

Row 8 (Increase row)**:** Ch 2, turn; hdc in next hdc and in each hdc across to last hdc, 2 hdc in last hdc: 33{34-37} hdc.

Sizes Small and Large only - Rows 9 thru 38{42}: Repeat Rows 5-8, 7{8} times; then repeat Row 5, 2 times **more**: 47{53} hdc.

Size Medium only - Rows 9-40: Repeat Rows 5-8, 7 times; repeat Rows 5-7 once; then repeat Row 5 once **more**: 49 hdc.

All Sizes - Row 39{41-43}: Ch 2, turn; hdc in next hdc and in each hdc across; do **not** finish off.

SLEEVE CAP

Rows 1 thru 23{25-27}: Turn; slip st in first hdc, hdc in next hdc and in each hdc across: 24{24-26} hdc.

Finish off.

Sew Sleeve seam beginning at Row 1 and ending at Row 39{41-43}.

TRIM

Row 1: With **right** side facing and working in end of rows, join yarn with sc in first row **(see Joining With Sc, page 205)**; work 34{37-40} sc evenly spaced across to seam, sc in seam, work 35{38-41} sc evenly spaced across ending in last row of opposite side: 71{77-83} sc.

To work Bobble, ★ YO, insert hook in sc indicated, YO and pull up a loop, YO and draw through 2 loops on hook; repeat from ★ 2 times **more**, YO and draw through all 4 loops on hook, ch 1 to close. Push Bobble to **right** side.

Row 2: Ch 1, turn; sc in first 5 sc, (work Bobble in next sc, sc in next 5 sc) across: 11{12-13} Bobbles.

Row 3: Ch 1, turn; sc in first 5 sc, skip next ch, sc in next Bobble, sc in next 5 sc, ★ skip next ch, sc in next Bobble, sc in next 5 sc; repeat from ★ across; finish off leaving a long end for sewing.

CUFF

Rnd 1: With **wrong** side facing and working in free loops of beginning ch **(Fig. 3b, page 205)**, join yarn with sc in seam; sc in each ch around; join with slip st to first sc: 28{30-32} sc.

Rnd 2: Ch 1, turn; sc in same st, work Bobble in next sc, (sc in next 5 sc, work Bobble in next sc) 4 times, sc in last 2{4-6} sc; join with slip st to first sc: 5 Bobbles.

Rnd 3: Ch 1, turn; sc in same st and in next 2{4-6} sc, skip next ch, sc in next Bobble, ★ sc in next 5 sc, skip next ch, sc in next Bobble; repeat from ★ around; join with slip st to first sc: 28{30-32} sc.

Rnds 4-7: Ch 1, turn; sc in same st and in each sc around; join with slip st to first sc.

Rnd 8: Ch 1, turn; sc in same st, work Bobble in next sc, (sc in next 5 sc, work Bobble in next sc) 4 times, sc in last 2{4-6} sc; join with slip st to first sc, finish off.

ARMHOLE EDGING

With **right** side facing and working in end of rows, join yarn with sc in first row; work 70{76-82} sc evenly spaced across ending in last row of opposite side; finish off: 71{77-83} sc.

Repeat for second armhole.

With **right** sides of Trim and Armhole Edging together, matching stitches, and working through **both** loops of each stitch on **both** pieces, whipstitch each Sleeve in place **(Fig. 9b, page 206)**.

BAND

To decrease, pull up a loop in each of next 2 hdc, YO and draw through all 3 loops on hook **(counts as one sc)**.

Rnd 1: With **right** side facing, join yarn with sc in free loop of ch at base of first sc on Right Front (bottom corner); sc in same st; work 62{67-72} sc evenly spaced across end of rows on Right Front; working across last row on Right Front, 3 sc in first hdc, sc in each hdc on to Armhole Edging; sc in end of each row on Armhole Edging and Trim; working across last row of Sleeve Cap, decrease 12{12-13} times; sc in end of each row on Trim and Armhole Edging; sc in each hdc across Back; sc in end of each row on Armhole Edging and Trim; working across last row Sleeve Cap, decrease 12{12-13} times; sc in end of each row on Trim and Armhole Edging; working across last row on Left Front, sc in each hdc across to last hdc, 3 sc in last hdc; work 62{67-72} sc evenly spaced across Left Front; working in free loops of beginning ch, 3 sc in first ch, sc in each ch across, sc in same ch as first sc; join with slip st to first sc: 328{360-386} sc.

Rnd 2: Ch 1, turn; 3 sc in same st, sc in next 1{1-2} sc, work Bobble, (sc in next 5 sc, work Bobble) 20{22-24} times, sc in next 0{2-3} sc, 3 sc in next sc, ★ sc in each sc across to center sc of next corner 3-sc group, 3 sc in center sc; repeat from ★ once **more**, sc in each sc across; join with slip st to first sc: 21{23-24} Bobbles.

Rnd 3: Ch 1, turn; sc in same st, ★ sc in each sc across to center sc of next corner 3-sc group, 3 sc in center sc; repeat from ★ 2 times **more**, sc in each sc and in Bobble across to center sc of next corner 3-sc group, 3 sc in center sc; join with slip st to first sc.

Rnd 4: Ch 1, turn; sc in same st and in next sc, 3 sc in next sc, ★ sc in each sc across to center sc of next corner 3-sc group, 3 sc in center sc; repeat from ★ 2 times **more**, ch 3, skip next sc **(button loop made)**, sc in each sc across; join with slip st to first sc: one button loop.

Rnd 5: Ch 1, turn; sc in same st and in each sc around working 5 sc in button loop and 3 sc in center sc of each 3-sc group; join with slip st to first sc, finish off.

Add button.

Design by Frankie Reece.

CHINESE JACKET

Designed with a mandarin collar and frog closures, this exotic jacket features a distinctive pattern that's worked in warming worsted weight yarn. It's just right for cool autumn outings.

■■■■□ INTERMEDIATE

Finished Chest Measurements:
X-Small - 36" (91.5 cm)
Small - 40" (101.5 cm)
Medium - 44" (112 cm)
Large - 48" (122 cm)
X-Large - 52" (132 cm)
XX-Large - 56" (142 cm)

Size Note: Instructions are written for sizes X-Small, Small, and Medium in first set of braces { } and sizes Large, X-Large, and XX-Large in second set. Instructions will be easier to read if you circle all the numbers pertaining to your size. If only one number is given, it applies to all sizes.

MATERIALS
Medium/Worsted Weight Yarn
 [8 ounces, 452 yards
 (230 grams, 413 meters)
 per skein]:
 Burgundy - {2-2-2}{3-3-3} skeins
 Black - {1-1-1}{2-2-2} skein(s)
Crochet hooks, sizes H (5 mm) **and**
 G (4 mm) **or** sizes needed for gauge
Yarn needle

GAUGE: With larger size hook,
in pattern, 14 dc = 4" (10 cm);
Rows 1-9 = 3³⁄₄" (9.5 cm)

Note: Use larger size hook unless otherwise instructed.

BODY
With Burgundy, ch {129-143-157}{171-185-199}.

Row 1 (Right side)**:** Dc in fourth ch from hook **(3 skipped chs count as first dc)** and in each ch across; finish off: {127-141-155}{169-183-197} dc.

Note: Mark Row 1 as **right** side.

Row 2: With **wrong** side facing, join Black with slip st in first dc; (dc in next dc, slip st in next dc) across; finish off.

Row 3: With **right** side facing, join Burgundy with slip st in first slip st; ch 3 **(counts as first dc, now and throughout)**, dc in next dc and in each st across; finish off.

Repeat Rows 2 and 3 until Body measures 11" (28 cm) from beginning ch, ending by working Row 3.

LEFT FRONT
Row 1: With **wrong** side facing, join Black with slip st in first dc; (dc in next dc, slip st in next dc) {15-17-19}{20-22-24} times, leave remaining {96-106-116}{128-138-148} dc unworked; finish off: {31-35-39}{41-45-49} sts.

Row 2: With **right** side facing, join Burgundy with slip st in first slip st; ch 3, dc in next dc and in each st across; finish off.

Row 3: With **wrong** side facing, join Black with slip st in first dc; (dc in next dc, slip st in next dc) across; finish off.

Rows 4 thru {18-18-22}{20-22-22}: Repeat Rows 2 and 3, {7-7-9}{8-9-9} times; then repeat Row 2 once **more**.

NECK SHAPING
Row 1: With **wrong** side facing, skip first {8-10-10}{8-10-12} dc and join Black with slip st in next dc; (dc in next dc, slip st in next dc) across; finish off: {23-25-29}{33-35-37} sts.

To decrease (uses next 2 sts), ★ YO, insert hook in **next** st, YO and pull up a loop, YO and draw through 2 loops on hook; repeat from ★ once **more**, YO and draw through all 3 loops on hook **(counts as one dc)**.

Row 2 (Decrease row)**:** With **right** side facing, join Burgundy with slip st in first slip st; ch 3, dc in next dc and in each st across to last 2 sts, decrease; finish off: {22-24-28}{32-34-36} dc.

Row 3 (Decrease row)**:** With **wrong** side facing, skip first dc and join Black with slip st in next dc; (dc in next dc, slip st in next dc) across; finish off: {21-23-27}{31-33-35} sts.

Rows 4 and 5: Repeat Rows 2 and 3: {19-21-25}{29-31-33} sts.

SIZES X-SMALL, SMALL, AND MEDIUM ONLY
Row 6: With **right** side facing, join Burgundy with slip st in first slip st; ch 3, dc in next dc and in each st across; finish off leaving a long end for sewing.

SIZES LARGE, X-LARGE, AND XX-LARGE ONLY
Row 6: With **right** side facing, join Burgundy with slip st in first slip st; ch 3, dc in next dc and in each st across; finish off.

Instructions continued on page 116.

Continued from page 114.

Row 7: With **wrong** side facing, join Black with slip st in first dc; (dc in next dc, slip st in next dc) across; finish off.

Row 8: With **right** side facing, join Burgundy with slip st in first slip st; ch 3, dc in next dc and in each st across; finish off leaving a long end for sewing.

BACK

Row 1: With **wrong** side facing, skip next dc from Left Front and join Black with slip st in next dc; (dc in next dc, slip st in next dc) {31-34-37}{42-45-48} times, leave remaining {32-36-40}{42-46-50} dc unworked; finish off: {63-69-75}{85-91-97} sts.

Row 2: With **right** side facing, join Burgundy with slip st in first slip st; ch 3, dc in next dc and in each st across; finish off.

Row 3: With **wrong** side facing, join Black with slip st in first dc; (dc in next dc, slip st in next dc) across; finish off.

Rows 4 thru {24-24-28}{28-30-30}: Repeat Rows 2 and 3, {10-10-12}{12-13-13} times; then repeat Row 2 once **more**.

RIGHT FRONT

Row 1: With **wrong** side facing, skip next dc from Back and join Black with slip st in next dc; (dc in next dc, slip st in next dc) across; finish off: {31-35-39}{41-45-49} sts.

Row 2: With **right** side facing, join Burgundy with slip st in first slip st; ch 3, dc in next dc and in each st across; finish off.

Row 3: With **wrong** side facing, join Black with slip st in first dc; (dc in next dc, slip st in next dc) across; finish off.

Rows 4 thru {18-18-22}{20-22-22}: Repeat Rows 2 and 3, {7-7-9}{8-9-9} times; then repeat Row 2 once **more**.

NECK SHAPING

Row 1: With **wrong** side facing, join Black with slip st in first dc; (dc in next dc, slip st in next dc) {11-12-14}{16-17-18} times, leave remaining {8-10-10}{8-10-12} dc unworked; finish off: {23-25-29}{33-35-37} sts.

Row 2 (Decrease row): With **right** side facing, join Burgundy with slip st in first slip st; ch 2, dc in next dc and in each st across; finish off: {22-24-28}{32-34-36} dc.

Row 3 (Decrease row): With **wrong** side facing, join Black with slip st in first dc; (dc in next dc, slip st in next dc) across to last dc, leave last dc unworked; finish off: {21-23-27}{31-33-35} sts.

Rows 4 and 5: Repeat Rows 2 and 3: {19-21-25}{29-31-33} sts.

SIZES X-SMALL, SMALL, AND MEDIUM ONLY

Row 6: With **right** side facing, join Burgundy with slip st in first slip st; ch 3, dc in next dc and in each st across; finish off leaving a long end for sewing.

SIZES LARGE, X-LARGE, AND XX-LARGE ONLY

Row 6: With **right** side facing, join Burgundy with slip st in first slip st; ch 3, dc in next dc and in each st across; finish off.

Row 7: With **wrong** side facing, join Black with slip st in first dc; (dc in next dc, slip st in next dc) across; finish off.

Row 8: With **right** side facing, join Burgundy with slip st in first slip st; ch 3, dc in next dc and in each st across; finish off leaving a long end for sewing.

SLEEVE (Make 2)

Note: To change colors as you join with slip st, insert hook in first st, hook new yarn and draw through st and loop on hook *(Fig. 7c, page 206)*. To change colors in last dc, work last dc to within one step of completion, hook new yarn and draw through both loops on hook *(Fig. 7b, page 206)*.

With Burgundy, ch {30-30-34}{34-36-36}; being careful not to twist ch, join with slip st to form a ring.

Rnd 1 (Right side): Ch 3, dc in next ch and in each ch around; join with slip st to first dc changing to Black: {30-30-34}{34-36-36} dc.

Note: Mark Rnd 1 as **right** side.

Rnd 2: Ch 3, turn; slip st in next dc, (dc in next dc, slip st in next dc) around; join with slip st to first dc changing to Burgundy.

Rnd 3 (Increase rnd): Ch 3, turn; 2 dc in next slip st, dc in each st around to last slip st, 2 dc in last slip st changing to Black in last dc; join with slip st to first dc: {32-32-36}{36-38-38} dc.

Rnd 4: Turn; dc in next dc, (slip st in next dc, dc in next dc) around; join with slip st to first slip st changing to Burgundy.

Rnd 5 (Increase rnd): Ch 3, turn; 2 dc in next dc, dc in each st around to last dc, 2 dc in last dc; join with slip st to first dc changing to Black: {34-34-38}{38-40-40} dc.

Rnds 6 thru {36-36-44}{44-48-48}: Repeat Rnds 2-5, {7-7-9}{9-10-10} times; then repeat Rnds 2-4 once **more**: {64-64-76}{76-82-82} sts.

SIZES X-SMALL AND SMALL ONLY

Rnd {37-37}: Ch 3, turn; dc in next slip st and in each st around; join with slip st to first dc changing to Black.

Rnd {38-38}: Ch 3, turn; slip st in next dc, (dc in next dc, slip st in next dc) around; join with slip st to first dc changing to Burgundy.

Rnd {39-39}: Ch 3, turn; dc in next slip st and in each st around; join with slip st to first dc, finish off.

SIZES MEDIUM, LARGE, X-LARGE, AND XX-LARGE ONLY

Rnd {45}{45-49-49}: Ch 3, turn; dc in next slip st and in each st around; join with slip st to first dc, finish off.

FINISHING

Sew shoulder seams.

Sew each Sleeve to Jacket, matching center of last round on Sleeve to shoulder seam.

COLLAR

Row 1: With **right** side facing, using smaller size hook, and working in unworked dc on Row {18-18-22}{20-22-22} of Right Front, join Black with sc in first dc *(see Joining With Sc, page 205)*; sc in next {7-9-9}{7-9-11} dc; work {9-9-9}{12-12-12} sc evenly spaced across end of rows along right neck edge, sc in seam, sc in next {25-27-25}{27-29-31} dc across Back, sc in seam; work {9-9-9}{12-12-12} sc evenly spaced across end of rows along left neck edge, sc in next {8-10-10}{8-10-12} unworked dc on Row {18-18-22}{20-22-22} of Left Front: {61-67-65}{69-75-81} sc.

Rows 2 and 3: Ch 3, turn; dc in next st and in each st across.

Finish off.

BODY EDGING

Rnd 1: With **right** side facing and using smaller size hook, join Burgundy with sc in center dc at Back neck edge; sc evenly around entire Jacket increasing as necessary to keep piece lying flat; join with slip st to first sc.

Rnd 2: Ch 1, working from **left** to **right**, work reverse sc *(Figs. 8a-d, page 206)* in each sc around; join with slip st to first st, finish off.

SLEEVE EDGING

Rnd 1: With **right** side facing, using smaller size hook, and working in free loops of beginning ch *(Fig. 3b, page 205)*, join Burgundy with sc in same ch as joining; sc in each ch around; join with slip st to first sc: {30-30-34}{34-36-36} sc.

Rnd 2: Ch 1, working from **left** to **right**, work reverse sc in each sc around; join with slip st to first st, finish off.

Repeat for second Sleeve.

FROG HOOK (Make 5)

Foundation (Right side)**:** With Black, using smaller size hook, and leaving a long end for sewing, ch 31, slip st in back ridge of tenth ch from hook *(Fig. 1, page 205)* and next 3 chs **(Loop made)**, ch 18; finish off leaving a long end for sewing.

Note: Mark Foundation as **right** side.

Row 1: With **right** side facing and working in top loops only, join Black with slip st in first ch; slip st in next 15 chs, place marker in last slip st made for st placement *(see Markers, page 205)*, slip st in next 22 sts, place marker in last slip st made for st placement, slip st in last 15 chs; finish off.

ASSEMBLY

First End: With **right** side facing and holding Loop at top, thread needle with long yarn end at right. Using photo as a guide, roll end in a **counterclockwise** manner, sewing piece together through all thicknesses as you roll and end at marked slip st, remove marker and do **not** cut yarn end.

Second End: Thread needle with remaining yarn end. With **right** side facing and using photo as a guide, roll end in a **clockwise** manner, sewing piece together through all thicknesses as you roll and end at marked slip st, remove marker and do **not** cut yarn end.

FROG BUTTON (Make 5)

Foundation (Right side)**:** With Black, using smaller size hook, and leaving a long end for sewing, ch 36, slip st in back ridge of ninth ch from hook and next 9 chs **(Loop made)**, ch 18; finish off leaving a long end for sewing.

Note: Mark Foundation as **right** side.

Row 1: With **right** side facing and working in top loops only, join Black with slip st in first ch; slip st in next 15 chs, place marker in last slip st made for st placement, slip st in next 33 sts, place marker in last slip st made for st placement, slip st in last 15 chs; finish off.

ASSEMBLY

Work same as Assembly for Frog Hook.

To form button, use photo as a guide and tie center of Loop in a knot. Wrap end over knot and tack in place on **wrong** side.

Using photo as a guide for placement, sew Frog Buttons to Left Front of Jacket and Frog Hooks to Right Front.

Design by Darla Sims.

STYLISH HAT & SCARF

Ridges formed by post stitches highlight this sophisticated hat and scarf. For extra appeal, a ribbon winds through the brim, and fringe hangs from both ends of the scarf.

■■□□ **EASY**

Finished Sizes:
Hat - 22" (56 cm) diameter
Scarf - 6¹/₂" x 44" (16.5 cm x 112 cm)

MATERIALS
Medium/Worsted Weight Yarn
[6 ounces, 348 yards **MEDIUM 4**
(170 grams, 318 meters)
per skein]:
Hat - 1 skein
Scarf - 1 skein
Crochet hooks, sizes H (5 mm) **and**
I (5.5 mm) **or** sizes needed for gauge
For Hat only:
⁵/₈" (16 mm) wide Ribbon - 1 yard
(.9 meters)
Vest buckle

HAT
GAUGE: With larger size hook,
Rnds 1-3 = 3¹/₄" (8.25 cm)

CROWN
Rnd 1 (Right side): With larger size hook, ch 4, 11 dc in fourth ch from hook; join with slip st to top of beginning ch: 12 sts.

Note: Mark Rnd 1 as **right** side.

To work Front Post double crochet (abbreviated FPdc), YO, insert hook from **front** to **back** around post of st indicated on rnd **below (Fig. 4, page 205)**, YO and pull up a loop (3 loops on hook), (YO and draw through 2 loops on hook) twice.

Rnd 2: Ch 3 **(counts as first dc, now and throughout)**, work FPdc around same st as dc just made, ★ dc in next dc, work FPdc around same st as dc just made; repeat from ★ around; join with slip st to first dc: 24 sts.

Rnd 3: Ch 3, dc in next FPdc, work FPdc around same st as dc just made, ★ dc in next dc and in next FPdc, work FPdc around same st as last dc made; repeat from ★ around; join with slip st to first dc: 36 sts.

Rnd 4: Ch 3, dc in next dc and in next FPdc, work FPdc around same st as last dc made, ★ dc in next 2 dc and in next FPdc, work FPdc around same st as last dc made; repeat from ★ around; join with slip st to first dc: 48 sts.

Rnd 5: Ch 3, dc in next 2 dc and in next FPdc, work FPdc around same st as last dc made, ★ dc in next 3 dc and in next FPdc, work FPdc around same st as last dc made; repeat from ★ around; join with slip st to first dc: 60 sts.

Rnd 6: Ch 3, dc in next 3 dc and in next FPdc, work FPdc around same st as last dc made, ★ dc in next 4 dc and in next FPdc, work FPdc around same st as last dc made; repeat from ★ around; join with slip st to first dc: 72 sts.

Rnd 7: Ch 3, dc in next 4 dc and in next FPdc, work FPdc around same st as last dc made, ★ dc in next 5 dc and in next FPdc, work FPdc around same st as last dc made; repeat from ★ around; join with slip st to first dc: 84 sts.

Rnd 8: Ch 3, dc in next 5 dc and in next FPdc, work FPdc around same st as last dc made, ★ dc in next 6 dc and in next FPdc, work FPdc around same st as last dc made; repeat from ★ around; join with slip st to first dc: 96 sts.

Rnd 9: Ch 3, dc in next 6 dc and in next FPdc, work FPdc around same st as last dc made, ★ dc in next 7 dc and in next FPdc, work FPdc around same st as last dc made; repeat from ★ around; join with slip st to first dc: 108 sts.

Rnd 10: Ch 3, dc in next 7 dc and in next FPdc, work FPdc around same st as last dc made, ★ dc in next 8 dc and in next FPdc, work FPdc around same st as last dc made; repeat from ★ around; join with slip st to first dc: 120 sts.

Rnd 11: Ch 3, dc in next 8 dc and in next FPdc, work FPdc around same st as last dc made, ★ dc in next 9 dc and in next FPdc, work FPdc around same st as last dc made; repeat from ★ around; join with slip st to first dc, do **not** finish off: 132 sts.

BRIM
Rnd 1: Ch 1, sc in same st, skip next dc, (sc in next st, skip next st) around; join with slip st to first sc: 66 sc.

Rnd 2: Ch 1, sc in same st and in each sc around; join with slip st to first sc.

To work treble crochet (abbreviated tr), YO twice, insert hook in sc indicated, YO and pull up a loop (4 loops on hook), (YO and draw through 2 loops on hook) 3 times.

Rnd 3: Ch 4 **(counts as first tr)**, tr in next sc and in each sc around; join with slip st to first tr.

Instructions continued on page 120.

Continued from page 118.

Rnd 4: Ch 1, sc in same st and in next 43 tr, place marker around last sc made for Neckband placement *(see Markers, page 205)*, sc in each tr around; join with slip st to Front Loop Only of first sc *(Fig. 2, page 205)*.

Change to smaller size hook.

Rnd 5: Ch 1, 2 sc in Front Loop Only of same st and each sc around; join with slip st to **both** loops of first sc: 132 sc.

Rnds 6-15: Ch 1, **turn**; sc in both loops of same st and each sc around; join with slip st to first sc.

Finish off.

NECKBAND

Row 1: With **right** side of Crown toward you, smaller size hook, and working **behind** Brim and in free loops on Rnd 4 *(Fig. 3a, page 205)*, join yarn with sc in marked sc *(see Joining With Sc, page 205)*; sc in next 45 sc, leave remaining 20 sc unworked: 46 sc.

Rows 2-9: Ch 1, turn; skip first sc, sc in each sc across: 38 sc.

Finish off.

EDGING

With **right** side facing and smaller size hook, join yarn with sc in end of first row; sc evenly across entire Neckband working 3 sc in each corner; finish off.

Beginning and ending at center back, weave ribbon through Rnd 3 on Brim and thread ribbon ends through buckle.

Design by Ada Dillard.

SCARF
GAUGE:
With larger size hook, in pattern, 14 sts and 8 rows = 4" (10 cm)

With larger size hook, ch 22.

Row 1 (Wrong side)**:** Sc in second ch from hook and in each ch across: 21 sc.

Note: Mark **back** of any stitch on Row 1 as **right** side.

Rows 2-5: Ch 1, turn; sc in each sc across.

To work treble crochet (abbreviated tr), YO twice, insert hook in sc indicated, YO and pull up a loop (4 loops on hook), (YO and draw through 2 loops on hook) 3 times.

Row 6: Ch 5 **(counts as first tr plus ch 1, now and throughout)**, turn; skip next sc, tr in next sc, ★ ch 1, skip next sc, tr in next sc; repeat from ★ across: 10 ch-1 sps and 11 tr.

Row 7: Ch 1, turn; sc in each tr and in each ch-1 sp across: 21 sc.

Rows 8-10: Ch 1, turn; sc in each sc across.

Row 11: Ch 3 **(counts as first dc, now and throughout)**, turn; dc in next sc and in each sc across.

To work Front Post double crochet (abbreviated FPdc), YO, insert hook from **front** to **back** around post of st indicated *(Fig. 4, page 205)*, YO and pull up a loop (3 loops on hook), (YO and draw through 2 loops on hook) twice.

Row 12: Ch 3, turn; dc in next dc, work FPdc around next dc, (dc in next 3 dc, work FPdc around next dc) 4 times, dc in last 2 dc.

To work Back Post double crochet (abbreviated BPdc), YO, insert hook from **back** to **front** around post of FPdc indicated *(Fig. 4, page 205)*, YO and pull up a loop (3 loops on hook), (YO and draw through 2 loops on hook) twice.

Row 13: Ch 3, turn; dc in next dc, work BPdc around next FPdc, (dc in next 3 dc, work BPdc around next FPdc) 4 times, dc in last 2 dc.

Row 14: Ch 3, turn; dc in next dc, work FPdc around next BPdc, (dc in next 3 dc, work FPdc around next BPdc) 4 times, dc in last 2 dc.

Rows 15-83: Repeat Rows 13 and 14, 34 times; then repeat Row 13 once **more**.

Rows 84-87: Ch 1, turn; sc in each st across.

Row 88: Ch 5, turn; skip next sc, tr in next sc, ★ ch 1, skip next sc, tr in next sc; repeat from ★ across: 10 ch-1 sps and 11 tr.

Row 89: Ch 1, turn; sc in each tr and in each ch-1 sp across: 21 sc.

Rows 90-93: Ch 1, turn; sc in each sc across; do **not** finish off.

EDGING
Ch 1, turn; sc evenly around entire Scarf working 3 sc in each corner; join with slip st to first sc, finish off.

Holding seven 11" (28 cm) strands of yarn together for each fringe, add fringe across short edges of Scarf *(Figs. 12a & b, page 207)*.

COSMOPOLITAN WRAP

When winter's in the air, bundle up in our chic, versatile wrap.
Its Tunisian-knit look is crocheted using an afghan hook.

Instructions begin on page 122.

COSMOPOLITAN WRAP
Shown on page 121.

■■□□ **EASY**

Finished Size: Adult

MATERIALS
Medium/Worsted Weight Yarn
[6 ounces, 330 yards
(170 grams, 302 meters)
per skein]: 11 skeins

MEDIUM **4**

Note: The photo model is 34" (86.5 meters) long, if you want your piece to be shorter or longer, you will need to adjust the yarn amounts accordingly.

Afghan hook, size J (6 mm) **or** size needed for gauge
Crochet hook, size J
Yarn needle

GAUGE: In pattern,
13 sts and 17 rows = 4" (10 cm)

FRONT (Make 2)
Ch 69.

Row 1 (Right side)**:** Working in top loops only, insert hook in second ch from hook, YO and pull up a loop (2 loops on hook) *(Fig. A)*, pull up a loop in each ch across *(Fig. B)*, keeping all loops on hook and working from **left** to **right**, YO and draw through first loop on hook, ★ YO and draw through 2 loops on hook *(Fig. C)*; repeat from ★ across until one loop remains on hook. This is the first stitch of the **next** row: 69 sts.

Fig. A

Fig. B

Fig. C

Row 2: Working from **right** to **left** and with yarn in back, skip first vertical strand, ★ insert hook from **front** to **back** between both vertical stands of next loop *(Figs. D & E)*, YO and pull up a loop even with loop on hook; repeat from ★ across, working from **left** to **right**, YO and draw through first loop on hook, (YO and draw through 2 loops on hook) across.

Fig. D

Fig. E

Repeat Row 2 until Front measures 34" (86.5 cm) from beginning ch **or** to desired length.

Last Row: Working from **right** to **left** and with yarn in back, skip first vertical strand, ★ insert hook from **front** to **back** between both vertical stands of next loop, YO and draw **loosely** through strands **and** loop on hook; repeat from ★ across; finish off.

FRONT HEM FACING
Row 1: With **right** side facing, working in free loops of beginning ch *(Fig. 3b, page 205)* and using crochet hook, join yarn with sc in first ch on either Front *(see Joining With Sc, page 205)*; sc in each ch across: 69 sc.

Rows 2-5: Ch 1, turn; sc in each sc across.

Finish off, leaving a long end for sewing.

Repeat for second Front.

Turn Hem Facing to **wrong** side and sew in place.

BACK
Ch 138.

Work same as Front.

BACK HEM FACING
Work same as Front Hem Facing.

ASSEMBLY
With **right** sides and last rows together and working from outer edge towards center of Back, sew one Front to Back for approximately 17" (43 cm).

Repeat for second Front.

FRONT EDGING
With **right** side facing, working through **both** thicknesses along edge of Hem Facing, and using crochet hook, join yarn with sc at bottom edge of right Front; sc in end of each row across; 3 sc in first st on Last Row, sc in each st across and in shoulder seam, sc in each st across Back and in shoulder seam, sc in each st across Last Row to last st, 3 sc in last st; sc in each row across; finish off.

SIDE EDGING
With **right** side facing, working through **both** thicknesses along edge of Hem Facing, and using crochet hook, join yarn with sc at bottom edge of right Front; sc in each row across working one sc in shoulder seam; finish off.

Repeat for left side.

PONCHO POWER

Back by popular demand, the granny square poncho is now a family affair!
Ours are sized for mothers and daughters, but don't forget cousins,
aunts, even grandmothers ... everybody will want one!

Instructions begin on page 124.

PONCHO POWER
Shown on page 123.

■■□□ **EASY**

Finished Measurements
Across Widest Point:
Small - 25" (63.5 cm)
Medium - 30" (76 cm)
Large - 39" (99 cm)
Ex-Large - 52" (132 cm)

MATERIALS
Medium/Worsted Weight Yarn
[6 ounces, 348 yards
(170 grams, 318 meters) (Seascape)
or 8 ounces, 452 yards
(230 grams, 413 meters)
per skein (all other colors)]:
Adult Sizes Large/Ex-Large
Aran - 1/1 skein
Seascape - 1/2 skein(s)
Cornmeal - 1/1 skein
Medium Sage - 1/2 skein(s)
Windsor Blue - 3/3 skeins
Child Sizes Small/Medium
Aran - 1/1 skein
Seascape - 1/1 skein
Light Sage - 1/1 skein
Country Blue - 2/2 skeins
Crochet hook, size G (4 mm) **or** size
  needed for gauge
Yarn needle

GAUGE:
Large Square = 6¹⁄₂" (16.5 cm)
Small Square = 5" (12.75 cm)

ADULT'S PONCHO
LARGE SQUARE
Note: For size Large, make 24; for size
Ex-Large, make 44.

With Aran, ch 5; join with slip st to form
a ring.

Rnd 1 (Right side)**:** Ch 3 **(counts as
first dc, now and throughout),** 2 dc
in ring, ch 1, (3 dc in ring, ch 1) 3 times;
join with slip st to first dc, finish off: 4
ch-1 sps.

Note: Mark Rnd 1 as **right** side.

Rnd 2: With **right** side facing, join
Seascape with sc in any ch-1 sp *(see
Joining With Sc, page 205)*; ch 3, sc
in same sp, ch 3, (sc, ch 3) twice in each
ch-1 sp around; join with slip st to first
sc, finish off: 8 ch-3 sps.

Rnd 3: With **right** side facing; join
Cornmeal with slip st in any corner ch-3
sp; ch 3, (2 dc, ch 1, 3 dc) in same sp,
ch 1, 3 dc in next ch-3 sp, ch 1, ★ (3 dc,
ch 1) twice in next corner ch-3 sp, 3 dc
in next ch-3 sp, ch 1; repeat from ★ 2
times **more**; join with slip st to first dc,
finish off: 12 ch-1 sps.

Rnd 4: With **right** side facing, join
Seascape with sc in any corner ch-1 sp;
ch 3, sc in same sp, ch 3, (sc in next
ch-1 sp, ch 3) across to next corner ch-1
sp, ★ (sc, ch 3) twice in corner ch-1 sp,
(sc in next ch-1 sp, ch 3) across to next
corner ch-1 sp; repeat from ★ 2 times
more; join with slip st to first sc, finish
off: 16 ch-3 sps.

Rnd 5: With **right** side facing, join
Medium Sage with slip st in any corner
ch-3 sp; ch 3, (2 dc, ch 1, 3 dc) in same
sp, ch 1, (3 dc in next ch-3 sp, ch 1)
across to next corner ch-3 sp, ★ (3 dc,
ch 1) twice in corner ch-3 sp, (3 dc in
next ch-3 sp, ch 1) across to next corner
ch-3 sp; repeat from ★ 2 times **more**;
join with slip st to first dc, finish off: 20
ch-1 sps.

Rnd 6: Repeat Rnd 4: 24 ch-3 sps.

Rnd 7: With Windsor Blue, repeat Rnd
5, leaving a long end for sewing: 84 dc
and 28 ch-1 sps.

LARGE HALF SQUARE
Note: For size Large, make 16; for size
Ex-Large, make 22.

With Aran, ch 4; join with slip st to form
a ring.

Row 1 (Right side)**:** Ch 4 **(counts as
first dc plus ch 1)**, (3 dc, ch 1, 3 dc,
ch 1, dc) in ring; finish off: 3 ch-1 sps.

Note: Mark Row 1 as **right** side.

Row 2: With **right** side facing, join
Seascape with sc in first dc; ch 3, (sc,
ch 3) twice in next ch-1 sp, sc in last dc;
finish off: 3 ch-3 sps.

Row 3: With **right** side facing, join
Cornmeal with slip st in first sc; ch 3, 2
dc in same st, ch 1, 3 dc in next ch-3 sp,
ch 1, (3 dc, ch 1) twice in next ch-3 sp,
3 dc in next ch-3 sp, ch 1, 3 dc in last
sc; finish off: 5 ch-1 sps.

Row 4: With **right** side facing, join
Seascape with sc in first dc; ch 3, (sc in
next ch-1 sp, ch 3) twice, (sc, ch 3) twice
in next ch-1 sp, (sc in next ch-1 sp, ch-3)
twice, sc in last dc; finish off: 7 ch-3 sps.

Row 5: With **right** side facing, join
Medium Sage with slip st in first sc; ch 3,
2 dc in same st, ch 1, (3 dc in next ch-3
sp, ch 1) 3 times, (3 dc, ch 1) twice in
next ch-3 sp, (3 dc in next ch-3 sp, ch 1)
3 times, 3 dc in last sc; finish off: 9 ch-1
sps.

Row 6: With **right** side facing, join
Seascape with sc in first dc; ch 3, (sc in
next ch-1 sp, ch 3) 4 times, (sc, ch 3)
twice in next ch-1 sp, (sc in next ch-1 sp,
ch 3) 4 times, sc in last dc; finish off: 11
ch-3 sps.

*To work treble crochet (abbreviated
tr),* YO twice, insert hook in sc
indicated, YO and pull up a loop (4
loops on hook), (YO and draw through 2
loops on hook) 3 times.

Row 7: With **right** side facing, join
Windsor Blue with slip st in first sc; ch 4
(counts as first tr), 3 dc in same st,
ch 1, (3 dc in next ch-3 sp, ch 1) 5
times, (3 dc, ch 1) twice in next ch-3 sp,
(3 dc in next ch-3 sp, ch 1) 5 times, (3
dc, tr) in last sc; finish off leaving a long
end for sewing: 44 sts and 13 ch-1 sps.

CHILD'S PONCHO
SMALL SQUARE

Note: For size Small, make 14; for size Medium, make 24.

Rnds 1 and 2: Work same as Large Square: 8 ch-3 sps.

Rnd 3: With Light Sage, work same as Large Square: 12 ch-1 sps.

Rnd 4: Work same as Large Square: 16 ch-3 sps.

Rnd 5: With Country Blue, work same as Large Square, leaving a long end for sewing: 60 dc and 20 ch-1 sps.

SMALL HALF SQUARE

Note: For size Small, make 14; for size Medium, make 16.

Rows 1 and 2: Work same as Large Half Square: 3 ch-3 sps.

Row 3: With Light Sage, work same as Large Half Square: 5 ch-1 sps.

Row 4: Work same as Large Half Square: 7 ch-3 sps.

Row 5: With **right** side facing, join Country Blue with slip st in first sc; ch 4 **(counts as first tr)**, 3 dc in same st, ch 1, (3 dc in next ch-3 sp, ch 1) 3 times, (3 dc, ch 1) twice in next ch-3 sp, (3 dc in next ch-3 sp, ch 1) 3 times, (3 dc, tr) in last sc; finish off leaving a long end for sewing: 32 sts and 9 ch-1 sps.

FINISHING
ASSEMBLY

Note: On each chart, solid lines represent edges to be joined; dotted lines represent edges to be left unjoined. Arrows indicate front and back edges to be joined.

Following chart for desired size and working through **both** loops, whipstitch Squares and Half Squares together **(Fig. 9a, page 206)**, beginning in first corner ch or tr and ending in next corner ch or tr leaving neck opening at front unsewn.

EDGINGS

Bottom: With **right** side facing, join either Windsor Blue or Country Blue with sc in any ch-1 sp; sc evenly around; join with slip st to first sc, finish off.

Neck: With **right** side facing, join either Windsor Blue or Country Blue with sc in any ch-1 sp; sc evenly around; join with slip st to first sc, finish off.

FRINGE

Cut a piece of cardboard 3" (7.5 cm) wide and 5" (12.5 cm) long. Wind Windsor Blue or Country Blue **loosely** and **evenly** around the cardboard lengthwise until the card is filled, then cut across one end; repeat as needed. Hold 2 strands of yarn together and fold in half. With **wrong** side facing and using a crochet hook, draw the folded end up through a stitch and pull the loose ends through the folded end **(Fig. A)**; draw the knot up **tightly (Fig. B)**. Repeat in each sc around. Lay flat on a hard surface and trim the ends.

Fig. A

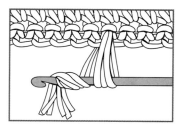

Fig. B

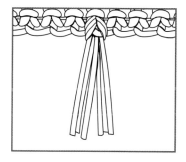

EX-LARGE CHART

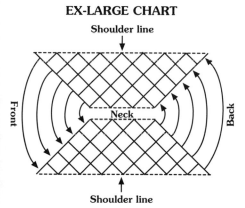

MEDIUM/LARGE CHART

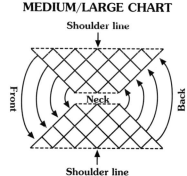

SMALL CHART

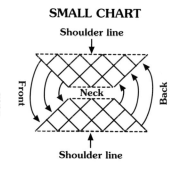

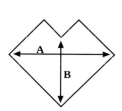

A – {25-30}{39-52}"
B – {15-20}{26-32$\frac{1}{2}$}"

SCHOOL-DAYS SWEATER

This pullover earns high marks for style! Vibrant granny squares contrast with the solid back and sleeves. Crocheted with lightweight yarn, the sweater can be made in sizes 6 to 12.

⬤⬤⬤◻ INTERMEDIATE

Finished Chest Measurement:
Size 6 - 28" (71 cm)
Size 8 - 30" (76 cm)
Size 10 - 32" (81.5 cm)
Size 12 - 35" (89 cm)

Size Note: Instructions are written for size 6 with sizes 8, 10, and 12 in braces { }. Instructions will be easier to read if you circle all the numbers pertaining to your size. If only one number is given, it applies to all sizes.

MATERIALS
Light/Worsted Weight Yarn
[2¹/₂ ounces, 250 yards (70 grams, 229 meters) per skein]:
Black - 5{6-6-7} skeins
White - 1 skein
Purple - 1 skein
Yellow - 1 skein
Emerald - 1 skein
Skipper Blue - 1 skein
Cherry Red - 1 skein
Crochet hooks, sizes C (2.75 mm) **and** E (3.5 mm) **or** sizes needed for gauge
Yarn needle

GAUGE: Each Square = 3¹/₂" (9 cm)
With larger size hook,
3 3-dc groups and 5 rows = 2" (5 cm)

FRONT
SQUARE A

For sizes 6, 8, and 10 only, make **one** Square of each color combination given below. For size 12 only, make **two** Squares each of combinations 1, 3, 4, and 5, and **one** Square each of combinations 2, 6, 7, and 8.

Combination	Rnd 1	Rnd 2	Rnd 3
1	WHITE	EMERALD	RED
2	WHITE	BLUE	EMERALD
3	WHITE	PURPLE	RED
4	EMERALD	RED	BLUE
5	PURPLE	YELLOW	RED
6	RED	YELLOW	BLUE
7	BLUE	EMERALD	PURPLE
8	RED	BLUE	YELLOW

With larger size hook and first color, ch 4; join with slip st to form a ring.

Rnd 1 (Right side)**:** Ch 3 **(counts as first dc, now and throughout)**, 2 dc in ring, ch 1, (3 dc in ring, ch 1) 3 times; join with slip st to first dc, finish off: 4 ch-1 sps.

Note: Mark Rnd 1 as **right** side.

Rnd 2: With **right** side facing and larger size hook, join next color with slip st in any ch-1 sp; ch 3, (2 dc, ch 1, 3 dc) in same sp, (3 dc, ch 1, 3 dc) in each ch-1 sp around; join with slip st to first dc, finish off: 24 dc.

Rnd 3: With **right** side facing and larger size hook, join next color with slip st in any corner ch-1 sp; ch 3, (2 dc, ch 1, 3 dc) in same sp, 3 dc in sp **between** next 2 3-dc groups *(Fig. 5, page 205)*, ★ (3 dc, ch 1, 3 dc) in next ch-1 sp, 3 dc in sp **between** next 2 3-dc groups; repeat from ★ around; join with slip st to first dc, finish off: 36 dc.

Rnd 4: With **right** side facing and larger size hook, join Black with slip st in any corner ch-1 sp; ch 3, (2 dc, ch 1, 3 dc) in same sp, 3 dc in each sp **between** 3-dc groups across to next corner ch-1 sp, ★ (3 dc, ch 1, 3 dc) in corner ch-1 sp, 3 dc in each sp **between** 3-dc groups across to next corner ch-1 sp; repeat from ★ around; join with slip st to first dc, finish off: 48 dc and 4 ch-1 sps.

SQUARE B

For sizes 6, 8, and 10 only, make **one** Square of each color combination given below. For size 12 only, make **two** Squares each of combinations 1, 2, 3, 5, and 6, and **one** Square each of combinations 4, 7, and 8.

Combination	Rnd 1	Rnd 2	Rnd 3
1	RED	YELLOW	PURPLE
2	YELLOW	BLUE	PURPLE
3	EMERALD	PURPLE	YELLOW
4	YELLOW	PURPLE	RED
5	EMERALD	WHITE	YELLOW
6	BLUE	WHITE	EMERALD
7	PURPLE	RED	BLUE
8	PURPLE	EMERALD	WHITE

With larger size hook and first color, ch 4; join with slip st to form a ring.

Rnd 1 (Right side)**:** Ch 3, 2 dc in ring, ch 1, (3 dc in ring, ch 1) 3 times; join with slip st to first dc, finish off: 4 ch-1 sps.

Note: Mark Rnd 1 as **right** side.

Rnd 2: With **right** side facing and larger size hook, join next color with slip st in same st as joining; ch 3, dc in same st, hdc in next dc, 2 dc in next dc, ch 3, ★ 2 dc in next dc, hdc in next dc, 2 dc in next dc, ch 3; repeat from ★ around; join with slip st to first dc, finish off: 20 sts and 4 ch-3 sps.

Instructions continued on page 128.

Continued from page 126.

Rnd 3: With **right** side facing and larger size hook, join next color with slip st in same st as joining; ch 3, hdc in same st and in next dc, 2 hdc in next hdc, hdc in next dc, (hdc, dc) in next dc, ch 3, ★ (dc, hdc) in next dc, hdc in next dc, 2 hdc in next hdc, hdc in next dc, (hdc, dc) in next dc, ch 3; repeat from ★ around; join with slip st to first dc, finish off: 32 sts and 4 ch-3 sps.

Rnd 4: With **right** side facing and larger size hook, join Black with slip st in any corner ch-3 sp; ch 3, (2 dc, ch 1, 3 dc) in same sp, skip next 2 sts, (3 dc in next hdc, skip next 2 sts) twice, ★ (3 dc, ch 1, 3 dc) in next ch-3 sp, skip next 2 sts, (3 dc in next hdc, skip next 2 sts) twice; repeat from ★ around; join with slip st to first dc, finish off: 48 dc and 4 ch-1 sps.

JOINING

With Black, using diagram as a guide (numbers correspond to color combinations), and working through **inside** loops, whipstitch Squares together forming 4{4-4-5} strips of 4{4-4-5} Squares each *(Fig. 9c, page 206)*, beginning and ending in corner chs; then whipstitch strips together in same manner.

Sizes 6, 8, and 10 Only

1	1	2	2
3	3	4	4
5	5	6	6
7	7	8	8

Size 12 Only

1	1	2	2	3
3	3	4	4	4
5	5	6	6	5
7	7	8	8	3
6	5	2	1	1

KEY
☐ **Square A**
▨ **Square B**

SIZE 6 ONLY
Neck Foundation Row: With **right** side facing and larger size hook, join Black with slip st in top right corner ch-1 sp; ch 3, 3 dc in same sp and in each of next 3 sps **between** 3-dc groups, 3 dc in next joining, ch 2, skip next 3 dc, sc in next 9 dc, sc in next sp and in next joining, sc in next sp and in next 9 dc, ch 2, skip next 3 dc, 3 dc in next joining and in each of next 3 sps **between** 3-dc groups, 4 dc in next corner ch-1 sp; do **not** finish off: 32 dc and 21 sc.

SIZE 8 ONLY
Border - Rnd 1: With **right** side facing and larger size hook, join Black with slip st in top right corner ch-1 sp; ch 4 **(counts as first dc plus ch 1, now and throughout)**, 3 dc in same sp, 3 dc in each sp **between** 3-dc groups and in each joining across to next corner ch-1 sp, ★ (3 dc, ch 1, 3 dc) in corner ch-1 sp, 3 dc in each sp **between** 3-dc groups and in each joining across to next corner ch-1 sp; repeat from ★ 2 times **more**, 2 dc in same sp as first dc; join with slip st to first dc: 68 3-dc groups.

Neck Foundation Row: Slip st in first corner ch-1 sp, ch 3, 3 dc in same sp and in each of next 4 sps **between** 3-dc groups, ch 2, skip next 2 dc, sc in next 23 dc, ch 2, skip next 2 dc, 3 dc in each of next 4 sps **between** 3-dc groups, 4 dc in next corner ch-1 sp, leave remaining sts unworked; do **not** finish off: 32 dc and 23 sc.

SIZE 10 ONLY
Border - Rnd 1: With **right** side facing and larger size hook, join Black with slip st in top right corner ch-1 sp; ch 4 **(counts as first dc plus ch 1, now and throughout)**, 3 dc in same sp, 3 dc in each sp **between** 3-dc groups and in each joining across to next corner ch-1 sp, ★ (3 dc, ch 1, 3 dc) in corner ch-1 sp, 3 dc in each sp **between** 3-dc groups and in each joining across to next corner ch-1 sp; repeat from ★ 2 times **more**, 2 dc in same sp as first dc; join with slip st to first dc: 68 3-dc groups.

Rnd 2: Slip st in first corner ch-1 sp, ch 4, 3 dc in same sp and in each sp **between** 3-dc groups across to next corner ch-1 sp, ★ (3 dc, ch 1, 3 dc) in corner ch-1 sp, 3 dc in each sp **between** 3-dc groups across to next corner ch-1 sp; repeat from ★ 2 times **more**, 2 dc in same sp as first dc; join with slip st to first dc: 72 3-dc groups.

Neck Foundation Row: Slip st in first corner ch-1 sp, ch 3, 3 dc in same sp and in each of next 4 sps **between** 3-dc groups, ch 2, skip next 2 dc, sc in next 26 dc, ch 2, skip next 2 dc, 3 dc in each of next 4 sps **between** 3-dc groups, 4 dc in next corner ch-1 sp, leave remaining sts unworked; do **not** finish off: 32 dc and 26 sc.

SIZE 12 ONLY
Neck Foundation Row: With **right** side facing and larger size hook, join Black with slip st in top right corner ch-1 sp; ch 3, 3 dc in same sp and in each of next 3 sps **between** 3-dc groups, 3 dc in next joining and in next sp **between** 3-dc groups, ch 2, skip next 3 dc, sc in next 6 dc and in next sp, skip next joining, sc in next sp, sc in next 12 dc and in next sp, skip next joining, sc in next sp and in next 6 dc, ch 2, skip next 3 dc, 3 dc in next sp **between** 3-dc groups, 3 dc in next joining and in each of next 3 sps **between** 3-dc groups, 4 dc in next corner ch-1 sp; do **not** finish off: 38 dc and 28 sc.

RIGHT SHOULDER
Row 1: Ch 4 **(counts as first dc plus ch 1, now and throughout)**, turn; skip next 3 dc, 3 dc in each of next 4{4-4-5} sps **between** 3-dc groups, ch 1, dc in next ch-2 sp, leave remaining sts unworked: 4{4-4-5} 3-dc groups.

Row 2: Ch 3, turn; 3 dc in next ch-1 sp and in each of next 3{3-3-4} sps **between** 3-dc groups, 3 dc in next ch-1 sp, dc in last dc: 5{5-5-6} 3-dc groups.

Row 3: Ch 4, turn; skip next 3 dc, 3 dc in each of next 4{4-4-5} sps **between** 3-dc groups, ch 1, skip next 3 dc, dc in last dc: 4{4-4-5} 3-dc groups.

Row 4: Ch 3, turn; 3 dc in next ch-1 sp and in each of next 3{3-3-4} sps **between** 3-dc groups, 3 dc in next ch-1 sp, dc in last dc: 5{5-5-6} 3-dc groups.

Row 5: Turn; skip first dc, slip st in next 2 dc, sc in next dc, hdc in sp **before** next dc, (2 hdc, dc) in next sp **between** 3-dc groups, 3 dc in each of next 2{2-2-3} sps **between** 3-dc groups, ch 1, skip next 3 dc, dc in last dc: 15{15-15-18} sts.

Sizes 6, 8, and 10 only - Row 6: Ch 3, turn; 3 dc in next ch-1 sp and in next sp **between** 3-dc groups, skip next 3 dc, (dc, hdc, sc) in sp **before** next dc, skip next 3 sts, sc in sp **before** next hdc, slip st in next hdc, leave remaining 3 sts unworked; finish off: 12 sts.

Size 12 only - Row 6: Ch 3, turn; 3 dc in next ch-1 sp and in each of next 2 sps **between** 3-dc groups, skip next 3 dc, (dc, hdc, sc) in sp **before** next dc, skip next 3 sts, sc in sp **before** next hdc, slip st in next hdc, leave remaining 3 sts unworked; finish off: 15 sts.

LEFT SHOULDER

Row 1: With **wrong** side facing and larger size hook, skip next 21{23-26-28} sc from Right Shoulder and join Black with slip st in next ch-2 sp; ch 4, skip next 3 dc, 3 dc in each of next 4{4-4-5} sps **between** 3-dc groups, ch 1, skip next 3 dc, dc in last dc: 4{4-4-5} 3-dc groups.

Rows 2-4: Work same as Right Shoulder.

Row 5: Ch 4, turn; skip next 3 dc, 3 dc in each of next 2{2-2-3} sps **between** 3-dc groups, (dc, 2 hdc) in next sp **between** 3-dc groups, hdc in next sp **between** 3-dc groups, sc in next dc, leave remaining 3 dc unworked: 13{13-13-16} sts.

Sizes 6, 8, and 10 only - Row 6: Turn; skip first sc, slip st in next hdc, sc in sp **before** next hdc, skip next 3 sts, (sc, hdc, dc) in sp **before** next dc, 3 dc in next sp **between** 3-dc groups and in next ch-1 sp, dc in last dc; finish off: 12 sts.

Size 12 only - Row 6: Turn; skip first sc, slip st in next hdc, sc in sp **before** next hdc, skip next 3 sts, (sc, hdc, dc) in sp **before** next dc, 3 dc in each of next 2 sps **between** 3-dc groups and in next ch-1 sp, dc in last dc; finish off: 15 sts.

RIBBING
Foundation Row: With **right** side of bottom edge facing and larger size hook, join Black with sc in first corner ch-1 sp *(see Joining With Sc, page 205)*; work 64{66-72-78} sc evenly spaced across to next corner ch-1 sp, sc in corner ch-1 sp: 66{68-74-80} sc.

Change to smaller size hook.

Row 1: Ch 9{12-12-12}, sc in back ridge of second ch from hook *(Fig. 1, page 205)* and each ch across, slip st in first 2 sc on Foundation Row: 10{13-13-13} sts.

Row 2: Turn; skip first 2 slip sts, sc in Back Loop Only of each sc across *(Fig. 2, page 205)*: 8{11-11-11} sc.

Row 3: Ch 1, turn; sc in Back Loop Only of each sc across, slip st in **both** loops of next 2 sc on Foundation Row: 10{13-13-13} sts.

Repeat Rows 2 and 3 across, ending by working Row 2; finish off.

BACK
RIBBING
With Black and smaller size hook, ch 9{12-12-12}.

Row 1: Sc in back ridge of second ch from hook and each ch across: 8{11-11-11} sc.

Row 2: Ch 1, turn; sc in Back Loop Only of each sc across.

Repeat Row 2 until 33{34-37-40} ribs [66{68-74-80} rows] are complete; do **not** finish off.

BODY
Change to larger size hook.

Size 6 only - Row 1 (Right side): Ch 1, working in end of rows, 2 sc in first row, sc in each row across: 67 sc.

Note: Mark Row 1 as **right** side.

Sizes 8, 10, and 12 only - Row 1 (Right side): Ch 1, working in end of rows, 2 sc in first row, sc in each row across to last row, 2 sc in last row: {70-76-82} sc.

Note: Mark Row 1 as **right** side.

ALL SIZES
Row 2: Ch 3, turn; (skip next 2 sc, 3 dc in next sc) across to last 3 sc, skip next 2 sc, dc in last sc: 21{22-24-26} 3-dc groups.

Row 3: Ch 4, turn; skip next 3 dc, 3 dc in each sp **between** 3-dc groups across to last 4 dc, ch 1, skip next 3 dc, dc in last dc: 20{21-23-25} 3-dc groups.

Row 4: Ch 3, turn; 3 dc in next ch-1 sp and in each sp **between** 3-dc groups across to last ch-1 sp, 3 dc in last ch-1 sp, dc in last dc: 21{22-24-26} 3-dc groups.

Repeat Rows 3 and 4 for pattern until Back measures approximately 17 1/2{19-19 1/2-21 1/2}"/44.5{48.5-49.5-54.5} cm from bottom of Ribbing, ending by working Row 4; do **not** finish off: 21{22-24-26} 3-dc groups.

Instructions continued on page 130.

SHOULDERS

Row 1: Turn; skip first dc, slip st in next 2 dc, sc in next dc, hdc in sp **before** next dc, (2 hdc, dc) in next sp **between** 3-dc groups, 3 dc in each of next 16{17-19-21} sps **between** 3-dc groups, (dc, 2 hdc) in next sp **between** 3-dc groups, hdc in next sp **between** 3-dc groups, sc in next dc, leave remaining 3 dc unworked: 16{17-19-21} 3-dc groups.

Row 2: Turn; skip first sc, slip st in next hdc, sc in sp **before** next hdc, skip next 3 sts, (sc, hdc, dc) in sp **before** next dc, 3 dc in each of next 15{16-18-20} sps **between** 3-dc groups, skip next 3 dc, (dc, hdc, sc) in sp **before** next dc, skip next 3 sts, sc in sp **before** next hdc, slip st in next hdc, leave remaining 3 sts unworked; finish off: 55{58-64-70} sts.

SLEEVE (Make 2)
RIBBING

With Black and smaller size hook, ch 12{15-15-15}.

Row 1: Sc in back ridge of second ch from hook and each ch across: 11{14-14-14} sc.

Row 2: Ch 1, turn; sc in Back Loop Only of each sc across.

Repeat Row 2 until 18{19-21-21} ribs [36{38-42-42} rows] are complete; do **not** finish off.

BODY

Change to larger size hook.

Sizes 6, 10, and 12 only - Row 1 (Right side)**:** Ch 1, working in end of rows, 2 sc in first row, sc in each row across: 37{43-43} sc.

Note: Mark Row 1 as **right** side.

Size 8 only - Row 1 (Right side)**:** Ch 1, working in end of rows, 2 sc in first row, sc in each row across to last row, 2 sc in last row: 40 sc.

Note: Mark Row 1 as **right** side.

ALL SIZES

Row 2: Ch 3, turn; (skip next 2 sc, 3 dc in next sc) across to last 3 sc, skip next 2 sc, dc in last sc: 11{12-13-13} 3-dc groups.

Row 3: Ch 3, turn; 3 dc in sp **before** first 3-dc group and in each sp **between** 3-dc groups across, 3 dc in sp **before** last dc, dc in last dc: 12{13-14-14} 3-dc groups.

Rows 4 and 5: Ch 3, turn; skip next 3 dc, 3 dc in each sp **between** 3-dc groups across, 3 dc in sp **before** last dc, dc in last dc.

Row 6 (Increase row)**:** Ch 3, turn; 3 dc in sp **before** first 3-dc group and in each sp **between** 3-dc groups across, 3 dc in sp **before** last dc, dc in last dc: 13{14-15-15} 3-dc groups.

Rows 7 thru 24{27-30-33}: Repeat Rows 4-6, 6{7-8-9} times: 19{21-23-24} 3-dc groups.

Repeat Row 4 until Sleeve measures approximately 13{14$\frac{1}{2}$-16-17$\frac{1}{2}$}"/ 33{37-40.5-44.5} cm from bottom of Ribbing, ending by working a **wrong** side row; finish off.

FINISHING

Sew shoulder seams.

Sew each Sleeve to sweater, matching center of last row on Sleeve to shoulder seam and beginning approximately 6$\frac{1}{2}${7-7$\frac{1}{2}$-8}"/16.5{18-19-20.5} cm down from seam.

Sew each underarm and side in one continuous seam.

NECK RIBBING

Foundation Rnd: With **right** side facing and smaller size hook, join Black with sc in first dc from shoulder seam at Back neck edge; work 67{71-79-83} sc evenly spaced around entire neck edge; join with slip st to first sc: 68{72-80-84} sc.

Row 1: Ch 6{6-7-7}, sc in back ridge of second ch from hook and each ch across, slip st in first 2 sc on Foundation Rnd: 7{7-8-8} sts.

Row 2: Turn; skip first 2 slip sts, sc in Back Loop Only of each sc across: 5{5-6-6} sc.

Row 3: Ch 1, turn; sc in Back Loop Only of each sc across, slip st in **both** loops of next 2 sc on Foundation Rnd: 7{7-8-8} sts.

Repeat Rows 2 and 3 around, ending by working Row 2; finish off leaving a long end for sewing.

Sew Ribbing seam.

KIDS' CARDIGAN SETS

These colorful cardigans will brighten the gray days of winter while keeping children warm and toasty. The boys' and girls' sweaters both have matching caps for protecting little heads from the cold.

Instructions begin on page 132.

KIDS' CARDIGAN SETS
Shown on page 131.

◼◼◼◻ **INTERMEDIATE**

Finished Chest Measurements:
Size 1 - 23³/₄" (60.5 cm)
Size 2 - 26" (66 cm)
Size 4 - 28¹/₄" (72 cm)
Size 6 - 30¹/₂" (77.5 cm)

Size Note: Instructions are written for size 1 with sizes 2, 4, and 6 in braces { }. Instructions will be easier to read if you circle all numbers pertaining to your child's size. If only one number is given, it applies to all sizes. If a zero is given, it means to do nothing.

MATERIALS
Light/Worsted Weight Yarn
[5 ounces, 500 yards (140 grams, 457 meters) per skein]:
Girl's Set
Raspberry - 2{3-4-5} skeins
White - 1 skein
Boy's Set
Skipper Blue - 2{2-3-4} skeins
White - 1 skein
Crochet hook, size F (3.75 mm) **or** size needed for gauge
Yarn needle
Safety pin
¹/₂" Buttons - 6 (for Girl's set)
¹/₂" Buttons - 4 (for Boy's set)
Sewing needle and thread

GIRL'S CARDIGAN
GAUGE: In pattern, 8 sts = 2" (5 cm); 10 rows = 3¹/₂" (9 cm)

BODY
With Raspberry, ch 92{101-110-119}.

Row 1 (Right side): Sc in second ch from hook and in each ch across: 91{100-109-118} sc.

Note: Mark Row 1 as **right** side.

Row 2: Ch 3 **(counts as first dc, now and throughout)**, turn; dc in next sc and in each sc across.

Row 3: Ch 1, turn; sc in each dc across.

Row 4: Ch 3, turn; dc in next sc and in each sc across; finish off.

To work Front Post double crochet (abbreviated FPdc), YO, insert hook from **front** to **back** around post of sc indicated *(Fig. 4, page 205)*, YO and pull up a loop (3 loops on hook), (YO and draw through 2 loops on hook) twice.

To work Front Post treble crochet (abbreviated FPtr), YO twice, insert hook from **front** to **back** around post of dc indicated *(Fig. 4, page 205)*, YO and pull up a loop (4 loops on hook), (YO and draw through 2 loops on hook) 3 times.

Row 5: With **right** side facing, join White with sc in first dc *(see Joining With Sc, page 205)*; ch 2, skip next 2 dc, sc in next dc, ★ † work 2 FPdc around sc one row **below** next dc, skip dc behind FPdc, work FPtr around dc 2 rows **below** next dc, working **behind** FPtr, work 2 FPdc around sc one row **below** same dc, skip dc behind FPdc, sc in next dc †, (ch 2, skip next 2 dc, sc in next dc) twice; repeat from ★ 8{9-10-11} times **more**, then repeat from † to † once, ch 2, skip next 2 dc, sc in last dc; finish off: 40{44-48-52} FPdc, 10{11-12-13} FPtr, and 20{22-24-26} ch-2 sps.

Row 6: With **wrong** side facing, join Raspberry with sc in first sc; working **behind** ch-2, dc in next 2 skipped dc on Row 4, sc in next sc, ★ † skip next FPdc, insert hook in next skipped dc on Row 4 **and** next FPdc on Row 5, YO and pull up a loop, YO and draw through both loops on hook, skip next FPtr, insert hook in next skipped dc on Row 4 **and** next FPdc on Row 5, YO and pull up a loop, YO and draw through both loops on hook, skip next FPdc, sc in next sc †, (working **behind** ch-2, dc in next 2 skipped dc on Row 4, sc in next sc) twice; repeat from ★ 8{9-10-11} times **more**, then repeat from † to † once, working **behind** ch-2, dc in next 2 skipped dc on Row 4, sc in last sc; do **not** finish off: 91{100-109-118} sts.

Row 7: Ch 3, turn; dc in next dc and in each st across.

Row 8: Ch 1, turn; sc in each dc across.

Row 9: Ch 3, turn; dc in next sc and in each sc across; finish off.

Row 10: With **right** side facing, join White with sc in first dc; ch 3, skip next 3 dc, sc in next dc, ch 2, skip next 2 dc, sc in next dc, ★ † work 2 FPdc around sc one row **below** next dc, skip dc behind FPdc, work FPtr around dc 2 rows **below** next dc, working **behind** FPtr just made, work 2 FPdc around sc one row **below** same dc, skip dc behind FPdc, sc in next dc †, (ch 2, skip next 2 dc, sc in next dc) twice; repeat from ★ 7{8-9-10} times **more**, then repeat from † to † once, ch 2, skip next 2 dc, sc in next dc, ch 3, skip next 3 dc, sc in last 2 dc; finish off: 36{40-44-48} FPdc, 9{10-11-12} FPtr, and 20{22-24-26} sps.

Row 11: With **wrong** side facing, join Raspberry with sc in first sc; sc in next sc, working **behind** ch-3, dc in next 3 skipped dc on Row 9, sc in next sc, working **behind** ch-2, dc in next 2 skipped dc on Row 9, sc in next sc, ★ † skip next FPdc, insert hook in next skipped dc on Row 9 **and** next FPdc on Row 10, YO and pull up a loop, YO and draw through both loops on hook, skip next FPtr, insert hook in next skipped dc on Row 9 **and** next FPdc on Row 10, YO and pull up a loop, YO and draw through both loops on hook, skip next FPdc, sc in next sc †, (working **behind** ch-2, dc in next 2 skipped dc on Row 9, sc in next sc) twice; repeat from ★ 7{8-9-10} times **more**, then repeat from † to † once, working **behind** ch-2, dc in next 2 skipped dc on Row 9, sc in next sc, working **behind** ch-3, dc in next 3 skipped dc on Row 9, sc in last sc; do **not** finish off: 91{100-109-118} sts.

Row 12: Ch 3, turn; dc in next dc and in each st across.

Row 13: Ch 1, turn; sc in each dc across.

Row 14: Ch 3, turn; dc in next sc and in each sc across.

Repeat Rows 13 and 14 until Body measures approximately 7¼{8-8¾-9½}"/18.5{20.5-22-24} cm from beginning ch, ending by working Row 13; do **not** finish off.

RIGHT FRONT
Row 1: Ch 3, turn; dc in next 21{23-25-27} sc, leave remaining 69{76-83-90} sc unworked: 22{24-26-28} dc.

Row 2: Ch 1, turn; sc in each dc across.

Row 3: Ch 3, turn; dc in next sc and in each sc across.

Rows 4 thru 9{11-11-13}: Repeat Rows 2 and 3, 3{4-4-5} times; do **not** finish off.

NECK SHAPING
To sc decrease, pull up a loop in each of next 2 sts, YO and draw through all 3 loops on hook (**counts as one sc**).

Row 1 (Decrease row)**:** Ch 1, turn; sc in first 14{16-18-20} dc, sc decrease, leave remaining 6 dc unworked: 15{17-19-21} sc.

Row 2 (Decrease row)**:** Ch 2, turn; dc in next sc and in each sc across: 14{16-18-20} dc.

Row 3 (Decrease row)**:** Ch 1, turn; sc in each dc across to last 2 dc, sc decrease: 13{15-17-19} sc.

Rows 4 thru 5{5-7-7}: Repeat Rows 2 and 3, 1{1-2-2} time(s): 11{13-13-15} sc.

Finish off.

BACK
Row 1: With **right** side facing, skip next sc on last row of Body from Right Front and join Raspberry with slip st in next sc; ch 3, dc in next 44{49-54-59} sc, leave remaining 23{25-27-29} sc unworked: 45{50-55-60} dc.

Row 2: Ch 1, turn; sc in each dc across.

Row 3: Ch 3, turn; dc in next sc and in each sc across.

Rows 4 thru 14{16-18-20}: Repeat Rows 2 and 3, 5{6-7-8} times; then repeat Row 2 once **more**; finish off leaving a long end for sewing.

LEFT FRONT
Row 1: With **right** side facing, skip next sc on last row of Body from Back and join Raspberry with slip st in next sc; ch 3, dc in next sc and in each sc across: 22{24-26-28} dc.

Row 2: Ch 1, turn; sc in each dc across.

Row 3: Ch 3, turn; dc in next sc and in each sc across.

Rows 4 thru 9{11-11-13}: Repeat Rows 2 and 3, 3{4-4-5} times; do **not** finish off.

NECK SHAPING
Row 1 (Decrease row)**:** Turn; slip st in first 6 dc, ch 1, sc decrease, sc in each dc across: 15{17-19-21} sc.

To dc decrease (uses last 2 sc), ★ YO, insert hook in **next** sc, YO and pull up a loop, YO and draw through 2 loops on hook; repeat from ★ once **more**, YO and draw through all 3 loops on hook (**counts as one dc**).

Row 2 (Decrease row)**:** Ch 3, turn; dc in next sc and in each sc across to last 2 sc, dc decrease: 14{16-18-20} dc.

To work beginning sc decrease, pull up a loop in each of first 2 dc, YO and draw through all 3 loops on hook (**counts as one sc**).

Row 3 (Decrease row)**:** Ch 1, turn; work beginning sc decrease, sc in each dc across: 13{15-17-19} sc.

Rows 4 thru 5{5-7-7}: Repeat Rows 2 and 3, 1{1-2-2} time(s): 11{13-13-15} sc.

Finish off, leaving a long end for sewing.

SLEEVE (Make 2)
BODY
With Raspberry, ch 27{27-36-36}; being careful not to twist ch, join with slip st to form a ring.

Rnd 1 (Right side)**:** Ch 1, sc in each ch around; join with slip st to first sc: 27{27-36-36} sc.

Note: Mark Rnd 1 as **right** side.

Instructions continued on page 134.

Rnd 2: Ch 3, turn; dc in next sc and in each sc around; join with slip st to first dc.

Rnd 3: Ch 1, turn; sc in same st and in each dc around; join with slip st to first sc.

Rnd 4: Ch 3, turn; dc in next sc and in each sc around; join with slip st to first dc, finish off.

Rnd 5: With **right** side facing, join White with sc in same st as joining; ch 2, skip next 2 dc, sc in next dc, ★ † work 2 FPdc around sc one rnd **below** next dc, skip dc behind FPdc, work FPtr around dc 2 rnds **below** next dc, working **behind** FPtr just made, work 2 FPdc around sc one rnd **below** same dc, skip dc behind FPdc, sc in next dc †, (ch 2, skip next 2 dc, sc in next dc) twice; repeat from ★ 1{1-2-2} time(s) **more**, then repeat from † to † once, ch 2, skip last 2 dc; join with slip st to first sc, finish off: 12{12-16-16} FPdc, 3{3-4-4} FPtr, and 6{6-8-8} ch-2 sps.

Rnd 6: With **wrong** side facing, join Raspberry with sc in same st as joining; working **behind** ch-2, dc in next 2 skipped dc on Rnd 4, sc in next sc, ★ † skip next FPdc, insert hook in next skipped dc on Rnd 4 **and** next FPdc on Rnd 5, YO and pull up a loop, YO and draw through both loops on hook, skip next FPtr, insert hook in next skipped dc on Rnd 4 **and** next FPdc on Rnd 5, YO and pull up a loop, YO and draw through both loops on hook, skip next FPdc, sc in next sc †, (working **behind** ch-2, dc in next 2 skipped dc on Rnd 4, sc in next sc) twice; repeat from ★ 1{1-2-2} time(s) **more**, then repeat from † to † once, working **behind** ch-2, dc in last 2 skipped dc on Rnd 4; join with slip st to first sc, do **not** finish off: 27{27-36-36} sts.

Rnd 7: Ch 3, turn; dc in next dc and in each st around; join with slip to first dc.

Rnd 8: Ch 1, turn; sc in same st and in each dc around; join with slip to first sc.

Rnd 9: Ch 3, turn; dc in next 4 sc, place marker around last dc made for st placement, dc in next sc and in each sc around; join with slip to first dc, finish off.

Rnd 10: With **right** side facing, join White with sc in marked dc; ch 2, skip next 2 dc, sc in next dc, ★ † work 2 FPdc around sc one rnd **below** next dc, skip dc behind FPdc, work FPtr around dc 2 rnds **below** next dc, working **behind** FPtr just made, work 2 FPdc around sc one rnd **below** same dc, skip dc behind FPdc, sc in next dc †, (ch 2, skip next 2 dc, sc in next dc) twice; repeat from ★ 1{1-2-2} time(s) **more**, then repeat from † to † once, ch 2, skip last 2 dc; join with slip to first sc, finish off: 12{12-16-16} FPdc, 3{3-4-4} FPtr, and 6{6-8-8} ch-2 sps.

Rnd 11: With **wrong** side facing, join Raspberry with sc in same st as joining; working **behind** ch-2, dc in next 2 skipped dc on Rnd 9, sc in next sc, ★ † skip next FPdc, insert hook in next skipped dc on Rnd 9 **and** next FPdc on Rnd 10, YO and pull up a loop, YO and draw through both loops on hook, skip next FPtr, insert hook in next skipped dc on Rnd 9 **and** next FPdc on Rnd 10, YO and pull up a loop, YO and draw through both loops on hook, skip next FPdc, sc in next sc †, (working **behind** ch-2, dc in next 2 skipped dc on Rnd 9, sc in next sc) twice; repeat from ★ 1{1-2-2} time(s) **more**, then repeat from † to † once, working **behind** ch-2, dc in last 2 skipped dc on Rnd 9; join with slip to first sc, do **not** finish off: 27{27-36-36} sts.

Rnd 12 (Increase rnd)**:** Ch 3, turn; dc in same st and in each st around to last st, 2 dc in last st; join with slip st to first dc: 29{29-38-38} dc.

Rnd 13 (Increase rnd)**:** Ch 1, turn; 2 sc in same st, sc in each dc around to last dc, 2 sc in last dc; join with slip st to first sc: 31{31-40-40} sc.

Rnds 14-16: Repeat Rnds 12 and 13 once, then repeat Rnd 12 once **more**: 37{37-46-46} dc.

Rnd 17: Ch 1, turn; sc in same st and in each dc around; join with slip st to first sc.

Rnd 18 (Increase rnd)**:** Ch 3, turn; dc in same st and in each sc around to last sc, 2 dc in last sc; join with slip st to first dc, do **not** finish off: 39{39-48-48} dc.

SIZE 1 ONLY
Rnd 19: Ch 1, turn; sc in same st and in each dc around; join with slip to first sc.

Rnd 20: Ch 3, turn; dc in next sc and in each sc around; join with slip st to first dc.

Rnds 21 and 22: Repeat Rnds 19 and 20.

Finish off, leaving a long end for sewing.

SIZES 2, 4, AND 6 ONLY
Rnds 19 thru {22-20-26}: Repeat Rnds 17 and 18, {2-1-4} time(s): {43-50-56} dc.

Rnd {23-21-27}: Ch 1, turn; sc in same st and in each dc around; join with slip st to first sc.

Rnd {24-22-28}: Ch 3, turn; dc in next sc and in each sc around; join with slip st to first dc.

SIZE 2 ONLY
Finish off, leaving a long end for sewing.

SIZES 4 AND 6 ONLY
Rnds {23-29} thru {26-30}: Repeat Rnds {21-27} and {22-28}, {2-1} time(s).

Finish off, leaving a long end for sewing.

EDGING - ALL SIZES
Rnd 1: With **right** side facing and working in free loops of beginning ch **(Fig. 3b, page 205)**, join Raspberry with sc in any ch; sc decrease, (sc in next ch, sc decrease) around; join with slip st to first sc: 18{18-24-24} sc.

Rnds 2 and 3: Ch 1, sc in same st and in each sc around; join with slip st to first sc.

Rnd 4: Ch 2, hdc in same st, skip next sc, ★ (slip st, ch 2, hdc) in next sc, skip next sc; repeat from ★ around; join with slip st to same st as joining, finish off.

FINISHING
Sew shoulder seams.

Sew each Sleeve to Cardigan, matching center of last round on Sleeve to shoulder seam.

BODY EDGING
Rnd 1: With **right** side facing, join Raspberry with sc in sc at center of Back neck edge; sc evenly around entire Cardigan working 3 sc in each corner and being careful to space sc so Edging will lie flat and making sure to have an even number of sc; join with slip st to first sc.

Rnd 2: Ch 1, sc in same st and in each sc around working 3 sc in center sc of each corner 3-sc group; join with slip st to first sc, place loop from hook onto safety pin to keep piece from unraveling while placing buttonhole markers.

With **right** side of Rnd 2 on Right Front facing, place a marker around sc 1/2" (12 mm) from bottom edge for first buttonhole placement; place another marker around sc 1/4" (7 mm) down from neck edge for sixth buttonhole placement. Place four additional buttonhole markers around sc evenly spaced between first and sixth markers.

Rnd 3 (Buttonhole rnd): Place loop from safety pin onto hook; with **right** side facing, ch 1, sc in same st, ★ sc in each sc across to center sc of next corner 3-sc group, 3 sc in center sc; repeat from ★ 2 times **more**, † sc in each sc across to next marker, ch 2, skip marked sc and next sc **(buttonhole made)** †, repeat from † to † 5 times **more**, sc in each sc across to center sc of next corner 3-sc group, 3 sc in center sc, sc in each sc across; join with slip st to first sc.

Rnd 4: Ch 1, sc in same st and in each st around working 3 sc in center sc of each corner 3-sc group; join with slip st to first sc.

Rnd 5: Ch 2, hdc in same st, skip next sc, ★ (slip st, ch 2, hdc) in next sc, skip next sc; repeat from ★ around; join with slip st to same st as joining, finish off.

Sew buttons to Cardigan.

GIRL'S CAP
CROWN
Rnd 1 (Right side): With Raspberry, ch 4, 9{11-13-13} dc in fourth ch from hook **(3 skipped chs count as first dc)**; join with slip st to first dc: 10{12-14-14} dc.

Note: Mark Rnd 1 as **right** side.

Rnd 2: Ch 1, turn; 2 sc in same st and in each dc around; join with slip st to first sc: 20{24-28-28} sc.

Rnd 3: Ch 3 **(counts as first dc, now and throughout)**, turn; dc in next 3{4-5-5} sc, 2 dc in next sc, ★ dc in next 4{5-6-6} sc, 2 dc in next sc; repeat from ★ around; join with slip st to first dc: 24{28-32-32} dc.

Rnd 4: Ch 1, turn; 2 sc in same st, sc in next dc, (2 sc in next dc, sc in next dc) around; join with slip st to first sc: 36{42-48-48} sc.

Rnd 5: Ch 3, turn; dc in next sc and in each sc around; join with slip st to first dc.

Rnd 6: Ch 1, turn; 2 sc in same st, sc in next dc, (2 sc in next dc, sc in next dc) around; join with slip st to first sc: 54{63-72-72} sc.

Rnd 7: Ch 3, turn; dc in next sc and in each sc around; join with slip st to first dc.

Instructions continued on page 136.

Rnd 8: Ch 1, turn; 2 sc in same st, sc in next 5{6-7-7} dc, ★ 2 sc in next dc, sc in next 5{6-7-7} dc; repeat from ★ around; join with slip st to first sc: 63{72-81-81} sc.

Rnd 9: Ch 3, turn; dc in next sc and in each sc around; join with slip st to first dc.

Rnd 10: Ch 1, turn; sc in same st and in each dc around; join with slip st to first sc.

Rnds 11 thru 19{21-23-23}: Repeat Rnds 9 and 10, 4{5-6-6} times; then repeat Rnd 9 once **more**; do **not** finish off.

BRIM

Rnd 1: Ch 1, turn; sc in same st, sc in Back Loop Only of each dc around *(Fig. 2, page 205)*; join with slip st to **both** loops of first sc: 63{72-81-81} sc.

Rnd 2: Ch 3, turn; dc in both loops of next sc and each sc around; join with slip st to first dc.

Rnd 3: Ch 1, turn; sc in same st and in each dc around; join with slip st to first sc.

Rnd 4: Ch 3, turn; dc in next sc and in each sc around; join with slip st to first sc, finish off.

Rnd 5: With **wrong** side facing, join White with sc in same st as joining *(see Joining With Sc, page 205)*; ch 2, skip next 2 dc, sc in next dc, ★ † work 2 FPdc around sc one rnd **below** next dc, skip dc behind FPdc, work FPtr around dc 2 rnds **below** next dc, working **behind** FPtr just made, work 2 FPdc around sc one rnd **below** same dc, skip dc behind FPdc, sc in next dc †, (ch 2, skip next 2 dc, sc in next dc) twice; repeat from ★ 5{6-7-7} times **more**, then repeat from † to † once, ch 2, skip last 2 dc; join with slip st to first sc, finish off: 28{32-36-36} FPdc, 7{8-9-9} FPtr, and 14{16-18-18} ch-2 sps.

Rnd 6: With **right** side facing, join Raspberry with sc in same st as joining; working **behind** ch-2, dc in next 2 skipped dc on Rnd 4, sc in next sc, ★ † skip next FPdc, insert hook in next skipped dc on Rnd 4 **and** next FPdc on Rnd 5, YO and pull up a loop, YO and draw through both loops on hook, skip next FPtr, insert hook in next skipped dc on Rnd 4 **and** next FPdc on Rnd 5, YO and pull up a loop, YO and draw through both loops on hook, skip next FPdc, sc in next sc †, (working **behind** ch-2, dc in next 2 skipped dc on Rnd 4, sc in next sc) twice; repeat from ★ 5{6-7-7} times **more**, then repeat from † to † once, working **behind** ch-2, dc in last 2 skipped dc on Rnd 4; join with slip st to first sc, do **not** finish off: 63{72-81-81} sts.

Rnd 7: Ch 1, turn; sc in same st, sc decrease 1{0-1-1} time(s), sc in each st around; join with slip st to first sc: 62{72-80-80} sc.

Rnd 8: Ch 2, hdc in same st, skip next sc, ★ (slip st, ch 2, hdc) in next sc, skip next sc; repeat from ★ around; join with slip st to same st as joining, finish off.

Turn Brim up.

Trim: With **right** side facing, top toward you, and working in free loops of Rnd 19{21-23-23} of Crown *(Fig. 3a, page 205)*, join Raspberry with slip st in any dc; ch 2, hdc in same st, skip next 0{1-0-0} dc, ★ (slip st, ch 2, hdc) in next dc, skip next dc; repeat from ★ around; join with slip st to joining slip st, finish off.

With Raspberry, make pom-pom *(Figs. 10a-c, page 207)*; then sew pom-pom to top of Cap.

BOY'S CARDIGAN
GAUGE: In pattern,
8 dc and 5 rows = 2" (5 cm)

BODY
With Skipper Blue, ch 93{102-111-120}.

Row 1 (Right side)**:** Dc in fourth ch from hook **(3 skipped chs count as first dc)** and in each ch across: 91{100-109-118} dc.

Note: Mark Row 1 as **right** side.

Rows 2 and 3: Ch 3 **(counts as first dc, now and throughout)**, turn; dc in next dc and in each dc across.

Finish off.

To work treble crochet (abbreviated tr), YO twice, insert hook in dc indicated, YO and pull up a loop (4 loops on hook, (YO and draw through 2 loops on hook) 3 times. Push tr to **right** side of work.

Row 4: With **wrong** side facing, join White with sc in first dc *(see Joining With Sc, page 205)*; (sc, tr) in next dc and in each dc across to last 2 dc, sc in last 2 dc; finish off: 91{100-109-118} sc and 88{97-106-115} tr.

Row 5: With **right** side facing, join Skipper Blue with slip st in first sc; ch 3, dc in next sc, (skip next tr, dc in next sc) across to last 3 sts, skip next tr, dc in last 2 sc; do **not** finish off: 91{100-109-118} dc.

Rows 6 and 7: Ch 3, turn; dc in next dc and in each dc across.

Finish off.

Rows 8 thru 16{20-24-24}: Repeat Rows 4-7, 2{3-4-4} times; then repeat Row 4 once **more**: 91{100-109-118} sc and 88{97-106-115} tr.

RIGHT FRONT

Row 1: With **right** side facing, join Skipper Blue with slip st in first sc; ch 2, dc in next sc, (skip next tr, dc in next sc) 20{22-24-26} times, leave remaining 137{151-165-179} sts unworked: 21{23-25-27} dc.

To decrease (uses last 2 dc), ★ YO, insert hook in **next** dc, YO and pull up a loop, YO and draw through 2 loops on hook; repeat from ★ once **more**, YO and draw through all 3 loops on hook **(counts as one dc).**

Row 2 (Decrease row): Ch 3, turn; dc in next dc and in each dc across to last 2 dc, decrease: 20{22-24-26} dc.

Row 3 (Decrease row): Ch 2, turn; dc in next dc and in each dc across; finish off: 19{21-23-25} dc.

Row 4: With **wrong** side facing, join White with sc in first dc; (sc, tr) in next dc and in each dc across to last 2 dc, sc in last 2 dc; finish off: 19{21-23-25} sc and 16{18-20-22} tr.

Row 5 (Decrease row): With **right** side facing, join Skipper Blue with slip st in first sc; ch 2, dc in next sc, (skip next tr, dc in next sc) across to last 3 sts, skip next tr, dc in last 2 sc; do **not** finish off: 18{20-22-24} dc.

Rows 6 thru 13{15-15-17}: Repeat Rows 2-5, 2{2-2-3} times; then repeat Rows 2 and 3, 0{1-1-0} time(s) **more**; finish off leaving a long end for sewing: 12{12-14-15} dc.

BACK

Row 1: With **right** side facing, skip next 3 sts on last row of Body from Right Front and join Skipper Blue with slip st in next sc; ch 3, (skip next tr, dc in next sc) 44{49-54-59} times, leave remaining 45{49-53-57} sts unworked: 45{50-55-60} dc.

Rows 2 and 3: Ch 3, turn; dc in next dc and in each dc across.

Finish off.

Row 4: With **wrong** side facing, join White with sc in first dc; (sc, tr) in next dc and in each dc across to last 2 dc, sc in last 2 dc; finish off: 45{50-55-60} sc and 42{47-52-57} tr.

Row 5: With **right** side facing, join Skipper Blue with slip st in first sc; ch 3, dc in next sc, (skip next tr, dc in next sc) across to last 3 sts, skip next tr, dc in last 2 sc; do **not** finish off: 45{50-55-60} dc.

Rows 6 thru 13{15-15-17}: Repeat Rows 2-5, 2{2-2-3} times; then repeat Rows 2 and 3, 0{1-1-0} time(s) **more**; finish off leaving a long end for sewing.

LEFT FRONT

Row 1: With **right** side facing, skip next 3 sts on last row of Body from Back and join Skipper Blue with slip st in next sc; ch 3, (skip next tr, dc in next sc) across to last 3 sts, skip next tr, decrease: 21{23-25-27} dc.

Row 2 (Decrease row): Ch 2, turn; dc in next dc and in each dc across: 20{22-24-26} dc.

Row 3 (Decrease row): Ch 3, turn; dc in next dc and in each dc across to last 2 dc, decrease; finish off: 19{21-23-25} dc.

Row 4: With **wrong** side facing, join White with sc in first dc; sc in next dc, (tr, sc) in next dc and in each dc across to last dc, sc in last dc; finish off: 19{21-23-25} sc and 16{18-20-22} tr.

Row 5 (Decrease row): With **right** side facing, join Skipper Blue with slip st in first sc; ch 3, dc in next sc, (skip next tr, dc in next sc) across to last 3 sts, skip next tr, decrease; do **not** finish off: 18{20-22-24} dc.

Rows 6 thru 13{15-15-17}: Repeat Rows 2-5, 2{2-2-3} times; then repeat Rows 2 and 3, 0{1-1-0} time(s) **more**; finish off: 12{12-14-15} dc.

Sew shoulder seams.

SLEEVE
BODY

Rnd 1: With **right** side facing, join Skipper Blue with slip st in sc at underarm; ch 3, skip next tr, dc in same st as first dc on Row 1 of Back **or** Left Front on Body; work 19{22-22-24} dc evenly spaced across end of rows to shoulder seam, dc in shoulder seam; work 19{22-22-24} dc evenly spaced across end of rows, dc in same st as last dc on Row 1 of Right Front **or** Back on Body; join with slip st to first dc: 42{48-48-52} dc.

Rnds 2 and 3 (Decrease rnds): Ch 2, turn; dc in next dc and in each dc around to last 2 dc, decrease; join with slip st to first dc: 38{44-44-48} dc.

Rnd 4: Ch 3, turn; dc in next dc and in each dc around; join with slip st to first dc, do **not** finish off.

Instructions continued on page 138.

SIZES 1 AND 2 ONLY

Rnds 5 thru 13{10}: Repeat Rnds 2-4, 3{2} times: 26{36} dc.

SIZES 2, 4 AND 6 ONLY

Rnds {11-5-5} thru {17-17-17}: Repeat Rnds 3 and 4, {3-6-6} times; then repeat Rnd 3 once **more**: {28-30-34} dc.

ALL SIZES

Rnds 14{18-18-18} thru 19{21-25-27}: Ch 3, turn; dc in next dc and in each dc around; join with slip st to first dc, do **not** finish off.

EDGING

Rnd 1: Ch 1, do **not** turn; sc in same st and in each dc around; join with slip st to first sc.

Rnds 2 and 3: Ch 1, sc in same st and in each sc around; join with slip st to first sc.

To work Front Post double crochet (*abbreviated FPdc*), YO, insert hook from **front** to **back** around post of sc indicated *(Fig. 4, page 205)*, YO and pull up a loop (3 loops on hook), (YO and draw through 2 loops on hook) twice. Skip sc behind FPdc.

Rnd 4: Ch 1, sc in same st, work FPdc around sc 2 rnds **below** next sc, ★ sc in next sc, work FPdc around sc 2 rnds **below** next sc; repeat from ★ around; join with slip st to first sc, finish off.

Repeat for second Sleeve.

BODY EDGING

Rnd 1: With **right** side facing, join Skipper Blue with sc in dc at center of Back neck edge; being careful to space sc so Edging will lie flat, sc evenly across to beginning ch; working in free loops of beginning ch *(Fig. 3b, page 205)*, 3 sc in first ch, 2 sc in 0{1-0-1} ch(s), sc in next 87{97-107-115} chs, 3 sc in next ch; sc evenly across; join with slip st to first sc.

Rnd 2: Ch 1, sc in same st and in each sc around working 3 sc in center sc of each corner 3-sc group; join with slip st to first sc, place loop from hook onto safety pin to keep piece from unraveling while placing buttonhole markers.

With **right** side of Rnd 2 on Left Front facing, place a marker around sc ¹/₂" (12 mm) from bottom edge for first buttonhole placement; place another marker around sc even with underarm for fourth buttonhole placement. Place two additional buttonhole markers around sc evenly spaced between first and fourth markers.

Rnd 3 (Buttonhole rnd)**:** Place loop from safety pin onto hook; with **right** side facing, ch 1, sc in same st, ★ sc in each sc across to next marker, ch 2, skip marked sc and next sc; repeat from ★ 3 times **more**, † sc in each sc across to center sc of next corner 3-sc group, 3 sc in center sc †, repeat from † to † once **more**, sc in each sc across; join with slip st to first sc.

Rnd 4: Ch 1, sc in same st and in each st across to center sc of next corner 3-sc group, 3 sc in center sc, sc in next sc, ★ work FPdc around sc 2 rnds **below** next sc, sc in next sc; repeat from ★ across to center sc of next corner 3-sc group, 3 sc in center sc, sc in each sc across; join with slip st to first sc, finish off.

Sew buttons to Cardigan.

BOY'S CAP
CROWN

Rnd 1 (Right side)**:** With Skipper Blue, ch 4, 15{17-19-19} dc in fourth ch from hook **(3 skipped chs count as first dc)**; join with slip st to first dc, finish off: 16{18-20-20} dc.

Note: Mark Rnd 1 as **right** side.

Rnd 2: With **wrong** side facing, join White with sc in same st as joining *(see Joining With Sc, page 205)*; tr in same st, (sc, tr) in next dc and in each dc around; join with slip st to first sc, finish off: 32{36-40-40} sts.

Rnd 3: With **right** side facing, join Skipper Blue with slip st in same st as joining; ch 3, dc in same st, skip next tr, (2 dc in next sc, skip next tr) around; join with slip st to first dc, do **not** finish off: 32{36-40-40} dc.

Rnd 4: Ch 3, dc in same st and in next dc, (2 dc in next dc, dc in next dc) around; join with slip st to first dc: 48{54-60-60} dc.

Rnd 5: Ch 3, dc in next dc and in each dc around; join with slip st to first dc, finish off.

Rnd 6: With **wrong** side facing, join White with sc in same st as joining; tr in same st, (sc, tr) in next dc and in each dc around; join with slip st to first sc, finish off: 96{108-120-120} sts.

Rnd 7: With **right** side facing, join Skipper Blue with slip st in same st as joining; ch 3, skip next tr, (dc in next sc, skip next tr) 4 times, 2 dc in next sc, skip next tr, ★ (dc in next sc, skip next tr) 5 times, 2 dc in next sc, skip next tr; repeat from ★ around; join with slip st to first dc, do **not** finish off: 56{63-70-70} dc.

Rnds 8 and 9: Ch 3, dc in next dc and in each dc around; join with slip st to first dc.

Finish off.

Rnd 10: With **wrong** side facing, join White with sc in same st as joining; tr in same st, (sc, tr) in next dc and in each dc around; join with slip st to first sc, finish off: 112{126-140-140} sts.

Rnd 11: With **right** side facing, join Skipper Blue with slip st in same st as joining; ch 3, skip next tr, (dc in next sc, skip next tr) 5 times, 2 dc in next sc, skip next tr, ★ (dc in next sc, skip next tr) 6 times, 2 dc in next sc, skip next tr; repeat from ★ around; join with slip st to first dc, do **not** finish off: 64{72-80-80} dc.

Rnds 12-14: Repeat Rnds 8-10: 128{144-160-160} sts.

Rnd 15: With **right** side facing, join Skipper Blue with slip st in same st as joining; ch 3, skip next tr, (dc in next sc, skip next tr) around; join with slip st to first dc, do **not** finish off: 64{72-80-80} dc.

SIZE 2 ONLY
Rnd 16: Ch 3, dc in next dc and in each dc around; join with slip st to first dc, do **not** finish off.

SIZES 4 AND 6 ONLY
Rnds 16 and 17: Ch 3, dc in next dc and in each dc around; join with slip st to first dc, do **not** finish off.

BAND - ALL SIZES
Rnd 1: Ch 1, sc in same st and in each dc around; join with slip st to first sc: 64{72-80-80} sc.

Rnds 2 and 3: Ch 1, sc in same st and in each sc around; join with slip st to first sc.

Rnd 4: Ch 1, sc in same st, work FPdc around sc 2 rnds **below** next sc, ★ sc in next sc, work FPdc around sc 2 rnds **below** next sc; repeat from ★ around; join with slip st to first sc, finish off.

EAR FLAP (Make 2)
Rnd 1 (Right side)**:** With Skipper Blue, ch 2, 6 sc in second ch from hook; do **not** join, place marker *(see Markers, page 205)*.

Rnd 2: 2 Sc in each sc around: 12 sc.

Rnd 3: (2 Sc in each of next 2 sc, sc in next 4 sc) twice: 16 sc.

Rnd 4: Sc in next sc, 2 sc in each of next 2 sc, sc in next 6 sc, 2 sc in each of next 2 sc, sc in next 5 sc: 20 sc.

Rnd 5: Sc in next 2 sc, 2 sc in each of next 2 sc, sc in next 8 sc, 2 sc in each of next 2 sc, sc in next 6 sc; do **not** finish off: 24 sc.

SIZES 4 AND 6 ONLY
Rnd 6: Sc in next 3 sc, 2 sc in each of next 2 sc, sc in next 10 sc, 2 sc in each of next 2 sc, sc in next 7 sc; do **not** finish off: 28 sc.

ALL SIZES
Rnds 6{6-7-7} thru 11{11-12-12}: Sc in each sc around.

Rnd 12{12-13-13}: Sc in each sc around; slip st in next sc, finish off leaving a long end for sewing.

FINISHING
Fold Cap in half with joining at fold and to the back, place marker around stitch on last round 1³/₄{2-2¹/₄-2³/₄}"/4.5{5-5.75-7} cm from **each** side of joining. Flatten one Ear Flap, working through **all** thicknesses, sew Ear Flap to Cap, beginning in marked stitch and working toward front of Cap.

Repeat for second Ear Flap.

Tie: Cut a 3¹/₂ yard (3.25 meter) length of Skipper Blue and fold strand in half; insert hook in bottom point on one Ear Flap and pull folded end through stitch. Using both strands held together, make a chain; finish off.

Repeat for second Tie.

With Skipper Blue, make pom-pom *(Figs. 10a-c, page 207)*; then sew pom-pom to top of Cap.

Designs by Jennine Korejko.

KIDS' COZY MITTEN SET

Snuggled up in our scarf and mittens, boys and girls can have fun building a snowman without becoming one! The lightweight coordinates can be crocheted in a flurry — the same pattern creates your choice of colorful stripes or frosty solids.

■■□□ **EASY**

MATERIALS
Light/Worsted Weight Yarn [5 ounces, 500 yards (140 grarms, 457 meters) per skein]:
Solid Set
Off-White - 3 skeins
Striped Set
Off-White - 2 skeins
Royal - 2 skeins
Crochet hook, size G (4 mm) **or** size needed for gauge
Yarn needle

GAUGE: In pattern,
8 sts and 7 rows = 2" (5 cm)

MITTENS

Size	Palm Circumference	Hand Length
Small	5"	3³/₄"
Medium	6"	4¹/₂"
Large	6"	5³/₄"

Size Note: Instructions are written for size Small with sizes Medium and Large in braces { }. Instructions will be easier to read if you circle all the numbers pertaining to your child's size. If only one number is given, it applies to all sizes.

Note: For striped Mittens, follow Stripe Sequence below, changing colors in joining slip st on rounds or in last st on rows *(Figs. 7a-c, page 206)*.

Stripe Sequence: ★ Work 2 rnds/rows with Royal, 2 rnds/rows with Off-White; repeat from ★ 2{3-4} times **more.**

HAND
With Off-White for solid Mitten or Royal for striped Mitten, ch 6.

Rnd 1 (Right side)**:** Sc in second ch from hook, dc in next ch, sc in next ch, dc in next ch, (sc, dc, sc) in last ch; working in free loops of beginning ch *(Fig. 3b, page 205)*, dc in next ch, sc in next ch, dc in next ch, (sc, dc) in same ch as first sc; join with slip st to first sc: 12 sts.

Note: Mark Rnd 1 as **right** side.

Rnd 2: Ch 1, turn; sc in same st, (dc, sc, dc) in next dc, sc in next sc, (dc in next dc, sc in next sc) twice, (dc, sc, dc) in next dc, (sc in next sc, dc in next dc) twice; join with slip st to first sc: 16 sts.

Rnd 3: Ch 1, turn; sc in same st, dc in next dc, (sc in next sc, dc in next dc) twice, (sc, dc, sc) in next sc, dc in next dc, (sc in next sc, dc in next dc) 3 times, (sc, dc, sc) in next sc, dc in last dc; join with slip st to first sc, do **not** finish off: 20 sts.

SIZES MEDIUM AND LARGE ONLY
Rnd 4: Ch 1, turn; sc in same st, dc in next dc, sc in next sc, (dc, sc, dc) in next dc, sc in next sc, (dc in next dc, sc in next sc) 4 times, (dc, sc, dc) in next dc, (sc in next sc, dc in next dc) 3 times; join with slip st to first sc; do **not** finish off: 24 sts.

ALL SIZES
Rnds 4{5-5} thru 6{10-14}: Ch 1, turn; sc in same st, dc in next dc, (sc in next sc, dc in next dc) around; join with slip st to first sc.

Finish off.

SIZE SMALL ONLY
Row 1: With **right** side facing, join Off-White with sc in first sc to right of joining *(see Joining With Sc, page 205)*; (dc in next dc, sc in next sc) 9 times, leave remaining dc unworked: 19 sts.

Rows 2-4: Ch 1, turn; sc in first sc, (dc in next dc, sc in next sc) across.

Note: Begin working in rounds.

Rnd 1 (Joining rnd)**:** Ch 1, turn; sc in first sc, (dc in next dc, sc in next sc) across, ch 1; join with slip st to first sc: 19 sts and one ch.

Rnd 2: Ch 1, turn; sc in same st, dc in next ch, (sc in next sc, dc in next dc) around; join with slip st to first sc, do **not** finish off: 20 sts.

SIZES MEDIUM AND LARGE ONLY
Row 1: With **right** side facing, join Off-White with slip st in second dc to right of joining; ch 3 **(counts as first dc, now and throughout)**, (sc in next sc, dc in next dc) 11 times, leave remaining sc unworked: 23 sts.

Rows 2-4: Ch 3, turn; (sc in next sc, dc in next dc) across.

Instructions continued on page 142.

Continued from page 140.

Note: Begin working in rounds.

Rnd 1 (Joining rnd)**:** Ch 3, turn; (sc in next sc, dc in next dc) across, ch 1; join with slip st to first dc: 23 sts and one ch.

Rnd 2: Ch 3, turn; sc in next ch, (dc in next dc, sc in next sc) around; join with slip st to first dc, do **not** finish off: 24 sts.

RIBBING - ALL SIZES
To decrease, pull up a loop in each of next 2 sts, YO and draw through all 3 loops on hook **(counts as one sc)**.

Foundation Rnd: Ch 1, turn; sc in same st and in next 7{9-9} sts, decrease, sc in next 8{10-10} sts, decrease; join with slip st to first sc: 18{22-22} sc.

Row 1: Ch 9{11-11}, sc in back ridge of second ch from hook **(Fig. 1, page 205)** and each ch across, slip st in first 2 sc on Foundation Rnd: 10{12-12} sts.

Row 2: Ch 1, turn; skip first 2 slip sts, sc in Back Loop Only of each sc across **(Fig. 2, page 205)**: 8{10-10} sc.

Row 3: Ch 1, turn; sc in Back Loop Only of each sc across, slip st in **both** loops of next 2 sc on Foundation Rnd: 10{12-12} sts.

Rows 4 thru 18{22-22}: Repeat Rows 2 and 3, 7{9-9} times; then repeat Row 2 once **more**.

Finish off, leaving a long end for sewing.

Sew Ribbing seam.

THUMB
Rnd 1: With **right** side facing, join Off-White for solid Mitten or Royal for striped Mitten with sc in skipped st on Rnd 6{10-14} of Hand; working in end of rows, sc in next 2 rows, hdc in next row, 2 dc in each of next 2 rows; dc in free loops of next ch; working in end of rows, 2 dc in each of next 2 rows, hdc in next row, sc in last 2 rows; join with slip st to first sc: 16 sts.

To work beginning decrease, pull up a loop in same st and in next sc, YO and draw through all 3 loops on hook **(counts as one sc)**.

Rnd 2: Ch 1, turn; work beginning decrease, decrease, dc in next dc, (sc in next dc, dc in next dc) 4 times, sc in next hdc, decrease; join with slip st to first sc: 13 sts.

Rnd 3: Ch 1, turn; work beginning decrease, decrease, sc in next sc, (dc in next dc, sc in next sc) 3 times, decrease; join with slip st to first sc: 10 sts.

Rnd 4: Ch 1, turn; sc in same st, dc in next st, (sc in next sc, dc in next st) around; join with slip st to first sc.

Repeat Rnd 4 until Thumb measures approximately 1½{1¾-2}"/3.75{4.5-5} cm **or** desired length; do **not** finish off.

Last Rnd: Ch 1, turn; work beginning decrease, decrease around; join with slip st to first sc, finish off leaving a long end for sewing.

Thread needle with long end and weave through stitches on last round; gather tightly and secure end.

SCARF
Finished Size:
5¼" x 32" (13.5 cm x 81.5 cm)

Note #1: Each row is worked across length of Scarf.

Note #2: For striped Scarf, follow Stripe Sequence below, changing colors in last sc on designated rows **(Fig. 7a, page 206)**.

Stripe Sequence: Work 2 rows with Royal, ★ 2 rows with Off-White, 2 rows with Royal; repeat from ★ throughout.

With Off-White for solid Scarf or Royal for striped Scarf, ch 128.

Row 1 (Right side)**:** Sc in second ch from hook, (dc in next ch, sc in next ch) across: 127 sts.

Note: Mark Row 1 as **right** side.

Row 2: Ch 1, turn; sc in first sc, (dc in next dc, sc in next sc) across.

Repeat Row 2 until Scarf measures approximately 5¼" (13.5 cm) from beginning ch; finish off.

Add fringe across short edges of Scarf **(Figs. 12a & b, page 207)**.

"DOGGONE" CUTE SWEATER

This cozy canine sweater will give your "best friend" an extra winter coat! The pooch pullover can be made in four sizes to simply slip over the head and button across the chest.

Instructions begin on page 144.

"DOGGONE" CUTE SWEATER
Shown on page 143.

■■□□ **EASY**

Finished Size:
11{16½-22-25}"/28{42-56-63.5} cm from neck to base of tail

Size Note: Instructions are written for size Small with sizes Medium, Large, and X-Large in braces { }. Instructions will be easier to read if you circle all the numbers pertaining to your dog's size. If only one number is given, it applies to all sizes.

MATERIALS
Medium/Worsted Weight Yarn
  [6 ounces, 348 yards
  (170 grams, 318 meters)
  per skein]: 1{1-2-2} skein(s)
Crochet hook, size J (6 mm) **or** size
  needed for gauge
Yarn needle
¾" Buttons - 2{3-3-4}
Sewing needle and thread
Elastic thread (optional)

GAUGE: In pattern,
13 sts and 10 rows = 4" (10 cm)

BODY
Ch 20{30-40-46}.

Row 1 (Right side): Sc in back ridge of second ch from hook *(Fig. 1, page 205)* and each ch across: 19{29-39-45} sc.

Note: Mark Row 1 as **right** side.

Row 2: Ch 1, turn; sc in first sc, (dc in next sc, sc in next sc) across.

Row 3: Ch 1, turn; working in Back Loops Only *(Fig. 2, page 205)*, sc in first sc, (dc in next dc, sc in next sc) across.

Row 4: Ch 1, turn; working in both loops, sc in first sc, (dc in next dc, sc in next sc) across.

Row 5: Ch 1, turn; working in Back Loops Only, sc in first sc, (dc in next dc, sc in next sc) across.

Row 6 (Increase row): Ch 1, turn; working in both loops, (sc, dc) in each of first 2 sts, sc in next sc, (dc in next dc, sc in next sc) across to last 2 sts, (dc, sc) in each of last 2 sts: 23{33-43-49} sts.

Row 7: Ch 1, turn; working in Back Loops Only, sc in first sc, (dc in next dc, sc in next sc) across.

Row 8: Ch 1, turn; working in both loops, sc in first sc, (dc in next dc, sc in next sc) across.

Rows 9-13: Repeat Rows 7 and 8 twice, then repeat Row 7 once **more**.

Rows 14 thru 21{29-37-45}: Repeat Rows 6-13, 1{2-3-4} time(s): 27{41-55-65} sts.

Row 22{30-38-46}: Ch 1, turn; working in both loops, sc in first sc, (dc in next dc, sc in next sc) across.

Repeat Rows 7 and 8 until Body measures approximately 11{16½-22-25}"/28{42-56-63.5} cm from beginning ch or until desired length from neck to tail, ending by working Row 7; do **not** finish off.

With **right** side facing, place marker for Band placement in end of row on left side of Body 2½{5-6-8½}"/6.5{12.5-15-21.5} from top of last row made.

LEFT NECK SHAPING
To sc decrease, pull up a loop in each of next 2 sts, YO and draw through all 3 loops on hook **(counts as one sc)**.

To dc decrease (uses next 2 sts), ★ YO, insert hook in **next** st, YO and pull up a loop, YO and draw through 2 loops on hook; repeat from ★ once **more**, YO and draw through all 3 loops on hook **(counts as one dc)**.

SIZE SMALL ONLY
Row 1: Ch 1, turn; working in both loops, sc in first sc, (dc in next dc, sc in next sc) 4 times, leave remaining 18 sts unworked: 9 sts.

Row 2: Ch 1, turn; working in Back Loops Only, sc in first sc, (dc in next dc, sc in next sc) across.

Row 3: Ch 1, turn; working in both loops, sc in first sc, (dc in next dc, sc in next sc) twice, dc decrease, sc decrease: 7 sts.

Row 4: Ch 1, turn; working in Back Loops Only, sc in first sc, (dc in next dc, sc in next sc) across.

Row 5: Ch 1, turn; working in both loops, sc in first sc, (dc in next dc, sc in next sc) across.

Repeat Rows 4 and 5 until Shaping measures approximately 3½" (9 cm) from neck edge or until desired length (allowing for ease), ending by working Row 5; finish off.

SIZES MEDIUM, LARGE, AND X-LARGE ONLY
Row 1: Ch 1, turn; working in both loops, sc in first sc, (dc in next dc, sc in next sc) {6-8-10} times, leave remaining {28-38-44} sts unworked: {13-17-21} sts.

Row 2: Ch 1, turn; working in Back Loops Only, sc in first sc, (dc in next dc, sc in next sc) across.

Row 3 (Decrease row): Ch 1, turn; working in both loops, sc in first sc, (dc in next dc, sc in next sc) across to last 4 sts, dc decrease, sc decrease: {11-15-19} sts.

Rows 4 thru {5-5-7}: Repeat Rows 2 and 3, {1-1-2} time(s): {9-13-15} sts.

Row {6-6-8}: Ch 1, turn; working in Back Loops Only, sc in first sc, (dc in next dc, sc in next sc) across.

Row {7-7-9}: Ch 1, turn; working in both loops, sc in first sc, (dc in next dc, sc in next sc) across.

Repeat Rows {6-6-8} and {7-7-9} until Shaping measures approximately {5¼-6¾-8½}"/{13.5-17-21.5} cm from neck edge or until desired length (allowing for ease), ending by working Row {7-7-9}; finish off.

RIGHT NECK SHAPING
SIZE SMALL ONLY
Row 1: With **wrong** side facing and working in both loops, skip next 9 sts from Left Neck Shaping and join yarn with sc in next sc *(see Joining With Sc, page 205)*; (dc in next dc, sc in next sc) across: 9 sts.

Row 2: Ch 1, turn; working in Back Loops Only, sc in first sc, (dc in next dc, sc in next sc) across.

Row 3: Ch 1, turn; working in both loops, sc decrease, dc decrease, sc in next sc, (dc in next dc, sc in next sc) twice: 7 sts.

Complete same as Left Neck Shaping, leaving a long end for sewing as you finish off.

Working through **inside** loops on both pieces, sew neck seam.

SIZES MEDIUM, LARGE, AND X-LARGE ONLY
Row 1: With **wrong** side facing and working in both loops, skip next {15-21-23} sts from Left Neck Shaping and join yarn with sc in next sc; (dc in next dc, sc in next sc) across: {13-17-21} sts.

Row 2: Ch 1, turn; working in Back Loops Only, sc in first sc, (dc in next dc, sc in next sc) across.

Row 3 (Decrease row)**:** Ch 1, turn; working in both loops, sc decrease, dc decrease, sc in next sc, (dc in next dc, sc in next sc) across: {11-15-19} sts.

Rows 4 thru {5-5-7}: Repeat Rows 2 and 3, {1-1-2} time(s): {9-13-15} sts.

Complete same as Left Neck Shaping, leaving a long end for sewing as you finish off.

Working through **inside** loops on both pieces, sew neck seam.

FINISHING
NECK EDGING
Rnd 1: With **right** side facing, join yarn with sc in seam at neck opening; sc evenly around; join with slip st to first sc.

Rnds 2 and 3: Ch 1, sc in same st and in each sc around; join with slip st to first sc.

Finish off.

If desired, weave elastic thread through tops of stitches on wrong side of Rnds 1 and 3; knot thread to secure and trim ends.

BAND
Sizes Small and X-Large only - Row 1: With **right** side facing and working in end of rows, join yarn with slip st in marked row; ch 3 **(counts as first dc, now and throughout)**, dc in same row and in next row, 2 dc in next row, (dc in next row, 2 dc in next row) 2{7} times, leave remaining rows unworked: 11{26} dc.

Size Medium only - Row 1: With **right** side facing and working in end of rows, join yarn with slip st in marked row; ch 3 **(counts as first dc, now and throughout)**, dc in same row, 2 dc in next row, (dc in next row, 2 dc in next row) 4 times, leave remaining rows unworked: 16 dc.

Size Large only - Row 1: With **right** side facing and working in end of rows, join yarn with slip st in marked row; ch 3 **(counts as first dc, now and throughout)**, dc in next 2 rows, 2 dc in next row, (dc in next row, 2 dc in next row) 5 times, leave remaining rows unworked: 20 dc.

ALL SIZES
Row 2: Ch 3, turn; dc in next dc and in each dc across.

Repeat Row 2 until Band fits snugly around dog's chest, ending by working a **right** side row; do **not** finish off.

BUTTONHOLES
Row 1: Ch 1, turn; sc in each dc across.

Row 2: Ch 1, turn; sc in first 2{2-3-3} sc, ch 2, ★ skip next 2 sc, sc in next 3{3-4-4} sc, ch 2; repeat from ★ 0{1-1-2} time(s) **more**, skip next 2 sc, sc in last 2{2-3-3} sc: 2{3-3-4} ch-2 sps.

Row 3: Ch 1, turn; sc in each sc and in each ch across: 11{16-20-26} sc.

Row 4: Ch 1, turn; sc in each sc across; do **not** finish off.

BODY EDGING
Ch 1, do **not** turn; sc evenly around entire Sweater working 3 sc in each outer corner; join with slip st to first sc, finish off.

Add buttons.

ANGELS DIVINE

Designed to watch over a loved one, our clothespin angel will look precious whether hanging from the bedpost or standing guard on the night table. She makes a divine gift for all ages!

■■□□ EASY

Finished Size: 4 1/4" (11 cm) tall

MATERIALS
Beadspread Weight Cotton Thread (size 10) [150 yards (137 meters) (colors) or 225 yards (206 meters) (Cream) per ball]:
  MC (Periwinkle **or** Almond Pink) - 1 ball
  CC (Cream) - 1 ball
Steel crochet hook, size 5 (1.9 mm) **or** size needed for gauge
3 3/4" (9.5 cm) Round, slotted clothespin
Glue
1/8" (3 mm) Ribbon - 6" (15 cm) for bow
Optional: Wooden doll pin stand **or** 12" (30.5 cm) of 1/8" (3 mm) ribbon for hanger

GAUGE: 16 dc and 8 rows = 2" (5 cm)

DRESS
BODICE
With MC, ch 14; being careful not to twist ch, join with slip st to form a ring.

Rnd 1 (Right side)**:** Ch 3 **(counts as first dc, now and throughout)**, dc in same st, 2 dc in next ch, † ch 1, (dc, ch 1) 3 times in next ch, (dc, ch 1) twice in next ch, (dc, ch 1) 3 times in next ch †, 2 dc in each of next 4 chs, repeat from † to † once, 2 dc in each of last 2 chs; join with slip st to first dc: 32 dc and 18 ch-1 sps.

Note: Mark Rnd 1 as **right** side.

Rnd 2: Ch 3, dc in next 3 dc, ch 1, skip next 9 ch-1 sps (armhole), dc in next 8 dc, ch 1, skip next 9 ch-1 sps (armhole), dc in last 4 dc; join with slip st to first dc, do **not** finish off: 16 dc and 2 ch-1 sps.

SKIRT
Rnd 1: Ch 1, sc in same st and in next 3 dc, skip next ch-1 sp, sc in next 8 dc, skip next ch-1 sp, sc in last 4 dc; join with slip st to first sc: 16 sc.

To work Cluster, YO, insert hook in **same** sc or sp as last st worked, YO and pull up a loop, YO and draw through 2 loops on hook, YO, insert hook in **next** sc or sp, YO and pull up a loop, YO and draw through 2 loops on hook, YO and draw through all 3 loops on hook.

Rnd 2: Ch 2, dc in next sc **(ch 2 and first dc count as first Cluster, now and throughout)**, ch 1, (work Cluster, ch 1) around working last leg of last Cluster in st at base of beginning ch-2; join with slip st to first dc: 16 Clusters and 16 ch-1 sps.

Rnd 3: Slip st in first ch-1 sp, ch 2, dc in next ch-1 sp, ch 2, (work Cluster, ch 2) around working last leg of last Cluster in same sp as beginning ch-2; join with slip st to first dc.

Rnds 4 and 5: Slip st in first ch-2 sp, ch 2, dc in next ch-2 sp, ch 2, (work Cluster, ch 2) around working last leg of last Cluster in same sp as beginning ch-2; join with slip st to first dc.

Rnd 6: Slip st in first ch-2 sp, ch 2, dc in next ch-2 sp, ch 3, (work Cluster, ch 3) around working last leg of last Cluster in same sp as beginning ch-2; join with slip st to first dc.

Rnd 7: Slip st in first ch and in same sp, ch 2, dc in next ch-3 sp, ch 3, (work Cluster, ch 3) around working last leg of last Cluster in same sp as beginning ch-2; join with slip st to first dc.

Rnd 8: Slip st in first ch and in same sp, ch 2, dc in next ch-3 sp, ch 4, (work Cluster, ch 4) around working last leg of last Cluster in same sp as beginning ch-2; join with slip st to first dc.

Rnd 9: Slip st in first 2 chs and in same sp, ch 2, dc in next ch-4 sp, ch 4, (work Cluster, ch 4) around working last leg of last Cluster in same sp as beginning ch-2; join with slip st to first dc, finish off.

BOTTOM TRIM
With **right** side facing, join CC with sc in any ch-4 sp on Rnd 9 of Skirt *(see Joining With Sc, page 205)*; ch 3, sc in same sp, ch 1, ★ (sc, ch 3, sc) in next ch-4 sp, ch 1; repeat from ★ around; join with slip st to first sc, finish off.

TOP TRIM
With **right** side facing, Bodice toward you, and working in ch-2 sps on Rnd 5 **between** Clusters, join CC with sc in any ch-2 sp; ch 3, sc in same sp, ch 1, ★ (sc, ch 3, sc) in next ch-2 sp, ch 1; repeat from ★ around; join with slip st to first sc, finish off.

CENTER TRIM
With **right** side facing, Bodice toward you, and working in ch-3 sps on Rnd 7 **between** Clusters, join CC with sc in any ch-3 sp; ch 3, sc in same sp, ch 1, ★ (sc, ch 3, sc) in next ch-3 sp, ch 1; repeat from ★ around; join with slip st to first sc, finish off.

WING
Rnd 1: With **right** side facing, join CC with sc in skipped ch-1 sp on Rnd 2 of Bodice (at underarm); sc in side of next dc on Rnd 2, ch 1, working in ch-1 sps on Rnd 1, (sc in next ch-1 sp, ch 1) 9 times, sc in side of next dc on Rnd 2; join with slip st to first sc: 12 sc and 10 ch-1 sps.

Rnd 2: Ch 1, (sc, ch 3, sc) in same st, skip next sc, (sc, ch 3, sc) in each ch-1 sp around, skip last sc; join with slip st to first sc: 11 ch-3 sps.

Rnd 3: Slip st in first ch-3 sp, ch 1, sc in same sp, ch 3, (sc in next ch-3 sp, ch 3) around; join with slip st to first sc.

To work treble crochet (abbreviated tr), YO twice, insert hook in sp indicated, YO and pull up a loop (4 loops on hook), (YO and draw through 2 loops on hook) 3 times.

Rnd 4: Slip st in first ch-3 sp, ch 1, (sc, hdc, dc, tr) in same sp, ★ sc in next ch-3 sp, (sc, hdc, dc, tr) in next ch-3 sp; repeat from ★ around; join with slip st to first sc, finish off.

Repeat for second Wing.

HALO

Rnd 1 (Right side)**:** With CC, ch 2, (sc, ch 3) 6 times in second ch from hook; join with slip st to first sc: 6 ch-3 sps.

Rnd 2: Slip st in first ch-3 sp, ch 5, hdc in same sp, ch 3, (hdc, ch 3) twice in each ch-3 sp around; join with slip st to second ch of beginning ch-5, finish off.

Using photo as a guide for placement:

Place Dress on clothespin.
Weave ribbon through Rnd 2 of Bodice and tie ends in a bow at front.
Glue Halo to clothespin at back of Dress.
Place Angel in stand or add ribbon hanger if desired.

Designs by Patty Kowaleski.

SACHET BLOSSOM

Whispers of fragrance arise from this beribboned floral sachet to provide a fresh scent of spring! The color sequence gives the impression of a delicate flower cradled in a bed of leaves.

■■□□ **EASY**

Finished Size:
5" (12.5 cm) diameter

MATERIALS
Bedspread Weight Cotton Thread
  (size 10) **[**225 yards (206 meters) per
  ball (Natural) or 150 yards
  (137 meters) per ball (all other colors)**]**:
  Natural - 1 ball
  Maize - 1 ball
  Spruce - 1 ball
Steel crochet hook, size 6 (1.8 mm) **or**
  size needed for gauge
Fabric for pouch - 6" x 12"
  (15 cm x 30.5 cm)
Sewing needle and thread
Potpourri **or** small amount of polyester
  fiberfill and scented oil
1/4" (7 mm) wide Ribbon - 1 yard
  (.9 meters)

GAUGE: Rnds 1-6 = 2" (5 cm)

FRONT
Rnd 1 (Right side)**:** With Maize, ch 2, 10 sc in second ch from hook; join with slip st to Back Loop Only of first sc **(Fig. 2, page 205)**.

Note: Mark Rnd 1 as **right** side.

Rnd 2: Ch 1, 2 sc in Back Loop Only of same st and each sc around; join with slip st to first sc: 20 sc.

Rnd 3: Ch 1, working in Back Loops Only, 2 sc in same st, sc in next sc, (2 sc in next sc, sc in next sc) around; join with slip st to **both** loops of first sc, finish off: 30 sc.

Rnd 4: With **right** side facing and working in free loops of sc on Rnd 1 **(Fig. 3a, page 205)**, join Maize with sc in any sc **(see Joining With Sc, page 205)**; ch 5, (sc in next sc, ch 5) around; join with slip st to **both** loops of first sc: 10 ch-5 sps.

To work Small Petal, ch 5, sc in second ch from hook, dc in last 3 chs.

Rnd 5: Ch 1, working in free loops of sc on Rnd 2, slip st in first sc, ch 1, sc in same st, work Small Petal, skip next sc, ★ sc in next sc, work Small Petal, skip next sc; repeat from ★ around; join with slip st to **both** loops of first sc: 10 Small Petals.

To work Large Petal, ch 5, hdc in second ch from hook, dc in last 3 chs.

Rnd 6: Ch 1, working in both loops of sc on Rnd 3, slip st in first sc, ch 1, sc in same st, work Large Petal, skip next sc, ★ sc in next sc, work Large Petal, skip next sc; repeat from ★ around; join with slip st to first sc, finish off: 15 Large Petals.

To work tr Cluster, ch 4, YO twice, insert hook in fourth ch from hook, YO and pull up a loop, (YO and draw through 2 loops on hook) twice, YO twice, insert hook in same ch, YO and pull up a loop, (YO and draw through 2 loops on hook) twice, YO and draw through all 3 loops on hook.

Rnd 7: With **right** side facing, join Spruce with sc in end of any Large Petal; work tr Cluster, (sc in end of next Large Petal, work tr Cluster) around; join with slip st to first sc: 15 sc.

To work treble crochet (abbreviated tr), YO twice, insert hook in st indicated, YO and pull up a loop (4 loops on hook), (YO and draw through 2 loops on hook) 3 times.

To work dc Cluster, ch 3, YO, insert hook in third ch from hook, YO and pull up a loop, YO and draw through 2 loops on hook, YO, insert hook in same ch, YO and pull up a loop, YO and draw through 2 loops on hook, YO and draw through all 3 loops on hook.

Rnd 8: Ch 6, tr in same st, work dc Cluster, ★ (tr, ch 2, tr) in next sc, work dc Cluster; repeat from ★ around; join with slip st to fourth ch of beginning ch-6, finish off: 15 ch-2 sps.

Rnd 9: With **right** side facing, join Natural with slip st in any ch-2 sp; ch 3 **(counts as first dc, now and throughout)**, 4 dc in same sp, ch 3, (5 dc in next ch-2 sp, ch 3) around; join with slip st to first dc: 75 dc and 15 ch-3 sps.

Rnd 10 (Eyelet rnd): Ch 4 **(counts as first dc plus ch 1)**, skip next dc, working in dc and in chs, ★ dc in next st, ch 1, skip next st; repeat from ★ around; join with slip st to first dc: 60 dc.

Rnd 11: Ch 1, sc in same st, ch 4, skip next dc, ★ sc in next dc, ch 4, skip next dc; repeat from ★ around; join with slip st to first sc: 30 ch-4 sps.

Rnd 12: (Slip st, ch 3, 4 dc) in first ch-4 sp and in each ch-4 sp around; join with slip st to first slip st, finish off.

BACK

Work same as Front through Rnd 10; finish off: 60 dc.

FINISHING

Using Back for pattern, cut two circles from fabric. With **right** sides together and using a 1/4" (7 mm) seam allowance, sew circles together leaving an opening for turning. Being careful not to cut stitching and leaving seam allowance at opening uncut, clip seam allowance at regular intervals. Turn pouch right side out and stuff with potpourri or scented polyester fiberfill. Sew opening closed.

With **wrong** sides of Front and Back together, weave ribbon through Eyelet rounds, inserting pouch before closing. Tie ribbon ends in a bow.

Design by Anne Halliday.

HEARTSTRING BAG

Why wear your heart on your sleeve when it looks so lovely on this drawstring tote? The simple mesh pattern is crocheted holding two strands of lightweight cotton yarn.

Shown on page 151.

■■□□ **EASY**

Finished Size: 14" high x 9 1/2" diameter (35.5 cm x 24 cm)

MATERIALS
Light/Worsted Weight Yarn [2 1/2 ounces, 160 yards (70 grams, 146 meters) per skein]: 4 skeins
Crochet hook, size G (4 mm) **or** size needed for gauge

GAUGE: Rnds 1-3 = 3 3/4" (9.5 cm)

Note: Bottom and Sides are worked holding two strands of yarn together. Ties are worked holding four strands of yarn together.

BOTTOM
Rnd 1 (Right side): Ch 4, 11 dc in fourth ch from hook; join with slip st to top of beginning ch: 12 sts.

Rnd 2: Ch 3 **(counts as first dc, now and throughout)**, dc in same st, 2 dc in next dc and in each dc around; join with slip st to first dc: 24 dc.

Rnd 3: Ch 3, dc in same st and in next dc, (2 dc in next dc, dc in next dc) around; join with slip st to first dc: 36 dc.

Rnd 4: Ch 3, dc in same st and in next 2 dc, (2 dc in next dc, dc in next 2 dc) around; join with slip st to first dc: 48 dc.

Rnd 5: Ch 3, dc in same st and in next 3 dc, (2 dc in next dc, dc in next 3 dc) around; join with slip st to first dc: 60 dc.

Rnd 6: Ch 3, dc in same st and in next 4 dc, (2 dc in next dc, dc in next 4 dc) around; join with slip st to first dc: 72 dc.

Rnd 7: Ch 3, dc in same st and in next 5 dc, (2 dc in next dc, dc in next 5 dc) around; join with slip st to first dc: 84 dc.

Rnd 8: Ch 3, dc in same st and in next 6 dc, (2 dc in next dc, dc in next 6 dc) around; join with slip st to first dc: 96 dc.

Rnd 9: Ch 1, 2 sc in same st, sc in next 7 dc, (2 sc in next dc, sc in next 7 dc) around; join with slip st to Back Loop Only of first sc, do **not** finish off: 108 sc.

SIDES
Rnd 1: Ch 1, sc in Back Loop Only of same st *(Fig. 2, page 205)* and each sc around; join with slip st to **both** loops of first sc.

Rnd 2: Ch 3, dc in both loops of next sc and each sc around; join with slip st to first dc.

Rnd 3: Ch 3, dc in next 3 dc, ch 2, skip next 2 dc, (dc in next dc, ch 2, skip next 2 dc) 14 times, (dc in next 4 dc, ch 2, skip next 2 dc) twice, (dc in next dc, ch 2, skip next 2 dc) 14 times, dc in next 4 dc, ch 2, skip last 2 dc; join with slip st to first dc: 44 dc and 32 ch-2 sps.

Instructions continued on page 150.

Rnds 4 and 5: Ch 3, dc in next 3 dc, ch 2, (dc in next dc, ch 2) 14 times, (dc in next 4 dc, ch 2) twice, (dc in next dc, ch 2) 14 times, dc in last 4 dc, ch 2; join with slip st to first dc.

Rnd 6: Ch 3, dc in next 3 dc, † (ch 2, dc in next dc) 7 times, 2 dc in next ch-2 sp, (dc in next dc, ch 2) 7 times, dc in next 4 dc, ch 2 †, dc in next 4 dc, repeat from † to † once; join with slip st to first dc.

Rnd 7: Ch 3, dc in next 3 dc, † (ch 2, dc in next dc) 6 times, 2 dc in next ch-2 sp, dc in next 4 dc, 2 dc in next ch-2 sp, (dc in next dc, ch 2) 6 times, dc in next 4 dc, ch 2 †, dc in next 4 dc, repeat from † to † once; join with slip st to first dc.

Rnd 8: Ch 3, dc in next 3 dc, † (ch 2, dc in next dc) 5 times, 2 dc in next ch-2 sp, dc in next 10 dc, 2 dc in next ch-2 sp, (dc in next dc, ch 2) 5 times, dc in next 4 dc, ch 2 †, dc in next 4 dc, repeat from † to † once; join with slip st to first dc.

Rnd 9: Ch 3, dc in next 3 dc, † (ch 2, dc in next dc) 4 times, 2 dc in next ch-2 sp, dc in next 16 dc, 2 dc in next ch-2 sp, (dc in next dc, ch 2) 4 times, dc in next 4 dc, ch 2 †, dc in next 4 dc, repeat from † to † once; join with slip st to first dc.

Rnd 10: Ch 3, dc in next 3 dc, † (ch 2, dc in next dc) 3 times, 2 dc in next ch-2 sp, dc in next 22 dc, 2 dc in next ch-2 sp, (dc in next dc, ch 2) 3 times, dc in next 4 dc, ch 2 †, dc in next 4 dc, repeat from † to † once; join with slip st to first dc.

Rnds 11-14: Ch 3, dc in next 3 dc, ch 2, † (dc in next dc, ch 2) twice, dc in next 28 dc, ch 2, (dc in next dc, ch 2) twice †, (dc in next 4 dc, ch 2) twice, repeat from † to † once, dc in last 4 dc, ch 2; join with slip st to first dc.

Rnd 15: Ch 3, dc in next 3 dc, ch 2, † (dc in next dc, ch 2) twice, dc in next 13 dc, ch 2, skip next 2 dc, dc in next 13 dc, ch 2, (dc in next dc, ch 2) twice †, (dc in next 4 dc, ch 2) twice, repeat from † to † once, dc in last 4 dc, ch 2; join with slip st to first dc.

Rnd 16: Ch 3, dc in next 3 dc, ch 2, † (dc in next dc, ch 2) 3 times, skip next 2 dc, dc in next 7 dc, ch 2, skip next 2 dc, (dc in next dc, ch 2) twice, skip next 2 dc, dc in next 7 dc, ch 2, skip next 2 dc, (dc in next dc, ch 2) 3 times †, (dc in next 4 dc, ch 2) twice, repeat from † to † once, dc in last 4 dc, ch 2; join with slip st to first dc.

Rnd 17: Ch 3, dc in next 3 dc, ch 2, † (dc in next dc, ch 2) 4 times, skip next 2 dc, dc in next dc, ch 2, skip next 2 dc, (dc in next dc, ch 2) 4 times, skip next 2 dc, dc in next dc, ch 2, skip next 2 dc, (dc in next dc, ch 2) 4 times †, (dc in next 4 dc, ch 2) twice, repeat from † to † once, dc in last 4 dc, ch 2; join with slip st to first dc.

Rnds 18 and 19: Ch 3, dc in next 3 dc, ch 2, (dc in next dc, ch 2) 14 times, (dc in next 4 dc, ch 2) twice, (dc in next dc, ch 2) 14 times, dc in last 4 dc, ch 2; join with slip st to first dc.

Rnd 20: Ch 3, dc in next 3 dc, † 2 dc in next ch-2 sp, (dc in next dc, 2 dc in next ch-2 sp) 14 times, dc in next 4 dc, ch 2 †, dc in next 4 dc, repeat from † to † once; join with slip st to first dc.

Rnd 21: Ch 5 **(counts as first dc plus ch 2, now and throughout)**, † skip next 2 dc, dc in next dc, ch 2 †, repeat from † to † 16 times **more**, dc in next dc, ch 2, repeat from † to † 17 times; join with slip st to first dc.

Rnds 22 and 23: Ch 5, (dc in next dc, ch 2) around; join with slip st to first dc.

Rnd 24: Slip st in first ch-2 sp, ch 1, (sc, ch 3, sc) in same sp and in each ch-2 sp around; join with slip st to first sc, finish off.

Drawstrings: Holding four strands of yarn together for each ch, make two 44" (112 cm) long chains.

Beginning and ending at right edge, weave one Drawstring through ch-2 sps on Rnd 23; tie ends together.

Beginning and ending at left edge, weave second Drawstring through same sps as first Drawstring; tie ends together.

Design by Jennine Korejko.

THE FINER THINGS

These gracefully edged linen handkerchiefs are ideal for the woman who appreciates the finer things in life. The genteel trims are crocheted using size 30 cotton thread.

■■■□ INTERMEDIATE

MATERIALS

Cotton Thread (size 30) **[**500 yards (457 meters) per ball**]**: 1 ball
Note: Thread amount is sufficient to make both edgings.
Steel crochet hook, size indicated below **or** size needed for gauge
Edging #1 - size 7 (1.65 mm)
Edging #2 - size 11 (1.1 mm)
11" (28 cm) square hemstitched linen handkerchief - one for **each** Edging
Sewing needle and thread - for Edging #2 only
Tapestry needle

EDGING #1

Finished Size: 1" (2.5 cm) wide

Gauge: 11 dc = 1" (2.5 cm)

Rnd 1 (Right side): Working through edge of handkerchief, join thread with sc in any corner *(see Joining With Sc, page 205)*; sc in same sp, work 109 sc evenly spaced across to next corner, (3 sc in corner, work 109 sc evenly spaced across to next corner) 3 times, sc in same sp as first sc; join with slip st to first sc: 448 sc.

Rnd 2: Ch 3 **(counts as first dc, now and throughout)**, 2 dc in same st, dc in next sc and in each sc across to center sc of next corner 3-sc group, (5 dc in center sc, dc in next sc and in each sc across to center sc of next corner 3-sc group) 3 times, 2 dc in same st as first dc; join with slip st to first dc: 464 dc.

Rnd 3: Ch 3, dc in same st, ★ † 2 dc in next dc, ch 2, (skip next dc, dc in next 7 dc, ch 2) 14 times, skip next dc †, 3 dc in next dc, 2 dc in next dc; repeat from ★ 2 times **more**, then repeat from † to † once, dc in same st as first dc; join with slip st to first dc: 420 dc and 60 ch-2 sps.

Rnd 4: Ch 3, 2 dc in same st, ★ ♥ ch 2, dc in next dc, ch 2, skip next dc, (dc in next dc, ch 2) twice, † skip next dc, dc in next 3 dc, ch 2, skip next dc, (dc in next dc, ch 2) twice †; repeat from † to † 13 times **more**, skip next dc, dc in next dc, ch 2 ♥, 3 dc in next dc; repeat from ★ 2 times **more**, then repeat from ♥ to ♥ once; join with slip st to first dc: 308 dc and 188 ch-2 sps.

To decrease (uses next 3 dc), ★ YO, insert hook in **next** dc, YO and pull up a loop, YO and draw through 2 loops on hook; repeat from ★ 2 times **more**, YO and draw through all 4 loops on hook.

To work Cluster, ★ YO, insert hook in dc indicated, YO and pull up a loop, YO and draw through 2 loops on hook; repeat from ★ once **more**, YO and draw through all 3 loops on hook.

Rnd 5: Ch 5 **(counts as first dc plus ch 2)**, ★ † work Cluster in next dc, ch 2, (dc in next dc, ch 2) 4 times, decrease, ch 2, [(dc in next dc, ch 2) twice, decrease, ch 2] 13 times †, (dc in next dc, ch 2) 4 times; repeat from ★ 2 times **more**, then repeat from † to † once, (dc in next dc, ch 2) 3 times; join with slip st to first dc: 196 sts and 196 ch-2 sps.

Rnd 6: Slip st in first ch-2 sp, ch 1, sc in same sp, ch 5, (sc in next ch-2 sp, ch 5) around; join with slip st to first sc, finish off.

EDGING #2
Finished Size: 1⅛" (3 cm) wide

Gauge: 8 rows = 1⅜" (3.5 cm)

Row 1 (Wrong side): Ch 18, dc in fourth ch from hook and in next 2 chs **(3 skipped chs count as first dc)**, ch 2, skip next 2 chs, dc in next ch and in each ch across: 14 dc and one ch-2 sp.

Note: Mark **back** of any dc on Row 1 as **right** side.

Row 2: Ch 5 **(counts as first dc plus ch 2, now and throughout)**, turn; skip next 2 dc, dc in next dc, (ch 2, skip next 2 dc, dc in next dc) twice, 2 dc in next ch-2 sp, dc in next dc, ch 2, skip next 2 dc, dc in last dc.

Row 3: Ch 5, turn; dc in next dc, ch 2, skip next 2 dc, dc in next dc, 2 dc in next ch-2 sp, dc in next dc, (ch 2, dc in next dc) twice.

Row 4: Ch 5, turn; dc in next dc, 2 dc in next ch-2 sp, dc in next dc, ch 2, skip next 2 dc, dc in next dc, (ch 2, dc in next dc) twice.

Row 5: Ch 3 **(counts as first dc, now and throughout)**, turn; (2 dc in next ch-2 sp, dc in next dc) 3 times, ch 2, skip next 2 dc, dc in next dc, 2 dc in next ch-2 sp, dc in last dc.

Row 6: Ch 5, turn; skip next 2 dc, dc in next dc, 2 dc in next ch-2 sp, dc in next dc, (ch 2, skip next 2 dc, dc in next dc) across.

Row 7: Ch 5, turn; dc in next dc, ch 2, dc in next dc, 2 dc in next ch-2 sp, dc in next dc, ch 2, skip next 2 dc, dc in next dc, ch 2, dc in last dc.

Row 8: Ch 5, turn; (dc in next dc, ch 2) twice, skip next 2 dc, dc in next dc, 2 dc in next ch-2 sp, dc in next dc, ch 2, dc in last dc.

Row 9: Ch 3, turn; 2 dc in next ch-2 sp, dc in next dc, ch 2, skip next 2 dc, dc in next dc, (2 dc in next ch-2 sp, dc in next dc) across.

Instructions continued on page 154.

THE FINER THINGS
Continued from page 152.

Rows 10-36: Repeat Rows 2-9, 3 times; then repeat Rows 2-4 once **more**.

Row 37: Ch 3, turn; 2 dc in next ch-2 sp, dc in next dc, ch 2, dc in next dc, 2 dc in next ch-2 sp, dc in next 4 dc, 2 dc in next ch-2 sp, dc in last dc.

Row 38: Ch 5, turn; skip next 2 dc, dc in next dc, (ch 2, skip next 2 dc, dc in next dc) twice, 2 dc in next ch-2 sp, dc in next dc, ch 2, skip next 2 dc, dc in last dc.

Row 39: Ch 3, turn; 2 dc in next ch-2 sp, dc in next dc, ch 2, skip next 2 dc, dc in next dc, 2 dc in next ch-2 sp, dc in next dc, (ch 2, dc in next dc) twice.

Row 40: Ch 5, turn; dc in next dc, 2 dc in next ch-2 sp, dc in next dc, ch 2, skip next 2 dc, dc in next dc, ch 2, dc in last 4 dc.

Row 41: Ch 3, turn; dc in next 3 dc, ch 2, (dc in next dc, ch 2) twice, skip next 2 dc, dc in next dc, 2 dc in next ch-2 sp, dc in last dc, place marker around dc just made for Edging placement first time only.

Row 42: Turn; slip st in each dc and in each ch across; ch 5, working in end of rows, skip first row, 4 dc in next row, (ch 2, skip next row, dc in top of next row) 3 times, leave remaining rows unworked: 8 dc and 4 ch-2 sps.

Rows 43-45: Repeat Rows 7-9.

Rows 46-104: Repeat Rows 2-9, 7 times; then repeat Rows 2-4 once **more**.

Rows 105-249: Repeat Rows 37-104 twice; then repeat Rows 37-45 once **more**.

Rows 250-272: Repeat Rows 2-9 twice, then repeat Rows 2-8 once **more**.

Finish off, leaving a long end for sewing.

With **right** side together and matching stitches, sew Row 272 to free loops of beginning ch.

With sewing needle and thread, sew Edging to handkerchief, easing to fit as needed.

Edging: With **right** side facing, join thread with slip st around post of marked dc; ch 4, (dc, ch 1) 4 times in same sp, ★ † skip next ch-2 sp, (dc, ch 1) 5 times in next ch-2 sp, skip ch-2 sp and next 2 dc, sc in next dc, ch 1, skip first row, (dc, ch 1) 5 times in next row †, [skip next row, sc in next row, ch 1, skip next row, (dc, ch 1) 5 times in next row] across to last 2 rows, skip next row, (dc, ch 1) 5 times in last row; repeat from ★ 2 times **more**, then repeat from † to † once, skip next row, [sc in next row, ch 1, skip next row, (dc, ch 1) 5 times in next row, skip next row] across; join with slip st to third ch of beginning ch-4, finish off.

Designs by Alice Heim.

GRACEFUL GOTHIC CROSS

Mark a special occasion for a faithful friend by presenting a gift of grace. Our Gothic cross bookmark calls for size 10 cotton thread.

●●□□□ EASY

MATERIALS
Bedspread Weight Cotton Thread (size 10) [225 yards (206 meters) per ball]: 25 yards
Steel crochet hook, size 6 (1.8 mm)

CENTER
Ch 4; join with slip st to form a ring.

Rnd 1 (Right side)**:** Ch 3 **(counts as first dc, now and throughout)**, dc in ring, (ch 2, 2 dc in ring) 3 times, hdc in first dc to form last ch-2 sp: 8 dc and 4 ch-2 sps.

Note: Mark Rnd 1 as **right** side.

Rnd 2: Ch 3, (dc, ch 3, 2 dc) in same sp, ch 1, ★ (2 dc, ch 3, 2 dc) in next ch-2 sp, ch 1; repeat from ★ 2 times **more**; join with slip st to first dc, do **not** finish off: 16 dc and 8 sps.

FIRST POINT
Row 1: Ch 4 **(counts as first dc plus ch 1, now and throughout)**, (3 dc, ch 3, 3 dc) in next ch-2 sp, ch 1, skip next dc and next ch-1 sp, dc in next dc, leave remaining dc and sps unworked: 8 dc and 3 sps.

Row 2: Ch 4, **turn**; (4 dc, ch 4, 4 dc) in next ch-3 sp, ch 1, skip next 3 dc and next ch-1 sp, dc in last dc: 10 dc and 3 sps.

Row 3: Ch 4, turn; (5 dc, ch 3, 5 dc) in next ch-4 sp, ch 1, skip next 4 dc and next ch-1 sp, dc in last dc; finish off: 12 dc and 3 sps.

SECOND & THIRD POINTS
Row 1: With **right** side facing, join thread with slip st in next dc on Rnd 2 of Center from last Point made; ch 4, (3 dc, ch 3, 3 dc) in next ch-2 sp, ch 1, skip next dc, dc in next dc, leave remaining dc and sps unworked: 8 dc and 3 sps.

Rows 2 and 3: Work same as First Point.

FOURTH POINT

Row 1: With **right** side facing, join thread with slip st in next dc on Rnd 2 of Center from last Point made; ch 4, (3 dc, ch 3, 3 dc) in next ch-2 sp, ch 1, skip next dc, dc in last dc: 8 dc and 3 sps.

Row 2: Ch 4, turn; (4 dc, ch 4, 4 dc) in next ch-3 sp, ch 1, skip next 3 dc and last ch-1 sp, dc in last dc: 10 dc and 3 sps.

Row 3: Ch 4, turn; (5 dc, ch 5, 5 dc) in next ch-4 sp, ch 1, skip next 4 dc and last ch-1 sp, dc in last dc: 12 dc and 3 sps.

Row 4: Ch 4, turn; (6 dc, ch 6, 6 dc) in next ch-5 sp, ch 1, skip next 5 dc and last ch-1 sp, dc in last dc: 14 dc and 3 sps.

Row 5: Ch 4, turn; (7 dc, ch 3, 7 dc) in next ch-6 sp, ch 1, skip next 6 dc and last ch-1 sp, dc in last dc; do **not** finish off: 16 dc and 3 sps.

EDGING

To work Picot, ch 3, slip st in third ch from hook.

Rnd 1: Ch 1, do **not** turn; † working in end of rows on same Point and next Point, (sc, work Picot, sc) in first 8 rows †; working across Row 3 of same Point, skip first dc, sc in next 5 dc, (sc, work Picot, sc) in next ch-3 sp, sc in next 5 dc, skip last dc; ★ working in end of rows on same Point and next Point, (sc, work Picot, sc) in next 6 rows; working across Row 3 of same Point, skip first dc, sc in next 5 dc, (sc, work Picot, sc) in next ch-3 sp, sc in next 5 dc, skip last dc; repeat from ★ once **more**, then repeat from † to † once; working across Row 5 of same Point, skip first dc, sc in next 7 dc, (sc, ch 3, sc) in next ch-3 sp, sc in next 7 dc, skip last dc; join with slip st to first sc, finish off.

Add tassel *(Figs. 11a & b, page 207)* to ch-3 sp at bottom of Fourth Point.

Design by Betty Parish.

BRIGHT BOOKMARKS

These bright bookmarks make reading exciting for all ages! Combine colorful scraps of thread for the granny-square styles, or use variegated thread to make the granny strip all in one piece.

▰▰▱▱ **EASY**

MATERIALS
Bedspread Weight Cotton Thread
  (size 10) [400 yards (366 meters)
  per ball]:
  Granny Strip
  Mexicana - 35 yards
  Cluster Granny
  Victory Red - 10 yards
  Goldenrod - 10 yards
  True Blue - 10 yards
  Pumpkin - 10 yards
  Purple - 10 yards
  Mexicana - 15 yards
  Classic Granny
  Victory Red - 5 yards
  Goldenrod - 5 yards
  True Blue - 5 yards
  Pumpkin - 5 yards
  Myrtle Green - 5 yards
  Purple - 5 yards
  Black - 20 yards
Steel crochet hook, size 7 (1.65 mm)
Tapestry needle and nylon thread
  (Classic Granny only)

GRANNY STRIP

Foundation Row: With Mexicana, ★ ch 4, YO, insert hook in third ch from hook, YO and pull up a loop, YO and draw through 2 loops on hook, YO, insert hook in **same** ch, YO and pull up a loop, YO and draw through 2 loops on hook, YO and draw through all 3 loops on hook **(Cluster made)**; repeat from ★ 16 times **more**: 17 Clusters and 17 chs.

Rnd 1: Ch 3 **(counts as first dc, now and throughout)**, do **not** turn; (2 dc, ch 3, 3 dc) in top of same st, ch 2; working in chs **between** Clusters across Foundation Row, (3 dc in next ch, ch 2) 16 times, 3 dc in ch at base of first Cluster, (ch 3, 3 dc in same ch) twice, ch 2; working in same chs on opposite side of Foundation Row, (3 dc in next ch, ch 2) across, 3 dc in same st as first dc, ch 1, hdc in first dc to form last ch-3 sp: 38 sps.

Rnd 2: Ch 3, 2 dc in same sp, ch 2, (3 dc, ch 3, 3 dc) in next ch-3 sp, ch 2, (3 dc in next ch-2 sp, ch 2) across to next ch-3 sp, [(3 dc, ch 3, 3 dc) in next ch-3 sp, ch 2] twice, (3 dc in next ch-2 sp, ch 2) across, 3 dc in same sp as first dc, ch 1, hdc in first dc to form last ch-3 sp: 42 sps.

Rnd 3: Ch 3, 2 dc in same sp, ch 2, 3 dc in next ch-2 sp, ch 2, (3 dc, ch 3, 3 dc) in next ch-3 sp, ch 2, (3 dc in next ch-2 sp, ch 2) across to next ch-3 sp, (3 dc, ch 3, 3 dc) in ch-3 sp, ch 2, 3 dc in next ch-2 sp, ch 2, (3 dc, ch 3, 3 dc) in next ch-3 sp, ch 2, (3 dc in next ch-2 sp, ch 2) across, 3 dc in same sp as first dc, ch 3; join with slip st to first dc: 138 dc and 46 sps.

Rnd 4: Ch 1, working in Back Loops Only of each dc and each ch **(Fig. 2, page 205)**, sc in each st around working 3 sc in center ch of each corner ch-3; join with slip st to **both** loops of first sc, finish off.

CLUSTER GRANNY
FIRST SQUARE

To work beginning Cluster, ch 2, ★ YO, insert hook in sp indicated, YO and pull up a loop, YO and draw through 2 loops on hook; repeat from ★ once **more**, YO and draw through all 3 loops on hook.

To work Cluster, ★ YO, insert hook in sp indicated, YO and pull up a loop, YO and draw through 2 loops on hook; repeat from ★ 2 times **more**, YO and draw through all 4 loops on hook.

With Victory Red, ch 6; join with slip st to form a ring.

Rnd 1 (Right side)**:** Work beginning Cluster in ring, ch 1, (work Cluster in ring, ch 1) 7 times; join with slip st to top of beginning Cluster: 8 ch-1 sps.

Note: Mark Rnd 1 as **right** side.

Rnd 2: Slip st in first ch-1 sp, work (beginning Cluster, ch 2, Cluster) in same sp, ch 1, work Cluster in next ch-1 sp, ch 1, ★ work (Cluster, ch 2, Cluster) in next ch-1 sp, ch 1, work Cluster in next ch-1 sp, ch 1; repeat from ★ 2 times **more**; join with slip st to top of beginning Cluster: 12 sps.

Rnd 3: Slip st in first ch-2 sp, work (beginning Cluster, ch 2, Cluster) in same sp, ch 1, (work Cluster in next ch-1 sp, ch 1) twice, ★ work (Cluster, ch 2, Cluster) in next ch-2 sp, ch 1, (work Cluster in next ch-1 sp, ch 1) twice; repeat from ★ 2 times **more**; join with slip st to top of beginning Cluster, finish off: 16 sps.

Rnd 4: With **right** side facing, join Mexicana with sc in any corner ch-2 sp *(see Joining With Sc, page 205)*; ch 5, place marker around ch-5 just made for joining placement, sc in same sp, ch 3, (sc in next ch-1 sp, ch 3) across to next corner ch-2 sp, ★ (sc, ch 5, sc) in corner ch-2 sp, ch 3, (sc in next ch-1 sp, ch 3) across to next corner ch-2 sp; repeat from ★ 2 times **more**; join with slip st to first sc, finish off: 20 sps.

Instructions continued on page 158.

Continued from page 156.

SECOND SQUARE

With Goldenrod, ch 6; join with slip st to form a ring.

Rnd 1 (Right side): Work beginning Cluster in ring, ch 1, (work Cluster in ring, ch 1) 7 times; join with slip st to top of beginning Cluster: 8 ch-1 sps.

Note: Mark Rnd 1 as **right** side.

Rnd 2: Slip st in first ch-1 sp, work (beginning Cluster, ch 2, Cluster) in same sp, ch 1, work Cluster in next ch-1 sp, ch 1, ★ work (Cluster, ch 2, Cluster) in next ch-1 sp, ch 1, work Cluster in next ch-1 sp, ch 1; repeat from ★ 2 times **more**; join with slip st to top of beginning Cluster: 12 sps.

Rnd 3: Slip st in first ch-2 sp, work (beginning Cluster, ch 2, Cluster) in same sp, ch 1, (work Cluster in next ch-1 sp, ch 1) twice, ★ work (Cluster, ch 2, Cluster) in next ch-2 sp, ch 1, (work Cluster in next ch-1 sp, ch 1) twice; repeat from ★ 2 times **more**; join with slip st to top of beginning Cluster, finish off: 16 sps.

Rnd 4 (Joining rnd): With **right** side facing, join Mexicana with sc in any corner ch-2 sp; ch 5, place marker around ch-5 just made for joining placement, sc in same sp, ch 3, (sc in next ch-1 sp, ch 3) across to next corner ch-2 sp, sc in corner ch-2 sp, ch 2, holding Squares with **wrong** sides together, hdc in marked corner ch-5 sp on **previous Square**, ch 2, sc in same sp on **new Square**, ch 1, hdc in next ch-3 sp on **previous Square**, ch 1, ★ sc in next ch-1 sp on **new Square**, ch 1, hdc in next ch-3 sp on **previous Square**, ch 1; repeat from ★ 2 times **more**, sc in next corner ch-2 sp on **new Square**, ch 2, hdc in next corner ch-5 sp on **previous Square**, ch 2, sc in same sp on **new Square**, ch 3, (sc in next ch-1 sp, ch 3) across to next corner ch-2 sp, (sc, ch 5, sc) in corner ch-2 sp, ch 3, (sc in next ch-1 sp, ch 3) across; join with slip st to first sc, finish off.

THIRD SQUARE

Substituting True Blue for Goldenrod, work same as Second Square.

FOURTH SQUARE

Substituting Pumpkin for Goldenrod, work same as Second Square.

FIFTH SQUARE

Substituting Purple for Goldenrod, work same as Second Square; on Rnd 4, do **not** place marker and do **not** finish off.

EDGING

Slip st in first ch-5 sp, ch 1, (sc, ch 3) twice in same sp, † (sc in next ch-3 sp, ch 3) 4 times, ★ sc in next 2 sps, ch 3, (sc in next ch-3 sp, ch 3) 4 times; repeat from ★ 3 times **more**, (sc, ch 3) twice in next corner ch-5 sp, (sc in next ch-3 sp, ch 3) 4 times †, (sc, ch 3) twice in next corner ch-5 sp, repeat from † to † once; join with slip st to first sc, finish off.

CLASSIC GRANNY SQUARE (Make one **each** using Victory Red, Goldenrod, True Blue, Pumpkin, Myrtle Green, and Purple for Rnd 1 **and** Rnd 3)

With color indicated, ch 6; join with slip st to form a ring.

Rnd 1 (Right side): Ch 3 **(counts as first dc, now and throughout)**, 2 dc in ring, ch 3, (3 dc in ring, ch 3) 3 times; join with slip st to first dc, finish off: 4 ch-3 sps.

Note: Mark Rnd 1 as **right** side.

Rnd 2: With **right** side facing, join Black with slip st in any ch-3 sp; ch 3, (2 dc, ch 3, 3 dc) in same sp, ch 1, ★ (3 dc, ch 3, 3 dc) in next ch-3 sp, ch 1; repeat from ★ 2 times **more**; join with slip st to first dc, finish off.

Rnd 3: With **right** side facing, join color indicated with slip st in any corner ch-3 sp; ch 3, (2 dc, ch 3, 3 dc) in same sp, ch 1, 3 dc in next ch-1 sp, ch 1, ★ (3 dc, ch 3, 3 dc) in next corner ch-3 sp, ch 1, 3 dc in next ch-1 sp, ch 1; repeat from ★ 2 times **more**; join with slip st to first dc, finish off.

JOINING

Using photo as a guide for placement and nylon thread, with **wrong** sides together and working through **inside** loops, whipstitch Squares together *(Fig. 9c, page 206)*, beginning in center ch of first corner ch-3 and ending in center ch of next corner ch-3, forming a strip.

EDGING

With **right** side facing and working in Back Loops Only *(Fig. 2, page 205)* of each dc and each ch around, join Black with sc in any st *(see Joining With Sc, page 205)*; sc in each st around working 2 sc in center ch of each corner ch-3; join with slip st to first sc, finish off.

With Black, make an 1¹/₂" (4 cm) long tassel *(Figs. 11a & b, page 207)*.

Using photo as a guide for placement, attach tassel to one end of strip.

Design by Mary Bland.

SOOTHING RICE ROLLS

Comfort a friend with a gift of relaxation — a reusable, therapeutic neck roll. The crocheted accessory contains a rice-filled cloth pouch that can be heated in a microwave for soothing muscle relief.

Instructions begin on page 160.

SOOTHING RICE ROLLS
Shown on page 159.

■■☐☐ **EASY**

MATERIALS
Medium/Worsted Weight Yarn
[5 ounces, 253 yards
(140 grams, 231 meters)
per skein]:
For Lady's
Light Sage - 1 skein
For Gent's
Dark Sage - 1 skein
Light Sage - 25 yards
Crochet hook, size I (5.5 mm) **or**
size needed for gauge
Fabric - two 4" x 18" (10 cm x 45.5 cm)
pieces for **each** Rice Bag
Sewing machine
Sewing needle and thread
Uncooked rice - 3¹/₃ cups (.8 liter) for
each Rice Bag
¹/₈" (3 mm) wide Ribbon - two 18"
(45.5 cm) lengths (for Lady's only)

GAUGE: (sc, ch 1) 4 times = 2" (5 cm)

RICE BAG
Matching right sides and raw edges, use a ¹/₄" (7 mm) seam allowance to sew fabric pieces together, leaving an opening at one short edge for turning and filling. Turn bag right side out. Pour uncooked rice into bag and sew final closure by hand.

LADY'S RICE ROLL
With Light Sage, ch 32; being careful not to twist ch, join with slip st to form a ring.

Rnd 1 (Right side): Ch 1, sc in same st and in each ch around; join with slip st to first sc: 32 sc.

Note: Mark Rnd 1 as **right** side.

Rnd 2: Ch 1, turn; sc in same st, ch 1, skip next sc, ★ sc in next sc, ch 1, skip next sc; repeat from ★ around; join with slip st to first sc: 16 ch-1 sps.

Rnd 3: Ch 1, turn; sc in first ch-1 sp, ch 1, (sc in next ch-1 sp, ch 1) around; join with slip st to first sc: 32 sc.

Repeat Rnd 3 until Rice Roll measures approximately 18" (45.5 cm) from beginning ch, ending by working a **wrong** side round.

Last Rnd: Ch 1, turn; sc in same st and in each ch-1 sp and each sc around; join with slip st to first sc, do **not** finish off: 32 sc.

To work Picot, ch 3, slip st in top of last dc made.

TRIM
First End: Ch 1, do **not** turn; sc in same st, skip next sc, (2 dc, work Picot, dc) in next sc, skip next sc, ★ sc in next sc, skip next sc, (2 dc, work Picot, dc) in next sc, skip next sc; repeat from ★ around; join with slip st to first sc, finish off.

Second End: With **right** side facing and working in free loops of beginning ch *(Fig. 3b, page 205)*, join Light Sage with sc in same ch as joining; skip next ch, (2 dc, work Picot, dc) in next ch, skip next ch, ★ sc in next ch, skip next ch, (2 dc, work Picot, dc) in next ch, skip next ch; repeat from ★ around; join with slip st to first sc, finish off.

Using photo as a guide, weave one ribbon length through ch-1 sps on each end of Rice Roll. Insert Rice Bag. Tie ribbon at each end in a bow.

GENT'S RICE ROLL
With Dark Sage, ch 32; being careful not to twist ch, join with slip st to form a ring.

Rnd 1 (Right side): Ch 1, sc in same st and in each ch around; join with slip st to first sc: 32 sc.

Note: Mark Rnd 1 as **right** side.

Rnd 2: Ch 1, turn; sc in same st, ch 1, skip next sc, ★ sc in next sc, ch 1, skip next sc; repeat from ★ around; join with slip st to first sc: 16 ch-1 sps.

Rnd 3: Ch 1, turn; sc in first ch-1 sp, ch 1, (sc in next ch-1 sp, ch 1) around; join with slip st to first sc changing to Light Sage *(Fig. 7c, page 206)*.

Rnd 4: Ch 1, turn; sc in first ch-1 sp, ch 1, (sc in next ch-1 sp, ch 1) around; join with slip st to first sc changing to Dark Sage.

Rnd 5: Ch 1, turn; sc in first ch-1 sp, ch 1, (sc in next ch-1 sp, ch 1) around; join with slip st to first sc.

Rnds 6 and 7: Repeat Rnds 3 and 4.

Repeat Rnd 5 until Rice Roll measures approximately 15¹/₂" (39.5 cm) from beginning ch, ending by working a **right** side round.

Next 5 Rnds: Repeat Rnds 3-7.

Next 2 Rnds: Ch 1, turn; sc in first ch-1 sp, ch 1, (sc in next ch-1 sp, ch 1) around; join with slip st to first sc.

Last Rnd: Ch 1, turn; sc in same st and in each ch-1 sp and each sc around; join with slip st to first sc, finish off: 32 sc.

TRIM
First End: With **right** side facing, join Light Sage with slip st in same st as joining; slip st **loosely** in each sc around; join with slip st to joining slip st, finish off.

Second End: With **right** side facing and working in free loops of beginning ch *(Fig. 3b, page 205)*, join Light Sage with slip st in first ch; slip st **loosely** in each ch around; join with slip st to joining slip st, finish off.

DRAWSTRING (Make 2)
With Light Sage, make a chain 18" (45.5 cm) long; slip st **loosely** in second ch from hook and in each ch across; finish off.

Holding two 5" (12.5 cm) pieces of Light Sage together for each fringe, add fringe to ends of each Drawstring *(Figs. 12a & b, page 207)*.

Using photo as a guide, weave one Drawstring through ch-1 sps on each end of Rice Roll. Insert Rice Bag and tie Drawstring at each end in a bow.

CROCHET CADDY TISSUE COVER

Organize your crochet supplies while displaying your love of the craft! This fun and functional tissue box cover will capture your heart with its charming needle cushion and accessory pockets.

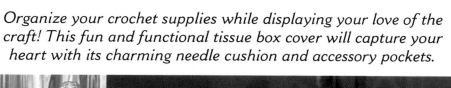

Instructions begin on page 162.

CROCHET CADDY TISSUE COVER

Shown on page 161.

■■□□ **EASY**

Finished Size:
To fit a Boutique Tissue Box

MATERIALS
Medium/Worsted Weight Yarn
 [8 ounces, 452 yards
 (230 grams, 413 meters)
 per skein]:
 Soft White - 1 skein
 Country Rose - 15 yards (13.5 meters)
Crochet hook, size H (5 mm) **or** size
 needed for gauge
Yarn needle
Polyester fiberfill

GAUGE: 8 sc and 8 rows = 2" (5 cm)

FRONT AND BACK
With Soft White, ch 17.

Row 1 (Wrong side)**:** Sc in second ch
from hook and in each ch across: 16 sc.

Note: Mark **back** of any sc on Row 1 as
right side.

Rows 2-28: Ch 1, turn; sc in each sc
across.

Edging: Ch 1, do **not** turn; 3 sc in last
sc on last row; † working in end of rows,
skip first row, sc in next row and in each
row across to last row, skip last row †;
working in free loops of beginning ch
(Fig. 3b, page 205), 3 sc in ch at base
of first sc, sc in each ch across to last ch,
3 sc in last ch, repeat from † to † once;
working across last row, 3 sc in first sc,
sc in each sc across; join with slip st to
first sc, finish off: 92 sc.

SIDE (Make 2)
With Soft White, ch 15.

Row 1 (Wrong side)**:** Sc in second ch
from hook and in each ch across: 14 sc.

Note: Mark **back** of any sc on Row 1 as
right side.

Rows 2-20: Ch 1, turn; sc in each sc
across.

Edging: Ch 1, do **not** turn; 3 sc in last
sc on Row 20; working in end of rows,
skip first row, sc in last 19 rows; working
in free loops of beginning ch, 3 sc in ch
at base of first sc, sc in next 12 chs, 3 sc
in last ch; working in end of rows, sc in
first 19 rows, skip last row; working
across Row 20, 3 sc in first sc, sc in last
12 sc; join with slip st to first sc, finish
off: 74 sc.

RULER POCKET
With Soft White, ch 5.

Row 1 (Wrong side)**:** Sc in second ch
from hook and in each ch across: 4 sc.

Note: Mark **back** of any sc on Row 1 as
right side.

Rows 2-16: Ch 1, turn; sc in each sc
across.

Edging: Work same as Front and Back
leaving a long end for sewing: 44 sc.

PAD AND PEN POCKET
With Soft White, ch 15.

Row 1 (Wrong side)**:** Sc in second ch
from hook and in each ch across: 14 sc.

Note: Mark **back** of any sc on Row 1 as
right side.

Rows 2-18: Ch 1, turn; sc in each sc
across.

Edging: Work same as Front and Back
leaving a long end for sewing: 68 sc.

HOOKS POCKET
With Soft White, ch 15.

Row 1 (Wrong side)**:** Sc in second ch
from hook and in each ch across: 14 sc.

Note: Mark **back** of last sc on Row 1 as
right side and bottom corner (point A).

Rows 2-12: Ch 1, turn; sc in Back
Loop Only of each sc across *(Fig. 2,
page 205)*.

Edging: Ch 1, do **not** turn; 3 sc in last
sc on Row 18; working in end of rows,
skip first row, sc in next 10 rows, skip
last row; working in free loops of
beginning ch, 3 sc in ch at base of first
sc, sc in last 13 chs, ch 20 (loop to hang
markers); skip next 12 rows (top edge);
working across Row 12, sc in first 13 sc;
join with slip st to first sc, finish off
leaving a long end for sewing: 42 sc.

SCISSORS POCKET

Row 1: With Ecru, ch 2, 2 sc in second ch from hook.

Row 2 (Right side): Ch 1, turn; 2 sc in each of first 2 sc: 4 sc.

Note: Mark Row 2 as **right** side.

Rows 3-12: Ch 1, turn; sc in each sc across.

Row 13: Ch 1, turn; 2 sc in first sc, sc in next 2 sc, 2 sc in last sc: 6 sc.

Row 14: Ch 1, turn; sc in each sc across.

Edging: Ch 1, do **not** turn; 3 sc in last sc on Row 14; working in end of rows, skip first row, sc in next 12 rows, skip last row; 3 sc in free loops of ch at base of sc; working in end of rows, skip first row, sc in next 12 rows, skip last row; working across Row 14, 3 sc in first sc, sc in last 4 sc; join with slip st to first sc, finish off leaving a long end for sewing: 37 sc.

HEART PINCUSHION
BODY

Row 1: With Country Rose, ch 2, 2 sc in second ch from hook.

Row 2 (Right side): Ch 1, turn; 2 sc in each of first 2 sc: 4 sc.

Note: Mark Row 2 as **right** side.

Row 3: Ch 1, turn; 2 sc in first sc, sc in next 2 sc, 2 sc in last sc: 6 sc.

Row 4: Ch 1, turn; sc in each sc across.

Row 5: Ch 1, turn; 2 sc in first sc, sc in each sc across to last sc, 2 sc in last sc: 8 sc.

Rows 6-10: Repeat Rows 4 and 5 twice, then repeat Row 4 once **more**: 12 sc.

LEFT SIDE

Row 1: Ch 1, turn; sc in first 6 sc, leave remaining 6 sc unworked: 6 sc.

To work beginning decrease, pull up a loop in each of first 2 sc, YO and draw through all 3 loops on hook **(counts as one sc)**.

To work ending decrease, pull a loop in each of last 2 sc, YO and draw through all 3 loops on hook **(counts as one sc)**.

Row 2: Ch 1, turn; work beginning decrease, sc in next 2 sc, work ending decrease: 4 sc.

Row 3: Ch 1, turn; sc in each sc across.

Row 4: Ch 1, turn; work beginning decrease, work ending decrease; finish off: 2 sc.

RIGHT SIDE

Row 1: With **wrong** side facing, join Country Rose with sc in first unworked sc on Row 10 of Body; sc in last 5 sc: 6 sc.

Rows 2-4: Work same as Left Side; do **not** finish off.

EDGING

Rnd 1: Ch 1, do **not** turn; sc evenly around entire piece working 3 sc in point; join with slip st to first sc, finish off.

Rnd 2: With **right** side facing, join Soft White with sc in center sc of 3-sc group at point; 2 sc in same st, sc in each sc around; join with slip st to first sc.

Rnd 3: Ch 1, do **not** turn; sc in same st, ch 5, (sc in next sc, ch 5) around; join with slip st to first sc, finish off leaving a long end for sewing.

ASSEMBLY

Using diagram as a guide for placement:

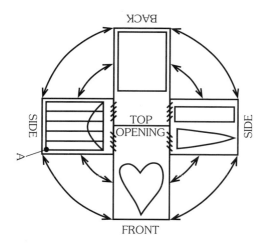

Sew Scissors Pocket and Ruler Pocket to one Side.

Sew Hooks Pocket to remaining Side. Sew across every other row from bottom to top to form six pockets.

Sew Rnd 2 of Edging on Heart Pincushion to Front, stuffing lightly before closing.

Sew Pad and Pen Pocket to Back.

With **wrong** sides together and working through **inside** loops, whipstitch Sides to Front and Back *(Fig. 9d, page 206)*.

Design by Theresa Jones.

GOLF CLUB COZIES

Avid golfers are sure to appreciate these club cozies for their all-important woods! Accented with felt symbols and handmade pom-poms, they can be crocheted in any color scheme.

⬛⬛◻◻ **EASY**

Finished Size: 12" (30.5 cm) long

MATERIALS
Medium/Worsted Weight Yarn
[6 ounces, 348 yards
(170 grams, 318 meters)
per skein (Kaleidoscope) or
3 ounces, 170 yards
(90 grams, 155 meters)
per skein (Paddy Green)]:
Kaleidoscope - 1 skein
Paddy Green - 1 skein
Crochet hook, size H (5 mm) **or** size
needed for gauge
Yarn needle
Felt (one color for numbers and circle;
one color for diamonds)
Glue

GAUGE: 10 dc = 3" (7.5 cm) and
3 dc rnds = 2¹/₄" (5.75 cm)

HEAD COVER (Make 3)
BODY
With Kaleidoscope, ch 5; join with slip st to form a ring.

Rnd 1 (Wrong side)**:** Ch 3 **(counts as first dc, now and throughout)**, 13 dc in ring; join with slip st to first dc: 14 dc.

Note #1: Mark **back** of any dc on Rnd 1 as **right** side.

Note #2: Work in Back Loops Only throughout **(Fig. 2, page 205)**.

Rnd 2: Ch 3, 2 dc in next dc, (dc in next dc, 2 dc in next dc) around; join with slip st to first dc: 21 dc.

Rnd 3: Ch 3, dc in next dc, 2 dc in next dc, (dc in next 2 dc, 2 dc in next dc) around; join with slip st to first dc: 28 dc.

Rnds 4-6: Ch 3, dc in next dc and in each dc around; join with slip st to first dc.

Rnd 7: Ch 1, sc in same st and in each dc around; do **not** join, place marker *(see Markers, page 205)*.

To decrease, pull up a loop in each of next 2 sc, YO and draw through all 3 loops on hook **(counts as one sc)**.

Rnd 8: (Sc in next 5 sc, decrease) around: 24 sc.

Rnd 9: (Sc in next 10 sc, decrease) twice: 22 sc.

Rnd 10: (Sc in next 9 sc, decrease) twice: 20 sc.

Rnds 11-21: Sc in each sc around.

Rnd 22: Sc in each sc around; slip st in next sc, finish off.

CUFF
Note: Work in Back Loops Only unless otherwise instructed.

Rnd 1: With **wrong** side facing, join Paddy Green with sc in same st as slip st *(see Joining With Sc, page 205)*; sc in each sc around to last 2 sc, decrease; join with slip st to first sc: 19 sc.

Rnds 2 and 3: Ch 3, dc in next st and in each st around; join with slip st to first dc.

Rnd 4: Ch 1, sc in same st and in each dc around; join with slip st to **both** loops of first sc, finish off.

FINISHING
Turn Head Covers right side out and turn up Cuffs.

Trace diamond pattern and cut three from felt; trace circle and number patterns and cut from felt. Using photo as a guide for placement, glue felt pieces to Head Covers.

POM-POM
Cut fifty 5" (12.5 cm) strands of Kaleidoscope and fifty 5" (12.5 cm) strands of Paddy Green. Holding all strands together, tie another strand tightly around center and knot to secure. Sew pom-pom to center top of one Head Cover. Repeat for remaining Head Covers.

Designs by Kim A. Harmon.

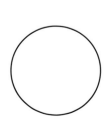
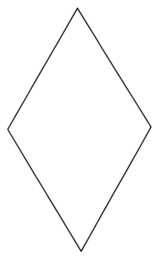

GEOMETRIC BABIES

These bright shapes and friendly faces are sure to fascinate little ones! The durable toys are a snap to crochet, and the embroidered features are safe for babies.

■■□□ EASY

MATERIALS
Medium/Worsted Weight Yarn
[3 ounces, 170 yards
(90 grams, 155 meters)
per skein]:

4 MEDIUM

Square
Hot Red - 1 skein
Bright Yellow - 1 skein
Black - small amount
Triangle
Parakeet - 1 skein
Vibrant Orange - 1 skein
Bright Yellow - 1 skein
Black - small amount
Circle
Spring Green - 1 skein
Lavender - 1 skein
Black - small amount
Crochet hook, size B (2.25 mm)
Polyester fiberfill
Yarn needle

SQUARE
BODY
BACK
With Bright Yellow, ch 21.

Row 1 (Right side): Sc in second ch from hook and in each ch across: 20 sc.

Note: Mark Row 1 as **right** side and bottom edge.

Rows 2-20: Ch 1, turn; sc in each sc across; do **not** finish off.

Edging: Ch 1, turn; 3 sc in first sc, sc in each sc across to last sc, 3 sc in last sc; work 18 sc evenly spaced across end of rows; working in free loops of beginning ch *(Fig. 3b, page 205)*, 3 sc in first ch, sc in next 18 chs, 3 sc in next ch; work 18 sc evenly spaced across end of rows; join with slip st to first sc, finish off: 84 sc.

FRONT
Work same as Back; do **not** finish off.

JOINING
With **wrong** sides facing, Front toward you, and working through **inside** loops of each stitch on **both** pieces, slip st in each sc around stuffing with fiberfill before closing; join with slip st to **both** loops of first slip st, finish off.

ARM (Make 2)
Rnd 1 (Right side): With Hot Red, ch 2, 6 sc in second ch from hook; do **not** join, place marker *(see Markers, page 205)*.

Rnd 2: 2 Sc in each sc around: 12 sc.

Rnds 3 and 4: Sc in each sc around.

To decrease, pull up a loop in each of next 2 sc, YO and draw through all 3 loops on hook **(counts as one sc)**.

Rnd 5: Decrease around: 6 sc.

Stuff hand firmly with fiberfill.

Rnds 6-19: Sc in each sc around.

Rnd 20: Sc in each sc around; slip st in next sc, finish off leaving a long end for sewing.

LEG (Make 2)
Rnd 1 (Right side): With Hot Red, ch 2, 6 sc in second ch from hook; do **not** join, place marker.

Rnd 2: 2 Sc in each sc around: 12 sc.

Rnds 3 and 4: Sc in each sc around.

Rnd 5: Decrease around: 6 sc.

Stuff foot firmly with fiberfill.

Rnds 6-22: Sc in each sc around.

Rnd 23: Sc in each sc around; slip st in next sc, finish off leaving a long end for sewing.

FINISHING
Using photo as a guide for placement:

Flatten top edge of each Arm and sew opening closed; flatten top edge of each Leg and sew opening closed. Sew Arms and Legs to Body.

For tassel, cut seven 7" (18 cm) strands each of Hot Red and Bright Yellow. Hold strands together and use crochet hook to draw through stitches at one top corner of Body; tie ends in a knot. Tightly wrap an 8" (20.5 cm) strand of Bright Yellow around base of knot; knot ends securely. Tightly wrap another 8" (20.5 cm) strand of Bright Yellow around all strands above knot; knot ends securely. Trim the ends of the tassel evenly. Repeat for second tassel.

With Black, add straight stitches *(Fig. A, page 169)* for eyes and mouth; add satin stitches *(Fig. 14, page 208)* for nose.

Instructions continued on page 168.

Continued from page 166.

TRIANGLE
BODY
BACK
With Parakeet, ch 28.

Row 1 (Right side): Sc in second ch from hook and in each ch across: 27 sc.

Note: Mark Row 1 as **right** side and bottom edge.

To decrease, pull up a loop in each of next 2 sc, YO and draw through all 3 loops on hook **(counts as one sc).**

Row 2: Ch 1, turn; decrease, sc in each sc across to last 2 sc, decrease: 25 sc.

Row 3: Ch 1, turn; sc in each sc across.

Rows 4-25: Repeat Rows 2 and 3, 11 times: 3 sc.

Row 26: Ch 1, turn; pull up a loop in next 3 sc, YO and draw through all 4 loops on hook; do **not** finish off.

Edging: Ch 1, turn; work 31 sc evenly spaced across end of rows; working in free loops of beginning ch **(Fig. 3b, page 205)**, 3 sc in first ch, sc in next 25 chs, 3 sc in next ch; work 31 sc evenly spaced across end of rows; 3 sc in top corner; join with slip st to first sc, finish off: 96 sc.

FRONT
Work same as Back; do **not** finish off.

JOINING
With **wrong** sides facing, Front toward you, and working through **inside** loops of each stitch on **both** pieces, slip st in each sc around stuffing with fiberfill before closing; join with slip st to **both** loops of first slip st, finish off.

ARM (Make 2)
Rnd 1 (Right side): With Vibrant Orange, ch 2, 6 sc in second ch from hook; do **not** join, place marker **(see Markers, page 205)**.

Rnd 2: 2 Sc in each sc around: 12 sc.

Rnds 3 and 4: Sc in each sc around.

Rnd 5: Decrease around changing to Bright Yellow in last sc **(Fig. 7a, page 206)**: 6 sc.

Stuff hand firmly with fiberfill.

Rnds 6-19: Sc in each sc around.

Rnd 20: Sc in each sc around; slip st in next sc, finish off leaving a long end for sewing.

LEG (Make 2)
Rnd 1 (Right side): With Vibrant Orange, ch 2, 6 sc in second ch from hook; do **not** join, place marker.

Rnd 2: 2 Sc in each sc around: 12 sc.

Rnds 3 and 4: Sc in each sc around.

Rnd 5: Decrease around changing to Bright Yellow in last sc: 6 sc.

Stuff foot firmly with fiberfill.

Rnds 6-22: Sc in each sc around.

Rnd 23: Sc in each sc around; slip st in next sc, finish off leaving a long end for sewing.

FINISHING
Using photo as a guide for placement:

Flatten top edge of each Arm and sew opening closed; flatten top edge of each Leg and sew opening closed. Sew Arms and Legs to Body.

For tassel, cut five 7" (18 cm) strands each of Vibrant Orange, Parakeet, and Bright Yellow. Hold strands together and use crochet hook to draw through stitches at top of Body; tie ends in a knot. Tightly wrap an 8" (20.5 cm) strand of Parakeet around base of knot; knot ends securely. Tightly wrap another 8" (20.5 cm) strand of Parakeet around all strands above knot; knot ends securely. Trim the ends of the tassel evenly.

With Black, add straight stitches **(Fig. A, page 169)** for eyes and mouth; add satin stitches **(Fig. 14, page 208)** for nose.

CIRCLE

BODY

BACK

Rnd 1 (Right side): With Spring Green, ch 2, 6 sc in second ch from hook; do **not** join, place marker *(see Markers, page 205)*.

Note: Mark Rnd 1 as **right** side.

Rnd 2: 2 Sc in each sc around: 12 sc.

Rnd 3: (Sc in next sc, 2 sc in next sc) around: 18 sc.

Rnd 4: (2 Sc in next sc, sc in next 2 sc) around: 24 sc.

Rnd 5: Sc in next 2 sc, 2 sc in next sc, (sc in next 3 sc, 2 sc in next sc) 5 times, sc in next sc: 30 sc.

Rnd 6: (2 Sc in next sc, sc in next 4 sc) around: 36 sc.

Rnd 7: Sc in next 3 sc, 2 sc in next sc, (sc in next 5 sc, 2 sc in next sc) 5 times, sc in next 2 sc: 42 sc.

Rnd 8: (2 Sc in next sc, sc in next 6 sc) around: 48 sc.

Rnd 9: Sc in next 4 sc, 2 sc in next sc, (sc in next 7 sc, 2 sc in next sc) 5 times, sc in next 3 sc: 54 sc.

Rnd 10: (2 Sc in next sc, sc in next 8 sc) around: 60 sc.

Rnd 11: Sc in next 5 sc, 2 sc in next sc, (sc in next 9 sc, 2 sc in next sc) 5 times, sc in next 4 sc: 66 sc.

Rnd 12: (2 Sc in next sc, sc in next 10 sc) around: 72 sc.

Rnd 13: Sc in each sc around; slip st in next sc, finish off.

FRONT

Work same as Back; do **not** finish off.

JOINING

With **wrong** sides facing, Front toward you, and working through **inside** loops of each stitch on **both** pieces, slip st in each sc around stuffing with fiberfill before closing; join with slip st to **both** loops of first slip st, finish off.

ARM (Make 2)

Rnd 1 (Right side): With Lavender, ch 2, 6 sc in second ch from hook; do **not** join, place marker.

Rnd 2: 2 Sc in each sc around: 12 sc.

Rnds 3 and 4: Sc in each sc around.

To decrease, pull up a loop in each of next 2 sc, YO and draw through all 3 loops on hook **(counts as one sc)**.

Rnd 5: Decrease around: 6 sc.

Stuff hand firmly with fiberfill.

Rnds 6-19: Sc in each sc around.

Rnd 20: Sc in each sc around; slip st in next sc, finish off leaving a long end for sewing.

LEG (Make 2)

Rnd 1 (Right side): With Lavender, ch 2, 6 sc in second ch from hook; do **not** join, place marker.

Rnd 2: 2 Sc in each sc around: 12 sc.

Rnds 3 and 4: Sc in each sc around.

Rnd 5: Decrease around: 6 sc.

Stuff foot firmly with fiberfill.

Rnds 6-22: Sc in each sc around.

Rnd 23: Sc in each sc around; slip st in next sc, finish off leaving a long end for sewing.

FINISHING

Using photo as a guide for placement:

Flatten top edge of each Arm and sew opening closed; flatten top edge of each Leg and sew opening closed. Sew Arms and Legs to Body.

For tassel, cut seven 7" (18 cm) strands each of Spring Green and Lavender. Hold strands together and use crochet hook to draw through stitches at top of Body; tie ends in a knot. Tightly wrap an 8" (20.5 cm) strand of Spring Green around base of knot; knot ends securely. Tightly wrap another 8" (20.5 cm) strand of Spring Green around all strands above knot; knot ends securely. Trim the ends of the tassel evenly.

With Black, add straight stitches *(Fig. A)* for eyes and mouth; add satin stitches *(Fig. 14, page 208)* for nose.

Designs by Donna Cordero.

STRAIGHT STITCH

Straight Stitch is just what the name implies, a single, straight stitch. Come up at 1 and go down at 2 *(Fig. A)*.

Fig. A

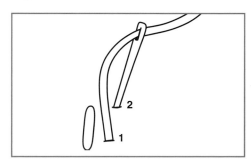

PINEAPPLE GARDEN DOILY

Our oval doily features a "garden" of lovely crochet stitches: clusters, shells, V-stitches, and picots. Size 20 thread lends delicacy.

■■■□ EXPERIENCED

Finished Size:
11¹/₂" x 18¹/₂" (29 cm x 47 cm)

MATERIALS
Cotton Thread (size 20) [400 yards
 (366 meters) per ball]: 1 ball
Steel crochet hook, size 9 (1.4 mm) **or**
 size needed for gauge

GAUGE: Rnds 1-3 = 1¹/₂" x 8¹/₂"
(3.75 cm x 21.5 cm)

Ch 96.

Rnd 1 (Right side)**:** 11 Dc in fourth ch from hook **(3 skipped chs count as first dc, now and throughout)**, † skip next 3 chs, sc in next ch, (ch 5, skip next 4 chs, sc in next ch) 3 times, ★ skip next 3 chs, 8 dc in next ch, skip next 3 chs, sc in next ch, (ch 5, skip next 4 chs, sc in next ch) 3 times; repeat from ★ 2 times **more**, skip next 3 chs †, 12 dc in last ch; working in free loops of beginning ch **(Fig. 3b, page 205)**, repeat from † to † once; join with slip st to first dc: 72 dc and 24 loops.

Note: Mark Rnd 1 as **right** side.

Rnd 2: Ch 6 **(counts as first dc plus ch 3)**, dc in next dc, (ch 3, dc in next dc) 10 times, † sc in next loop, (ch 5, sc in next loop) twice, ★ dc in next dc, (ch 1, dc in next dc) 7 times, sc in next loop, (ch 5, sc in next loop) twice; repeat from ★ 2 times **more** †, dc in next dc, (ch 3, dc in next dc) 11 times, repeat from † to † once; join with slip st to first dc: 64 sps and 16 loops.

To work beginning Cluster, slip st in first ch-3 sp, ch 2, ★ YO, insert hook in same sp, YO and pull up a loop, YO and draw through 2 loops on hook; repeat from ★ once **more**, YO and draw through all 3 loops on hook.

To work Cluster, ★ YO, insert hook in sp indicated, YO and pull up a loop, YO and draw through 2 loops on hook; repeat from ★ 2 times **more**, YO and draw through all 4 loops on hook.

Rnd 3: Work beginning Cluster, † (ch 3, work Cluster in next ch-3 sp) 10 times, sc in next loop, ch 5, sc in next loop, ★ work Cluster in next ch-1 sp, (ch 3, work Cluster in next ch-1 sp) 6 times, sc in next loop, ch 5, sc in next loop; repeat from ★ 2 times **more** †, work Cluster in next ch-3 sp, repeat from † to † once; join with slip st to top of beginning Cluster: 64 Clusters.

To work Large Picot, ch 4, slip st in side of last sc made.

Rnd 4: Slip st in first ch-3 sp, ch 1, (2 sc, work Large Picot, 2 sc) in same sp, ch 2, 2 sc in next ch-3 sp, work Large Picot, place marker around Picot just made for joining placement, 2 sc in same sp, ch 2, [(2 sc, work Large Picot, 2 sc) in next ch-3 sp, ch 2] 8 times, † (sc, work Large Picot, sc) in next loop, ch 2, ★ [(2 sc, work Large Picot, 2 sc) in next ch-3 sp, ch 2] 6 times, (sc, work Large Picot, sc) in next loop, ch 2; repeat from ★ 2 times **more** †, [(2 sc, work Large Picot, 2 sc) in next ch-3 sp, ch 2] 10 times, repeat from † to † once; join with slip st to first sc, finish off: 64 Large Picots.

To work 3-dc Shell, (3 dc, ch 3, 3 dc) in sp or loop indicated.

To work dtr Cluster (uses next 3 Picots), ★ YO 3 times, insert hook in **next** Picot, YO and pull up a loop, (YO and draw through 2 loops on hook) 3 times; repeat from ★ 2 times **more**, YO and draw through all 4 loops on hook.

To work treble crochet (abbreviated tr), YO twice, insert hook in st, sp, or loop indicated, YO and pull up a loop (4 loops on hook), (YO and draw through 2 loops on hook) 3 times.

Rnd 5: Ch 4, (2 dc, ch 3, 3 dc) in fourth ch from hook, place marker around last dc made for st placement, ch 3; with **right** side facing, dc in marked Picot, ♥ ch 3, **turn**; work 3-dc Shell in next Shell (ch-3 sp), ch 7, **turn**; work 3-dc Shell in next Shell, ch 3, dc in next Picot, ch 3, **turn**; work 3-dc Shell in next Shell, ch 7, **turn**; work 3-dc Shell in next Shell, ch 3, ★ dc in next Picot, ch 3, **turn**; work 3-dc Shell in next Shell, ch 7, **turn**; work 3-dc Shell in next Shell, ch 3, dc in same Picot, ch 3, **turn**; work 3-dc Shell in next Shell, ch 7, **turn**; work 3-dc Shell in next Shell, ch 3; repeat from ★ 3 times **more**, [dc in next Picot, ch 3, **turn**; work 3-dc Shell in next Shell, ch 7, **turn**; work 3-dc Shell in next Shell, ch 3] twice, work dtr Cluster, † ch 3, **turn**; work 3-dc Shell in next Shell, ch 7, **turn**; work 3-dc Shell in next Shell, ch 3, dc in next Picot, ch 3, **turn**; work 3-dc Shell in next Shell, ch 7, **turn**; work 3-dc Shell in next Shell, ch 3, skip next Picot, dc in next ch-2 sp, ch 3, **turn**; work 3-dc Shell in next Shell, ch 7, **turn**; work 3-dc Shell in next Shell, ch 3, skip next Picot, dc in next Picot, ch 3, **turn**; work 3-dc Shell in next Shell, ch 7, **turn**; work 3-dc Shell in next Shell, ch 3, work dtr Cluster †, repeat from † to † 2 times **more** ♥, ch 3, **turn**; work 3-dc Shell in

Instructions continued on page 172.

Continued from page 170.

next Shell, ch 7, **turn**; work 3-dc Shell in next Shell, ch 3, dc in next Picot, repeat from ♥ to ♥ once, ch 3, **turn**; 3 dc in next Shell, slip st in base of marked dc, ch 1, skip next 4 dc on first Shell, slip st in base of next dc, 3 dc in same sp on last Shell, ch 3, **turn**; tr in top of first dc to form last loop: 50 loops.

Rnd 6: Ch 7 **(counts as first tr plus ch 3)**, tr in same loop, † [ch 7, (tr, ch 3, tr) in next loop] 12 times †, (ch 3, tr) twice in each of next 13 loops, repeat from † to † once, ch 3, (tr, ch 3) twice in each of last 12 loops; join with slip st to first tr: 76 ch-3 sps and 24 loops.

To work 2-dc Shell, (2 dc, ch 2, 2 dc) in ch or sp indicated.

Rnd 7: Slip st in first ch-3 sp, ch 3 **(counts as first dc, now and throughout)**, (dc, ch 2, 2 dc) in same sp, † (work 2-dc Shell in center ch of next loop, work 2-dc Shell in next ch-3 sp) 12 times †, (skip next ch-3 sp, work 2-dc Shell in next ch-3 sp) 13 times, repeat from † to † once, skip next ch-3 sp, (work 2-dc Shell in next ch-3 sp, skip next ch-3 sp) 12 times; join with slip st to first dc: 74 Shells.

To work beginning 2-dc Shell, slip st in next dc and in next ch-2 sp, ch 3, (dc, ch 2, 2 dc) in same sp.

Rnds 8 and 9: Work beginning 2-dc Shell, work 2-dc Shell in each Shell (ch-2 sp) around; join with slip st to first dc.

Rnd 10: Slip st in next dc and in next ch-2 sp, ch 1, 3 sc in same sp, ch 4, slip st in second ch from hook, ch 2, sc in next Shell, ch 11, sc in tenth ch from hook, place marker around loop just made for joining placement, sc in next ch and in same Shell, ch 4, slip st in second ch from hook, ch 2, [sc in next Shell, ch 11, sc in tenth ch from hook, sc in next ch and in same Shell, ch 4, slip st in second ch from hook, ch 2] 22 times, 3 sc in next Shell, ch 12, sc in tenth ch from hook and in next ch, ch 1, 3 sc in next Shell, ch 4, slip st in second ch from hook, ch 2, ★ sc in next Shell, ch 11, sc in tenth ch from hook, sc in next ch and in same Shell, ch 4, slip st in second ch from hook, ch 2, 3 sc in next Shell, ch 12, sc in tenth ch from hook and in next ch, ch 1, 3 sc in next Shell, ch 4, slip st in second ch from hook, ch 2; repeat from ★ 3 times **more**, [sc in next Shell, ch 11, sc in tenth ch from hook, sc in next ch and in same Shell, ch 4, slip st in second ch from hook, ch 2] 23 times, 3 sc in next Shell, ch 12, sc in tenth ch from hook and in next ch, ch 1, † 3 sc in next Shell, ch 4, slip st in second ch from hook, ch 2, sc in next Shell, ch 11, sc in tenth ch from hook, sc in next ch and in same Shell, ch 4, slip st in second ch from hook, ch 2, 3 sc in next Shell, ch 12, sc in tenth ch from hook and in next ch, ch 1 †, repeat from † to † 3 times **more**; join with slip st to first sc, finish off: 64 loops.

Rnd 11: With **right** side facing, join thread with slip st in marked loop; ch 3, (2 dc, ch 3, 3 dc) in same loop, † (ch 3, sc in center ch of next loop, ch 3, work 3-dc Shell in next loop) 11 times †, (ch 5, sc in center ch of next loop, ch 5, work 3-dc Shell in next loop) 5 times, repeat from † to † once, ch 5, sc in center ch of next loop, ch 5, (work 3-dc Shell in next loop, ch 5, sc in center ch of next loop, ch 5) 4 times; join with slip st to first dc: 32 Shells.

To work beginning 3-dc Shell, slip st in next 2 dc and in next ch-3 sp, ch 3, (2 dc, ch 3, 3 dc) in same sp.

To work V-St, (dc, ch 3, dc) in st or sp indicated.

Rnd 12: Work beginning 3-dc Shell, † (ch 3, work V-St in next sc, ch 3, work 3-dc Shell in next Shell) 11 times †, (ch 4, work V-St in next sc, ch 4, work 3-dc Shell in next Shell) 5 times, repeat from † to † once, ch 4, work V-St in next sc, ch 4, (work 3-dc Shell in next Shell, ch 4, work V-St in next sc, ch 4) 4 times; join with slip st to first dc.

Rnd 13: Work beginning 3-dc Shell, † [ch 3, work V-St in next V-St (ch-3 sp), ch 3, work 3-dc Shell in next Shell] 11 times †, (ch 4, work V-St in next V-St, ch 4, work 3-dc Shell in next Shell) 5 times, repeat from † to † once, ch 4, work V-St in next V-St, ch 4, (work 3-dc Shell in next Shell, ch 4, work V-St in next V-St, ch 4) 4 times; join with slip st to first dc.

Rnd 14: Work beginning 3-dc Shell, † (ch 2, skip next ch-3 sp, dc in next dc, 5 dc in next ch-3 sp, dc in next dc, ch 2, work 3-dc Shell in next Shell) 11 times †, (ch 3, skip next ch-4 sp, dc in next dc, 5 dc in next ch-3 sp, dc in next dc, ch 3, work 3-dc Shell in next Shell) 5 times, repeat from † to † once, ch 3, skip next ch-4 sp, dc in next dc, 5 dc in next ch-3 sp, dc in next dc, ch 3, (work 3-dc Shell in next Shell, ch 3, skip next ch-4 sp, dc in next dc, 5 dc in next ch-3 sp, dc in next dc, ch 3) 4 times; join with slip st to first dc: 416 dc.

Rnd 15: Work beginning 3-dc Shell, ch 1, skip next ch-2 sp, (dc in next dc, ch 1) 7 times, ★ work 3-dc Shell in next Shell, ch 1, skip next sp, (dc in next dc, ch 1) 7 times; repeat from ★ around; join with slip st to first dc.

Rnd 16: Work beginning 3-dc Shell, ch 2, skip next ch-1 sp, (sc in next ch-1 sp, ch 2) 6 times, ★ work 3-dc Shell in next Shell, ch 2, skip next ch-1 sp, (sc in next ch-1 sp, ch 2) 6 times; repeat from ★ around; join with slip st to first dc: 256 sps.

Rnd 17: Work beginning 3-dc Shell, ch 3, skip next ch-2 sp, sc in next ch-2 sp, (ch 2, sc in next ch-2 sp) 4 times, ch 3, ★ work 3-dc Shell in next Shell, ch 3, skip next ch-2 sp, sc in next ch-2 sp, (ch 2, sc in next ch-2 sp) 4 times, ch 3; repeat from ★ around; join with slip st to first dc: 224 sps.

Rnd 18: Ch 3, dc in next dc, ch 2, dc in next ch-3 sp, ch 2, skip next dc, dc in next 2 dc, ch 3, skip next ch-3 sp, sc in next ch-2 sp, (ch 2, sc in next ch-2 sp) 3 times, ch 3, ★ dc in next 2 dc, ch 2, dc in next ch-3 sp, ch 2, skip next dc, dc in next 2 dc, ch 3, skip next ch-3 sp, sc in next ch-2 sp, (ch 2, sc in next ch-2 sp) 3 times, ch 3; repeat from ★ around; join with slip st to first dc.

Rnd 19: Ch 3, dc in next dc, ch 3, work V-St in next dc, ch 3, dc in next 2 dc, ch 3, skip next ch-3 sp, sc in next ch-2 sp, (ch 2, sc in next ch-2 sp) twice, ch 3, ★ dc in next 2 dc, ch 3, work V-St in next dc, ch 3, dc in next 2 dc, ch 3, skip next ch-3 sp, sc in next ch-2 sp, (ch 2, sc in next ch-2 sp) twice, ch 3; repeat from ★ around; join with slip st to first dc.

To work Small Picot, ch 3, slip st in third ch from hook.

Rnd 20: Ch 3, dc in next dc, ♥ ch 3, dc in next dc, work Small Picot, (dc, work Small Picot) 4 times in next ch-3 sp, dc in next dc, ch 3, dc in next 2 dc, ch 3, skip next ch-3 sp, sc in next ch-2 sp, ch 2, sc in next ch-2 sp, ch 3, ★ dc in next 2 dc, ch 3, dc in next dc, work Small Picot, (dc, work Small Picot) 4 times in next ch-3 sp, dc in next dc, ch 3, dc in next 2 dc, ch 3, skip next ch-3 sp, sc in next ch-2 sp, ch 2, sc in next ch-2 sp, ch 3; repeat from ★ 10 times **more**, † dc in next 2 dc, ch 3, dc in next dc, work Small Picot, (dc, work Small Picot) twice in next ch-3 sp, dc in next dc, ch 3, dc in next 2 dc, ch 3, skip next ch-3 sp, sc in next ch-2 sp, ch 2, sc in next ch-2 sp, ch 3 †, repeat from † to † 3 times **more** ♥, dc in next 2 dc, repeat from ♥ to ♥ once; join with slip st to first dc: 304 dc.

Rnd 21: Ch 3, dc in next dc, ♥ ch 3, tr in next dc, (ch 5, tr in next dc) 5 times, ch 3, dc in next 2 dc, skip next ch-3 sp, tr in next ch-2 sp, ★ dc in next 2 dc, ch 3, tr in next dc, (ch 5, tr in next dc) 5 times, ch 3, dc in next 2 dc, skip next ch-3 sp, tr in next ch-2 sp; repeat from ★ 10 times **more**, † dc in next 2 dc, ch 3, tr in next dc, ch 5, tr in next dc, ch 7, tr in next dc, ch 5, tr in next dc, ch 3, dc in next 2 dc, skip next ch-3 sp, tr in next ch-2 sp †, repeat from † to † 3 times **more** ♥, dc in next 2 dc, repeat from ♥ to ♥ once; join with slip st to first dc: 144 loops and 64 ch-3 sps.

Rnd 22: Slip st in next dc, ch 1, sc in same st, ♥ 3 sc in next ch-3 sp, sc in next tr, [ch 4, (tr, work Small Picot, tr) in center ch of next loop, ch 4, sc in next tr] 5 times, 3 sc in next ch-3 sp, sc in next dc, ch 4, slip st in third ch from hook, ch 1, ★ skip next 3 sts, sc in next dc, 3 sc in next ch-3 sp, sc in next tr, [ch 4, (tr, work Small Picot, tr) in center ch of next loop, ch 4, sc in next tr] 5 times, 3 sc in next ch-3 sp, sc in next dc, ch 4, slip st in third ch from hook, ch 1; repeat from ★ 10 times **more**, † skip next 3 sts, sc in next dc, 3 sc in next ch-3 sp, sc in next tr, ch 4, (tr, work Small Picot, tr) in center ch of next loop, ch 4, sc in next tr, ch 4, [skip next ch, (tr, work Small Picot, tr) in next ch, ch 4, skip next ch, sc in next st, ch 4] twice, (tr, work Small Picot, tr) in center ch of next loop, ch 4, sc in next tr, 3 sc in next ch-3 sp, sc in next dc, ch 4, slip st in third ch from hook, ch 1 †, repeat from † to † 3 times **more**, skip next 3 sts ♥, sc in next dc, repeat from ♥ to ♥ once; join with slip st to first sc, finish off.

Design by C. Strohmeyer.

CLASSIC SQUARE DOILY

Offering a hint of nature with its symmetrical pattern of leaves, this graceful doily will infuse your home with harmony and balance.

■■■□ INTERMEDIATE

Finished Size: 11½" (29 cm)

MATERIALS
Bedspread Weight Cotton Thread
 (size 10) [150 yards (137 meters)
 per ball]: 2 balls
Steel crochet hook, size 9 (1.4 mm) **or**
 size needed for gauge

GAUGE: Rnds 1-5 = 2½" (6.25 cm)

Ch 8; join with slip st to form a ring.

Rnd 1 (Right side)**: Ch 4 (counts as first dc plus ch 1)**, (5 dc in ring, ch 1) 3 times, 4 dc in ring; join with slip st to first dc: 20 dc and 4 ch-1 sps.

Rnd 2: Slip st in first ch-1 sp, ch 5 **(counts as first dc plus ch 2)**, dc in same sp, ★ † 2 dc in next dc, dc in next 3 dc, 2 dc in next dc †, (dc, ch 2, dc) in next ch-1 sp; repeat from ★ 2 times **more**, then repeat from † to † once; join with slip st to first dc: 36 dc and 4 ch-2 sps.

Rnd 3: Slip st in first ch-2 sp, ch 3 **(counts as first dc, now and throughout)**, (dc, ch 3, 2 dc) in same sp, ★ † skip next dc, 2 dc in next dc, dc in next 5 dc, 2 dc in next dc †, (2 dc, ch 3, 2 dc) in next ch-2 sp; repeat from ★ 2 times **more**, then repeat from † to † once; join with slip st to first dc: 52 dc and 4 ch-3 sps.

Rnd 4: Slip st in next dc and in next ch-3 sp, ch 3, (dc, ch 3, 2 dc) in same sp, ★ † skip next 2 dc, 2 dc in next dc, dc in next 7 dc, 2 dc in next dc †, (2 dc, ch 3, 2 dc) in next ch-3 sp; repeat from ★ 2 times **more**, then repeat from † to † once; join with slip st to first dc: 60 dc and 4 ch-3 sps.

Rnd 5: Slip st in next dc and in next ch-3 sp, ch 3, (dc, ch 3, 2 dc) in same sp, ★ † skip next 2 dc, (dc, ch 1, dc) in next dc, [skip next dc, (dc, ch 1, dc) in next dc] 5 times †, (2 dc, ch 3, 2 dc) in next ch-3 sp; repeat from ★ 2 times **more**, then repeat from † to † once; join with slip st to first dc: 64 dc and 28 sps.

Rnd 6: Slip st in next dc and in next ch-3 sp, ch 3, (dc, ch 3, 2 dc) in same sp, ★ † skip next 2 dc, 2 dc in next dc, dc in next ch-1 sp, (dc in next 2 dc and in next ch-1 sp) twice, dc in next dc, ch 1, dc in next dc and in next ch-1 sp, (dc in next 2 dc and in next ch-1 sp) twice, 2 dc in next dc †, (2 dc, ch 3, 2 dc) in next ch-3 sp; repeat from ★ 2 times **more**, then repeat from † to † once; join with slip st to first dc: 96 dc and 8 sps.

Rnd 7: Slip st in next dc and in next ch-3 sp, ch 3, (dc, ch 3, 2 dc) in same sp, ★ † skip next 2 dc, 2 dc in next dc, dc in next 8 dc, ch 1, dc in next ch-1 sp, ch 1, skip next dc, dc in next 8 dc, 2 dc in next dc †, (2 dc, ch 3, 2 dc) in next ch-3 sp; repeat from ★ 2 times **more**, then repeat from † to † once; join with slip st to first dc: 100 dc and 12 sps.

Rnd 8: Slip st in next dc and in next ch-3 sp, ch 3, (dc, ch 3, 2 dc) in same sp, ★ † skip next 2 dc, 2 dc in each of next 2 dc, dc in next 7 dc, ch 1, (dc in next ch-1 sp, ch 1) twice, skip next dc, dc in next 7 dc, 2 dc in each of next 2 dc †, (2 dc, ch 3, 2 dc) in next ch-3 sp; repeat from ★ 2 times **more**, then repeat from † to † once; join with slip st to first dc: 112 dc and 16 sps.

Rnd 9: Slip st in next dc and in next ch-3 sp, ch 3, (dc, ch 3, 2 dc) in same sp, ★ † ch 1, skip next 2 dc, 2 dc in next dc, dc in next 9 dc, ch 1, (dc in next ch-1 sp, ch 1) 3 times, skip next dc, dc in next 9 dc, 2 dc in next dc, ch 1 †, (2 dc, ch 3, 2 dc) in next ch-3 sp; repeat from ★ 2 times **more**, then repeat from † to † once; join with slip st to first dc: 116 dc and 28 sps.

Rnd 10: Slip st in next dc and in next ch-3 sp, ch 3, (dc, ch 3, 2 dc) in same sp, ★ † ch 1, 2 dc in next ch-1 sp, dc in next 11 dc and in next ch-1 sp, (ch 1, dc in next ch-1 sp) 3 times, dc in next 11 dc, 2 dc in next ch-1 sp, ch 1 †, (2 dc, ch 3, 2 dc) in next ch-3 sp; repeat from ★ 2 times **more**, then repeat from † to † once; join with slip st to first dc: 136 dc and 24 sps.

Rnd 11: Slip st in next dc and in next ch-3 sp, ch 3, (dc, ch 3, 2 dc) in same sp, ★ † ch 1, 2 dc in next ch-1 sp, dc in next 14 dc and in next ch-1 sp, (ch 1, dc in next ch-1 sp) twice, dc in next 14 dc, 2 dc in next ch-1 sp, ch 1 †, (2 dc, ch 3, 2 dc) in next ch-3 sp; repeat from ★ 2 times **more**, then repeat from † to † once; join with slip st to first dc: 156 dc and 20 sps.

To sp or dc decrease (uses next 2 sps or next 2 dc), ★ YO, insert hook in **next** sp or **next** dc, YO and pull up a loop, YO and draw through 2 loops on hook; repeat from ★ once **more**, YO and draw through all 3 loops on hook **(counts as one dc)**.

Rnd 12: Slip st in next dc and in next ch-3 sp, ch 3, (dc, ch 3, 2 dc) in same sp, ★ † ch 1, 2 dc in next ch-1 sp, dc in each dc across to next ch-1 sp, sp decrease, dc in each dc across to next ch-1 sp, 2 dc in next ch-1 sp, ch 1 †, (2 dc, ch 3, 2 dc) in next ch-3 sp; repeat from ★ 2 times **more**, then repeat from † to † once; join with slip st to first dc: 172 dc and 12 sps.

Instructions continued on page 176.

Continued from page 174.

Rnd 13: Slip st in next dc and in next ch-3 sp, ch 3, (dc, ch 3, 2 dc) in same sp, ★ † (ch 1, dc) twice in next ch-1 sp, skip next dc, [(dc, ch 1, dc) in next dc, skip next dc] across to next ch-1 sp, (dc, ch 1) twice in next ch-1 sp †, (2 dc, ch 3, 2 dc) in next ch-3 sp; repeat from ★ 2 times **more**, then repeat from † to † once; join with slip st to first dc: 184 dc and 96 sps.

Rnd 14: Slip st in next dc and in next ch-3 sp, ch 3, (dc, ch 3, 2 dc) in same sp, ★ † ch 1, 2 dc in next ch-1 sp, dc in next dc and in next ch-1 sp, (dc decrease, dc in next ch-1 sp) 20 times, dc in next dc, 2 dc in next ch-1 sp, ch 1 †, (2 dc, ch 3, 2 dc) in next ch-3 sp; repeat from ★ 2 times **more**, then repeat from † to † once; join with slip st to first dc: 204 dc and 12 sps.

Rnd 15: Slip st in next dc and in next ch-3 sp, ch 3, (dc, ch 3, 2 dc) in same sp, ★ † ch 1, dc in next ch-1 sp, dc in next dc and in each dc across to next ch-1 sp, dc in next ch-1 sp, ch 1 †, (2 dc, ch 3, 2 dc) in next ch-3 sp; repeat from ★ 2 times **more**, then repeat from † to † once; join with slip st to first dc: 212 dc and 12 sps.

Rnd 16: Slip st in next dc and in next ch-3 sp, ch 3, (dc, ch 3, 2 dc) in same sp, ★ † ch 1, 2 dc in next ch-1 sp, dc in next dc and in each dc across to next ch-1 sp, 2 dc in next ch-1 sp, ch 1 †, (2 dc, ch 3, 2 dc) in next ch-3 sp; repeat from ★ 2 times **more**, then repeat from † to † once; join with slip st to first dc: 228 dc and 12 sps.

Rnd 17: Slip st in next dc and in next ch-3 sp, ch 3, (dc, ch 2, 2 dc, ch 4, 2 dc, ch 2, 2 dc) in same sp, ★ † (2 dc, ch 2, 2 dc) in next ch-1 sp, skip next 2 dc, (2 dc, ch 2, 2 dc) in next dc, [skip next 3 dc, (2 dc, ch 2, 2 dc) in next dc] 12 times, skip next 2 dc, (2 dc, ch 2, 2 dc) in next ch-1 sp †, in next ch-3 sp work (2 dc, ch 2, 2 dc, ch 4, 2 dc, ch 2, 2 dc); repeat from ★ 2 times **more**, then repeat from † to † once; join with slip st to first dc: 272 dc and 72 sps.

Rnd 18: Slip st in next dc and in next ch-2 sp, ch 3, (dc, ch 2, 2 dc) in same sp, 6 dc in next ch-4 sp, ★ (2 dc, ch 2, 2 dc) in next ch-2 sp, 6 dc in next sp; repeat from ★ around; join with slip st to first dc: 36 6-dc groups and 36 ch-2 sps.

Rnd 19: Slip st in next dc and in next ch-2 sp, ch 3, (dc, ch 2, 2 dc) in same sp, skip next 2 dc, 2 dc in each of next 3 dc, ch 1, 2 dc in each of next 3 dc, ★ (2 dc, ch 2, 2 dc) in next ch-2 sp, [skip next 2 dc, dc in next 6 dc, (2 dc, ch 2, 2 dc) in next ch-2 sp] 8 times, skip next 2 dc, 2 dc in each of next 3 dc, ch 1, 2 dc in each of next 3 dc; repeat from ★ 2 times **more**, [(2 dc, ch 2, 2 dc) in next ch-2 sp, skip next 2 dc, dc in next 6 dc] across; join with slip st to first dc: 40 6-dc groups and 40 sps.

Rnd 20: Slip st in next dc and in next ch-2 sp, ch 3, (dc, ch 2, 2 dc) in same sp, skip next 2 dc, dc in next 2 dc, dc decrease, dc in next 2 dc, ch 3, ★ dc in next 2 dc, dc decrease, dc in next 2 dc, † (2 dc, ch 2, 2 dc) in next ch-2 sp, skip next 2 dc, dc in next 2 dc, dc decrease, dc in next 2 dc †; repeat from † to † 8 times **more**, ch 3; repeat from ★ 2 times **more**, dc in next 2 dc, dc decrease, dc in next 2 dc, repeat from † to † across; join with slip st to first dc.

Rnd 21: Slip st in next dc and in next ch-2 sp, ch 3, [(dc, (ch 2, 2 dc) twice] in same sp, skip next 2 dc, dc decrease, dc in next dc, dc decrease, [2 dc, (ch 2, 2 dc) twice] in next ch-3 sp, dc decrease, dc in next dc, dc decrease, ★ † [2 dc, (ch 2, 2 dc) twice] in next ch-2 sp, skip next 2 dc, dc decrease, dc in next dc, dc decrease †; repeat from † to † 8 times **more**, [2 dc, (ch 2, 2 dc) twice] in next ch-3 sp, dc decrease, dc in next dc, dc decrease; repeat from ★ 2 times **more**, then repeat from † to † across; join with slip st to first dc.

To work Cluster (uses next 3 sts), ★ YO, insert hook in **next** st, YO and pull up a loop, YO and draw through 2 loops on hook; repeat from ★ 2 times **more**, YO and draw through all 4 loops on hook.

To work treble crochet (abbreviated *tr*), YO twice, insert hook in st or sp indicated, YO and pull up a loop (4 loops on hook), (YO and draw through 2 loops on hook) 3 times.

Rnd 22: Slip st in next dc and in next ch-2 sp, ch 3, (dc, ch 2, 2 dc) in same sp, ch 1, (2 dc, ch 2, 2 dc) in next ch-2 sp, skip next 2 dc, work Cluster, (2 tr, ch 2, 2 tr) in next ch-2 sp, ch 3, (2 tr, ch 2, 2 tr) in next ch-2 sp, skip next 2 dc, work Cluster, ★ † (2 dc, ch 2, 2 dc) in next ch-2 sp, ch 1, (2 dc, ch 2, 2 dc) in next ch-2 sp, skip next 2 dc, work Cluster †; repeat from † to † 8 times **more**, (2 tr, ch 2, 2 tr) in next ch-2 sp, ch 3, (2 tr, ch 2, 2 tr) in next ch-2 sp, skip next 2 dc, work Cluster; repeat from ★ 2 times **more**, then repeat from † to † across; join with slip st to first dc.

Rnd 23: Slip st in next dc, ch 3, 2 dc in next ch-2 sp, dc in next 2 dc and in next ch-1 sp, dc in next 2 dc, 2 dc in next ch-2 sp, dc in next dc, work Cluster, tr in next tr, 2 tr in next ch-2 sp, tr in next 2 tr, 7 tr in next ch-3 sp, tr in next 2 tr, 2 tr in next ch-2 sp, tr in next tr, work Cluster, ★ † dc in next dc, 2 dc in next ch-2 sp, dc in next 2 dc and in next ch-1 sp, dc in next 2 dc, 2 dc in next ch-2 sp, dc in next dc, work Cluster †; repeat from † to † 8 times **more**, tr in next tr, 2 tr in next ch-2 sp, tr in next 2 tr, 7 tr in next ch-3 sp, tr in next 2 tr, 2 tr in next ch-2 sp, tr in next tr, work Cluster; repeat from ★ 2 times **more**, then repeat from † to † across; join with slip st to first dc, finish off.

Design by Mary Werst.

ELEGANT FROST DOILY

Mirroring the lacy fingers of frost on a wintry windowpane, this classic white doily will bring pristine beauty to any table.

Instructions begin on page 178.

ELEGANT FROST DOILY
Shown on page 177.

■■□□ EASY

Finished Size:
12¹⁄₂" (32 cm) diameter

MATERIALS
Bedspread Weight Cotton Thread
  (size 10) [225 yards (206 meters)
  per ball]: 1 ball
Steel crochet hook, size 7 (1.65 mm) **or**
  size needed for gauge

GAUGE: Rnds 1-4 = 1³⁄₄" (4.5 cm)

Ch 7; join with slip st to form a ring.

Rnd 1 (Right side)**:** Ch 5 **(counts as first dc plus ch 2, now and throughout)**, (dc in ring, ch 2) 13 times; join with slip st to first dc: 14 dc and 14 ch-2 sps.

Rnd 2: Ch 3 **(counts as first dc, now and throughout)**, 2 dc in next ch-2 sp, (dc in next dc, 2 dc in next ch-2 sp) around; join with slip st to first dc: 42 dc.

Rnd 3: Ch 1, sc in sp **before** joining **(Fig. 5, page 205)**, ★ ch 3, skip next 3 dc, sc in sp **before** next dc; repeat from ★ around to last 3 dc, ch 1, skip last 3 dc, hdc in first sc to form last ch-3 sp: 14 ch-3 sps.

Rnd 4: Ch 1, 2 sc in last ch-3 sp made, (ch 3, 2 sc in next ch-3 sp) around, ch 1, hdc in first sc to form last ch-3 sp.

Rnd 5: Ch 5, dc in last ch-3 sp made, ch 2, (dc, ch 2) twice in next ch-3 sp and in each ch-3 sp around; join with slip st to first dc: 28 ch-2 sps.

Rnd 6: Slip st in first ch-2 sp, ch 6 **(counts as first dc plus ch 3, now and throughout)**, (dc in next ch-2 sp, ch 3) around; join with slip st to first dc.

Rnd 7: Slip st in first ch-3 sp, ch 3, 3 dc in same sp, 4 dc in next ch-3 sp and in each ch-3 sp around; join with slip st to first dc: 112 dc.

Rnd 8: Ch 1, sc in sp **before** joining, ch 7, skip next 4 dc, ★ sc in sp **before** next dc, ch 7, skip next 4 dc; repeat from ★ around; join with slip st to first sc: 28 ch-7 sps.

Rnd 9: Slip st in first ch-7 sp, ch 3, 8 dc in same sp, sc in next ch-7 sp, ★ 9 dc in next ch-7 sp, sc in next ch-7 sp; repeat from ★ around; join with slip st to first dc: 140 sts.

Rnd 10: Ch 1, sc in same st, (ch 4, skip next 3 dc, sc in next dc) twice, ★ ch 4, skip next sc, sc in next dc, (ch 4, skip next 3 dc, sc in next dc) twice; repeat from ★ around to last sc, ch 1, skip last sc, dc in first sc to form last ch-4 sp: 42 ch-4 sps.

Rnd 11: Ch 5, dc in last ch-4 sp made, ch 2, (dc, ch 2) twice in next ch-4 sp and in each ch-4 sp around; join with slip st to first dc: 84 ch-2 sps.

Rnd 12: Slip st in first ch-2 sp, ch 6, skip next ch-2 sp, dc in next ch-2 sp, ★ ch 3, skip next ch-2 sp, dc in next ch-2 sp; repeat from ★ around to last ch-2 sp, ch 1, skip last ch-2 sp, hdc in first dc to form last ch-3 sp: 42 ch-3 sps.

Rnd 13: Ch 3, dc in same sp, ch 1, ★ (2 dc, ch 2, 2 dc) in next ch-3 sp, ch 1; repeat from ★ around, 2 dc in same sp as first dc, ch 1, sc in first dc to form last ch-2 sp: 84 sps.

Rnd 14: Ch 3, dc in last ch-2 sp made, sc in next ch-1 sp, ★ (2 dc, ch 2, 2 dc) in next ch-2 sp, sc in next ch-1 sp; repeat from ★ around, 2 dc in same sp as first dc, ch 1, sc in first dc to form last ch-2 sp: 42 ch-2 sps.

Rnd 15: Ch 3, dc in last ch-2 sp made, ch 1, (2 dc, ch 1) twice in next ch-2 sp and in each ch-2 sp around, 2 dc in same sp as first dc, sc in first dc to form last ch-1 sp: 84 ch-1 sps.

Rnd 16: Ch 3, dc in last ch-1 sp made, sc in next ch-1 sp, ★ (2 dc, ch 2, 2 dc) in next ch-1 sp, sc in next ch-1 sp; repeat from ★ around, 2 dc in same sp as first dc, ch 1, sc in first dc to form last ch-2 sp: 42 ch-2 sps.

Rnd 17: Ch 3, dc in last ch-2 sp made, ch 1, ★ (2 dc, ch 2, 2 dc) in next ch-2 sp, ch 1; repeat from ★ around, 2 dc in same sp as first dc, ch 1, sc in first dc to form last ch-2 sp: 84 sps.

Rnd 18: Ch 3, dc in last ch-2 sp made, sc in next ch-1 sp, ★ (2 dc, ch 2, 2 dc) in next ch-2 sp, sc in next ch-1 sp; repeat from ★ around, 2 dc in same sp as first dc, ch 1, sc in first dc to form last ch-2 sp: 42 ch-2 sps.

Rnd 19: Ch 3, dc in last ch-2 sp made, ch 2, (2 dc, ch 2) twice in next ch-2 sp and in each ch-2 sp around, 2 dc in same sp as first dc, ch 1, sc in first dc to form last ch-2 sp: 84 ch-2 sps.

Rnd 20: Ch 3, dc in last ch-2 sp made, ch 1, sc in next ch-2 sp, ch 1, ★ (2 dc, ch 2, 2 dc) in next ch-2 sp, ch 1, sc in next ch-2 sp, ch 1; repeat from ★ around, 2 dc in same sp as first dc, ch 1, sc in first dc to form last ch-2 sp: 210 sts and 126 sps.

Rnd 21: Ch 1, sc in last ch-2 sp made and in next 2 dc and next ch-1 sp, skip next sc, sc in next ch-1 sp and in next 2 dc, ★ (sc, ch 3, sc) in next ch-2 sp, sc in next 2 dc and in next ch-1 sp, skip next sc, sc in next ch-1 sp and in next 2 dc; repeat from ★ around, sc in same sp as first sc, ch 3; join with slip st to first sc, finish off.

Design by Sue Galucki.

TAILOR-MADE TABLE RUNNER

This remarkable runner takes first place in style! We tell you how to adjust its length without breaking the continuity of the lacy picot and shell border or the lovely spider web diamond pattern.

Instructions begin on page 180.

TAILOR-MADE TABLE RUNNER
Shown on page 179.

■■■□ INTERMEDIATE

Finished Size: 17¹/₂" (44.5 cm) wide

MATERIALS
Bedspread Weight Cotton Thread
(size 10) [225 yards (206 meters)
per ball]: 5 balls (sufficient for 42"
(106.5 cm) long Runner; each
pattern repeat requires
approximately 40 yards (36.5
meters) of thread)
Steel crochet hook, size 8 (1.5 mm) **or**
size needed for gauge

GAUGE: (dc, ch 2) 9 times = 2¹/₂"
(6.25 cm); 10 rows = 2¹/₄" (5.75 cm)

Ch 160, place marker in last ch made
for st placement, ch 4: 164 chs.

Row 1: Dc in eighth ch from hook,
★ ch 2, skip next 2 chs, dc in next ch;
repeat from ★ across: 53 sps.

Row 2 (Right side): Ch 5 **(counts as
first dc plus ch 2, now and
throughout)**, turn; dc in next dc, (ch 2,
dc in next dc) 5 times, 2 dc in next ch-2
sp, ★ dc in next dc, (ch 2, dc in next dc)
7 times, 2 dc in next ch-2 sp; repeat
from ★ 4 times **more**, (dc in next dc,
ch 2) 6 times, skip next 2 chs, dc in next
ch: 47 ch-2 sps.

Row 3: Ch 5, turn; dc in next dc, (ch 2,
dc in next dc) 4 times, ★ 2 dc in next
ch-2 sp, dc in next dc, ch 8, skip next 2
dc, dc in next dc, 2 dc in next ch-2 sp,
dc in next dc, (ch 2, dc in next dc) 5
times; repeat from ★ across: 35 ch-2 sps
and 6 loops.

Row 4: Ch 5, turn; dc in next dc, (ch 2,
dc in next dc) 3 times, ★ † 2 dc in next
ch-2 sp, dc in next dc, ch 4, sc in next
loop, ch 4, skip next 3 dc, dc in next dc,
2 dc in next ch-2 sp, dc in next dc †,
(ch 2, dc in next dc) 3 times; repeat from
★ 4 times **more**, then repeat from † to
† once, (ch 2, dc in next dc) across: 23
ch-2 sps and 12 ch-4 sps.

Row 5: Ch 5, turn; dc in next dc, (ch 2,
dc in next dc) twice, 2 dc in next ch-2 sp,
dc in next dc, ★ † ch 5, sc in next ch-4
sp, sc in next sc and in next ch-4 sp,
ch 5, skip next 3 dc, dc in next dc, 2 dc
in next ch-2 sp, dc in next dc †, ch 2, dc
in next dc, 2 dc in next ch-2 sp, dc in
next dc; repeat from ★ 4 times **more**,
then repeat from † to † once, (ch 2, dc
in next dc) across: 11 ch-2 sps and 12
loops.

Row 6: Ch 5, turn; dc in next dc, ch 2,
dc in next dc, 2 dc in next ch-2 sp, dc in
next dc, ★ ch 7, sc in next loop, sc in
next 3 sc and in next loop, ch 7, skip
next 3 dc, dc in next dc, 2 dc in next
ch-2 sp, dc in next dc; repeat from ★
across to last 2 dc, (ch 2, dc in next dc)
twice: 4 ch-2 sps and 12 loops.

Row 7: Ch 5, turn; (dc in next dc, ch 2)
twice, skip next 2 dc, dc in next dc, ★ 3
dc in next loop, ch 7, skip next sc, sc in
next 3 sc, ch 7, 3 dc in next loop, dc in
next dc, ch 2, skip next 2 dc, dc in next
dc; repeat from ★ across to last 2 dc,
(ch 2, dc in next dc) twice: 11 ch-2 sps
and 12 loops.

Row 8: Ch 5, turn; (dc in next dc, ch 2)
3 times, skip next 2 dc, dc in next dc, 3
dc in next loop, ch 7, skip next sc, sc in
next sc, ch 7, 3 dc in next loop, dc in
next dc, ch 2, ★ skip next 2 dc, (dc in
next dc, ch 2) twice, skip next 2 dc, dc
in next dc, 3 dc in next loop, ch 7, skip
next sc, sc in next sc, ch 7, 3 dc in next
loop, dc in next dc, ch 2; repeat from ★
4 times **more**, skip next 2 dc, dc in next
dc, (ch 2, dc in next dc) across: 23 ch-2
sps and 12 loops.

Row 9: Ch 5, turn; (dc in next dc, ch 2)
4 times, skip next 2 dc, dc in next dc, 3
dc in next loop, ch 2, 3 dc in next loop,
dc in next dc, ch 2, ★ skip next 2 dc, (dc
in next dc, ch 2) 4 times, skip next 2 dc,
dc in next dc, 3 dc in next loop, ch 2, 3
dc in next loop, dc in next dc, ch 2;
repeat from ★ 4 times **more**, skip next
2 dc, dc in next dc, (ch 2, dc in next dc)
across: 41 ch-2 sps.

Row 10: Ch 5, turn; (dc in next dc,
ch 2) 5 times, ★ † skip next 2 dc, dc in
next dc, 2 dc in next ch-2 sp, dc in next
dc, ch 2 †, skip next 2 dc, (dc in next dc,
ch 2) 6 times; repeat from ★ 4 times
more, then repeat from † to † once,
skip next 2 dc, dc in next dc, (ch 2, dc in
next dc) across: 47 ch-2 sps.

Repeat Rows 3-10 until Runner is
desired length, ending by working Row
10.

Last Row: Ch 5, turn; (dc in next dc,
ch 2) 6 times, ★ skip next 2 dc, (dc in
next dc, ch 2) 8 times; repeat from ★ 4
times **more**, skip next 2 dc, dc in next
dc, (ch 2, dc in next dc) across; do **not**
finish off: 53 ch-2 sps.

EDGING

Rnd 1: Ch 3 **(counts as first dc, now and throughout)**, turn; dc in same st, **[**(2 dc in next ch-2 sp, dc in next dc) twice, dc in next ch-2 sp and in next dc**]** across to last 2 ch-2 sps, 2 dc in next ch-2 sp, dc in next dc, 2 dc in last ch-2 sp and in last dc; working in end of rows, dc in first sp, 2 dc in next sp and in each sp across; working in sps over beginning ch and in free loops of chs at base of Row 1 dc *(Fig. 3b, page 205)*, 2 dc in marked ch, **[**(2 dc in next sp, dc in next ch) twice, dc in next sp and in next ch**]** across to last 2 sps, 2 dc in next sp, dc in next ch, 2 dc in last sp and in last ch; working in end of rows, dc in first sp, 2 dc in next sp and in each sp across; join with slip st to first dc.

Rnd 2: Ch 5, do **not** turn; dc in next dc, ch 4, skip next 2 dc, sc in next dc, ch 4, skip next 2 dc, ★ dc in next dc, (ch 1, skip next dc, dc in next dc, ch 4, skip next 2 dc, sc in next dc, ch 4, skip next 2 dc, dc in next dc) across working last dc in first dc of next corner 2-dc group, ch 2, dc in next dc, ch 4, skip next 2 dc, sc in next dc, ch 4, skip next 2 dc; repeat from ★ 2 times **more**, † dc in next dc, ch 1, skip next dc, dc in next dc, ch 4, skip next 2 dc, sc in next dc, ch 4, skip next 2 dc †, repeat from † to † across; join with slip st to first dc.

To work beginning Shell, ch 3, (2 dc, ch 2, 3 dc) in sp indicated.

To work Shell, (3 dc, ch 2, 3 dc) in sp indicated.

Rnd 3: Slip st in first ch-2 sp, work beginning Shell in same sp, ch 6, skip next 2 ch-4 sps, ★ work Shell in next sp, ch 6, skip next 2 ch-4 sps; repeat from ★ around; join with slip st to first dc.

Rnd 4: Slip st in next 2 dc and in next ch-2 sp, work beginning Shell in same sp, ch 6, work Shell in next Shell (ch-2 sp), (ch 4, work Shell in next Shell) across working last Shell in Shell **before** corner Shell, ch 6, ★ work Shell in corner Shell, ch 6, work Shell in next Shell, (ch 4, work Shell in next Shell) across working last Shell in Shell **before** corner Shell, ch 6; repeat from ★ 2 times **more**; join with slip st to first dc.

To work Picot, ch 3, slip st in top of sc just made.

Rnd 5: Slip st in next 2 dc and in next ch-2 sp, work beginning Shell in same sp, ch 4, working around next sp, sc in sp on Rnd 3, work Picot, ch 4, work Shell in next Shell, † ch 2, working around next sp, sc in sp on Rnd 3, work Picot, ch 2, work Shell in next Shell †, repeat from † to † across to within one loop of next corner Shell, ch 4, working around next sp, sc in sp on Rnd 3, work Picot, ch 4, ★ work Shell in next Corner Shell, ch 4, working around next sp, sc in sp on Rnd 3, work Picot, ch 4, work Shell in next Shell, repeat from † to † across to within one loop of next corner Shell, ch 4, working around next sp, sc in sp on Rnd 3, work Picot, ch 4; repeat from ★ 2 times **more**; join with slip st to first dc, finish off.

Design by Katherine Satterfield.

COASTER REVERIE

This dreamy coaster was inspired by a flight of fancy. Crocheted with size 20 thread, it's also attractive as a mini doily during tea for two.

■■□□ **EASY**

Finished Size: 5¹/₂" (14 cm) diameter

MATERIALS
Cotton Thread (size 20) [400 yards
   (366 meters) per ball]: 1 ball
   (sufficient for six Coasters)
Steel crochet hook, size 9 (1.4 mm) **or**
   size needed for gauge

GAUGE: Rnds 1-3 = 1¹/₄" (3.25 cm)

Ch 10; join with slip st to form a ring.

Rnd 1 (Right side)**:** Ch 1, 16 sc in ring; join with slip st to first sc.

Rnd 2: Ch 1, sc in same st, ch 5, skip next sc, ★ sc in next sc, ch 5, skip next sc; repeat from ★ around; join with slip st to first sc: 8 ch-5 sps.

Rnd 3: Ch 1, sc in same st, 2 sc in next ch-5 sp, ch 5, ★ sc in next sc, 2 sc in next ch-5 sp, ch 5; repeat from ★ around; join with slip st to first sc: 24 sc.

Rnd 4: Slip st in next sc, ch 1, sc in same st and in next sc, 2 sc in next ch-5 sp, ch 5, skip next sc, ★ sc in next 2 sc, 2 sc in next ch-5 sp, ch 5, skip next st; repeat from ★ around; join with slip st to first sc: 32 sc.

Rnd 5: Slip st in next sc, ch 1, sc in same st and in next 2 sc, 2 sc in next ch-5 sp, ch 5, skip next sc, ★ sc in next 3 sc, 2 sc in next ch-5 sp, ch 5, skip next st; repeat from ★ around; join with slip st to first sc: 40 sc.

Rnd 6: Slip st in next sc, ch 1, sc in same st and in next 3 sc, 2 sc in next ch-5 sp, ch 5, skip next sc, ★ sc in next 4 sc, 2 sc in next ch-5 sp, ch 5, skip next st; repeat from ★ around; join with slip st to first sc: 48 sc.

Rnd 7: Slip st in next sc, ch 1, sc in same st and in next 4 sc, 2 sc in next ch-5 sp, ch 5, skip next sc, ★ sc in next 5 sc, 2 sc in next ch-5 sp, ch 5, skip next st; repeat from ★ around; join with slip st to first sc: 56 sc.

Rnd 8: Slip st in next sc, ch 1, sc in same st and in next 5 sc, 2 sc in next ch-5 sp, ch 5, skip next sc, ★ sc in next 6 sc, 2 sc in next ch-5 sp, ch 5, skip next st; repeat from ★ around; join with slip st to first sc: 64 sc.

Rnd 9: Slip st in next sc, ch 1, sc in same st and in next 6 sc, 2 sc in next ch-5 sp, ch 5, skip next sc, ★ sc in next 7 sc, 2 sc in next ch-5 sp, ch 5, skip next st; repeat from ★ around; join with slip st to first sc: 72 sc.

Rnd 10: Slip st in next sc, ch 1, sc in same st and in next 6 sc, ch 5, sc in next 7 sc, ch 5, sc in next ch-5 sp, ch 5, skip next st; repeat from ★ around; join with slip st to first sc: 64 sc.

Rnd 11: Slip st in next sc, ch 1, sc in same st and in next 4 sc, ch 5, (sc in next ch-5 sp, ch 5) twice, skip next sc, ★ sc in next 5 sc, ch 5, (sc in next ch-5 sp, ch 5) twice, skip next st; repeat from ★ around; join with slip st to first sc: 56 sc.

Rnd 12: Slip st in next sc, ch 1, sc in same st and in next 2 sc, ch 5, (sc in next ch-5 sp, ch 5) 3 times, skip next sc, ★ sc in next 3 sc, ch 5, (sc in next ch-5 sp, ch 5) 3 times, skip next st; repeat from ★ around; join with slip st to first sc: 48 sc.

Rnd 13: Slip st in next sc, ch 1, sc in same st, ch 5, ★ (sc in next ch-5 sp, ch 5) 4 times, skip next sc, sc in next sc, ch 5; repeat from ★ around to last 4 ch-5 sps, sc in next ch-5 sp, (ch 5, sc in next ch-5 sp) 3 times, ch 2, dc in first sc to form last ch-5 sp: 40 ch-5 sps.

Rnd 14: Ch 1, sc in last ch-5 sp made, ch 6, (sc in next ch-5 sp, ch 6) around; join with slip st to first sc.

Rnd 15: Slip st in first loop, ch 3 **(counts as first dc, now and throughout)**, 11 dc in same loop, sc in next loop, (ch 6, sc in next loop) 3 times, ★ 12 dc in next loop, sc in next loop, (ch 6, sc in next loop) 3 times; repeat from ★ around; join with slip st to first dc: 96 dc.

Rnd 16: Ch 3, dc in same st and in next dc, (2 dc in next dc, dc in next dc) 5 times, sc in next loop, (ch 6, sc in next loop) twice, ★ (2 dc in next dc, dc in next dc) 6 times, sc in next loop, (ch 6, sc in next loop) twice; repeat from ★ around; join with slip st to first dc: 144 dc.

To decrease (uses next 2 dc), ★ YO, insert hook in **next** dc, YO and pull up a loop, YO and draw through 2 loops on hook; repeat from ★ once **more**, YO and draw through all 3 loops on hook.

To work Picot, ch 3, slip st in top of st just made.

Rnd 17: Ch 2, dc in next dc, ch 2, decrease, (work Picot, ch 2, decrease) 7 times, sc in next loop, ch 6, slip st in fourth ch from hook, ch 3, sc in next loop, ★ decrease, ch 2, decrease, (work Picot, ch 2, decrease) 7 times, sc in next loop, ch 6, slip st in fourth ch from hook, ch 3, sc in next loop; repeat from ★ around; join with slip st to first dc, finish off.

Design by Shobha Govindan.

CHEERY PLACE SETTING

Brighten your breakfast table with classic blue and white. You'll use these appealing accessories — place mat, napkin ring, hot pad, and coaster — time and time again.

■■□□ EASY

MATERIALS
Light/Worsted Weight Yarn
[1³/₄ ounces, 150 yards (50 grams, 137 meters) per ball]:
Complete set
MC (White) - 3 balls
CC (Bluette) - 2 balls
Crochet hook, size E (3.5 mm) **or** size needed for gauge
Tapestry needle

GAUGE: In pattern, 2 Clusters and Rows 1-8 = 2¹/₂" (6.25 cm)

PATTERN STITCHES
Beginning Cluster *(uses first 4 sts)*
Ch 3, ★ YO, insert hook in **next** st, YO and pull up a loop, YO and draw through 2 loops on hook; repeat from ★ 2 times **more**, YO and draw through all 4 loops on hook.
Cluster *(uses next 7 sts)*
★ YO, insert hook in **next** st, YO and pull up a loop, YO and draw through 2 loops on hook; repeat from ★ 6 times **more**, YO and draw through all 8 loops on hook.
Ending Cluster *(uses last 4 sts)*
★ YO, insert hook in **next** st, YO and pull up a loop, YO and draw through 2 loops on hook; repeat from ★ 3 times **more**, YO and draw through all 5 loops on hook.

PLACEMAT
Finished Size:
13¹/₂" x 17" (34.5 cm x 43 cm)

With CC, ch 107.

Row 1 (Right side)**:** Sc in second ch from hook and in next ch, ★ skip next 3 chs, 7 dc in next ch, skip next 3 chs, sc in next 3 chs; repeat from ★ across to last 4 chs, skip next 3 chs, 4 dc in last ch; finish off: 10 7-dc groups.

Note: Mark Row 1 as **right** side.

Row 2: With **wrong** side facing, join MC with sc in first dc *(see Joining With Sc, page 205)*; sc in next dc, ch 3, ★ work Cluster, ch 3, sc in next 3 dc, ch 3; repeat from ★ across to last 4 sts, work ending Cluster: 11 Clusters.

Row 3: Ch 3, turn; 3 dc in first Cluster, (sc in next 3 sc, 7 dc in next Cluster) across to last 2 sc, sc in last 2 sc; finish off: 10 7-dc groups.

Row 4: With **wrong** side facing, join CC with slip st in first sc; work beginning Cluster, ch 3, ★ sc in next 3 dc, ch 3, work Cluster, ch 3; repeat from ★ across to last 2 sts, sc in last 2 sts: 11 Clusters.

Row 5: Ch 1, turn; sc in first 2 sc, (7 dc in next Cluster, sc in next 3 sc) across to last Cluster, 4 dc in last Cluster; finish off: 10 7-dc groups.

Rows 6-40: Repeat Rows 2-5, 8 times; then repeat Rows 2-4 once **more**.

Finish off.

EDGING
Rnd 1: With **right** side facing, join MC with sc in first sc on last row; sc in same st, † work 87 sc evenly spaced across to next corner, 3 sc in corner, work 63 sc evenly spaced across to next corner †, 3 sc in corner, repeat from † to † once, sc in same st as first sc; join with slip st to first sc: 312 sc.

Rnd 2: Ch 3, 6 dc in same st, skip next 2 sc, sc in next sc, skip next 2 sc, ★ 7 dc in next sc, skip next 2 sc, sc in next sc, skip next 2 sc; repeat from ★ around; join with slip st to top of beginning ch-3, finish off.

COASTER
Finished Size: 5" (12.5 cm) square

With CC, ch 27.

Rows 1-12: Work same as Placemat: 3 Clusters.

Finish off.

EDGING
Rnd 1: With **right** side facing, join MC with sc in first sc on last row; sc in same st, work 21 sc evenly spaced across to next corner, ★ 3 sc in corner, work 21 sc evenly spaced across to next corner; repeat from ★ around, sc in same st as first sc; join with slip st to first sc: 96 sc.

Rnd 2: Ch 1, sc in same st, skip next 2 sc, 7 dc in next sc, skip next 2 sc, ★ sc in next sc, skip next 2 sc, 7 dc in next sc, skip next 2 sc; repeat from ★ around; join with slip st to first sc, finish off.

Instructions continued on page 203.

DELIGHTFUL DISHCLOTHS

Kitchen duty will be delightful with these soft, durable, absorbent cloths crocheted using two strands of lightweight cotton yarn.

■■□□ EASY

MATERIALS
Light/Worsted Weight Yarn
[2½ ounces, 160 yards
(70 grams, 146 meters)
per skein]:
Dishcloth #1
Cream - 2 skeins
Periwinkle - 2 skeins
Dishcloth #2
Periwinkle - 2 skeins
Cream - 2 skeins
Dishcloth #3
Jade - 2 skeins
Cream - 2 skeins
Dishcloth #4
Lilac - 2 skeins
Cream - 2 skeins
Crochet hook, size I (5.5 mm)

Note: Each Dishcloth is worked holding two strands of yarn together.

DISHCLOTH #1
With Cream, ch 34.

Row 1 (Right side): Sc in second ch from hook, ★ skip next ch, (dc, ch 1, dc) in next ch, skip next ch, sc in next ch; repeat from ★ across: 9 sc and 8 ch-1 sps.

Note: Mark Row 1 as **right** side.

Row 2: Ch 4 **(counts as first dc plus ch 1)**, turn; sc in next ch-1 sp, ch 1, dc in next sc, ★ ch 1, sc in next ch-1 sp, ch 1, dc in next sc; repeat from ★ across: 17 sts and 16 ch-1 sps.

Row 3: Ch 1, turn; sc in first dc, ★ (dc, ch 1, dc) in next sc, sc in next dc; repeat from ★ across: 9 sc and 8 ch-1 sps.

Rows 4-21: Repeat Rows 2 and 3, 9 times.

Finish off.

EDGING
Rnd 1: With **right** side facing, join Periwinkle with sc in first sc **(see Joining With Sc, page 205)**; sc in same st, work 29 sc evenly spaced across to last sc, 3 sc in last sc; work 29 sc evenly spaced across end of rows; working in free loops of beginning ch **(Fig. 3b, page 205)**, 3 sc in first ch, work 29 sc evenly spaced across to ch at base of last sc, 3 sc in ch; work 29 sc evenly spaced across end of rows, sc in same st as first sc; join with slip st to first sc: 128 sc.

Rnd 2: Ch 3, (dc, ch 1, 2 dc) in same st, skip next sc, sc in next sc, skip next sc, ★ (2 dc, ch 1, 2 dc) in next sc, skip next sc, sc in next sc, skip next sc; repeat from ★ around; join with slip st to top of beginning ch-3, finish off.

DISHCLOTH #2
With Periwinkle, ch 32.

Row 1: (Sc, hdc) in second ch from hook, ★ skip next ch, (sc, hdc) in next ch; repeat from ★ across: 32 sts.

Row 2 (Right side): Ch 1, turn; sc in each st across.

Note: Mark Row 2 as **right** side.

Row 3: Ch 1, turn; skip first sc, (sc, hdc) in next sc, ★ skip next sc, (sc, hdc) in next sc; repeat from ★ across.

Row 4: Ch 1, turn; sc in each st across.

Rows 5-30: Repeat Rows 3 and 4, 13 times; do **not** finish off.

EDGING
Rnd 1: Ch 1, do **not** turn; sc evenly around entire Dishcloth working 3 sc in each corner; join with slip st to first sc, finish off.

Rnd 2: With **right** side facing, join Cream with slip st in any sc; ch 1, working from **left** to **right**, work reverse sc **(Figs. 8a-d, page 206)** in each sc around; join with slip st to first st, finish off.

DISHCLOTH #3
With Jade, ch 32.

Row 1: Sc in second ch from hook, ★ ch 2, skip next 2 chs, sc in next ch; repeat from ★ across: 11 sc.

Row 2 (Right side): Ch 3 **(counts as first dc, now and throughout)**, turn; dc in same st, 3 dc in next sc and in each sc across to last sc, 2 dc in last sc: 31 dc.

Note: Mark Row 2 as **right** side.

Row 3: Ch 1, turn; sc in first dc, ★ ch 2, skip next 2 dc, sc in next dc; repeat from ★ across: 11 sc.

Row 4: Ch 3, turn; dc in same st, 3 dc in next sc and in each sc across to last sc, 2 dc in last sc: 31 dc.

Rows 5-18: Repeat Rows 3 and 4, 7 times.

Finish off.

EDGING
Rnd 1: With **right** side facing, join Cream with sc in first dc **(see Joining With Sc, page 205)**; sc in same st, sc in each dc across to last dc, 3 sc in last dc; work 29 sc evenly spaced across end of rows; working in free loops of beginning ch **(Fig. 3b, page 205)**, 3 sc in ch at base of first sc, sc in each ch across to last ch, 3 sc in last ch; work 29 sc evenly spaced across end of rows, sc in same st as first sc; join with slip st to first sc: 128 sc.

Rnd 2: Ch 3, (dc, ch 2, 2 dc) in same st, skip next 3 sc, ★ (2 dc, ch 2, 2 dc) in next sc, skip next 3 sc; repeat from ★ around; join with slip st to first dc, finish off.

DISHCLOTH #4
With Lilac, ch 34.

Row 1 (Right side): 2 Dc in fourth ch from hook **(3 skipped chs count as first dc)**, ★ skip next 2 chs, (sc, 2 dc) in next ch; repeat from ★ across to last 3 chs, skip next 2 chs, sc in last ch: 31 sts.

Note: Mark Row 1 as **right** side.

Rows 2-19: Ch 3 **(counts as first dc)**, turn; 2 dc in same st, ★ skip next 2 dc, (sc, 2 dc) in next sc; repeat from ★ across to last 3 dc, skip next 2 dc, sc in last dc.

Finish off.

EDGING
Rnd 1: With **right** side facing, join Cream with sc in first dc *(see Joining With Sc, page 205)*; sc in same st, work 27 sc evenly spaced across to last sc, 3 sc in last sc; work 27 sc evenly spaced across end of rows; working in free loops of beginning ch *(Fig. 3b, page 205)*, 3 sc in first ch, work 27 sc evenly spaced across to ch at base of last dc, 3 sc in ch; work 27 sc evenly spaced across end of rows, sc in same st as first sc; join with slip st to first sc: 120 sc.

To work Picot, ch 3, slip st in third ch from hook.

Rnd 2: Ch 6, slip st in third ch from hook, (dc, work Picot, dc) in same st, skip next 2 sc, † (dc, work Picot, dc) in next sc, skip next 2 sc †, repeat from † to † 8 times **more**, ★ dc in next sc, (work Picot, dc in same st) twice, skip next 2 sc, repeat from † to † 9 times; repeat from ★ 2 times **more**; join with slip st to third ch of beginning ch-6, finish off.

Designs by Lorraine White.

SCRUB-A-DUB DISHCLOTH

Maximize your power to scour — this handy kitchen cloth incorporates a plastic mesh scrubbing pad!

■■□□ **EASY**

MATERIALS

Medium/Worsted Weight Yarn [225 yards (206 meters) per ball]: 1 ball
Crochet hook, size G (4 mm)
Round plastic mesh scouring pad [approximately 3^1/$_2$" (9 cm) diameter]

CORNER SQUARE

Rnd 1 (Right side): With knotted ends of pad at center and working through two layers of mesh at outer edge of pad, join yarn with sc *(see Joining With Sc, page 205)*; work 31 sc evenly spaced around; join with slip st to first sc: 32 sc.

Rnd 2: Ch 3 **(counts as first dc, now and throughout)**, dc in same st and in next 7 sc, ★ (2 dc, ch 2, 2 dc) in next sc, dc in next 7 sc; repeat from ★ 2 times **more**, 2 dc in same st as first dc, ch 1, sc in first dc to form last ch-2 sp; do **not** finish off: 44 dc and 4 ch-2 sps.

BODY

Row 1: Ch 3, dc in same sp, ch 2, † skip next 2 dc, ★ 3 dc in next dc, ch 2, skip next 2 dc; repeat from ★ across to next corner ch-2 sp †, (2 dc, ch 2) twice in corner ch-2 sp, repeat from † to † once, 2 dc in corner ch-2 sp, leave remaining 22 dc and one ch-2 sp unworked: 26 dc and 9 ch-2 sps.

Row 2: Ch 1, turn; skip first 2 dc, (sc, ch 2, 2 dc) in next ch-2 sp and in each ch-2 sp across to next corner ch-2 sp, (sc, ch 2, 2 dc) twice in corner ch-2 sp, (sc, ch 2, 2 dc) in each ch-2 sp across to last 2 dc, skip next dc, sc in last dc: 11 sc and 10 ch-2 sps.

Row 3: Ch 3, turn; sc in next ch-2 sp, ch 1, ★ dc in next sc, ch 1, sc in next ch-2 sp, ch 1; repeat from ★ across to next corner sc, (dc, ch 2, dc) in corner sc, ch 1, sc in next ch-2 sp, † ch 1, dc in next sc, ch 1, sc in next ch-2 sp †; repeat from † to † across to last sc, dc in last sc: 22 sts and 19 sps.

Row 4: Ch 3, turn; ★ 3 dc in next sc, ch 2, skip next dc; repeat from ★ across to next corner ch-2 sp, (2 dc, ch 2) twice in corner ch-2 sp, skip next dc, 3 dc in next sc, † ch 2, skip next dc, 3 dc in next sc †; repeat from † to † across to last dc, leave last dc unworked: 35 dc and 11 ch-2 sps.

Row 5: Ch 1, turn; (sc, ch 2, 2 dc) in first dc and in each ch-2 sp across to next corner ch-2 sp, (sc, ch 2, 2 dc) twice in corner ch-2 sp, (sc, ch 2, 2 dc) in each ch-2 sp across to last 4 dc, skip next dc, (sc, ch 2, 2 dc) in next dc, skip next dc, sc in last dc: 15 sc and 14 ch-2 sps.

Rows 6-10: Repeat Rows 3-5 once, then repeat Rows 3 and 4 once **more**; do **not** finish off: 59 dc and 19 ch-2 sps.

EDGING

Rnd 1: Ch 1, turn; (sc, ch 2, 2 dc) in first dc and in each ch-2 sp across to next corner ch-2 sp, (sc, ch 2, 2 dc) twice in corner ch-2 sp, (sc, ch 2, 2 dc) in each ch-2 sp across to last 4 dc, skip next 2 dc, (sc, ch 2, 2 dc) twice in next dc, skip last dc; working in end of rows, skip first row, (sc, ch 2, 2 dc) in next row, ★ skip next row, (sc, ch 2, 2 dc) in next row; repeat from ★ across to Corner Square; working in sts and sps on Rnd 2 of Corner Square, (sc, ch 2, 2 dc) in first corner ch-2 sp, skip next 2 dc, † (sc, ch 2, 2 dc) in next dc, skip next 2 dc †; repeat from † to † 2 times **more**, (sc, ch 2, 2 dc) twice in next corner ch-2 sp, skip next 2 dc, repeat from † to † 3 times, (sc, ch 2, 2 dc) in next corner ch-2 sp; working in end of rows on Body, (sc, ch 2, 2 dc) in first row, skip next row, [(sc, ch 2, 2 dc) in next row, skip next row] 4 times, (sc, ch 2, 2 dc) in same st as first sc; join with slip st to first sc, finish off.

Design by Joan E. Reeves.

KITCHEN COMPANIONS

For cooking and cleaning, as well as for cheering up the kitchen, call on these nifty companions. Made of lightweight cotton, the towel, dishcloth, and pot holder are both useful and decorative.

Instructions begin on page 190.

KITCHEN COMPANIONS
Shown on page 189.

▰▰▱▱ **EASY**

MATERIALS
Light/Worsted Weight Yarn
[2½ ounces, 160 yards (70 grams, 146 meters) per skein]:
Red - 4 skeins
White - 4 skeins
Crochet hook, size H (5 mm)
For Dishtowel only:
Button
Tapestry needle

Note: Each piece is worked holding two strands of yarn together.

DISHTOWEL
CORD (Make 6)
With White, ch 51, slip st in second ch from hook and in each ch across; finish off.

Note: Cords will be joined into Body; set Cords aside until needed.

BODY
With Red, ch 46.

Row 1 (Right side)**:** Dc in fourth ch from hook **(3 skipped chs count as first dc)** and in next 2 chs, ch 1, ★ skip next ch, dc in next 6 chs, ch 1; repeat from ★ across to last 5 chs, skip next ch, dc in last 4 chs: 38 dc and 6 ch-1 sps.

Note: Mark Row 1 as **right** side.

Row 2: Ch 3 **(counts as first dc, now and throughout)**, turn; dc in next 3 dc, ch 1, (dc in next 6 dc, ch 1) 5 times, dc in last 4 dc; finish off.

Row 3: With **right** side facing, join White with sc in first dc **(see Joining With Sc, page 205)**; sc in next 3 dc, ch 1, (sc in next 6 dc, ch 1) 5 times, sc in last 4 dc.

Row 4: Ch 1, turn; sc in first 4 sc, ch 1, (sc in next 6 sc, ch 1) 5 times, sc in last 4 sc; finish off.

Row 5: With **right** side facing, join Red with slip st in first sc; ch 3, dc in next 3 sc, ch 1, (dc in next 6 sc, ch 1) 5 times, dc in last 4 sc; finish off.

Row 6: With **wrong** side facing, join White with sc in first dc; sc in next 3 dc, ch 1, (sc in next 6 dc, ch 1) 5 times, sc in last 4 dc.

Rows 7-9: Ch 1, turn; sc in first 4 sc, ch 1, (sc in next 6 sc, ch 1) 5 times, sc in last 4 sc.

Finish off.

Row 10: With **wrong** side facing, join Red with slip st in first sc; ch 3, dc in next 3 sc, ch 1, (dc in next 6 sc, ch 1) 5 times, dc in last 4 sc; finish off.

Rows 11-13: Repeat Rows 3-5; at end of Row 13, do **not** finish off.

Rows 14-24: Ch 3, turn; dc in next 3 dc, ch 1, (dc in next 6 dc, ch 1) 5 times, dc in last 4 dc; do **not** finish off.

TRIM
Rnd 1: Ch 1, turn; sc in first dc and in each dc and each ch-1 sp across; work 40 sc evenly spaced across end of rows; working in free loops of beginning ch **(Fig. 3b, page 205)**, 2 sc in first ch, sc in next 42 chs, 2 sc in next ch; work 40 sc evenly spaced across end of rows; join with slip st to first sc, finish off: 170 sc.

Using photo as a guide for placement and beginning and ending on **wrong** side, weave one Cord vertically through first row of ch-1 sps on Body, keeping ends to **wrong** side of work.

Repeat for remaining 5 vertical rows of ch-1 sps.

Rnd 2 (Joining rnd)**:** With **right** side facing, join White with sc in same st as joining; sc in next 3 sc, † insert hook in next sc **and** Cord **behind** sc, YO and pull up a loop, YO and draw through both loops on hook, ★ sc in next 6 sc, insert hook in next sc **and** Cord **behind** sc, YO and pull up a loop, YO and draw through both loops on hook; repeat from ★ 4 times **more** †, sc in next 44 sc, 2 sc in next sc, sc in next 4 sc, repeat from † to † once, sc in next 4 sc, 2 sc in next sc, sc in each sc around; join with slip st to first sc, do **not** finish off.

STRAP
Row 1: Ch 1, sc in same st, skip next sc, (sc in next sc, skip next sc) 20 times, sc in next 2 sc, leave remaining sts unworked: 23 sc.

Row 2: Ch 3, turn; (skip next sc, dc in next sc) across: 12 dc.

Rows 3-5: Ch 1, turn; pull up a loop in first 2 sts, YO and draw through all 3 loops on hook **(counts as one sc)**, sc in each st across: 9 sc.

Row 6: Ch 3, turn; (skip next sc, dc in next sc) across: 5 dc.

Rows 7 and 8: Repeat Rows 3 and 4: 3 sc.

Rows 9-21: Ch 1, turn; sc in each sc across; do **not** finish off.

Edging: Ch 1, do **not** turn; working in end of rows and in unworked sc on Trim, sc evenly around entire Dishtowel to beginning of Row 21 of Strap, ch 3 **(buttonhole made)**, skip next 3 sc on Row 21; join with slip st to first sc, finish off.

With **right** side facing, sew button to center sc on Row 8 of Strap.

DISHCLOTH

CORD (Make 5)

With White, ch 34, slip st in second ch from hook and in each ch across; finish off.

Note: Cords will be joined into Body; set Cords aside until needed.

BODY

With Red, ch 31.

Row 1 (Right side): Dc in fourth ch from hook **(3 skipped chs count as first dc)** and in next 2 chs, ★ ch 1, skip next ch, dc in next 4 chs; repeat from ★ across: 24 dc and 5 ch-1 sps.

Note: Mark Row 1 as **right** side.

Rows 2-12: Ch 3 **(counts as first dc)**, turn; dc in next 3 dc, (ch 1, dc in next 4 dc) across; do **not** finish off.

EDGING

Rnd 1: Ch 1, turn; 2 sc in first dc, sc in each dc and in each ch-1 sp across to last dc, 3 sc in last dc; † working in end of rows, sc in first row, 2 sc in each of next 10 rows, sc in last row †; working in free loops of beginning ch *(Fig. 3b, page 205)*, 3 sc in first ch, sc in next 27 chs, 3 sc in next ch, repeat from † to † once, sc in same st as first sc; join with slip st to first sc, finish off: 110 sc.

Using photo as a guide for placement and beginning and ending on **wrong** side, weave one Cord vertically through first row of ch-1 sps on Body, keeping ends to **wrong** side of work.

Repeat for remaining 4 vertical rows of ch-1 sps.

Rnd 2 (Joining rnd): With **right** side facing, join White with sc in same st as joining *(see Joining With Sc, page 205)*; 2 sc in same st, † sc in next 4 sc, ★ insert hook in next sc **and** Cord **behind** sc, YO and pull up a loop, YO and draw through both loops on hook, sc in next 4 sc; repeat from ★ 4 times **more**, 3 sc in next sc, sc in each sc across to center sc of next corner 3-sc group †, 3 sc in center sc, repeat from † to † once; join with slip st to first sc.

Rnd 3: Ch 1, sc in same st and in each st around working 3 sc in center sc of each corner 3-sc group; join with slip st to first sc, finish off.

POT HOLDER

CORD (Make 8)

With White, ch 28, slip st in second ch from hook and in each ch across; finish off.

Note: Cords will be joined into Front and Back; set Cords aside until needed.

FRONT

With Red, ch 26.

Row 1 (Right side): Dc in fourth ch from hook **(3 skipped chs count as first dc)** and in next 2 chs, ★ ch 1, skip next ch, dc in next 4 chs; repeat from ★ across: 20 dc and 4 ch-1 sps.

Note: Mark Row 1 as **right** side.

Rows 2-10: Ch 3 **(counts as first dc)**, turn; dc in next 3 dc, (ch 1, dc in next 4 dc) across; do **not** finish off.

EDGING

Rnd 1: Ch 1, turn; 2 sc in first dc, sc in each dc and in each ch-1 sp across to last dc, 3 sc in last dc; † working in end of rows, sc in first row, 2 sc in each of next 8 rows, sc in last row †; working in free loops of beginning ch *(Fig. 3b, page 205)*, 3 sc in first ch, sc in next 22 chs, 3 sc in next ch, repeat from † to † once, sc in same st as first sc; join with slip st to first sc, finish off: 92 sc.

Using photo as a guide for placement and beginning and ending on **wrong** side, weave one Cord vertically through first row of ch-1 sps on Body, keeping ends to **wrong** side of work.

Repeat for remaining 3 vertical rows of ch-1 sps.

Rnd 2 (Joining rnd): With **right** side facing, join White with sc in same st as joining *(see Joining With Sc, page 205)*; 2 sc in same st, † sc in next 4 sc, ★ insert hook in next sc **and** Cord **behind** sc, YO and pull up a loop, YO and draw through both loops on hook, sc in next 4 sc; repeat from ★ 3 times **more**, 3 sc in next sc, sc in each sc across to center sc of next corner 3-sc group †, 3 sc in center sc, repeat from † to † once; join with slip st to first sc, finish off: 100 sts.

BACK

Work same as Front.

JOINING

With **wrong** sides together, Front facing, and working through **both** loops, join White with slip st in center sc of top right corner 3-sc group; slip st in each st around; join with slip st to first slip st, ch 10 (hanger), holding ch to **left** of hook, slip st in same st as joining and in each ch around; finish off.

Designs by Roberta Maier.

LOVELY & LACY TOWEL EDGINGS

With their timeless patterns in neutral tones of size 10 thread, these trimmings for linen guest towels will never go out of style.

⬛⬛◻◻ EASY

MATERIALS
Bedspread Weight Cotton Thread
 (size 10) [350 yards (320 meters)
 per ball]:
 New Ecru - 1 ball
 Natural - 1 ball
Steel crochet hook, size 5 (1.9 mm) **or**
 size needed for gauge
Linen - 18" x 14¹/₂" (45.5 cm x 37 cm)
 piece for **each** towel
Sewing machine
Sewing needle and thread

FINISHING
Press edges of linen ¹/₄" (7 mm) to wrong side; press ¹/₄" (7 mm) to wrong side again. Machine stitch across each edge of linen ³/₁₆" (5 mm) from outer pressed edges. Matching wrong side of Edging to right side of towel, refer to photo to pin Edging across bottom edge of towel. Hand sew Edging in place.

EDGING #1
GAUGE: Each repeat = 1¹/₂" (3.75 cm)

Foundation Row: With New Ecru, ch 10, dc in fourth ch from hook to form a ring, ★ ch 15, dc in back ridge of fourth ch from hook to form a ring **(Fig. 1, page 205)**; repeat from ★ 7 times **more**.

To work treble crochet (abbreviated *tr*), YO twice, insert hook in st or sp indicated, YO and pull up a loop (4 loops on hook), (YO and draw through 2 loops on hook) 3 times.

Row 1: Ch 7, sc in back ridge of second ch from hook, ★ ch 2, tr in next ring, (ch 1, tr in same ring) 6 times, ch 2, skip next 5 chs, sc in back ridge of next ch; repeat from ★ across.

Row 2 (Right side)**:** Ch 4 **(counts as first tr, now and throughout)**, turn; ★ tr in next tr, (ch 1, tr in next tr) 3 times, (ch 1, tr in same st) twice, (ch 1, tr in next tr) 3 times; repeat from ★ across to last sc, tr in last sc.

Note: Mark Row 2 as **right** side.

Row 3: Ch 4, turn; skip next tr, tr in next tr, (ch 1, tr in next tr) 3 times, (ch 1, tr in same st) twice, (ch 1, tr in next tr) 3 times, ★ skip next 2 tr, tr in next tr, (ch 1, tr in next tr) 3 times, (ch 1, tr in same st) twice, (ch 1, tr in next tr) 3 times; repeat from ★ across to last 2 tr, skip next tr, tr in last tr.

Row 4: Ch 1, turn; sc in first 2 tr, ch 3, (sc in next tr, ch 3) 3 times, (sc, ch 3) twice in next tr, (sc in next tr, ch 3) 3 times, ★ skip next tr, sc in sp **before** next tr, ch 3, skip next tr, (sc in next tr, ch 3) 3 times, (sc, ch 3) twice in next tr, (sc in next tr, ch 3) 3 times; repeat from ★ across to last 2 tr, sc in last 2 tr; finish off.

Follow Finishing to hem towel and attach Edging.

EDGING #2
GAUGE: 9 sc = 1" (2.5 cm)

With Natural, ch 119.

Row 1 (Right side)**:** Sc in second ch from hook and in each ch across: 118 sc.

Note: Mark Row 1 as **right** side.

Row 2: Ch 1, turn; sc in first 3 sc, ch 4, skip next 2 sc, sc in next 3 sc, ★ ch 7, skip next 2 sc, sc in next 3 sc, ch 4, skip next 2 sc, sc in next 3 sc; repeat from ★ across: 36 sc and 23 sps.

Row 3: Ch 1, turn; sc in first 3 sc and in next ch-4 sp, (ch 3, sc in same sp) twice, ★ skip next sc, sc in next sc and in next ch-7 sp, (ch 3, sc in same sp) 4 times, skip next sc, sc in next sc and in next ch-4 sp, (ch 3, sc in same sp) twice; repeat from ★ across to last 3 sc, sc in last 3 sc: 68 sps.

Row 4: Ch 1, turn; sc in first 2 sc, 2 sc in next ch-3 sp, ch 3, ★ 2 sc in each of next 2 ch-3 sps, ch 3, (2 sc in next ch-3 sp, ch 3) twice, 2 sc in each of next 2 ch-3 sps, ch 3; repeat from ★ across to last ch-3 sp, 2 sc in last ch-3 sp, skip next 2 sc, sc in last 2 sc: 45 sps.

Row 5: Ch 1, turn; sc in first 4 sc, (sc, ch 3, sc) in each ch-3 sp across to last 4 sc, sc in last 4 sc.

Row 6: Ch 1, turn; sc in first 5 sc, (sc, ch 4, sc) in each ch-3 sp across to last 5 sc, sc in last 5 sc.

To work Picot, ch 3, slip st in third ch from hook, ch 1.

Row 7: Ch 1, turn; sc in first 6 sc, (sc, work Picot, sc) in next ch-4 sp, ★ sc in next ch-4 sp, dc in next ch-4 sp, (work Picot, dc in same sp) 3 times, sc in next ch-4 sp, (sc, work Picot, sc) in next ch-4 sp; repeat from ★ across to last 6 sc, sc in last 6 sc; finish off.

Trim: With **right** side facing and working in free loops of beginning ch *(Fig. 3b, page 205)*, join thread with sc in first ch *(see Joining With Sc, page 205)*; work Picot, ★ skip next ch, sc in next ch, work Picot; repeat from ★ across to last 3 chs, skip next ch, sc in last 2 chs; finish off.

Follow Finishing to hem towel and attach Edging.

Design by Patricia Kristoffersen.

EDGING #3
GAUGE: Rows 1-6 = 1³/₈" (3.5 cm)

With New Ecru, ch 19.

Row 1: Working in back ridges of beginning ch *(Fig. 1, page 205)*, sc in eighth ch from hook, ★ ch 5, skip next 3 chs, sc in next ch; repeat from ★ once **more**, ch 2, skip next 2 chs, sc in last ch: 4 sps.

Row 2 (Right side): Ch 5, turn; sc in first ch-2 sp, (ch 5, sc in next ch-5 sp) twice, 7 dc in last sp: 7 dc and 3 ch-5 sps.

Note: Mark Row 2 as **right** side.

Row 3: Ch 5, turn; skip first dc, sc in next dc, ch 3, ★ skip next dc, sc in next dc, ch 3; repeat from ★ once **more**, sc in next ch-5 sp, ch 5, sc in next ch-5 sp, ch 2, dc in last ch-5 sp: 6 sps.

Row 4: Ch 5, turn; sc in first ch-2 sp, (ch 5, sc in next sp) twice, 7 dc in next ch-3 sp, leave remaining 2 sps unworked: 7 dc and 3 ch-5 sps.

Rows 5-59: Repeat Rows 3 and 4, 27 times, then repeat Row 3 once **more**.

Finish off.

Follow Finishing to hem towel and attach Edging.

Design by Terry Kimbrough.

BATH BASKETS

Quick and easy to make using 1" wide fabric strips, these handy baskets will help keep your bath necessities organized.

◼◼◻◻ **EASY**

Finished Size:
Round Basket - 7" (18 cm) diameter and 3" (7.5 cm) deep
Rectangular Basket - 8" (20.5 cm) long and 3" (7.5 cm) deep

MATERIALS

100% Cotton fabrics [44/45" (112/114.5 cm) wide]:
Round Basket
MC (yellow print) - $^2/_3$ yard (61 cm)
CC (blue check) - 1 yard (91.5 cm)
Rectangular Basket
MC (blue check) - $^3/_4$ yard (68.5 cm)
CC (white) – $^1/_2$ yard (45.5 cm)
Crochet hook, size K (6.5 mm) **or** size needed for gauge
Metal yarn needle
Rotary cutter and mat (optional)

GAUGE: 4 sc and 4 rows = 2" (5 cm)

PREPARING FABRICS

Wash, dry, and press fabrics. Cut off selvages and then tear or cut fabrics into 1" (2.5 cm) wide strips along the longest direction of fabric. For quick results, a rotary cutter and mat may be used to cut several layers of fabric at one time.

Note #1: When the color varies on the right and wrong sides of a fabric, fold the fabric strip in half as you crochet so the preferred color will show. If the fabric is the same color intensity on both sides, folding is unnecessary.

Note #2: Do not join at end of each round unless instructed. Using a 2" (5 cm) scrap piece of fabric, place marker at beginning of each round, moving marker after each round is complete.

ROUND BASKET

Rnd 1 (Right side): With CC, ch 2, 6 sc in second ch from hook; do **not** join, place marker.

Note: Mark Rnd 1 as **right** side.

Rnd 2: 2 Sc in each sc around: 12 sc.

Rnd 3: (Sc in next sc, 2 sc in next sc) around: 18 sc.

Rnd 4: (Sc in next 2 sc, 2 sc in next sc) around: 24 sc.

Rnd 5: (Sc in next 3 sc, 2 sc in next sc) around: 30 sc.

Rnd 6: (Sc in next 4 sc, 2 sc in next sc) around; slip st in Back Loop Only of next sc *(Fig. 2, page 205)*, finish off: 36 sts.

Rnd 7: With **right** side facing and working in Back Loops Only, join MC with sc in same st as slip st *(see Joining With Sc, page 205)*; sc in each sc around; do **not** join, place marker.

Rnds 8 and 9: Sc in both loops of each sc around.

Rnd 10: Sc in each sc around; slip st in next sc, finish off.

Rnd 11: With **right** side facing, join CC with sc in same st as slip st; ch 3, skip next sc, ★ sc in next sc, ch 3, skip next sc; repeat from ★ around; join with slip st to first sc, finish off.

Trim: With bottom of Basket facing away from you and working in free loops on Rnd 6 *(Fig. 3a, page 205)*, join CC with slip st in any sc; slip st in each sc around; join with slip st to first slip st, finish off.

RECTANGULAR BASKET

With MC, ch 15.

Rnd 1 (Right side): Dc in fourth ch from hook, (ch 1, 2 dc in same ch) twice, dc in next 10 chs, 2 dc in last ch, (ch 1, 2 dc in same ch) twice; working in free loops of beginning ch *(Fig. 3b, page 205)*, dc in next 10 chs; join with slip st to top of beginning ch: 32 sts and 4 ch-1 sps.

Note: Mark Rnd 1 as **right** side.

Rnd 2: Ch 1, sc in same st and in each dc around working 3 sc in each ch-1 sp; join with slip st to Back Loop Only of first sc *(Fig. 2, page 205)*: 44 sc.

To decrease, pull up a loop in each of next 2 sc, YO and draw through all 3 loops on hook **(counts as one sc)**.

Rnd 3: Ch 1, working in Back Loops Only, sc in same st and in next sc, decrease, sc in next 3 sc, decrease, sc in next 15 sc, decrease, sc in next 3 sc, decrease, sc in last 13 sc; do **not** join, place marker: 40 sc.

Rnds 4 and 5: Sc in both loops of each sc around.

Rnd 6: Sc in each sc around; slip st in next sc, finish off.

Rnd 7: With **right** side facing, join CC with sc in same st as slip st *(see Joining With Sc, page 205)*; sc in each sc around; join with slip st to first sc, finish off.

Trim: With bottom of Basket facing away from you and working in free loops on Rnd 2 *(Fig. 3a, page 205)*, join CC with slip st in any sc; slip st in each sc around; join with slip st to first slip st, finish off.

Designs by Maggie Weldon.

QUICK PILLOWS

Create quick comfort with our plush seating companions. Each is crocheted using a Q hook and three strands of worsted weight yarn

◼◼◻◻ **EASY**

Finished Size of each Pillow:
12" x 16" (30.5 cm x 40.5 cm)

MATERIALS
Medium/Worsted Weight Yarn
[5 ounces, 328 yards (140 grams, 300 meters) per skein]:
Pillow #1
New Aran - 3 skeins
Pillow #2
New Aran - 3 skeins
Camel - 3 skeins
Pillow #3
Camel - 3 skeins
Crochet hook, size Q (15 mm)
Yarn needle
12" x 16" (30.5 cm x 40.5 cm)
  Purchased pillow form
2 - 12¹⁄₂" x 16¹⁄₂" (32 cm x 42) Fabric
  pieces for pillow form cover
Sewing machine
Sewing needle and thread

GAUGE: In pattern, 7 sc = 4" (10 cm)

Note: Pillows are worked holding 3 strands of yarn together throughout.

PILLOW FORM COVER
Matching right sides and raw edges, use a ¹⁄₄" (7 mm) seam allowance to sew fabric pieces together, leaving bottom edge open. Clip seam allowances at corners. Turn cover right side out, carefully pushing corners outward. Insert pillow form and sew final closure by hand.

PILLOW #1
BODY (Make 2)
Row 1 (Right side)**:** Ch 24, sc in second ch from hook and in each ch across: 23 sc.

Note: Mark Row 1 as **right** side and bottom edge.

Rows 2-18: Ch 1, turn; sc in first sc, ★ skip next sc, sc in next sc, working in **front** of sc just made, sc in skipped sc; repeat from ★ across; at end of Row 18, do **not** finish off.

Edging: Ch 1, turn; sc in each sc across, ch 1; sc in end of each row across, ch 1; sc in free loops of each ch across beginning ch *(Fig. 3b, page 205)*, ch 1; sc in end of each row across, ch 1; join with slip st to first sc, finish off: 82 sc and 4 chs.

FINISHING
Cover pillow form with fabric.

Matching bottom edges, place Body pieces with **wrong** sides together. Working through **inside** loops, whipstitch pieces together around three sides *(Fig. 9d, page 206)*, insert pillow form, and whipstitch last side.

Make four 6" (15 cm) long tassels *(Figs. 11a & b, page 207)*; attach one tassel to each corner of Pillow.

Design by Carolyn Pfeifer.

PILLOW #2
BODY (Make 2)
Row 1 (Right side)**:** With New Aran, ch 23, sc in second ch from hook and in each ch across: 22 sc.

Note: Mark Row 1 as **right** side and bottom edge.

Rows 2-4: Ch 1, turn; sc in first sc, ★ sc in Back Loop Only of next sc *(Fig. 2, page 205)*, insert hook from **back** to **front** in free loop of same st *(Fig. 3a, page 205)*, YO and pull up a loop, YO and draw through **both** loops on hook, skip next sc, sc in **both** loops of next sc; repeat from ★ across.

Finish off.

Row 5: With **right** side facing, join Camel with sc in **both** loops of first sc *(see Joining With Sc, page 205)*; ★ sc in Back Loop Only of next sc, insert hook from **back** to **front** in free loop of same st, YO and pull up a loop, YO and draw through **both** loops on hook, skip next sc, sc in **both** loops of next sc; repeat from ★ across; do **not** finish off.

Row 6: Ch 1, turn; sc in **both** loops of first sc, ★ sc in Back Loop Only of next sc, insert hook from **back** to **front** in free loop of same st, YO and pull up a loop, YO and draw through **both** loops on hook, skip next sc, sc in **both** loops of next sc; repeat from ★ across; finish off.

Rows 7 and 8: With New Aran, repeat Rows 5 and 6.

Rows 9-15: Repeat Rows 5-8 once, then repeat Rows 5-7 once **more**.

Rows 16-18: Repeat Rows 2-4; do **not** finish off.

Edging: Ch 1, turn; sc in both loops of each sc across, ch 1; sc in end of each row across, ch 1; sc in free loops of each ch across beginning ch *(Fig. 3b, page 205)*, ch 1; sc in end of each row across, ch 1; join with slip st to first sc, finish off: 80 sc and 4 chs.

FINISHING
Cover pillow form with fabric.

Matching bottom edges, place Body pieces with **wrong** sides together. Working through **both** loops of both pieces, join New Aran with sc in any corner ch-1; working from **left** to **right**, work reverse sc in each st across three sides *(Figs. 8a-d, page 206)*, insert pillow form, and work reverse sc in each st across last side; join with slip st to first st, finish off.

Design by Carolyn Pfeifer.

PILLOW #3
BODY (Make 2)

Row 1: Ch 24, sc in second ch from hook and in each ch across: 23 sc.

To work extended sc (abbreviated ex sc), pull up a loop in next sc, YO and draw through one loop on hook, YO and draw through both loops on hook.

Row 2 (Right side): Ch 1, turn; sc in first 2 sc, (work ex sc, sc in next 2 sc) across.

Note: Mark Row 2 as **right** side and bottom edge.

Row 3: Ch 1, turn; sc in each st across.

Row 4: Ch 1, turn; sc in first 2 sc, (work ex sc, sc in next 2 sc) across.

Rows 5-19: Repeat Rows 3 and 4, 7 times; then repeat Row 3 once **more**; do **not** finish off.

Edging: Ch 1, turn; sc in each sc across, ch 1; sc in end of each row across, ch 1; working in free loops of beginning ch **(Fig. 3b, page 205),** sc in ch at base of first sc and in each ch across, ch 1; sc in end of each row across, ch 1; join with slip st to first sc, finish off: 84 sc and 4 chs.

FINISHING
Cover pillow form with fabric.

Matching bottom edges, place Body pieces with **wrong** sides together. Working through **inside** loops, whipstitch around three sides **(Fig. 9d, page 206),** insert pillow form, and whipstitch last side.

SO-EASY RUG

*Easy to make and easy on your feet, this eye-pleasing rug has
a cushy center crocheted using four strands of yarn held together.
The striking trim rounds are added using double strands.*

⬛⬛⬜⬜ **EASY**

Finished Size: 28" (71 cm)
(from straight edge to straight edge)

MATERIALS
Medium/Worsted Weight Yarn
[3 ounces, 170 yards
(90 grams, 155.5 meters) **4** MEDIUM
per skein]:
MC (Buff) - 5 skeins
Color A (Dark Teal) - 3 skeins
Color B (Med Coral Rose) - 3 skeins
Crochet hook, size N (9 mm) **or** size
needed for gauge

GAUGE: Rnds 1-5 = 5½" (14 cm)
(from straight edge to straight edge)

Note: Rug is worked holding **four**
strands of yarn together and Trim is
worked holding **two** strands of yarn
together. To form four working strands
from two skeins of yarn, follow label
instructions to pull out **both** ends of
yarn from **each** skein; remove labels
and work with ends from both skeins
held together.

Rnd 1 (Right side)**:** With MC, ch 2, 6 sc
in second ch from hook; join with slip st
to first sc.

Note: Mark Rnd 1 as **right** side.

Rnd 2: Ch 1, turn; 2 sc in same st and
in each sc around; join with slip st to first
sc: 12 sc.

Rnd 3: Ch 1, turn; 2 sc in same st, sc
in next sc, (2 sc in next sc, sc in next sc)
around; join with slip st to first sc: 18 sc.

Rnd 4: Ch 1, turn; 2 sc in same st, sc
in next 2 sc, (2 sc in next sc, sc in next
2 sc) around; join with slip st to first sc:
24 sc.

Rnd 5: Ch 1, turn; 2 sc in same st, sc
in next 3 sc, (2 sc in next sc, sc in next
3 sc) around; join with slip st to first sc:
30 sc.

Rnd 6: Ch 1, turn; 2 sc in same st, sc
in next 4 sc, (2 sc in next sc, sc in next
4 sc) around; join with slip st to first sc:
36 sc.

Rnd 7: Ch 1, turn; 2 sc in same st, sc
in next 5 sc, (2 sc in next sc, sc in next
5 sc) around; join with slip st to first sc:
42 sc.

Rnd 8: Ch 1, turn; 2 sc in same st, sc
in next 6 sc, (2 sc in next sc, sc in next
6 sc) around; join with slip st to first sc:
48 sc.

Rnd 9: Ch 1, turn; 2 sc in same st, sc
in next 7 sc, (2 sc in next sc, sc in next
7 sc) around; join with slip st to first sc:
54 sc.

Rnd 10: Ch 1, turn; 2 sc in same st, sc
in next 8 sc, (2 sc in next sc, sc in next
8 sc) around; join with slip st to first sc:
60 sc.

Rnd 11: Ch 1, turn; 2 sc in same st, sc
in next 9 sc, (2 sc in next sc, sc in next
9 sc) around; join with slip st to first sc:
66 sc.

Rnd 12: Ch 1, turn; 2 sc in same st, sc
in next 10 sc, (2 sc in next sc, sc in next
10 sc) around; join with slip st to first sc:
72 sc.

Rnd 13: Ch 1, turn; 2 sc in same st, sc
in next 11 sc, (2 sc in next sc, sc in next
11 sc) around; join with slip st to first sc:
78 sc.

Rnd 14: Ch 1, turn; 2 sc in same st, sc
in next 12 sc, (2 sc in next sc, sc in next
12 sc) around; join with slip st to first sc:
84 sc.

Rnd 15: Ch 1, turn; 2 sc in same st, sc
in next 13 sc, (2 sc in next sc, sc in next
13 sc) around; join with slip st to first sc:
90 sc.

Rnd 16: Ch 1, turn; 2 sc in same st, sc
in next 14 sc, (2 sc in next sc, sc in next
14 sc) around; join with slip st to first sc:
96 sc.

Rnd 17: Ch 1, turn; 2 sc in same st, sc
in next 15 sc, (2 sc in next sc, sc in next
15 sc) around; join with slip st to first sc:
102 sc.

Rnd 18: Ch 1, turn; 2 sc in same st, sc
in next 16 sc, (2 sc in next sc, sc in next
16 sc) around; join with slip st to first sc,
finish off: 108 sc.

Rnd 19: With **right** side facing, join
Color A with sc in same st as joining
(see Joining With Sc, page 205); sc
in same st and in next 17 sc, (2 sc in
next sc, sc in next 17 sc) around; join
with slip st to first sc: 114 sc.

Rnd 20: Ch 1, turn; 2 sc in same st, sc
in next 18 sc, (2 sc in next sc, sc in next
18 sc) around; join with slip st to first sc,
finish off: 120 sc.

Rnd 21: With **right** side facing, join
Color B with sc in same st as joining; sc
in same st and in next 19 sc, (2 sc in
next sc, sc in next 19 sc) around; join
with slip st to first sc: 126 sc.

Rnd 22: Ch 1, turn; 2 sc in same st, sc
in next 20 sc, (2 sc in next sc, sc in next
20 sc) around; join with slip st to first sc,
finish off: 132 sc.

Rnd 23: With **right** side facing, join MC with sc in same st as joining; sc in same st and in next 21 sc, (2 sc in next sc, sc in next 21 sc) around; join with slip st to first sc, finish off: 138 sc.

Rnd 24: With **right** side facing, join Color B with sc in same st as joining; sc in same st and in next 22 sc, (2 sc in next sc, sc in next 22 sc) around; join with slip st to first sc: 144 sc.

Rnd 25: Ch 1, turn; 2 sc in same st, sc in next 23 sc, (2 sc in next sc, sc in next 23 sc) around; join with slip st to first sc, finish off: 150 sc.

Rnd 26: With **right** side facing, join Color A with sc in same st as joining; sc in same st and in next 24 sc, (2 sc in next sc, sc in next 24 sc) around; join with slip st to first sc: 156 sc.

Rnd 27: Ch 1, turn; 2 sc in same st, sc in next 25 sc, (2 sc in next sc, sc in next 25 sc) around; join with slip st to first sc, finish off.

TRIM

With **right** side facing, join MC with sc around post of any sc on Rnd 20 **(Fig. 4, page 205)**; sc around post of each sc around; join with slip st to first sc, finish off.

Repeat on Rnd 25.

Design by Mary Lamb Becker.

SOFT STEPS RUG

*You'll be floored by how quickly you can create this super-soft rug!
Crocheted using a Q hook and five strands of yarn in solid and variegated
colors, the mat has a simple scalloped edging.*

EASY

Finished Size:
24" x 32" (61 cm x 81.5 cm)

MATERIALS
Medium/Worsted Weight Yarn
[8 ounces, 452 yards
(230 grams, 413 meters)
per skein (Medium Windsor Blue) or
2¹/₂ ounces, 145 yards
(70 grams, 133 meters)
per skein (Cottage Garden)]:
Medium Windsor Blue - 3 skeins
Cottage Garden - 2 skeins
Crochet hook, size Q (15 mm)

GAUGE: 5 sc and 5 rows = 4" (10 cm)

Note: Entire Rug is worked holding three strands of Medium Windsor Blue and two strands of Cottage Garden together.

Row 1 (Right side): Ch 38, sc in second ch from hook and in each ch across: 37 sc.

Rows 2-27: Ch 1, turn; sc in each sc across; do **not** finish off.

Edging: Ch 2 **(counts as first hdc)**, do **not** turn; 3 hdc in same st; † working in end of rows, skip first row, sc in next row, skip next row, (5 hdc in next row, skip next row, sc in next row, skip next row) across †; working in free loops of

beginning ch *(Fig. 3b, page 205)*, 7 hdc in first ch, skip next ch, sc in next ch, skip next ch, (5 hdc in next ch, skip next ch, sc in next ch, skip next ch) 8 times, 7 hdc in next ch, repeat from † to † once; working across Row 27, 7 hdc in first sc, skip next sc, sc in next sc, skip next sc, (5 hdc in next sc, skip next sc, sc in next sc, skip next sc) across, 3 hdc in same st as first hdc; join with slip st to first hdc, finish off.

Design by Judy Sajewski.

FLOWER GARDEN
TISSUE BOX COVER

With no weed-pulling or watering ever needed, this blossoming tissue box cover makes a pleasant indoor flower patch.

Instructions begin on page 202.

FLOWER GARDEN TISSUE BOX COVER

Shown on page 201.

◼◼◻◻◻ **EASY**

Finished Size: Fits a 4¹/₄" (11 cm) wide x 5¹/₄" (13.5 cm) high x 4¹/₄" (11 cm) deep boutique tissue box

MATERIALS

Medium/Worsted Weight Yarn
[3 ounces, 170 yards (90 grams, 155 meters) per skein]: **MEDIUM 4**
  Aran -1 skein
  Spruce - 1 skein
  Rose Pink - 1 skein
  Raspberry - 1 skein
  Lavender - 1 skein
  Cornmeal - 1 skein
Crochet hook, size I (5.5 mm) **or** size needed for gauge

GAUGE:

Each Side = 4¹/₂" (11.5 cm) square

SIDE (Make 4)

Rnd 1 (Right side)**:** With Cornmeal, ch 2, 8 sc in second ch from hook; join with slip st to first sc, finish off.

Note: Mark Rnd 1 as **right** side.

To work beginning Popcorn, ch 3 **(counts as first dc, now and throughout),** 3 dc in st or sp indicated, drop loop from hook, insert hook in first dc, hook dropped loop and draw through st.

To work Popcorn, 4 dc in st or sp indicated, drop loop from hook, insert hook in first dc of 4-dc group, hook dropped loop and draw through st.

Note: Using the following colors for Rnds 2 and 3, make 2 flowers **each** of Rose Pink and Raspberry.

Rnd 2: With **right** side facing, join color indicated with slip st in any sc; work beginning Popcorn in same st, ch 2, (work Popcorn in next sc, ch 2) around; join with slip st to top of beginning Popcorn: 8 Popcorns and 8 ch-2 sps.

Rnd 3: Slip st in first ch-2 sp, work (beginning Popcorn, ch 2, Popcorn) in same sp, ch 2, (work Popcorn, ch 2) twice in each ch-2 sp around; join with slip st to top of beginning Popcorn, finish off: 16 Popcorns and 16 ch-2 sps.

Rnd 4: With **right** side facing, join Aran with slip st in first ch-2 sp; ch 3, 4 dc in same sp, 3 hdc in next ch-2 sp, 3 sc in next ch-2 sp, 3 hdc in next ch-2 sp, ★ 5 dc in next ch-2 sp, 3 hdc in next ch-2 sp, 3 sc in next ch-2 sp, 3 hdc in next ch-2 sp; repeat from ★ around; join with slip st first dc: 56 sts.

Rnd 5: Ch 1, sc in same st and in next dc, (sc, ch 2, sc) in next dc, ★ sc in next 13 sts, (sc, ch 2, sc) in next dc; repeat from ★ 2 times **more,** sc in each st across; join with slip st to first sc, finish off: 60 sc and 4 ch-2 sps.

TOP

With Lavender, ch 24; being careful not to twist ch, join with slip st to back ridge of first ch to form a ring *(Fig. 1, page 205).*

Rnd 1 (Right side)**:** Ch 1, sc in back ridge of same ch and each ch around; join with slip st to first sc: 24 sc.

Note: Mark Rnd 1 as **right** side.

Rnd 2: Work (beginning Popcorn, ch 2, Popcorn) in same st, ch 2, skip next 2 sc, ★ (work Popcorn, ch 2) twice in next sc, skip next 2 sc; repeat from ★ around; join with slip st to top of beginning Popcorn, finish off: 16 Popcorns and 16 ch-2 sps.

Rnd 3: With **right** side facing, join Aran with slip st in first ch-2 sp; ch 3, 4 dc in same sp, 3 hdc in next ch-2 sp, 3 sc in next ch-2 sp, 3 hdc in next ch-2 sp, ★ 5 dc in next ch-2 sp, 3 hdc in next ch-2 sp, 3 sc in next ch-2 sp, 3 hdc in next ch-2 sp; repeat from ★ around; join with slip st first dc: 56 sts.

Rnd 4: Ch 1, sc in same st and in next dc, (sc, ch 3, sc) in next dc, ★ sc in next 13 sts, (sc, ch 3, sc) in next dc; repeat from ★ 2 times **more,** sc in each st across; join with slip st to first sc, finish off: 60 sc and 4 ch-3 sps.

Trim: With **right** side facing and working in free loops of beginning ch *(Fig. 3b, page 205),* join Cornmeal with slip st in any ch; ch 1, (slip st in next ch, ch 1) around; join with slip st to first slip st, finish off.

ASSEMBLY

Note: Alternate flower colors when joining Sides.

Join two Sides as follows: With **right** side facing, join Aran with slip st in second ch of any ch-2 on First Side; holding **second** Side with **right** side facing, slip st in second ch of any ch-2 on **second** Side, ★ slip st in next st on **first** Side, slip st in next st on **second** Side; repeat from ★ 15 times **more;** finish off.

Join remaining Sides in same manner, then join first Side to last Side in same manner.

Join Top to Sides as follows: With **right** side facing, join Aran with slip st in center ch of any ch-3; holding Sides with **right** side facing, slip st in any joining, slip st in next ch on Top, ★ (slip st in next st on **Side,** slip st in next st on **Top**) across to next joining, slip st in joining, slip st in next ch on Top; repeat from ★ 2 times **more,** slip st in next ch on **Side,** (slip st in next st on **Top,** slip st in next st on **Side**) across; join with slip st to first slip st, finish off.

BOTTOM BAND

Rnd 1: With **right** side facing, join Aran with sc in any Side joining **(see Joining With Sc, page 205)**; ch 1, sc in next sc, ch 1, ★ (skip next sc, sc in next sc, ch 1) across to next joining, sc in joining, ch 1, sc in next sc, ch 1; repeat from ★ 2 times **more**, (skip next sc, sc in next sc, ch 1) across; join with slip st to first sc, finish off: 36 ch-1 sps.

To work Stem, YO twice, working in front of sts, insert hook in next ch-2 sp to **right** of 3 sc on Rnd 3 of Side, YO and pull up a loop, YO and draw through 2 loops on hook, YO, insert hook in **same** sp to **left** of 3 sc, YO and pull up a loop, (YO and draw through 2 loops on hook) 4 times.

Rnd 2: With **right** side facing, join Spruce with sc in same st as joining; ★ ♥ working **around** next ch-1, dc in ch-1 sp on Rnd 5 of Side **below** ch-1, sc in next sc on Rnd 1 of Bottom Border, † working **around** next ch-1, dc in sc on Rnd 5 of Side **below** ch-1, sc in next sc on Rnd 1 of Bottom Border †, repeat from † to † twice **more**, work Stem, sc in next sc on Rnd 1 of Bottom Border, repeat from † to † 3 times, working **around** next ch-1, dc in sp on Rnd 5 of Side **below** ch-1 ♥, sc in next joining; repeat from ★ 2 times **more**, then repeat from ♥ to ♥ once; join with slip st to first sc: 72 sts.

Rnd 3: Ch 1, sc in same st and in each st around; join with slip st to first sc.

Rnd 4: Ch 1, (slip st in next sc, ch 1) around; join with slip st to joining slip st, finish off.

Design by Joan Beebe.

CHEERY PLACE SETTING
Continued from page 184.

HOT PAD
Finished Size:
7¹/₂" x 8" (19 cm x 20.5 cm)

With CC, ch 47.

Rows 1-20: Work same as Placemat, page 184: 5 Clusters.

Finish off.

EDGING
Rnd 1: With **right** side facing, join MC with sc in first sc on last row; sc in same st, work 33 sc evenly spaced across to next corner, ★ 3 sc in corner, work 33 sc evenly spaced across to next corner; repeat from ★ around, sc in same st as first sc; join with slip st to first sc: 144 sc.

Rnd 2: Ch 3, 6 dc in same st, skip next 2 sc, sc in next sc, skip next 2 sc, ★ 7 dc in next sc, skip next 2 sc, sc in next sc, skip next 2 sc; repeat from ★ around; join with slip st to top of beginning ch-3, finish off.

NAPKIN RING
Finished Size: 1¹/₂" (4 cm) diameter x 2¹/₂" (6.5 cm)

With CC, ch 27.

Rows 1-4: Work same as Placemat, page 184: 3 Clusters.

Finish off, leaving a long end for sewing.

Sew ends together.

EDGING
Rnd 1: With **right** side facing, join MC with sc in any st; work 23 sc evenly spaced around; join with slip st to first sc: 24 sc.

Rnd 2: Ch 1, sc in same st, skip next 2 sc, 7 dc in next sc, skip next 2 sc, ★ sc in next sc, skip next 2 sc, 7 dc in next sc, skip next 2 sc; repeat from ★ around; join with slip st to first sc, finish off.

Repeat for opposite edge.

Designs by Lorraine White.

GENERAL INSTRUCTIONS

ABBREVIATIONS

BPdc	Back Post double crochet(s)
BPtr	Back Post treble crochet(s)
CC	Contrasting Color
ch(s)	chain(s)
cm	centimeters
dc	double crochet(s)
ex sc	extended single crochet(s)
FPdc	Front Post double crochet(s)
FPtr	Front Post treble crochet(s)
hdc	half double crochet(s)
MC	Main Color
mm	millimeters
Rnd(s)	Round(s)
sc	single crochet(s)
sp(s)	space(s)
st(s)	stitch(es)
tr	treble crochet(s)
tr tr	triple treble crochet(s)
YO	yarn over

★ — work instructions following ★ as many **more** times as indicated in addition to the first time.

† to † or ♥ to ♥ — work all instructions from first † to second † **or** from first ♥ to second ♥ **as many** times as specified.

( ) or [ ] — work enclosed instructions **as many** times as specified by the number immediately following **or** work all enclosed instructions in the stitch or space indicated **or** contains explanatory remarks.

colon (:) — the number(s) given after a colon at the end of a row or round denote(s) the number of stitches or spaces you should have on that row or round.

GAUGE

Exact gauge is essential for proper size and fit. Hook sizes given in instructions are merely a guide and should never be used without first making a sample swatch approximately 4" (10 cm) square in the stitch, yarn/thread, and hook specified. Then measure the swatch, counting your stitches and rows or rounds carefully. If your swatch is larger or smaller than specified, **make another, changing hook size to get the correct gauge**. Keep trying until you find the size hook that will give you the specified gauge. If no gauge is given, use the size hook specified in the Materials.

CROCHET TERMINOLOGY	
UNITED STATES	**INTERNATIONAL**
slip stitch (slip st) =	single crochet (sc)
single crochet (sc) =	double crochet (dc)
half double crochet (hdc) =	half treble crochet (htr)
double crochet (dc) =	treble crochet (tr)
treble crochet (tr) =	double treble crochet (dtr)
double treble crochet (dtr) =	triple treble crochet (ttr)
triple treble crochet (tr tr) =	quadruple treble crochet (qtr)
skip =	miss

Yarn Weight Symbol & Names	SUPER FINE 1	FINE 2	LIGHT 3	MEDIUM 4	BULKY 5	SUPER BULKY 6
Type of Yarns in Category	Sock, Fingering Baby	Sport, Baby	DK, Light Worsted	Worsted, Afghan, Aran	Chunky, Craft, Rug	Bulky, Roving

ALUMINUM CROCHET HOOKS													
U.S.	B-1	C-2	D-3	E-4	F-5	G-6	H-8	I-9	J-10	K-10½	N	P	Q
Metric - mm	2.25	2.75	3.25	3.5	3.75	4	5	5.5	6	6.5	9	10	15

STEEL CROCHET HOOKS															
U.S.	00	0	1	2	3	4	5	6	7	8	9	10	11	12	13	14
Metric - mm	3.5	3.25	2.75	2.25	2.1	2	1.9	1.8	1.65	1.5	1.4	1.3	1.1	1	.85	.75

●□□□ BEGINNER	Projects for first-time crocheters using basic stitches. Minimal shaping.
●●□□ EASY	Projects using yarn with basic stitches, repetitive stitch patterns, simple color changes, and simple shaping and finishing.
●●●□ INTERMEDIATE	Projects using a variety of techniques, such as basic lace patterns or color patterns, mid-level shaping and finishing.
●●●● EXPERIENCED	Projects with intricate stitch patterns, techniques and dimension, such as non-repeating patterns, multi-color techniques, fine threads, small hooks, detailed shaping and refined finishing.

THREAD

Most of the photographed thread pieces were made using bedspread weight cotton thread (size 10). Any brand of the following brands may be used with good results:

Aunt Lydia's® Classic Crochet
Coats Opera 10
DMC® Baroque
DMC® Cebelia
DMC® Cordonnet Special
DMC® Traditions
Grandma's Best
J. & P. Coats® Knit-Cro-Sheen®
J. & P. Coats® South Maid®
Lily® Antique

YARN

Most of the photographed yarn pieces were made using Red Heart® or J. & P. Coats® products in the specified weights. Any comparable yarns that can be crocheted to gauge may be used with good results. It is best to refer to the yardage/meters when determining how many balls or skeins to buy.

MARKERS

Markers are used to help distinguish the beginning of each round being worked. Place a 2" (5 cm) scrap piece of yarn/thread before the first stitch of each round, moving marker after each round is complete.

JOINING WITH SC

When instructed to join with sc, begin with a slip knot on hook. Insert hook in stitch or space indicated, YO and pull up a loop, YO and draw through both loops on hook.

JOINING WITH DC

When instructed to join with dc, begin with a slip knot on hook. YO, holding loop on hook, insert hook in stitch or space indicated, YO and pull up a loop (3 loops on hook), (YO and draw through 2 loops on hook) twice.

BACK RIDGE

Work only in loops indicated by arrows *(Fig. 1)*.

Fig. 1

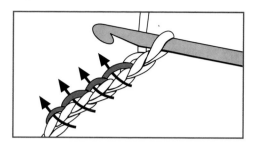

BACK OR FRONT LOOP ONLY

Work only in loop(s) indicated by arrow *(Fig. 2)*.

Fig. 2

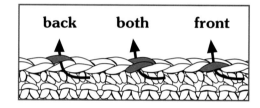

FREE LOOPS

After working in Back or Front Loops Only on a row or round, there will be a ridge of unused loops. These are called the free loops. Later, when instructed to work in the free loops of the same row or round, work in these loops *(Fig. 3a)*.

When instructed to work in free loops of a chain, work in loop indicated by arrow *(Fig. 3b)*.

Fig. 3a **Fig. 3b**

 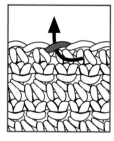

POST STITCH

Work around post of stitch indicated, inserting hook in direction of arrow *(Fig. 4)*.

Fig. 4

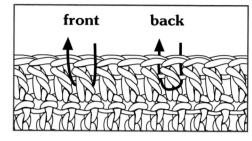

WORKING IN SPACE BEFORE A STITCH

When instructed to work in space **before** a stitch, insert hook in space indicated by arrow *(Fig. 5)*.

Fig. 5

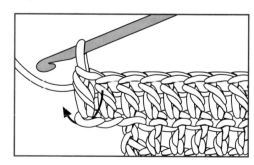

ADDING ON DC

YO, insert hook into base of last dc made *(Fig. 6)*, YO and pull up a loop (3 loops on hook), YO and draw through one loop on hook, (YO and draw through 2 loops on hook) twice. Repeat as many times as instructed.

Fig. 6

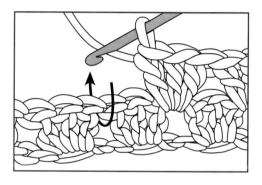

HINTS

As in all crocheted pieces, good finishing techniques make a big difference in the quality of the piece. Make a habit of taking care of loose ends as you work. Thread a yarn/tapestry needle with the yarn/thread end. With **wrong** side facing, weave the needle through several stitches, then reverse the direction and weave it back through several stitches. When ends are secure, clip them off close to work.

CHANGING COLORS

Work the last stitch to within one step of completion, hook new yarn **(Fig. 7a or 7b)** and draw through all loops on hook. When working in rounds, cut old yarn and join with slip stitch to first stitch using new yarn **(Fig. 7c)**.

Fig. 7a

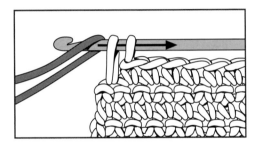

Fig. 7b

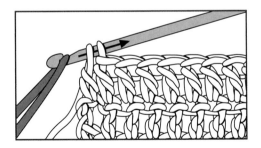

Fig. 7c

REVERSE SINGLE CROCHET

Working from **left** to **right**, ★ insert hook in stitch to right of hook **(Fig. 8a)**, YO and draw through, under and to left of loop on hook (2 loops on hook) **(Fig. 8b)**, YO and draw through both loops on hook **(Fig. 8c) (reverse sc made, Fig. 8d)**; repeat from ★ around.

Fig. 8a

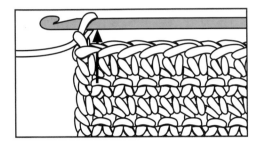

Fig. 8b

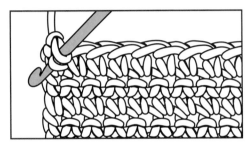

Fig. 8c

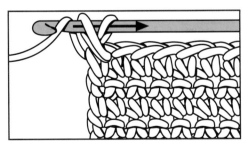

Fig. 8d

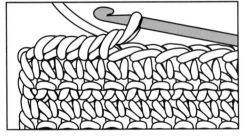

WHIPSTITCH

Place two pieces with **wrong** sides together. Sew through both pieces once to secure the beginning of the seam, leaving an ample yarn end to weave in later. Insert the needle from **front** to **back** through **both** loops on **both** pieces **(Fig. 9a or 9b)** or through **inside** loops only of each stitch on **both** pieces **(Fig. 9c or 9d)** and pull yarn through. Bring the needle around and insert it from **front** to **back** through next loops of both pieces. Continue in this manner across, keeping the sewing yarn fairly loose.

Fig. 9a

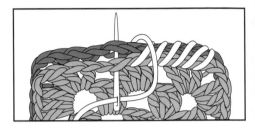

Fig. 9b

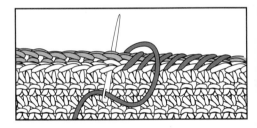

Fig. 9c

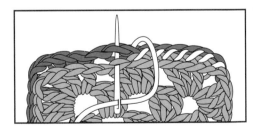

Fig. 9d

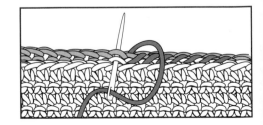

POM-POM

Cut a piece of cardboard 3" (7.5 cm) wide and as long as you want the diameter of your finished pom-pom to be.

Wind the yarn around the cardboard until it is approximately $1/2$" (7 mm) thick in the middle *(Fig. 10a)*. Carefully slip the yarn off the cardboard and firmly tie an 18" (45.5 cm) length of yarn around the middle *(Fig. 10b)*. Leave yarn ends long enough to attach the pom-pom. Cut the loops on both ends and trim the pom-pom into a smooth ball *(Fig. 10c)*.

Fig. 10a

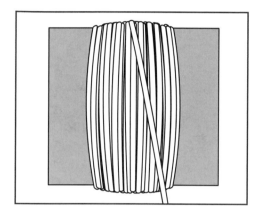

Fig. 10b

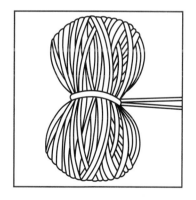

Fig. 10c

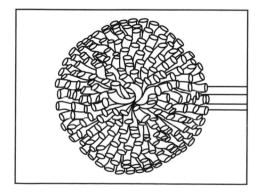

TASSEL

Cut a piece of cardboard 3" (7.5 cm) wide and as long as you want your finished tassel to be. Wind a double strand of yarn around the cardboard as many times as desired. Cut an 18" (45.5 cm) length of yarn and insert it under all of the strands at the top of the cardboard; pull up tightly and tie securely. Leave the yarn ends long enough to attach the tassel.

Cut the yarn at the opposite end of the cardboard and then remove it *(Fig. 11a)*. Cut an 8" (20.5 cm) length of yarn and wrap it tightly around the tassel twice, the desired distance below the top *(Fig. 11b)*; tie securely. Trim the ends.

Fig. 11a   **Fig. 11b**

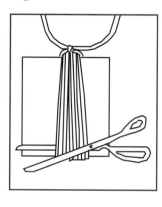

FRINGE

Cut a piece of cardboard 6" (15 cm) wide and half as long as strands specified in individual instructions. Wind the yarn **loosely** and **evenly** around the cardboard until the card is filled, then cut across one end; repeat as needed.

Hold the number of lengths specified for one knot together and fold in half.

With **wrong** side facing and using a crochet hook, draw the folded end up through a row, stitch or space and pull the loose ends through the folded end *(Fig. 12a or 12c)*; draw the knot up tightly *(Fig. 12b or 12d)*. Repeat, spacing as specified in individual instructions.

Lay flat on a hard surface and trim the ends.

Fig. 12a

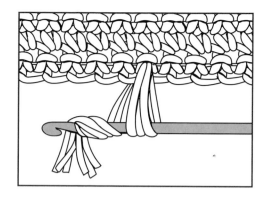

Fig. 12b

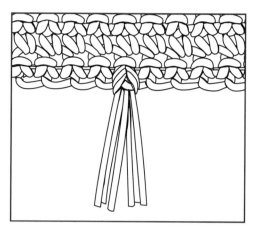

Fig. 12c

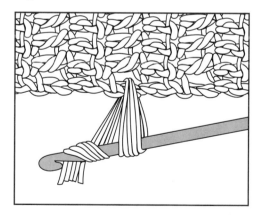

Fig. 12d

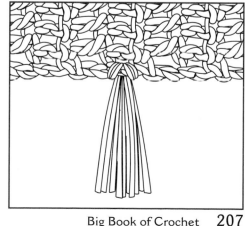

EMBROIDERY STITCHES

OUTLINE STITCH

Bring needle up at 1, leaving an end to be woven in later. Holding yarn **above** the needle with thumb, insert needle down at 2 and up again at 3 (halfway between 1 and 2) **(Fig. 13a)**; pull through. Insert needle down at 4 and up again at 2, making sure yarn is **above** needle **(Fig. 13b)**; pull through. Continue in this manner.

Fig. 13a

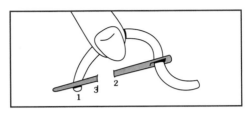

Fig. 13b

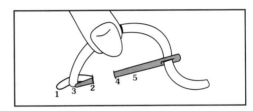

SATIN STITCH

Satin Stitch is a series of straight stitches worked side-by-side so they touch but do not overlap. Come up at odd numbers and go down at even numbers **(Fig. 14)**.

Fig. 14

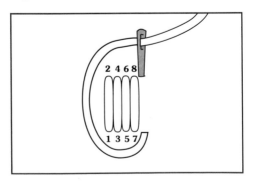

LAZY DAISY STITCH

Make all loops equal in length. Come up at 1 and make a counterclockwise loop with the yarn. Go down at 1 and come up at 2, keeping the yarn below the point of the needle **(Fig. 15)**. Secure loop by bringing yarn over loop and down at 3. Repeat for each flower or leaf.

Fig. 15

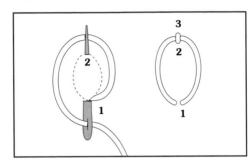

FRENCH KNOT

Bring needle up at 1. Wrap yarn around the needle the desired number of times and insert needle at 2, holding end of yarn with non-stitching fingers **(Fig. 16)**. Tighten knot; then pull needle through, holding yarn until it must be released.

Fig. 16

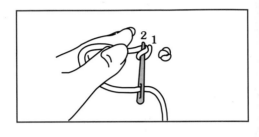

KEY for Cutie-Pie Bubble Suits, pages 66-69.

- ● Pastel Green French Knot
- Baby Yellow Lazy Daisy Stitch
- Pastel Green Lazy Daisy Stitch
- – – Pastel Green Outline Stitch
- / Baby Yellow Satin Stitch
- / Baby Blue Satin Stitch
- / Pastel Green Satin Stitch
- / Silver Satin Stitch